20 Questions
about Youth and the Media

This book is part of the Peter Lang Media and Communication list.
Every volume is peer reviewed and meets
the highest quality standards for content and production.

PETER LANG
New York • Bern • Berlin
Brussels • Vienna • Oxford • Warsaw

Praise for the First Edition of

20 Questions about Youth and the Media

"This readable, comprehensive compendium could be titled 'Everything You Ever Wanted to Know about Youth and Media.' Its broad scope covers politics, research, social aspects, and history, providing background, insights, and up-to-date information on numerous topics, from longtime debates over violence and television, to the recent controversy over indecency in broadcasting, to contemporary research on how young people are using the Internet and digital media. It is an essential resource for students, parents, policy makers, and the press."

Kathryn C. Montgomery, Professor, School of Communication, American University;

Author, *Generation Digital: Politics, Commerce, and Childhood in the Age of the Internet*

20 Questions
about Youth and the Media

REVISED EDITION

EDITED BY Nancy A. Jennings
AND Sharon R. Mazzarella

PETER LANG
New York • Bern • Berlin
Brussels • Vienna • Oxford • Warsaw

Library of Congress Cataloging-in-Publication Control Number: 2017034501

Bibliographic information published by **Die Deutsche Nationalbibliothek**.
Die Deutsche Nationalbibliothek lists this publication in the "Deutsche
Nationalbibliografie"; detailed bibliographic data are available
on the Internet at http://dnb.d-nb.de/.

ISBN 978-1-4331-4391-5 (paperback)
ISBN 978-1-4331-3935-2 (ebook pdf)
ISBN 978-1-4331-3936-9 (epub)
ISBN 978-1-4331-3937-6 (mobi)
DOI 10.3726/978-1-4331-3935-2

Cover design by Lisa Barfield

The paper in this book meets the guidelines for permanence and durability
of the Committee on Production Guidelines for Book Longevity
of the Council of Library Resources.

To our families whose love, laughter, and support
enable us to do the work we hold dear.

Contents

PART 1

THE PLAYERS: CORPORATIONS, GOVERNMENT, PARENTS & CHILD ADVOCACY ORGANIZATIONS & SCHOLARS

Illustration

Acknowledgments

Was it really a decade ago that the first edition of this book was published? While it seems like just yesterday, the ensuing years have wrought tremendous changes in the world of youth media and technology. The growth of social media, ubiquity of mobile phones, ever-increasing commodification of kid culture, shifting government regulations, evolving media content, consolidation of ownership of media companies, and so on make this topic ripe for updated analysis. Moreover, given the dynamic nature of academic inquiry in a field character-ized by scholars who continuously ask novel question, employ innovative methodologies, and have adopted a more global approach to the topic, we felt it was imperative to provide readers with the latest scholarship on these topics.

As with the first edition, we approached a stellar group of youth media scholars, asking them to think about what an undergraduate student might ask about a specific subtopic related to youth media. We gave them a tight timeline, restrictive word count, and highly specific formatting guidelines, and still they enthusiastically signed on! This book reflects their intel-lectual expertise, passion, and genuine dedication to the study of youth media. It has been a true pleasure to work with them, and we are honored to share their work with our readers.

We also would like to thank the editorial and production staff at Peter Lang Publishing. This edition was initially commissioned by acquisitions editor Mary Savigar whose enthusiasm and support in the early stages of this project were greatly appreciated. Kathryn Harrison came on board as acquisitions editor mid-way through this project, but has been an equally enthusi-astic supporter, patiently answering our questions about the minutiae of formatting, copyright permissions, and the like. We greatly appreciate her guidance and good humor. Thanks also to our production editor Janell Harris as well as Peter Lang's team of creative cover designers, detail-oriented copy-editors, and talented compositors. You make us look us good! Thank you to Cassie Peng for granting permission to use her hand-rendered digital drawing appearing in Chapter 19.

While Sharon was the sole editor of the first edition of this book, she was not intending to put together a revised edition until Nancy innocently (?) asked her if there were any plans for one. Somehow, by the end of that April 2016 phone call, Nancy had wheedled her way in not only as co-editor, but as *lead* co-editor at that! Seriously, Sharon was thrilled to collaborate with Nancy on this project and to have her take the lead. It's been a pure joy to work with her—well as much joy as editing any anthology can be. Nancy has been beyond words to work with such an outstanding and patient colleague in Sharon. She has truly been an inspiration.

We are both fortunate to have the support and encouragement of our educational institutions. Nancy appreciates the unconditional support of her writing circle colleagues, faculty, and staff in UC LEAF (University of Cincinnati Leadership, Empowerment, Advancement for Women STEM Faculty) and in the Department of Communication at the University of Cincinnati, particularly Dr. Steve Depoe, Department Head. Sharon appreciates the tremendous support of her colleagues in the School of Communication Studies at James Madison University, notably the School's Director Dr. Eric Fife as well as Dr. David Jeffrey, outgoing Dean of JMU's College of Arts & Letters.

Most importantly, no book on youth and media would exist without young people themselves. They are the reason we all are so dedicated to this field of inquiry.

Sometimes Things Do Change
Children and Media Studies Today

Ellen Wartella

It has been ten years since the last edition of this book was published and eleven years since I wrote the last introduction. At that time three topics seemed to describe the public discourse about children and media research: the influence of videogame violence on young players; the role of food marketing in the childhood obesity crisis; and the educational impact of a growing industry of baby videos on infants (Wartella, 2007). These three sets of public issues indeed dominated much of the last decade of policy discussions about media's influence and have led to changes in media practices. For instance, industry self-regulation through the Children's Food and Beverage Advertising Initiative (CFBAI) has led a majority of food marketers to pledge to only market healthier foods to children and, by and large, they have kept to these pledges (Hurwitz, Montague, & Wartella, 2017). There has been some suggestion that policies mandating more nutritious food in schools and levying soda taxes to reduce sugar sweetened beverage consumption have led to at least a leveling off of childhood obesity. Philadelphia, for example, is one city that has aggressively fought childhood obesity through policy initiatives (Jordan, 2017). On the other hand, no regulation of videogame violence came about and, indeed as pointed out in Chapter 8 of this book, the courts have deemed the research on videogame violence insufficient to warrant any restrictions of videogame sales to youth. Moreover, the issue of media violence has faded somewhat from public discussions of youth and media. Lastly, while baby videos are here to stay, the introduction of newer mobile digital technologies such as iPads and Apps have given rise to more infant directed media as well as adoption of these media by parents and caregivers (Wartella, Rideout, Lauricella, & Connell, 2014) even when concerns are raised about their appropriateness for young children.

I do not want to argue that these three public policy areas are unimportant today. Indeed they are taken up in this collection of essays. I do want to argue, however, that the context for the study of children and media has changed in the past ten years in at least two ways. First, the contemporary context of children's lives is globally in a state of crisis; and second, children and families are immersed now in a multi-platform, multi-media environment that can be accessed through a wide range of mobile, digital technologies. What we used to call "new media" are now "our media," and for today's children, using media technologies is like the air they breathe, something taken for granted and ever present.

It is not hard to find evidence of the dismal state of the world's children. Internationally, nearly 50 million children have been uprooted, with 28 million fleeing brutal conflicts as refugees (UNICEF, 2016). These children have lost homes and loved ones and seen horrific acts of violence. Moreover, it is estimated that nearly half (48%) of the world's children live in extreme poverty, which is defined as living on $1.90 a day (UNICEF, 2016). In addition, children around the world are not getting the schooling they should. In 2013 alone, 59 million of primary school aged children were out of school, with over half (33 million) living in sub-Saharan Africa (UNICEF, 2016). This has long term effects on children's lives and, in turn, on society.

The fact is that it is not just in other parts of the world that children are faring poorly—in the United States, 1 in 5 children live in poverty which is more than the number of adults living in poverty, and that trend has continued since the mid-1970s (Child Trends, 2016). Twelve million U.S. children live in households that lack the means to get enough nutritious food on a regular basis (No Kid Hungry, 2016). And one in every 30 children, or 2.5 million, are estimated to be homeless each year in the United States. Because of such deficiencies, children's educational attainment suffers: nearly 60% of all fourth and eighth grade U.S. public school students could not read or compute at grade level in 2013 (Children's Defense Fund, 2014).

These are worrying statistics because we know how important it is for children to have the very basics of support for healthy development: to have a place to live, to have nutritious food, and have emotional support and caring adults, not to mention access to education. What are the prospects for this generation of children to grow up healthy? We are learning more all of the time about the negative consequences of traumatic childhoods on the long term cognitive and social emotional development of youth.

Where in all of this should we locate concern about media and youth? Since the early 20th century there have been both naysayers against and advocates for media's role in children's development. The concerns have typically centered on how much time youth spend with media content that is considered inappropriate for its violence or commercialization. Advocates point to the evidence of the educational potential of media and technology for the development of informal learning, and as a way of supporting the education of young children as well as their readiness to enter schooling (Wartella, Lauricella, & Blackwell, 2016). What is clear is that media today are a dominant activity of childhood—not just here in the U.S.—but increasingly around the world. The Russian psychologist Lev Vygotsky (1978) argued that social interactions with others form the foundation for cognitive development and that cultural tools can mediate these social interactions. Dominant activities of children are those activities that are pervasive within a particular culture and which provide children pertinent information about social values and behaviors. Clearly, by virtue of their pervasiveness, media and technology influence the ways children make sense of their culture, values and expected behaviors. As such, media cannot be ignored as an important, pervasive influence on development. It is not just media scholars who are now interested in examining and understanding media's role in child development. There is a wide range of disciplinary homes for children and media research, perhaps best evidenced by the fact that, for the first time in its history, the Society for Research in Child Development (the largest interdisciplinary home for research on child development comprising a membership of about 8000 scholars) held a national conference on the role of technology in children's development in Fall 2016. And in May 2017, a special preconference on industry related research on children and media was held at the International Communication Association's annual meeting. Clearly, interest in and study of children and media issues continues and, indeed, may even be increasing, in interest by scholars and media professionals.

Furthermore, as this volume illustrates, the range of topics of interest regarding children and media issues has expanded (digital technologies, for instance) and evidences a deeper appreciation for the work that has come before. As I read these chapters I was struck by several themes that recur across the volume regarding attention to history, diversity of theory and method, and concern for a wide range of media beyond television.

First, there is clear attention to the importance of an historical understanding of an issue of media's influence. Just as violence in media has been of interest since the 19th century with concerns about children reading "penny dreadfuls"[1] and later public concerns about movies, radio and television, the historical precedents of violence research has been well known as Erica Scharrer points out in Chapter 8. Several other authors note the historical precedents for contemporary research on children and media issues. For instance, the historical development of the evolution of media industries is noted by J. Alison Bryant in the first chapter; Alison Alexander and Keisha L. Hoerrner examine government regulation and its historical development since the 1920s in Chapter 2; and, in Chapter 3, Sharon R. Mazzarella discusses the historical recurring moral panics about the impact of newer media forms on child audiences. Moreover, in Chapter 12, Jessica Taylor Piotrowski examines the historical development of educational media, while Nancy A. Jennings offers an historical context for the studies of children's parasocial relationships with media characters in Chapter 10. Two chapters on youth and commercialism, Matthew A. Lapierre and Chelsie Akers (Chapter 14) and Matthew P. McAllister and Azeta Hatef (Chapter 15), adopt an historical perspective and acknowledge the decades old concerns about commercialization of children's culture.

Second, this volume illustrates quite aptly the increased attention to diversity in media research. In Chapter 7, Dafna Lemish rightly points out that both quantitative and qualitative research traditions have made important contributions to our understanding of media's role in children's lives. For example, Cyndy Scheibe, in Chapter 6, examines the varying theoretical perspectives from developmental psychology that have been brought to the study of media's influence on children. Vikki S. Katz (Chapter 19) makes the case for more diversity among the child subjects we study; it is a plea for moving beyond studies of Anglo middle class youth. Rebecca C. Hains and Kyra Hunting conclude Chapter 11 with an argument for greater diversity in the perspectives used to study gender portrayals in children's media. Finally, in the book's concluding chapter Divya McMillin makes a strong argument for a global, comparative approach to studying youth media.

A third theme across this volume is its acknowledgement of the rapidly changing media landscape in which children are immersed. While much of the literature on children and media issues derives from studies of television's impact on children, there is a growing body of research on newer media. For instance, Sherri Hope Culver takes up some of these newer media platforms in her discussion of the role of media advocates in Chapter 4. In their Chapter 13 discussion of a positive media psychology, Rebecca N. H. de Leeuw and Moniek Buijzen examine social media and gaming as media that may impact children's sense of happiness. Valerie Steeves (Chapter 18) is concerned about the networked online environment and what that means for the rights of children as media users, while chapters by Susannah R. Stern and Olivia A. Gonzalez on teens use of the internet (Chapter 16), Sun Sun Lim & Yang Wang on mobile phone use (Chapter 17), and Sahara Byrne on risky behaviors in youth's use of media (Chapter 9), all considerably expand our understanding of the importance of digital and mobile technologies for young people today.

The volume is divided into three sections of book chapters: The Players, The Concerns and The Kids. These three sections neatly distinguish discussions of those institutions which are involved in the production, regulation, study, and critique of media for children; reviews of research on media's influence on children's development and behavior; and the youth culture that has developed with its attendant commercialization and new forms of cultural practices including a growing global youth culture.

The Players section covers how corporations, government, parents and child advocacy organizations and media and child development scholars have influenced both the development of children's media and the various critiques of media content produced for children. Chapter 1 (Bryant) sets the stage by offering a rich discussion of the various players in media produced for children including toy companies and advertisers and their influence on the development of media content. Chapter 2 (Alexander and Hoerrner) offer a nuanced examination of the complex balancing act of protecting the First Amendment rights of media producers and offering equal protection of children. They focus primarily on the television era of recurring public investigations and regulations regarding children and media, such as the adoption of the V-chip which gave parents the ability to screen out violent programming from their television sets. The examination of the recurring moral panics about media having a disproportionate effect on youth audiences—moral panics going back to the earliest days of the 20th century—are reviewed in Chapter 3 (Mazzarella). Chapter 4 (Culver) focuses on the various advocacy groups of parents, individuals and organizations that have publicly argued for and demanded that the rights of child media users be recognized by producers of children's media content. Related somewhat to the discussion of advocacy, Chapter 5 (Hobbs) addresses the historical development of media literacy education or the development of an international interest in incorporating education about media into youth's education and schooling.

The final two chapters in the first section introduce variable theories and methods used to study children and media. For instance, Chapter 6 (Scheibe) describes the contribution of developmental psychology to our understanding of media's influence on children's learning from media. It examines Bandura's social cognitive theory, Piaget's theory of cognitive development, as well as theories of moral development, and demonstrates their usefulness in helping us understand media's influence. The concluding chapter of this section (Lemish) presents a balanced discussion of the different approaches to studying children and media via quantitative and qualitative research methods. Differences are rooted in how these two research traditions view the child (in the process of becoming an adult or as people, as she says, "being in their own right at each stage of development"). The author wants to find a way to bridge the differences in approach, theory and methods of these two traditions to expand and better understand media's role in children's development.

The Concerns about media and youth are well known and of long standing. In this section the authors examine the research literature on many well studied topics in the history of youth media research. Chapter 8 (Scharrer) reviews the literature on media violence effects from television, movies and videogames, and asks whether we should still be concerned about media violence. Chapter 9 expands the focus on media's potential harmful effects (Byrne) by examining a range of risky behaviors associated with youth's media use, such as the influence of social media on children's identity, cyberbullying, and children's relatively easy access to unsavory online material. Addressing a less-studied but no less important topic Chapter 10 (Jennings) examines the development of children's attraction to and relationships with media characters, what is known as parasocial interactions and parasocial relationships. The chapter looks at the influence of parasocial relationships on children's learning through media. Chapter 11 (Hains and Hunting) reviews the relatively stereotypical ways gender is portrayed in the media, and calls for future researchers to go beyond the binary descriptions of gender portrayals as either male or female to a more elaborated examination of intersectional portrayals such as how gender and race/ethnicity interact to produce various portrayals. Chapter 12 (Piotrowski) reviews the literature, such as it is, on whether the newer media platforms and technologies offer useful educational content, and presents the best current evidence on the effects of educational media on child users. Addressing a relatively new topic in the youth media research field, Chapter 13 (de Leeuw and Buijzen) looks at the links between media use and happiness in young people, and calls for a research approach grounded in a positive media psychology. Lastly, Chapter 14 (Lapierre and Akers) review how media marketing, especially marketing directed at youth, has developed, expanded, and now influences not only youth's product consumption, but also, their dietary behavior and sense of well-being.

The final section of this book shifts the attention to **The Kids** and the development of cultural practices relating to youth and media. Complementing the previous chapter on the effects of media advertising, Chapter 15 (McAllister and Hatef) adds a cultural approach in addressing the commercialization of youth culture, for example, the power of media brands such as Disney and the proliferation of character licensing to sell children a wide range of consumer products. The next three chapters in this section address the relationship between young people and digital media. Chapter 16 (Stern and Gonzalez) focuses primarily on teens and their use of mobile digital technologies such as smartphones, tablets and computers. The power of these technologies to occupy teens time and attention is discussed as well as both the positive and potentially harmful effects of such use. Focusing specifically on mobile technologies, Chapter 17 (Lim and Wang) documents how young people's use of these technologies poses both benefits and concerns for parents. On one hand, youth now can be constantly connected to their families via mobile phones. However, parents fear youth are spending too much time and attention with these technologies. Chapter 18 (Steeves) takes an international perspective in examining the balancing act inherent in how the United Nations convention on the Rights of the Child attempts to protect children online while simultaneously encouraging their information rights. The final two chapters take up a call for expanding the focus on youth media scholarship—specifically moving beyond the historically narrow focus on White, Western, middle-class, Anglophone youth. The book purposely places these two chapters at the end as they provide food for thought as youth media scholars move into the future. Specifically, Chapter 19 (Katz) offers a critique of the contemporary body of research on children's media and points out that there is much more social and cultural diversity in U.S. society than we tend to see in our youth media studies. The author challenges us to include a focus on "social difference" in our youth media scholarship. Lastly, Chapter 20 (McMillin) too wants to expand our approach to youth media studies, and offers an introduction to the key concept of global media research. This only makes since approximately 85% of today's youth live in Asia, Africa and Latin America.

The second edition of *20 Questions about Youth and the Media* expands upon the first edition with several new chapters, and most importantly, with attention to newer concerns about media's role in youth's development. Some things have changed since the last volume, especially with regard to our growing understanding of the power of digital mobile media in children's lives and our understanding of the need for more diverse theories, methods and children to study. There is much to be learned in this volume and while some things do change, our fundamental concern to ensure the healthy development of children, and media's role in such development, is still in the forefront of our desire to understand the power of media in children's lives.

Note

1. Penny dreadfuls refers to inexpensive, serialized, weekly publications popular among working class youth in Great Britain in the mid- to late-19th century (Springhall, 1998).

References

Children's Defense Fund. (2014). *The State of America's Children 2014 report*. Retrieved from http://www. childrensdefense.org/library/state-of-americas-children/

Child Trends. (2016). *Children in poverty: Indicators of child and youth well-being*. Retrieved from https://www. childtrends.org/wp-content/uploads/2016/12/04_Poverty.pdf

Hurwitz, L. B., Montague, H., & Wartella, E. (2017). Food marketing to children online: A content analysis of food company websites. *Health Communication, 32*(3), 366–371. doi:http://dx.doi.org/10.1080/10410236. 2016.1138386

Jordan, A. (2017, April). *Children and media*. Van Zelst Lecture, Northwestern University.

No Kid Hungry. (2016). *Child hunger in America facts*. Retrieved from https://www.nokidhungry.org/problem/ hunger-facts

Springhall, J. (1998). *Youth, popular culture and moral panics: Penny gaffs to gangsta rap, 1830–1996*. New York, NY: St. Martin's.

UNICEF. (2016). *State of the World's Children 2016 report*. Retrieved from https://www.unicef.org/publications/ files/UNICEF_SOWC_2016.pdf

Vygotsky, L. (1978). *Mind in society: The development of higher psychological processes*. Cambridge, MA: Harvard University Press.

Wartella, E. (2007). Introduction: Where have we been and where are we going. In S. R. Mazzarella (Ed.), *20 questions about youth and the media* (pp. 1–10). New York, NY: Peter Lang.

Wartella, E., Lauricella, A. R., & Blackwell, C. K. (2016). *The ready to learn program: 2010–2015 policy brief.* Report for the Center on Media and Human Development School of Communication, Northwestern University. Retrieved from http://cmhd.northwestern.edu/wp-content/uploads/2016/04/RTL-Policy-Brief-2010-2015-Wartella-et-al-FINAL-March-2016.pdf

Wartella, E., Rideout, V., Lauricella, A., & Connell, S. (2014). *Revised parenting in the age of digital technology: A national survey.* Report of the Center on Media and Human Development, School of Communication, Northwestern University. Retrieved from http://cmhd.northwestern.edu/wp-content/uploads/2015/06/ ParentingAgeDigitalTechnology.REVISED.FINAL_.2014.pdf

PART 1

The Players: Corporations, Government, Parents & Child Advocacy Organizations & Scholars

CHAPTER 1

How Has the Kids' Media Industry Evolved?

J. Alison Bryant

The kids' media industry has changed dramatically over the last nine decades. From silent films to massive multiplayer online role-playing games to social networks and augmented reality, the ways in which children and adolescents can spend their leisure time have expanded exponentially. With this increase in choice has come an increase in the complexity of creating, distributing, and financing children's media. This chapter looks at what goes on "behind the curtain" in the kids' media industry and how that affects the media that kids have and use. This chapter will follow the children's media industry from the early days of film and radio to today's multimedia and immersive environment to look at the coevolution of the industry and the technology. In particular, it will look at the relationships among distributors, content creators, toy companies, and advertisers as children's media has changed over time, and will delve into the shifting dynamics among these organizational actors.

Early Days of Film and Radio (1920s–1940s)

The first two mass media to capture the eyes and ears of youth were motion pictures and radio programming. In the 1920s movie theaters became a major form of entertainment for kids, with the average child attending 1.6 movies per week in 1929 (Cressey, 1934). For young film viewers, the Saturday-afternoon matinee became a social ritual. Although originally these matinees were primarily short films and newsreels, once studios saw the revenue coming from their younger crowds, they began producing family films (Mitroff & Herr Stephenson, 2006). The first company to delve into this market is probably not a surprise to anyone today, since it continues to dominate the family-film genre. Disney released *Snow White and the Seven Dwarfs* in 1937 to great commercial success (Paik, 2001).

As film was gaining wide popularity in the 1920s, radio was still in its infancy. But by the 1930s, radio had firmly established itself as a kid-friendly medium. By 1930, 46% of American families had radios in their homes, and by 1940, 80% did (Paik, 2001). This in-home, easily accessible medium soon began to give film a run for its money—literally. As children curbed their cinema attendance, they greatly increased their radio listening time. By the mid-1930s, tweens (nine- to twelve-year-olds) were listening to two to three hours of radio a day, and in the New York City area alone there were fifty-two radio programs for kids (DeBoer, 1937; Eisenberg, 1936; Jersild, 1939; Paik, 2001).

As radio gained popularity, and status as the new family "hearth," there was a shift in the commercial interest paid to the medium. This shift manifested itself in two ways. First, networks were established in order to lure advertisers with the promise of larger audiences and to share costs, thus establishing the network model that would later be adopted by television (Alexander & Owers, 1998; Mitroff & Herr Stephenson, 2006). Second, advertisers began to see radio as an important medium, especially for reaching children (Pecora, 1998). Companies such as General Mills, Ovaltine, and Jell-O began to sponsor radio programs for kids (for example, *Jack Armstrong*, *Little Orphan Annie*, and *Wizard of Oz*, respectively) (Pecora, 1998; Summers, 1971). This form of radio sponsorship remained relatively unchanged until the 1950s, when television began to supplant radio as the kids' medium of choice.

TV Reigns Supreme (1950s–1970s)

In the 1940s and early 1950s, the purpose of television programs for children was to create the vision of the television as the new family hearth, and to therefore sell television sets to parents (Calabro, 1992; Melody, 1973; Schneider, 1987). The first daily thirty-minute program designed specifically for children, *Small Fry Club*, went on the air in 1947 (Mitroff & Herr Stephenson, 2006). It was soon followed by advertiser-sponsored shows such as *Kukla, Fran and Ollie*, and *Howdy Doody*, which were created by the broadcast networks, shown during prime-time hours, and meant to be entertaining for both children and adults. Although NBC, CBS, the now-defunct DuMont, and later ABC provided children's television programming as part of their lineup, for the most part programming for children was concentrated at the local level and was generally inexpensively produced (Schneider, 1987).

The advent of children's television programming and advertising as we know it today, however, occurred in the mid-1950s. In late 1954, ABC partnered with Disney to create *Disneyland*, an hour-long, high-quality program for children in which Disney was allowed to fully promote the new Disneyland amusement park and the collection of Disney films (Melody, 1973). This program met both ratings and critical success, and quickly became the model for children's programming—Hollywood studio programming sponsored through advertisements and program sponsorships. Disney's next venture, *The Mickey Mouse Club*, solidified this model. In November 1955, Walt Disney's *Mickey Mouse Club* became the first show to be aired every weekday during the child-targeted after-school time (Schneider, 1987). "No other show before it reached as many children with as much frequency. And no other show before it was used as effectively by advertisers of children's products" (Schneider, 1987, p. 12).

This new advertising model provided a wonderful opportunity for toy companies to take a strong position in children's television advertising. Mattel's Burp Gun became the first toy featured in a television commercial when it aired during *The Mickey Mouse Club* (Cross, 1997;

Schneider, 1987). For the first season of *The Mickey Mouse Club*, the cost of advertising sponsorship for the program was $500,000 per year (Schneider, 1987). For this amount, Mattel was given fifteen minutes to show three toy commercials. These commercials aired Wednesday evenings from 5:30 to 5:45, during *The Mickey Mouse Club*. At that time, there were no toy-industry giants as we know them today (such as Hasbro or Mattel), so this was a sizeable investment for a toy manufacturer. The wild success of the show proved to be worth the outrageous price tag. Sales of the Mattel Burp Gun, for example, doubled the company's entire previous annual profit in the few weeks between Thanksgiving and Christmas in 1955 (Schneider, 1987).

In 1958 Mattel introduced its first girl-directed toy, the Barbie doll. "Each commercial [for Barbie] was treated as a mini-episode in Barbie's glamorous life"; the advertising campaign was so successful that the television exposure of the doll had to be immediately cut back due to a demand for the doll that far outweighed the supply (Schneider, 1987, p. 30). The Barbie doll was soon followed by an array of successful tie-in products, such as the Barbie newsletter, Barbie magazine, and Barbie books, and the formation of the Barbie Fan Club (Schneider, 1987). These early successes for Mattel solidified the notion that commercials within children's programming were highly effective. By 1962, Hanna-Barbera, following this new model, was making over a million dollars from tie-in products alone (Barnouw, 1970, qtd. in Melody, 1973).

Non-toy advertising directed to children also began to emerge en force in the mid-1960s. Products such as Cheerios, Twinkies, and Star Brite Toothpaste all found their place in children's television programming (*Kid's Commercials*, 2003). General Foods' created *Linus the Lionhearted*, a vehicle for a spokescharacter of their cereals (Schneider, 1987).

During this period, advertising agencies began to specialize in the children's market and to understand the relative economic status and buying power of children within the household (Melody, 1973). Shortly after the advent of advertising-driven children's programming, two related but disparate forces changed the face of kids' programming. First, the homogenous viewing audience for television programming, which up to this point had been comprised of both adults and children, began to segment (Mitroff & Herr Stephenson, 2006). Programming watched by adults during prime hours became very lucrative for networks because it could command high advertising rates. This prompted the networks to relocate children's television in the 1960s to Saturday morning, a heretofore financially dismal time slot (Melody, 1973). Concurrently, the relative commercial success, now synonymous with advertising revenue, of shows like *The Mickey Mouse Club* made the networks recognize the untapped potential of the children's market. They began to pack this Saturday-morning time with inexpensive animated programming and extensive advertising (twice as much as in prime-time programming) (Melody, 1973). In the years following, producers and executives, such as Fred Silverman, introduced new production techniques and new higher-quality cartoons. These new cartoons, such as *The Jetsons*, garnered larger audiences than the old shows, and quickly became indispensable avenues of advertising for toys and other child-oriented products (Schneider, 1987). Stations realized huge profits from this programming (Schneider, 1987).

In the late 1960s, a new player entered the children's television broadcasting market—the Public Broadcasting System. Concurrent with the formation of PBS was the creation of Children's Television Workshop (CTW), whose program *Sesame Street* quickly became a highly heralded and highly watched educational program. The show was originally created to improve basic knowledge and social skills in preschool children, particularly minority and inner-city youth. The success of *Sesame Street* paved the way for an increase in educational programs on

PBS in the 1970s. *The Electric Company* came on the scene in 1971, and over the next several years other shows, including *Zoom, Big Blue Marble, Villa Alegre*, and *Vegetable Soup*, were created (Simensky, 2006). Most of these programs were relatively short-lived, however, in part due to their expensive, research-intensive live-action production costs. In the 1970s, the networks focused on animation instead.

Another change in the production-distribution system came when toy manufacturers entered the mix. Mattel was, again, the groundbreaker in this arena, entering into an alliance with ABC to create the first children's television program focused around a specific toy. *The Hot Wheels* show, created in 1969 by Mattel and programmed on Saturday mornings on ABC, was a thirty-minute program devoted to the product through the storylines (Schneider, 1987). It became the first in the genre of the "program-length commercial." The program did not air for long, but its influence would resurface again in the 1980s.

Although such barefaced toy tie-ins in entertainment programming were taboo in the 1970s, licensing of program-related products took off in the late 1970s (Pecora, 1998). In particular, licensing related to *Sesame Street* became an important archetype for providing for program longevity. Although originally funded by governmental bodies and philanthropic organizations, the program's producer, CTW, soon received pressure from the funders to find alternative sources of revenue to support the exorbitant production costs of the program (J. G. Cooney, personal communication, April 3, 2003). They quickly turned to licensing revenue, and partnered with the Jim Henson Production Company, which had created characters that were easily turned into plush, cuddly toys (Cross, 1997; J. G. Cooney, personal communication, April 3, 2003). Although it took several years for the licensing model to begin generating substantial revenue, by the mid-1970s licensing revenue was a major source of funding for the nonprofit organization (Pecora, 1998; J. G. Cooney, personal communication, April 3, 2003).

In addition to toy tie-ins, advertising for other children's products continued to move heavily into children's programming. By the early 1970s, Kellogg, Mattel, and General Mills accounted for 30% of all advertising revenues on the networks (Pearce, 1972). Moreover, the fast-food wars, between Ronald McDonald and the Burger "King," had begun in full force (McNeal, 1992).

TV Still Rules, but Pac-Man Begins to Gobble up Kids' Time (1980s)

Throughout the 1970s, children's television continued to consist mostly of inexpensive cartoons. In the 1980s, animation continued to dominate, but the organizations creating those cartoons changed to some extent. The deregulatory atmosphere of the Reagan administration, along with changes in the technological environment of television (specifically the marked increase in cable channels), provided an environment in which a new programming and sponsorship model for entertainment content arose. (See Chapter 2 for a complete history of the regulation of children's media in the United States.) In the 1980s, "program-length commercials" resurfaced and became the children's television standard, blurring "the line between sponsorship and program" (Pecora, 1998, p. 34).

Programs from the benign *Smurfs, Rainbow Brite*, and *My Little Pony* to the brutish *Transformers, He-Man*, and *Thundercats* proliferated in this environment. In many cases, content creators during this decade were so tightly aligned with toy manufacturers that it was hard to tell where one organization began and the other ended in the production of the programs. Two particularly telling examples show how this blurring of organizational boundaries occurred: *The Smurfs* and *He-Man and the Masters of the Universe* (Pecora, 1998).

The creation, financing, distribution, and licensing of *He-Man and the Masters of the Universe* is an extreme example of how the organizational boundaries blurred in the 1980s (Pecora, 1998). Filmation and its parent company, Group W, created and financed *He-Man* in conjunction with Mattel; Mattel retained licensing rights while Filmation/Group W retained syndication rights (Mattel, 1984; Pecora, 1998). The cartoon was shown on independent stations, which reaped the benefits in both ratings and product cost (Pecora, 1998). "Stations had a guaranteed commitment of advertising revenue from Mattel; Mattel, on the other hand, had up-front assurances of advertising time from the stations" (Pecora, 1998, p. 71). A barter relationship was created between the two: the stations provided the time and Mattel provided the programming.

The financial success of *He-Man* for all companies involved provided the example for the creation, financing, distribution, and licensing of toy-based entertainment programming for children throughout the decade. To highlight the extent of this trend toward toy-based programming, between 1980 and 1987 the percentage of toys sold in the United States that were based on licensed characters increased from 10% to 60% (Cross, 1997). The licensing frenzy of the 1980s also brought to light an important benefit of the relationship among toy manufacturers, content creators, and broadcasters—"by linking toys to television, the longevity of a product line can be enhanced" (Pecora, 1998, p. 51).

In addition to the change in the type and quality of children's programming being broadcast by the major networks, the 1980s also brought the launch of a fundamental change in the television landscape—the rise of cable. By 1983, "cable supplied almost 70% of children's programming hours" (Pecora, 1998, p. 82). By 1987, half of America had cable, so access to cable programming for children was a reality for half of American families (Calabro, 1992). Two major cable organizations, Nickelodeon and the Disney Channel, entered the children's television community during this time and were responsible for most of this dramatic change in children's television programming.

Nickelodeon, created as the program *Pinwheel* in 1979 and evolving into a cable channel by 1982, was the first cable channel aimed entirely at a child audience (Pecora, 1998). Although the channel was originally commercial-free, in 1983 it moved to an advertising-sponsored model (Calabro, 1992; Mifflin, 1999; Pecora, 1998; R. Weisskoff, personal communication, April 2, 2003). The programs were targeted to the six- to twelve-year-old set, and Nickelodeon successfully set its brand identity as the anti-adult channel (D. F. Meir, personal communication, March 28, 2003; Tracy, 2002).

Soon after Nickelodeon hit the cable lines, Disney launched a channel based on its megabrand (Kalagian, 2006). Unlike Nickelodeon, the Disney Channel began as a premium channel. Like Nickelodeon, the Disney Channel focuses on children, although 15 to 30% of its viewers are families without children (Pecora, 1998). Unlike Nickelodeon, however, the channel began with a strong footing because of the Disney conglomerate and its shear reach throughout the children's media and products. The channel was used to capitalize on the larger Disney brand image, and although the channel is technically commercial-free, the entire set of programming, from regular programs to movies to interstitials, was "one long advertisement for the Walt Disney empire" (Pecora, 1998, p. 84). Considering the vast holdings of the Walt Disney company, this "advertisement" had a large effect on the licensing of products, from theme park tickets to plush dolls, related to the programming (Pecora, 1998).

These new cable venues provided even more airtime for children's product advertising. In 1984 there were more than seventy-five corporations in the United States that provided services or products for children nationally (Schneider, 1987). These companies were spending over $500 million on advertising annually, most of which was concentrated on television advertisements (Schneider, 1987).

While television continued to flourish, a new medium began to gain ground in the lives of kids. Although arcade games had been around since the 1970s, it wasn't until the 1980s that video game consoles for home use became commonplace. The Atari 2600, which was released in 1977, suddenly exploded in popularity with the release of *Pac-Man* in 1980 (McDonald, 2005). Über-hits based on popular arcade games, like *Donkey Kong* and *Q*Bert*, soon followed. By 1981, video game consoles were a billion-dollar industry (Hart, 2000). After flourishing for a couple years, the video game industry floundered until 1985, when Nintendo released its Nintendo Entertainment System (NES) (Hart, 2000). A huge game catalogue, including *Super Mario Bros.*, *Legend of Zelda*, and *Final Fantasy*, secured Nintendo's dominance until the mid-1990s. The release of the Nintendo GameBoy in 1988 changed family road trips forever, with kids now able to take their video games with them anywhere.

The Decade of Consolidation (1990s)

The 1990s began with major changes in strategy by two key broadcasters that had a significant effect on the children's television community. The first transformation was PBS's revamping of its educational programming lineup. In 1991 PBS responded to the doldrums of children's programming by scheduling *Barney & Friends*, *Shining Time Station*, and *Lamb Chop's Play-Along*. *Barney*, in particular, was a huge success, and PBS took steps to add more programming. In 1992, through the Ready-to-Learn Act, PBS furthered its goal of providing a significant amount of educational programming by implementing its Ready-to-Learn (RTL) programming block (S. Petroff, personal communication, April 7, 2003). PBS's RTL combines eleven hours of educational programming throughout the day with community and parent outreach and resources, to address social and emotional development, physical well-being and motor development, approaches to learning, language skills, cognitive skills, and the general knowledge of two- to eight-year-olds. In order for a program to be part of RTL, it must have curriculum goals, as well as a formative and summative research plan, either in- or out-of-house.

In 1994, partly in response to RTL and partly out of the recognition that preschool-age children were still underserved, Nickelodeon made a major organizational change, deciding to invest $60 million and six hours a day in Nick Jr., a channel-within-a-channel focusing on educational programming for preschoolers (Andersen, 1998; Tracy, 2002). This foray into preschool educational programming got off to a stellar start, and *Blue's Clues*, the first in-house Nick Jr. production, was a financial coup for Nickelodeon. Nick Jr.'s successful model of educational production, channel branding, and product licensing became the gold standard in children's programming.

The success of Nickelodeon spurred several other large media corporations to take the plunge into children's television. The Cartoon Network by Time-Warner; Fox Kids Network by Fox; Noggin, a joint venture in educational television by CTW and Nickelodeon (which is now wholly owned by Nickelodeon and rebranded as Nick Jr.); DiscoveryKids by Discovery Channel; and the Kids Channel by PBS were examples of the boom in cable channels entering the population of children's television content programmers. This fundamentally altered the content programming landscape. In 1997, for example, basic cable provided 40% of children's programming; PBS provided 22%; premium channels provided 19%; small networks (FOX, UPN, WB) provided 17%; and the Big Three provided only 2% (Jordan & Woodard, 1997).

The larger industry trend toward vertical integration in the 1990s affected those organizations that program content for children. ABC, for example, became saturated with programming from its owner, Disney, and WB was able to program any Warner Bros. cartoons from its vast archive—and all at a huge profit margin. In addition, media conglomerates began to use their in-house resources to provide the educational and informational programming required by the Children's Television Act of 1990. For instance, CBS began airing programming from its Viacom sister-company, Nick Jr, and NBC began using Discovery Kids programming.

In addition to consolidation within and among media companies, the relationship between toy manufacturers and content creators remained strong in the 1990s. Programs such as *Teenage Mutant Ninja Turtles*, *Mighty Morphin Power Rangers*, and *Pokémon* continued the trend of successful licensing and toy-driven media products (Cross, 1997). A similar development was seen in the renewed and amplified fervor of successful licensing relationships between toy manufacturers and educational content. *Barney*, *Sesame Street*, and *Blue's Clues* all had phenomenally successful merchandising ventures (A. Cahn, personal communication, April 3, 2003; Pecora, 1998; M. Williams, personal communication, March 31, 2003). The Tickle-Me Elmo doll produced by Fisher-Price/Mattel in 1996 became a legend in merchandising history (Byrne, 2003; Fisher-Price, 2003). In 1998 *Teletubbies* generated $800 million in licensed product sales (Mifflin, 1999). In essence, toy licensing became a major factor (if not *the* major factor) in measuring the success of any children's television program.

Moreover, as a result of a series of mergers and acquisitions, by the end of the century, the three largest toy companies (Hasbro, Mattel, and LEGO) controlled nearly 85% of the marketplace (T. Conley, personal communication, April 4, 2003; T. Bartlett, personal communication, April 3, 2003).

Advertisers also saw an enhanced relationship with media companies during the 1990s. The most noteworthy change in the television landscape from the advertisers' perspective was the segmentation of the children's market by age and gender (McNeal, 1992). With more than a thousand hours of children's programming a week on network and cable channels, and programming being targeted to smaller niche age groups, audience fragmentation increased dramatically (Alexander & Owers, 2006). This fragmentation, in turn, gave advertisers greater choice in where to place their advertising, but made it harder to reach a large kids audience. From 1996 to 1999, the amount of advertiser revenue increased "at a double-digit rate annually, and it exceeded $1 billion for the 1998–99 season" (Mifflin, 1999, p. 4). The major players in advertising, however, remained the same: Hasbro, Mattel, Kraft, General Foods, and Kellogg (Alexander & Owers, 2006).

Just as the television audience grew fragmented because of an increase in programming choices, so did the market for video games in the 1990s. Although Nintendo entered the decade with a stranglehold on the market, for the first time it faced real competition. With the release of the Sega Genesis in 1989, Sega gained a foothold in the console market and had sold 1 million units by 1991 (Hart, 2000). Nintendo, realizing that its position of power was quickly waning, responded with the release of the Super Nintendo system. Although this system secured Nintendo's primacy in the market for the next few years, it was clear that the video game industry was changing. By the second half of the decade, the race for the most powerful gaming system and the largest share of the market had quickened. Sony entered the contest with their PlayStation in 1995, just as Sega was reentering the market with the Saturn. Nintendo countered by releasing the Nintendo 64 in 1996. At the close of the decade, Sega got in a final jab with the release of the Dreamcast system.

While console gaming systems flourished, another medium was beginning to compete for kids' attention—online games. As personal computers became more commonplace in homes, and the Internet extended its reach, kids and companies began to explore the possibilities of gaming that was also socially interactive. Although this type of gaming did not really catch on until the next century, the potential for combining the popularity of gaming with the power of the Internet was becoming clear.

Everything's Multiplatform (2000–2010)

As we entered the 21st century, the hallmark of children's media was that it was *multi*media. Even though linear television still reigned supreme, with the proliferation of devices in homes consumption of multiple media became more normative (Roberts, Foehr, & Rideout, 2005). Understanding that kids wanted to experience brands and characters on all the platforms they accessed drove the media industry to correspondingly develop, distribute, and market their content. Continuing on a wave of industry consolidation and cross-industry partnerships, the many media that kids used became more and more integrated and interrelated. In order to pitch a product for the children's entertainment market, it became increasingly important to work through the viability of the product, licensable figure, or brand in other media.

> The real profit in children's television is in the production/distribution arena, where ancillary marketing, aftermarkets, and international co-ventures and distribution are a multi-billion dollar industry. (Alexander & Owers, 2006, p. 72)

A continued increase in the number of television channels, especially in light of the move to digital television, coupled with new technologies that gave audiences more agency over their viewing, such as video-on-demand (VOD) and digital video recorders also began to fundamentally change the infrastructure and advertising underpinning that the industry had been accustomed to since the 1950s. The introduction (and quick adoption and retention by families) of Netflix—a subscription video service that began with DVDs and quickly moved to streaming video in 2007—meant true on-demand, anytime access to video content *without commercials* for children for a small monthly fee (Netflix, 2017). In 2005, YouTube debuted and very quickly rose to dominate the online video landscape for kids, providing access to alternative, user-generated and low-budget viewing options from the traditional high price-tag content that kids' brands had been creating for decades. The purchase of YouTube by Google in 2006 for $1.65 billion signaled to the industry that this wasn't just a passing fad (La Monica, 2006).

Other new technologies and Internet applications, such as MP3 players, handheld gaming systems (like the Nintendo GameBoy and DS), online games, and instant messaging, were also competing for kids' attention. And toward the end of the decade, mobile phones, which had been solely an adult technology, began to move into the hands of kids and teens as hand-me-down devices or "passed back" to them from their parents to keep them occupied. To give a sense of the dramatic adoption of these technologies, while 45% of U.S. teens had mobile phones by 2004, 71% had them only four years later in 2008 (Lenhart, 2009)! Moreover, by 2008 in the U.S.:

- 77% of teens owned a game console like an Xbox or a PlayStation
- 74% of teens owned an iPod or mp3 player
- 60% of teens "owned" a desktop or laptop computer (a number that was stable by about 2006)
- 55% of teens owned a portable gaming device. (Lenhart, 2009)

In response to this proliferation of devices and content, advertisers and the broadcasters that depended on their revenue began searching for new alternatives to the traditional ways of financially supporting their programming (although many in the industry would argue that they waited too long to begin that search). Product placement in every medium, from television to film to video games, became one popular solution to this issue of advertising. Another solution was the use of interactive advertising. This type of advertising was used extensively on the Internet, through vehicles such as "advergames" that highlight specific products (Pereira, 2004). On television, interactive advertising never really took off, as the TV viewing experience was more of a "lean back" experience that users weren't very interested in interacting with.

From a content and programming perspective, there was a trend toward embracing the dissolution of boundaries between the media and focusing on cross-platform branding as a means of reining in kids' attention and eventually their parent's wallets. Megaliths like Viacom and ABC/Disney, which had departments that managed content across TV, consumer products, and digital media, were able to offer kids their characters and brand experiences across platforms. From television to film to home video to publishing and beyond, licensing rights became even more important. They also became increasingly complex, as companies began to alter their licensing agreements for digital and multiplatform rights to their content (Castleman, 2005).

At the same time, maintaining control over one's product, and making a profit, became increasingly problematic and complex. Various "modes of digital distribution such as VOD, mobile and broadband [were] making inroads with consumers and threatening to supplant linear network broadcast" (Castleman, 2005, p. 93). Because the same program could be shown on broadcast, on-demand, online, and on mobile phones, content "windowing"—the delineation of where and when content is accessible on various platforms and services—became an important part of the programming world. In addition, defining how to monetize this windowed content across these platforms was a struggle for the traditional children's networks.

Similar issues were arising on the video game side of the children's media industry. In 2001 three video game consoles were released—Microsoft's Xbox, Nintendo's GameCube, and Sony's PlayStation 2—with the Xbox being the first console to integrate online gaming capabilities. In 2006, the Nintendo Wii was released with the first motion-based controller; and at the close of the decade Microsoft released its controller-less Kinect platform for Xbox. Although originally some of the games for these platforms were developed and distributed through smaller companies, there was also a trend toward consolidation within the large media conglomerates like Sony and Microsoft. Moreover, alternate revenue-generation methods—product placement and advertising in games, for example—became commonplace. Finally, other media tie-ins, such as character licensing for film and television, although not new to video gaming, became a more integrated part of the game-creation and product-license process.

Online gaming, both console- and computer-based, took hold in children's lives and moved from being solely in the living room to being virtual social spaces. Massive multiplayer online role-playing games and virtual worlds, such as Club Penguin, Neopets, Webkinz, and Poptropica; and connected capabilities of gaming consoles, such as Xbox Live; changed the ways in which children could communicate with other kids through gaming experiences. Club Penguin, in particular, saw huge success from being a "light" social platform for kids to communicate by sending quick chats to one another via their penguins in between playing games. It was so successful that Disney purchased it in 2007, when it had grown to about 12 million users (with very little promotion), including 700,000 paid subscribers that were generating $40 million in annual revenue (Walmsley, 2007).

Moreover, the rise of casual gaming—from Bejeweled to AddictingGames.com—meant that even if they weren't playing together, they were talking about their play the next day at school. Gaming became a core social currency for this generation of kids. And the currency for the industry in this space moved toward subscriptions and micropayments for virtual content.

Social and Virtual Realities (2010 and Beyond)

As fast-paced as the 2000s were with new technologies coming to market and disrupting the children's media industry, the short time since 2010 has seen even more dramatic changes in kids' access and use of these technologies and the implications for content and programming. On the television and video side, online streaming services such as Netflix, Hulu, and Amazon Prime, have seen significantly higher adoption and retention by families. In the U.S., 78% of families with kids 2–9 pay for these services, overindexing on these subscription video-on-demand (SVOD) services by 200% over the general population (PlayScience, 2015). Netflix and Amazon, in particular, have responded by starting to create their own content—in many ways starting to function like the early networks. In addition, as families have started to fully utilize the capabilities of Smart TV and platforms like Apple TV and Chromecast, which allow streaming of these SVOD services on the "big screen" in the living room, the lines between traditional linear viewing and on-demand viewing become increasing blurred. Kids today expect their favorite shows and movies to be available whenever they want them.

And they expect their videos, as well as all of their interactive content, to be available anywhere they are. Mobile devices, and especially tablets for use with kids, are now the norm for most families, even at the youngest ages (Kabali *et al.*, 2015). By 2013—only three years after the release of the first iPad and six years after the iPhone came out—three-fourths of kids under eight were using a tablet or smartphone (Common Sense Media, 2013). Children use them both on-the-go and at home and, although coviewing and big screen TV watching continues to be a mainstay, more personalized viewing and playing experiences are a part of everyday life.

In addition, YouTube has continued to be a dominant player for kids in this decade, and consistently ranks in the top 3 websites or apps for kids 5–14. Moving slightly away from its user-generated roots and advertising-driven revenue, YouTube has begun to augment its business model to incorporate more traditional "channel" viewing models with subscriptions and focusing on relationships with more professional or pro-am producers. In early 2015, they launched YouTube Kids, with the goal of more directly addressing the younger market and parents' concerns about advertising and content (Alba, 2015). Although the success of that venture remains to be seen, it was a significant move for such a dominant player in the kids' video space.

On the interactive side, social and gaming (and the intersection of the two) have found a large space in kids' lives and in the marketplace. The massive success of Minecraft—created by the small developer, Mojang, in Sweden and purchased by Microsoft in 2014 for $2.5 billion—showed that a multiplatform game with a strong kid audience could find financial success (Ovide & Rusli, 2014). It even broke many of the traditional education and entertainment barriers in gaming by blurring the B2C (business to consumer) and B2E (business to education) lines and finding significant use in schools. Casual games, such as *Candy Crush* and *Angry Birds*, have seen strong commercial success—in part because they appeal to a broader consumer audience as well as kids and families. *Angry Birds* has been an interesting example in the kids' space of a property that began as a casual game and has extended into other media, such as film, television, and even theme parks (Masters, 2016). And in social media, we have seen kids, and especially teens, moving from platform to platform—Facebook, Snapchat, Kik, and more—as new services and capabilities become available.

As we move through the second half of this decade, there is a significant amount of speculation as to which platforms and business models will be the next big thing. Virtual reality, augmented reality, and artificial intelligence are all moving mainstream; although they remain on the edges in the kids' space at this point. That said, the breakout success of Pokemon GO!, an augmented gaming version of the evergreen property that made $200 million in its first month, showed the potential that these new technologies and platforms can have for families (Etherington, 2016).

The next several years will continue to provide a challenge to those creating and providing media content to children and adolescents. The children's media industry is in constant transformation as new platforms and distribution opportunities continue to come to market. Although there is a lot of speculation as to what the technology and the industry will look like in ten years (or even two years), what will continue to be key is the importance of great characters and storytelling to drive compelling content, and social spaces for kids to communicate around that content.

Exercises

1. Create a timeline of the children's media industry. Make sure to include both changes in technology as well as the major players in the industry during each period. What have been the most interesting changes? What surprises you as remaining relatively constant?

2. Imagine you are Sony, a global media corporation with a huge consumer products base. What is your next move within the children's media industry? Come up with a business plan for the next five years. What partnerships within the industry would you try to forge? Which competitors will you have to worry about? How will you deal with the converging media environment?

3. Imagine that you are Disney. You own the rights to one of the largest catalogues of children's media content in the world. Come up with a business plan for the next five years. How would you go about capitalizing on your content? What have you learned from your

experiences over the past nine decades that will inform your decision-making?

4. Imagine that you are an advertising agency in today's media environment. You've just landed a major account with Kellogg to completely revamp its advertising strategies. What would be your pitch? Make sure to reflect on the issues raised in the chapter, such as branding and the challenges to advertising in the new environment of converging media.

5. If you are Amazon—with a very diverse set of business, including now kids programming—how would you address the cross-platform viewing and consumption habits of kids? Would you try to integrate the program and character touchpoints through your platforms or keep them separate, and why?

References

Alba, D. (2015). Google launches "YouTube Kids," a new family friendly app. *Wired*. Retrieved from https://www.wired.com/2015/02/youtube-kids

Alexander, A., & Owers, J. C. (1998). *Media economic theory and practice*. Mahwah, NJ: Lawrence Erlbaum.

Alexander, A., & Owers, J. C. (2006). *The economics of children's television*. In J. A. Bryant (Ed.), *The children's television community* (pp. 57–74). Mahwah, NJ: Lawrence Erlbaum.

Andersen, D. R. (1998). Educational television is not an oxymoron. *Annals of the American Academy of Political and Social Science, 557*(1), 24–38. doi:10.1177/0002716298557000003

Byrne, C. (2003). *Toys: Celebrating 100 years of the power of play*. New York, NY: Toy Industry Association.

Calabro, M. (1992). *Zap! A brief history of television*. New York, NY: Four Winds.

Castleman, L. (2005, October). Digital deal making: Between a right and a hard place. *KidScreen*, 93–97.

Common Sense Media. (2013). *Zero to 8: Children's media use in America 2013*. Retrieved from https://www.commonsensemedia.org/research/zero-to-eight-childrens-media-use-in-america-2013

Cressey, P. (1934). The motion picture as informal education. *Journal of Educational Sociology, 7*(8), 504–515.

Cross, G. (1997). *Kids' stuff: Toys and the changing world of American childhood*. Cambridge, MA: Harvard University Press.

DeBoer, J. J. (1937). The determination of children's interests in radio drama. *Journal of Applied Psychology, 21*(4), 456–463.

Eisenberg, A. (1936). *Children and radio programs*. New York, NY: Columbia University Press.

Etherington, D. (2016). Pokemon GO crosses 200M in global revenue one month into launch. *TechCrunch*. Retrieved from https://techcrunch.com/2016/08/07/pokemon-go-crosses-200m-in-global-revenue-one-month-into-launch

Fisher-Price. (2003). *About us*. Retrieved from http://www.fisher-price.com/us/hr/aboutus.asp#story

Hart, S. N. (2000). *A brief history of home video games*. Retrieved from http://www.geekcomix.com/vgh/

Jersild, A. T. (1939). Radio and motion pictures. In G. M. Wipple (Ed.), *The thirty-eighth yearbook of the National Society for the Study of Education* (pp. 153–160). Bloomington, IL: Public School.

Jordan, A. B., & Woodard, E. H. (1997). *The 1997 state of children's television report: Programming for children over broadcast and cable television* (no. 14). Philadelphia, PA: University of Pennsylvania, Annenberg Public Policy Center.

Kabali, H. K., Irigoyen, M. M., Nunez-Davis, R., Budacki, J. G., Mohanty, S. H., Leister, K. P., & Bonner, R. L. (2015). Exposure and use of mobile media devices by young children. *Pediatrics, 136*(6), 1044–1050. doi:10.1542/peds.2015-2151

Kalagian, T. (2006). Programming children's television: The cable model. In J. A. Bryant (Ed.), *The children's television community* (pp. 147–164). Mahwah, NJ: Lawrence Erlbaum.

Kid's Commercials. (2003). Retrieved from http://www.tvdays.com/Merchant2/merchant.mv?Screen=CTGY&Store_Code=VRA&Category_Code=kids

La Monica, P. R. (2006). Google to buy YouTube for $1.65 billion. (2006, October 9). *CNN*. Retrieved from http://money.cnn.com/2006/10/09/technology/googleyoutube_deal

Lenhart, A. (2009, August 19). Teens and mobile phones over the past five years: Pew Internet looks back. *Pew Internet & American Life Project*. Retrieved from http://www.pewinternet.org/2009/08/19/teens-and-mobile-phones-over-the-past-five-years-pew-internet-looks-back

Masters, D. (2016). 9 fun things Angry Birds has given the world from a film and a theme park to cook books and a plane. *Mirror*. Retrieved from http://www.mirror.co.uk/tv/tv-news/9-fun-things-angry-birds-7796328

Mattel. (1984). *Annual report*. El Segundo, CA: Author.

McDonald, G. (2005). *GameSpot presents: A brief history of video game music*. Retrieved from http://www.gamespot.com/gamespot/features/video/vg_music/index.html

McNeal, J. U. (1992). *Kids as customers: A handbook of marketing to children*. New York, NY: Lexington Books.

Melody, W. (1973). *Children's television: The economics of exploitation*. New Haven, CT: Yale University Press.

Mifflin, L. (1999, April 19). A growth spurt is transforming TV for children. *New York Times*, p. A1.

Mitroff, D., & Herr Stephenson, R. (2006). The television tug-of-war: A brief history of children's television programming in the United States. In J. A. Bryant (Ed.), *The children's television community* (pp. 3–34). Mahwah, NJ: Lawrence Erlbaum.

Netflix. (2017). *Netflix timeline*. Retrieved from https://media.netflix.com/en/about-netflix

Ovide, S., & Rusli, E. M. (2014). Microsoft gets "Minecraft" – Not the founders. *Wall Street Journal*. Retrieved from http://www.wsj.com/articles/microsoft-agrees-to-acquire-creator-of-minecraft-1410786190

Paik, H. (2001). The history of children's use of electronic media. In D. G. Singer & J. L. Singer (Eds.), *Handbook of children and the media* (pp. 7–28). Thousand Oaks, CA: Sage.

Pearce, A. (1972). *The economics of network children's television programming* (staff report). Washington, DC: Federal Communications Commission.

Pecora, N. (1998). *The business of children's entertainment*. New York, NY: Guilford.

Pereira, J. (2004, May 3). Junk-food games: Online arcades draw fire for immersing kids in ads; Ritz Bits wrestling, anyone? *Wall Street Journal*, p. B1.

PlayScience. (2015). *SVOD & media apps for families: A new day for "watch and play."* New York, NY: Author.

Roberts, D. F., Foehr, U. G., & Rideout, R. J. (2005). *Generation M: Media in the lives of 8–18 year-olds*. Menlo Park, CA: Kaiser Family Foundation Report.

Schneider, C. (1987). Children's television: The art, the business, and how it works. Lincolnwood, IL: NTC Business Books.

Simensky, L. (2006). Programming children's television: The PBS model. In J. A. Bryant (Ed.), *The children's television community* (pp. 131–146). Mahwah, NJ: Lawrence Erlbaum.

Summers, H. (1971). *A thirty year history of programs carried on national radio networks in the United States, 1926–1956*. New York, NY: Arno.

Tracy, D. (2002). *Blue's Clues for success: The 8 secrets behind a phenomenal business*. Chicago, IL: Dearborn Trade Publishing.

Walmsley, A. (2007, October 24). Kids' virtual worlds are maturing nicely. *Campaign*. Retrieved from http://www.campaignlive.co.uk/article/andrew-walmsley-digital-kids-virtual-worlds-maturing-nicely/756021?src_site=marketingmagazine

CHAPTER 2

How Does the U.S. Government Regulate Children's Media?

Alison Alexander and Keisha L. Hoerrner

There's no question that children are avid consumers of media content. National data show that the average American teen consumes more than nine hours of media each day, combining and often multitasking with television, the Internet, video games, social media, and other forms of mass media (Wallace, 2015). That is a dramatic 50% increase in media usage in one decade (Rideout, Roberts, & Foehr, 2005), driven primarily by mobile device access (Wallace, 2015). The love affair between media and its youngest audience members has been a staple of electronic media, especially television. While "children's television" refers to programs targeted primarily to children and designed to attract a majority of viewers who are children, it is only a small part of the total viewing of television by children. A popular prime-time situation comedy may attract many more child viewers than a "children's program" does, despite the fact that it is not targeted primarily to children, and children are not a majority of the audience.

Children's enjoyment of television began when the first television sets entered homes in the 1950s. It did not take long for children's interest in this new medium to spark governmental concern about its possible negative effects thereby igniting a debate over what role, if any, government should have in regulating television, especially content that reached the child audience. This debate has raged for more than sixty years.

While Chapter 1 provides a thorough history of the evolution of children's media, this chapter summarizes the complex set of legal concepts, players, and social issues that have defined this debate over the regulation of children's media. You might find that the intense discussion of government regulation over the last six decades has actually led to more questions than answers. Politicians, regulators, parents, advocacy groups, and media critics struggle to reach consensus on the following questions: Should the government regulate children's media? If so, how? If not, why not? After reading this chapter, decide how you would answer those questions.

First Amendment versus Vulnerable Audience: The Foundational Legal Concepts

Before delving into the specific issues of regulation and children's media, it is important to step back and briefly summarize broadcast regulation in general. All forms of mass media enjoy a certain degree of protection from governmental interference because of the First Amendment, which was added to the U.S. Constitution in 1791. Those forty-five words, which include "Congress shall make no law…abridging the freedom of speech or of the press," ensure that U.S. media outlets are not owned by the government, that they do not face daily censorship from government officials, and that they can criticize the government without facing onerous sanctions.

On the surface, the First Amendment sounds quite simple. Congress, and thereby the government, is prohibited from interfering with media content. But that's not how the First Amendment has been interpreted by the federal courts, especially when it comes to broadcasting. "No law" has never been interpreted as a complete prohibition on governmental regulation of broadcasting. Broadcast regulation experts Krattenmaker and Powe (1994) note that broadcasting has been treated differently by legislators and judges since its inception. It is the only form of mass communication, in fact, that faces direct content control by the federal government. Print media, the Internet and even violent video games enjoy significantly stronger constitutional protection than radio and television (Barbash, 2015).

The genesis for that control precedes the development of television. Beginning with the Radio Act of 1927, Congress has sought some control over broadcasting through the government's ownership of the electromagnetic spectrum. Reliance on spectrum space makes radio and television distinct from other forms of media and provides a ready rationale for governmental involvement in private industries. The Communications Act of 1934, which was overhauled extensively in 1996, provides Congress with a permanent justification for broadcast regulation.

Both the 1927 and 1934 acts explicitly stated that broadcasters must operate in the "public interest" in order to maintain their licenses for using the electromagnetic spectrum. Part of serving the public interest is to serve specific categories of audience members. One of those is children. Beginning in 1960, broadcasters have had a special obligation to serve their child audiences, ruled by regulators to be a vulnerable audience. A 1978 U.S. Supreme Court decision made it clear that "broadcasting is uniquely accessible to children, even those too young to read" and it is "uniquely pervasive," so it required closer scrutiny by the government, which has traditionally protected vulnerable members of society utilizing laws and regulations. The child labor laws are but one illustration of Congress's concern for children.

It is clear, then, that government regulation of broadcasting requires a balancing act between protection of First Amendment rights and protection of vulnerable members of the audience. A complex group of governmental and private entities struggles to maintain the balance.

The Broadcast Policy-Making Spectrum: The Major Players

In their influential work *The Politics of Broadcast Regulation*, Krasnow, Longley, and Terry (1982) explain the complex web of entities that determine broadcast regulation. They broadly categorize these entities into six groups: the Federal Communications Commission (FCC), the federal courts, the White House, Congress, the industry, and citizens' groups. It is useful to add the

Federal Trade Commission (FTC) when specifically discussing children and television issues. Following is a brief explanation of each of these groups.

- The FCC is a regulatory agency developed by Congress in 1934 to oversee broadcasting, telegraphs, and telephony. It now oversees cable, satellite, and digital communication. The FCC has five commissioners and thousands of employees.
- The federal courts, or the judicial branch of the government, hear challenges to FCC and FTC regulations as well as congressional legislation. The D.C. Circuit Court of Appeals reviews numerous cases involving the FCC and FTC.
- The White House, or executive branch of the government, both directly and indirectly influences broadcast regulation. Of course, the president must choose whether to sign any legislation that impacts broadcasting. That's a direct influence. More often, though, the president indirectly influences regulation by choosing to highlight or ignore issues related to media content.
- Congress, or the legislative branch of the government, can also directly and indirectly influence regulation. It can pass laws that direct agencies such as the FCC and FTC to develop specific regulations. It can also hold hearings to investigate issues, even if no legislation results from those hearings.
- The broadcasting industries are composed of individual station owners, corporate conglomerates, media professionals, and large trade organizations such as the National Association of Broadcasters (NAB).
- Citizens' groups are generally advocacy organizations. Groups of parents, educators, and critics band together for a specific purpose. Action for Children's Television (ACT), which formed in 1968 and disbanded in 1996, was the most influential citizens' group in terms of children and media issues. (See Chapter 4 for more information on advocacy.)
- The FTC is a regulatory agency that oversees commercial speech, or advertising. It ensures that the public is not misled by false or misleading advertising and promotes fair competition among advertisers. Like the FCC, the FTC has five commissioners, who are all political appointees, and thousands of employees.

Strolling through History: A Decade-by-Decade Review of Social Issues and Their Impact on Regulation of Children's Media

An examination of television's major changes by decade gives an overview of media development, social concerns, and public policy in the United States.

The 1950s

This decade is defined not only by poodle skirts and broadcast journalist Edward R. Murrow. It is the decade of the first congressional hearings concerning the possible negative effects of television on children. These hearings served as the template for congressional inquiries into the issue for the next four decades.

There was no regulation specifically targeting children's shows in the 1950s. The FCC was primarily concerned with stations' overall service to the "public interest." Congress, however, decided to grapple with the subject of television's impact on children, something it knew little about. In 1952 the House opened hearings to investigate "immoral and otherwise offensive matter" in radio and television programs, but ultimately concluded that "the television industry was in too great a state of flux to 'pass any conclusive judgment' upon it" (*Investigation*, 1952, p. 10).

The Senate took up the issue of television violence in 1954 and 1955. Actually, a Senate subcommittee was investigating causes and effects of juvenile delinquency. Two brief statements by witnesses turned the subcommittee's attention to television as one of the causes (Hoerrner, 1999). Senator Estes Kefauver, a Democrat from Tennessee, sparred with industry representatives over the negative effects of television crime and violence. Industry representatives repeatedly invoked the First Amendment as a protection against governmental interference in television content while at the same time promising to self-regulate and reduce the amount of violence. In response to these early hearings, the NAB adopted a Television Code noting industry responsibility to the child audience.

The results of congressional interest in negative effects of television content on child audiences were neither laws nor directives to the FCC. There were, however, results for the industry, researchers, and Congress as a whole. "Unwritten guidelines" were developed in these hearings that were utilized numerous times. Hoerrner (1999) refers to it as the development of a win-win situation: "The politicians scored points with their constituents for showing concern and outrage at any factor that contributed to crime and violence. The industry kept the government out of its daily affairs, allowing it to program the shows that would generate the greatest audience and result in more revenue."

The 1960s

During the 1960s children's programming became an extremely lucrative business. By the end of the decade, most children's programs were broadcast on Saturday mornings, a previously unprofitable time slot. Advertising minutes on Saturday-morning shows were high, up to sixteen minutes per hour in the early part of the decade (Kunkel & Wilcox, 2001), and advertisers increasingly recognized the importance of children as a potentially lucrative audience to whom they could sell toys, cereal, snacks, candy, and fast food.

In 1960 the FCC identified children's programs as one of fourteen program types usually necessary in order for broadcasters to meet their public-interest obligation (Kunkel & Wilcox, 2001). This was the first time the FCC had identified children as a "special audience" that deserved attention. Stations had to provide evidence that they were serving this special audience to facilitate the license renewal process, which had to be completed every eight years.

Congress was also paying attention to children and television in the 1960s. Five Senate hearings were held in that decade, led by Senator Thomas Dodd (Democrat from Connecticut) and Senator John Pastore (Democrat of Rhode Island). The 1969 Pastore hearings resulted in substantive action; the Secretary of Health, Education, and Welfare accepted the Senate subcommittee's request for a scientific study to determine whether a causal link existed between television violence and children's behaviors. The Surgeon General was asked to oversee this multiyear, million-dollar project. The results from this study were the subject of their own congressional hearings in the early 1970s.

The 1970s

The decade of the 1970s can be encapsulated as the "public advocacy decade." While concerned-citizens' groups were finding new ways to advocate for better children's programming, the industry seemed content to provide more of the same. Saturday morning remained the major programming block for children. Cable also became a part of the television landscape for children, with Nickelodeon debuting in 1979. Advertising to children continued unabated, and thirty-second spots dominated. The four categories of advertising to children (candy and snacks, cereals, toys, and fast food) continued to represent the majority of ads.

A group of mothers in Massachusetts banded together to promote better programming options for children. Formed in 1968 and headed by Peggy Charren, Action for Children's Television (ACT) was among the most vocal of citizens' groups calling for governmental action. ACT sought to change current programming and advertising practices by going directly to the governmental regulators charged with oversight of electronic media and the advertising industries, the FCC and the FTC (Clark, 2004).

ACT petitioned the FCC in the early 1970s to protect children from commercial persuasion and promote educational programming (Enis, Spencer, & Webb, 1980). The FCC responded in 1971 by issuing a notice of inquiry (NOI) and a notice of proposed rulemaking (NPRM), two official requests for public feedback on the issues. In 1974 the FCC instituted guidelines stating that each broadcaster was required to make a meaningful effort to provide programming for both preschool and school-aged children and that programs were to air during both weekday and weekend periods when children were likely to view.

The FCC also required broadcasters to maintain a "clear separation" between program content and commercial speech in order to simplify recognition of advertising messages. This meant that program-length commercials, shows designed to sell products like a new toy, were prohibited. Host selling, which occurs when a character on a show promotes a product during the program or in spot advertisements shown during the program, was also banned. "Bumpers," such as the familiar "We'll be back after these messages," were required. Finally, the FCC endorsed NAB amendments to its code limiting the amount of advertising during children's programs to twelve minutes per hour on weekdays and nine and a half on weekends (Kunkel & Wilcox, 2001).

When the FCC assessed compliance with the 1974 guidelines in 1979, the agency found three areas of concern: (1) total time devoted to children's programming was insufficient; (2) too little educational, informational, or age-specific programming was on the air; and (3) children's programs were still concentrated in a few time periods. The FCC promised to work on these concerns in the 1980s, but a change in leadership brought a change in the agency's focus (Alexander & Hoerrner, 2006).

ACT's next move was to petition the FTC to ban all commercials during children's programs. The FTC sent tremors through both the networks and advertisers in 1978 when it seemed to agree with the group. Because the FTC has congressional authority to protect consumers against unfair, deceptive, and fraudulent advertising, the regulators argued that children were being unfairly targeted by the ads they were too young to understand. In an unprecedented show of lobbying power, the television and advertising industries derailed the proposal by getting Congress to pass a law that specifically prohibited the agency from adopting the children's advertising rules (Alexander & Hoerrner, 2006).

While the FCC and FTC were imposing specific restrictions on programming and advertising targeting children, the Senate was concerned with broader "kidTV" issues. In 1972 the Report to the U.S. Surgeon General (widely known as the Surgeon General's Report) was released, cautiously linking children's violent behavior with television viewing. The Senate held hearings to discuss the report and its implications. Various proposals were explored, including the idea of rating television programs, but no legislative action resulted from the hearings.

The federal courts also had an impact on indecent content in television programs during this decade. The U.S. Supreme Court ruled in 1978 that the FCC had every right to enforce a "safe-harbor" restriction on content that met the agency's definition of "indecency."[1] The safe-harbor restriction kept programs with indecent content off the radio and television airwaves from 6 A.M. to 10 P.M., times when children were most likely to be in the audience. The courts and the FCC felt this was acceptable under the First Amendment because the government wasn't seeking to ban indecent content, just move it to hours when adults could view it but children were most likely to be asleep.

The 1980s

The 1980s have been characterized generally as the "deregulation decade," and that is certainly true in the area of children's television regulation. The marketplace was supposed to separate quality programs from junk, and it was supposed to punish advertisers who unfairly targeted children with deceptive messages. At least that was the opinion of the FCC under its new chairman, Mark Fowler.

Children were watching a variety of programs on an increasing number of channels in the 1980s and were perceived as primary consumers not only for shows but for a variety of products. They were also influential in their family's purchase of other products and services. Character licensing and the growth of specialty stores such as Toys "R" Us expanded the range of products available, and competition for the eyeballs of young viewers was intense.

The decade began with ACT expecting the FCC to work on quality educational programs for children and the diversification of time slots for children's shows. Those expectations would not be fulfilled when President Ronald Reagan appointed Fowler. Under his leadership the FCC removed time restrictions on advertising content during children's programming and redefined program-length commercials more narrowly as programs that include ads for the same characters as those shown in the program (Kunkel & Wilcox, 2001). As part of the streamlined licensing process, the FCC significantly reduced the information stations had to provide about how they served the public interest and their special audiences. Under Fowler's leadership, license renewals were quite easy to secure (Kunkel & Wilcox, 2001).

In 1982 a consent decree dictated by the federal courts eliminated the National Association of Broadcasters' self-regulatory advertising guidelines; the program guidelines were later abandoned. There was now less self-regulation and governmental regulation dictating programming content (Kunkel & Wilcox, 2001).

Congress, however, was still debating its role in broadcast regulation and how it could promote and/or mandate a reduction in the amount of inappropriate material on television. Senator Paul Simon (Democrat of Illinois) led the charge for the government to act to reduce both sexual and violent content. Simon and his like-minded colleagues authored five bills in the 1980s seeking to create an antitrust exemption for the television industry so representatives of the major networks, independent stations, local affiliates, cable channels, and trade organizations could develop industry-wide guidelines to reduce inappropriate content (Hoerrner, 1998). Simon argued that if all the players in the industry worked together to develop specific guidelines that they all employed at the same time, they would be willing to adhere to them. Simon, who was quite conscious of the First Amendment implications of any governmental regulation on media content, saw the antitrust exemption as promotion of self-regulation among broadcasters. None of the bills passed in the 1980s, but Simon did get his antitrust exemption in 1990.

The 1990s

The 1990s could clearly be categorized as the "decade of reckoning." The FCC changed leadership, and Congress changed its stance from simply talking about regulating television to actually passing laws that did just that.

The Children's Television Act of 1990 was the crowning achievement for ACT's years of work to push the government to improve the value of shows children were viewing (Kunkel & Wilcox, 2001). It mandated time restrictions on advertisements in children's programming, and it obligated stations to air educational/informational (E/I) programs for children sixteen or under. The first piece of legislation to actually regulate children's television content, the act focused on limiting the number of advertisements children were exposed to while increasing programming choices that furthered their cognitive learning and social/emotional needs. The act affected only traditional broadcast television, not the numerous cable channels that also aired popular programs for children (Kunkel, 1998).

The FCC designed the exact specifications for both the advertising and content rules. It quickly developed the advertising limits, requiring stations to show no more than ten and a half minutes of ads per hour on the weekend and twelve minutes per hour during the week for programs with a primarily child audience. Product placement is also prohibited during children's shows as a result of these advertising limitations (Kunkel, 1998).

After years of wrangling over how much programming and what type of programs met the E/I requirements of the act, the FCC in 1996 issued regulatory requirement to enforce the Children's Television Act of 1990 that specified stations should air three hours of educational programming each week. Stations are required to keep logs of those programs that can be viewed by the public and utilized by the FCC during license renewals. Shows that are designed to meet the educational requirements of the act are designated with a special E/I rating shown at the beginning of the show.

The second major piece of legislation relevant to children was the Telecommunications Act of 1996 that rewrote the 1934 Communications Act. Its primary focus was on opening competition within the industry, but it also included provisions requiring the adoption of a ratings system and the integration of a V-chip into television sets (Hoerrner, 1998). The V-chip is an electronic monitoring device that uses ratings to block specific programs and cannot operate without a rating system for television programming. Although a voluntary ratings system developed by the broadcast industries is called for in the legislation, there's also language that empowers the FCC to appoint an advisory board to assist in the establishment of a system should the industry choose not to do it on its own ("Telecommunications," 1996). Not surprisingly, the industry chose to voluntarily develop a ratings system, thereby negating the need for the FCC advisory board.

First, age-based ratings were developed, which mirrored the ratings scheme for motion pictures (Rice & Brown, 1996).[2] Several members of Congress spoke out immediately, charging that age-based ratings were not specific enough to provide parents with the information they needed to make informed programming choices (Fleming, 1997). A few months later, content designations were added to the ratings system. Those include "FV" for fantasy violence (a designator used for many animated children's cartoons), "V" for violence, "S" for sexual content, "L" for adult language, and "D" for suggestive dialogue. With a few exceptions, most networks and most cable channels were using age and content ratings by the end of 1997 (Albiniak, 1997).

At the end of the decade, a tragedy brought video game violence to the center of America's attention. In April 1999 the nation was stunned by the Columbine High School shootings, in which twelve high school students and a teacher were killed by two classmates. Several media reports noted that the two killers played the first-person shooter game *Doom* extensively, even constructing a shooting environment that bore many resemblances to their high school. The Entertainment Software Ratings Board (ESRB) rating system that had been in effect since 1994, and operated much like the MPAA system for film, were voluntary, self-managed rating systems, but could not shield the video game industry from public outcry that constant exposure to violent video games, particularly those first-person shooter games, was blurring the distinction between real and fantasy violence. Following Columbine and other school shootings, a handful of states tried to enact laws banning the purchase of violent or sexual video games to minors (Gledhill, 2005). The debate this tragedy engendered was a prelude to the concerns for privacy, decency, and safety that became the subjects of intense public and political concern in the 21st century.

The New Century: Same Song, New Verse

The new century has seen congressional interest and public concerns about an ever-expanding array of media choices and content that can now go with children wherever they go. In fact, the last decade has seen a demonstrative shift in how children interact with media. With a smartphone, they can engage with traditional media by streaming an episode of *The Daily Show* while also engaging in social media by posting a photo on Instagram or chatting with a small group of their friends on Snapchat. The very concepts of what is "mass" and what is "media" are causing regulators and legislators to pause. The concerns, however, seem to showcase a "same song, new verse" way of summarizing political interest: Congress, the FTC, and the FCC have been busy investigating issues of indecency, privacy and protection, violence, and educational programming (Shields, 2006) but few new regulations or laws have been enacted.

Concerned about the possible intersections of violent video games and violent acts like school shootings, California passed a law in 2005 that prohibited the sale of such games to minors. The video game and software industries sued and the case ultimately reached the Supreme Court in 2011, with the justices ruling 7–2 that the law did, in fact, infringe on free speech rights. The *Brown v. Entertainment Merchants Association* decision provided violent video games with a strong measure of protection similar to that enjoyed by books and other forms of print media. The opinion made it clear that no direct causal link existed between playing violent video games and performing acts of violence, and it also noted children had First Amendment rights that extended to violent media content they chose to consume. Justice Scalia, writing for the majority, reminded readers that "California's effort to regulate violent video games is the latest episode in a long series of failed attempts to censor violent entertainment for minors" (*Brown*, 2011, p. 17). What remains is the ESRB rating system discussed in the previous section, a self-regulatory board that rates video and computer games by age and content.

Legislators were more successful in the new century passing laws related to children's privacy and protection in use of the Internet. By 2000, when it was signed into law, the CIPA (Children's Internet Protection Act) was the third attempt by Congress to create legislation to protect children from indecent material on the Internet. This act required schools and libraries that receive federal funding and discounts for computer access to install filtering software and to enact policies regarding children's use of Internet. Also still in force is COPPA—the Children's Online Privacy Protection Act, enforced by the FTC, which applies to the online collection of personal information from children under thirteen. These rules outline requirements for a privacy policy, when and how to seek verifiable consent from a parent, and the responsibilities of a Web site operator to protect children's privacy and safety online. The FTC amended the COPPA requirements in 2013 to confirm the extension of COPPA into the world of popular social media sites such as Facebook, Twitter and Instagram, Internet access via smartphones and other mobile devices, and the prevalence of geolocation within mobile applications. The FTC reconfirmed the minimum age of 13 for most social media sites as well as requiring children 16 and under to have parental permission to use these sites (London & Silverman, 2013). Solutions are continually evolving as firms try to find ways to enforce the age and parental permission requirements.

The FTC reviewed marketing messages directed at young audiences in the new century. In 2000 the Commission issued a report exploring the marketing of violent media entertainment to children. It raised two issues: Do the industries promote products they themselves acknowledge warrant parental caution in venues where children make up a substantial percentage of the audience? In addition, are these advertisements intended to attract children and teenagers? The report found that "for all three segments of the entertainment industry, the answers are plainly 'yes'" ("FTC Report," 2000). The report found that film, video game, and music industries routinely target children under seventeen, despite content ratings identifying the content as inappropriately violent. The FTC recommended additional self-regulatory behaviors by the industry.

Another effort to protect children from the harmful effects of media content emerged over concern about unhealthy food marketing to children. Hearings before the FTC suggested possible regulatory action, but the advertising industry proposed the self-regulatory Children's Food and Beverage Advertising Initiative (CFBAI) in 2006. This initiative collects pledges from major food corporations to advertise to children only foods that meet CFBAI's nutritional standards. Housed at the same Better Business Bureau website, the Children's Advertising Review Unit (CARU), established in 1974, evaluates children's advertising for truthfulness, accuracy and consistency with their guidelines. The FTC continues to report and seek comments on food marketing to children, but so far any regulatory or rulemaking action has been forestalled.

In late 2004 the FCC issued a report making it clear to broadcasters that educational programming for children must remain part of the programming options as they move to digital broadcasting. Essentially, the FCC wanted to make it clear that the core requirements of the Children's Television Act—the three-hour minimum, the minimum length of the programs, and the E/I rating—transferred to the digital environment. The FCC's report also specified that the advertising limits remain intact in a digital world ("FCC Report," 2004). The FCC then updated its rules again in 2007 to add additional minimum requirements for stations that were multicasting in both analog and digital, clarify its prohibition on website addresses appearing during children's programming, and updating its definition of "commercial matter" in terms of stations promoting programming aimed at children.

The 2004 Super Bowl halftime show ignited a firestorm of protest when Justin Timberlake ripped the outfit of Janet Jackson, exposing her breast. The debate raised the old question of whether there should be some measure of control exerted over sexually provocative material. This social debate turned serious for the networks when Congress became involved. In June of 2006, President Bush signed into law the Broadcast Decency Act, which raised the ceiling on indecency fines from $32,500 to $325,000 per incident. The law allows cumulative fines of $3 million per day for multiple violations (Ahrens, 2006).

The challenges of protecting children from indecent content continue as children access a variety of media using a variety of devices. In his article appropriately titled "Netflix is coming for your kids," journalist Drew Harwell reminds readers that Web-centric entities like Netflix are not regulated like television and cable channels, and are vying for young viewers, understanding the importance of creating loyal subscribers. "The big-business battle for kids' distracted attention spans has never been more competitive—or eye-poppingly lucrative," Harwell (2016, para. 3) wrote.

Discussion

So how could you summarize the government's regulation of children's media? More than six decades of action—and inaction—have shown that Congress, the White House, and governmental agencies take cautious steps toward doing something about media content likely to be consumed by children, while not wanting to appear to infringe on First Amendment rights. It's almost like a parent threatening a child. Congress wants to persuade the film, video game, and television industries (especially the latter) to protect children, but legislators really want the industries to make the decision to "do the right thing" on their own. They threaten legislation more than they actually produce it, hoping that the mere threat will prompt corrective action.

Often these threatened legislative actions do result in media taking on a self-regulatory role. Sometimes when regulatory hearings seem to result in no action by the government, careful scrutiny will show that some umbrella organization has created a watchdog unit. Media industries can issue their own threats, however. They can threaten to appeal a congressional act, or an FTC or FCC regulation, to the federal courts, prompting a discussion of First Amendment rights and governmental interference. Court appeals can stall governmental initiatives, because laws and regulations are generally not enforced while the case is working its way through the court system.

Both the government and the media industries are at times more concerned with the court of public opinion than with the court of law. Americans seem to be concerned about the safety and privacy of children, but they are also reluctant to support governmental actions that seem to infringe on hallowed free press and free speech rights. Both sides can use those social concerns to their benefit, and they often do.

It's these seemingly conflicting societal concerns that lead to a great deal of talk but very little action regarding regulation of children's media. Certainly, the U.S. Supreme Court has made it clear that television and radio enjoy less First Amendment protection than other forms of mass media, a declaration that has not changed even with the development of cable, satellite, and other new methods of broadcast transmission. The few Court decisions regarding the Internet as well as video games have provided those forms of media with almost the same level of First Amendment protection that newspapers and other printed media enjoy. Media that children, tweens, and teens consume each day, however, have received little to no attention from legislators, regulators, or jurists. Facebook may boast usage by more than 70% of 12-to-17-year-olds, according to the Pew Research Center (Smith, 2014), but there's little in terms of regulation to protect children from content on Facebook. Social media in general enjoys practically no regulation. Mobile applications, including those critics call "advergames"—those created by companies to promote their products or brand, do not face the same restrictions as program-length commercials on television (Reid, 2014).

Practically all media industries that call children their consumers have learned from watching the film, television, and radio industries interact with Congress and the courts. They push the notion of self-regulation to avoid governmental interference whenever possible. Thus far, the strategy seems to have worked. As noted scholar and Director of the Media and the Developing Child sector of the Annenberg Public Policy Center Amy Jordan (2008) explained, "The need to protect both free speech and children has given rise to a fluid media policy mix of federal mandates and industry self-regulation" (p. 235). The fluidity is likely to increase in the next decade as new media options present new regulatory questions and concerns.

Discussion Questions

1. Are children a "special" audience in need of regulatory protection? Why or why not? What age group are you referencing when you think of "children"? Should media content directed at different age groups be regulated more or less stringently than others?

2. What type of media content, if any, seems to warrant more parental attention: television social media, or video games? Why? Should Congress also be more concerned about one type of media content than another? Provide a rationale for your argument.

Exercises

1. Before you begin reading, consider who should regulate content. Write as many arguments as you can for and against government regulation, self-regulation by media industry bodies, and parental control.

2. Divide the class into groups, with each assigned to watch at least three children's programs on a selected broadcast or cable network. Have each group report to the class about the content and advertising that they see. Compare these shows to the programs watched by the students when they were young children. Groups may also want to look at content and advertising in prime-time programs that children view regularly.

3. Do an in-home observation of a child watching television or video, or playing video or computer games. Note the level of attention and engagement (rapt or wandering attention), amount of time spent with the media, and any interaction with you or others about the media. What have you learned about children and media? How does the way children react to media compare to adult consumption patterns?

Notes

1. The Supreme Court's *FCC v. Pacifica Foundation* (1978) decision upheld the FCC's definition of "indecency," which is "language or material that, in context, depicts or describes, in terms patently offensive as measured by contemporary community standards for the broadcast medium, sexual or excretory organs or activities."
2. The ratings were TV-Y (all children), TV-Y7 (older children), TV-G (general audience), TV-PG (parental guidance suggested), TV-14 (parents strongly cautioned), and TV-M (mature audiences only).

References

Ahrens, F. (2006, July 11). Six-figure fines for four-letter words worry broadcasters. *Washington Post*, p. A01. Retrieved from http://www.washingtonpost.com/wp-dyn/content/article/2006/07/10/AR2006071001245_pf.html

Albiniak, P. (1997, October 6). NBC hangs tough on ratings. *Broadcasting & Cable*, p. 16. Retrieved from www.broadcastingcable.com

Alexander, A., & Hoerrner, K. (2006). Children's advertising. In J. Ciment (Ed.), *Social issues: An encyclopedia of social issues, histories, and debates* (pp. 37–44). Armonk, NY: M. E. Sharpe.

Barbash, F. (2015, September 18). Why two Supreme Court justices played a violent video game to help decide a major case. *The Washington Post*. Retrieved from https://www.washingtonpost.com/news/morning-mix/wp/2015/09/18/how-and-why-justices-kagan-and-breyer-faced-off-in-a-violent-video-game-to-help-decide-a-major-case/

Brown vs. Entertainment Merchants Association. 131 S. Ct. 2729 (2011). Retrieved from https://www.law.cornell.edu/supct/html/08-1448.ZS.html

Clark, N. (2004). The birth of an advocacy group: The first six years of Action for Children's Television. *Journalism History, 30*(2), 66–76. Retrieved from search.proquest.com

Enis, B. M., Spencer, D. R., & Webb, D. R. (1980). Television advertising and children: Regulatory vs. competitive perspectives. *Journal of Advertising, 9*(1), 19–42. doi:10.1080/00913367.1980.10673303

FCC Report (2004, November 23). FCC report and order (M. M. Docket 00–167), on children's television obligations of digital television broadcasters.

Fleming, H. (1997, January 13). TV ratings opponents get busy. *Broadcasting & Cable*, p. 6. Retrieved from www.broadcastingcable.com

FTC Report. (2000, September). FTC report on marketing violent entertainment to children.

Gledhill, L. (2005, December 23). Judge blocks ban on sale of violent video games to minors. *San Francisco Chronicle*, p. A1. Retrieved from http://www.sfchronicle.com/archive/

Harwell, D. (2016, March 28). Netflix is coming for your kids. *The Washington Post*. Retrieved from https://www.washingtonpost.com/news/the-switch/wp/2016/03/28/netflix/

Hoerrner, K. (1998). *Symbolic politics: An historical, empirical and legal discussion of congressional efforts and the issue of television violence* (Unpublished dissertation). University of Georgia.

Hoerrner, K. (1999). The forgotten battles: Congressional hearings on television violence in the 1950s. *Web Journal of Mass Communication Research, 2*(3). Retrieved from http://www.scripps.ohiou.edu/wjmcr/vol02/2-3a.htm

Investigation of Radio and Television Programs. (1952). 82nd Cong., 2nd sess., 1952. H. Rept. 2509. U.S. Congress. House. Committee on Interstate and Foreign Commerce.

Jordan, A. (2008). Children's media policy. *Future of Children, 18*(1), 235–253. doi:10.1353/foc.0.0003

Krasnow, E., Longley, L., & Terry, H. (1982). *The politics of broadcast regulation* (3rd ed.). Gordonville, VA: Palgrave-Macmillan.

Krattenmaker, T. G., & Powe, L. A. (1994). *Regulating broadcast programming*. Blue Ridge Summit, PA: National Book Network.

Kunkel, D. (1998). Policy battles over defining children's educational television. *Annals of the American Academy of Political and Social Science, 557*(1), 39–63. doi:10.1177/0002716298557000004

Kunkel, D., & Wilcox, B. (2001). Children and media policy. In D. S. Singer & J. L. Singer (Eds.), *Handbook of children and the media* (pp. 589–604). Thousand Oaks, CA: Sage.

London, R. G., & Silverman, D. M. (2013, January 17). FTC announces COPPA rule changes. Retrieved from http://www.dwt.com/FTC-Announces-COPPA-Rule-Changes-01-17-2013/

Reid, R. (2014). Embedded advertising to children: A tactic that requires a new regulatory approach. *American Business Law Journal, 51*(4), 721–777. doi:10.1111/ablj.12038

Rice, L., & Brown, R. (1996, December 30). Networks rolling out TV ratings. *Broadcasting & Cable*, p. 7. Retrieved from www.broadcastingcable.com

Rideout, V., Roberts, D., & Foehr, U. (2005). *Generation M: Media in the lives of 8–18 year-olds*. Menlo Park, CA: Kaiser Family Foundation. Retrieved from http://www.kff.org/entmedia/7251.cfm

Shields, T. (2006, January 2). Forecast 2006: Regulation. *Mediaweek*, p. 18. Retrieved from http://www.mediaweek.com/mw/index.jsp

Smith, A. (2014, February 3). 6 new facts about Facebook. *FactTank: News in the numbers*. Retrieved from http://www.pewresearch.org/fact-tank/2014/02/03/6-new-facts-about-facebook/

Telecommunications Act of 1996. (1996). Public Law No. 104–104.

Wallace, K. (2015, November 3). Teens spend a mind-boggling' 9 hours a day using media, report says. *CNN*. Retrieved from http://www.cnn.com/2015/11/03/health/teens-tweens-media-screen-use-report/index.html

CHAPTER 3

Why Is Everybody Always Pickin' on Youth?

Moral Panics about Youth, Media, and Culture

Sharon R. Mazzarella

When I first wrote this chapter over a decade ago, the media landscape was much less complicated than it is today. Young people were media consumers—watching, reading, and listening to content produced by professional media producers. In the interim, with the rise of the Internet, smartphones, and social media, young people have rapidly become both producers and consumers of media messages, and the range of issues of concern to adults has shifted dramatically. In this chapter, I outline a series of moral panics occurring across the 20th century—panics about young audiences that were remarkably similar in their basic, recurring features. I then look at how the nature of such panics has shifted as technology, and youth's role vis-à-vis that technology, has changed in the 21st century.

Following Joe Austin and Michael Nevin Willard's (1998) lead, "youth" in this chapter refers to young people roughly between the ages of twelve and twenty-four years. It is this age group upon whom I predominantly focus; however, at times I will discuss children of a younger age. This is not to imply that children and "youth" are one and the same, but rather is an acknowledgment that the issues related to their mediated representations and cultural constructions do overlap. I will return to the discussion of moral panics, but in order to understand this recurring phenomenon, I will first address the changing construction of childhood and adolescence that occurred in the United States during the late 19th and early 20th centuries (c.f., Hawes & Hiner, 1985), a change that created a climate in which adults could easily lapse into moral panic about youth culture.

Youth as a Construct

Quite simply, childhood and adolescence are socially constructed phenomena. The child, according to Lyn Spigel (1993), is a "cultural construct, a pleasing image that adults need in order to sustain their own identities. Childhood is the difference against which adults define themselves" (p. 259). Yet while the sociocultural construct of youth works toward defining adult identities, according to Henry Giroux (1996), it also "has become indeterminant, alien, and sometimes hazardous to the public eye" (p. 10). How did we get to this point?

Prior to the late 19th and early 20th centuries, children were not necessarily considered as a distinct cultural group, but rather as miniature adults who, in all but upper-class families, played vital economic roles within the family structure. As a result, with the exception of the children of the wealthy, most did not attend school beyond just a few years. With industrialization and urbanization, the structure of families began to change away from self-sufficiency; we became a nation of consumers rather than producers. As a result, children ceased to fill the same productive economic role within families, leaving them with more time on their hands, not to mention more things to consume.

Deriving from these changes was a belief in the innocence and naiveté of children that manifest in a wealth of social, cultural, and legislative initiatives including mandatory schooling laws, the institutionalization of public education, child labor laws, and the introduction of child/adolescent psychology (Wartella & Mazzarella, 1990). Paralleling the social construction of childhood innocence was an evolution in the leisure behaviors of young people over the course of the first half of the 20th century such that they spent more time in the company of their peers engaged in various commercialized or mediated forms of leisure (e.g., movies, record stores, soda shops, bowling alleys, and so on), all of which took them further away from the watchful eyes of their parents (Wartella & Mazzarella, 1990). Not surprisingly, youth's newfound leisure was alarming to moral reformers who "were concerned that such ill-spent leisure would lead to moral degeneration, particularly in the absence of control by family, church, and school" (Wartella & Mazzarella, 1990, p. 177).

In the midst of this leisure revolution and its attendant public outcry, a new youth culture was born. Wartella and Mazzarella (1990) contend that, by the 1940s, high schoolers had been constituted as "the subject of popular attention and concern" (p. 181). The label "teenager" first appeared in a 1941 issue of the magazine *Popular Science* (Hine, 1999), and *Seventeen* magazine was founded in 1944 as one of many attempts to exploit and capitalize on the newly emergent postwar middle-class youth culture and its vast disposable income (Palladino, 1996). Sternheimer (2015) submits that the social construction of youth has "mutated dramatically over the past century" and, as such, youth "have become a potent source of fear and concern, and a ripe subject for moral crusaders" (Sternheimer, 2015, p. 146).

Moral Panic

In 1985, Ellen Wartella and Byron Reeves conducted an exhaustive literature review of the research done on children and media during the first half of the 20th century. They found that the introduction into U.S. society of each of the major electronic technologies of film, radio, and television was accompanied by considerable public discussion and debate over their perceived impact on audiences, in particular youth. Sternheimer (2015) more recently adds that each technological innovation brings "new worries that they would bring harm, that vulnerable populations would learn the wrong values in an ever-enticing media environment" (p. 6). These cycles of concern derive directly from the way the U.S. culture has, since the early 20th century, defined youth as innocent, and constitutes what James Gilbert (1986) calls an "episodic notion" (p. 4).

As defined by Sternheimer (2015) a moral panic is "a widespread fear that arises which is dramatically out of proportion with the actual threat" (p. 6). Stanley Cohen (1980), in his now-classic definition, elaborates that a moral panic occurs when

> a condition, episode, person or group of persons emerges to become defined as a threat to societal values and interests; its nature is presented in a stylized and stereotypical fashion by the mass media; the moral barricades are manned by editors, bishops, politicians and other right-thinking people; socially accredited experts pronounce their diagnoses and solutions; ways of coping are evolved or (more often) resorted to; the condition then disappears, submerges or deteriorates and becomes more visible. (p. 9)

In the case of child and youth culture, moral panic has resided along generational fault lines. In fact, as McRobbie (1994) notes, such panics over youth culture serve as "a means of attempting to discipline the young through terrifying their parents," a phenomenon she describes as "a powerful emotional strategy" (p. 199).

While a moral panic can occur over anything, in this chapter I focus specifically on moral panics surrounding the relationship between young people and media. Classic, recurring 20th century moral panics about youth and media were characterized by the following:

- adults' fears of losing control over "vulnerable" youth;
- the need to find a simple solution to a complex problem involving youth (whether real or perceived);
- the perceived link to popular culture often grounded in a focus on manifest content of media/culture (for example, song lyrics) (i.e., the creation of "folk devils"; Cohen, 1980; Sternheimer, 2015)
- little or no actual evidence of a link between this content and the perceived problem of youth;
- claims made by "elites" (aka "moral crusaders"; Sternheimer, 2015) (e.g., doctors, politicians, clergy, and the like);
- a wave of often exaggerated press coverage;
- government hearings to investigate the so-called problem; and
- media industry fears of government regulation leading instead to voluntary self-regulation.

In the following subsections, I examine how these features manifested in three specific instances of moral panic over young audiences: the comic book/juvenile delinquency scare of the 1950s, the controversies over popular music (e.g., heavy metal) in the 1980s, and the perceived link between school shootings and video games in the 1990s. As I will show in the last section of this chapter, the concerns have morphed of late as young people's role in media production has changed. This can be seen in the current outcries over cyberbullying and sexting.

Comics and Music and Videogames, Oh My!

Juvenile Delinquency in the 1950s

A media-centered youth culture came to full fruition during the 1950s, as did the contradictory belief in the "innocence" of children and the necessity for parents to "mold" their children (Spigel, 1993). The clash between these two beliefs led adults who witnessed youths' new look, argot, and leisure to label such behaviors as delinquent, with the result that the decade produced a massive moral panic over juvenile delinquency and the alleged contribution of mass culture (for example, television, comic books, and rock 'n' roll). (See, for example, Beaty, 2005; Gilbert, 1986; Spigel, 1993; Springhall, 1998; Sternheimer, 2015.) Spigel (1993) argues that the primary concern in this struggle was "a marked desire to keep childhood as a period distinct from adulthood" and that television "might abolish such distinctions by making children privy to adult secrets" (p. 271).

While Spigel is specifically referring to the early panic over children and television, there was, at the time, an even more visible moral panic—one focusing on the role of comic books in promoting juvenile delinquency, and equally related to adult fears of losing control. Historians typically cite literary critic Sterling North's May 1940 *Chicago Daily News* editorial "A National Disgrace" as planting the seed of the anti-comic book crusade (Beaty, 2005; Sternheimer, 2015). Throughout the 1940s and into the 1950s, concern over the relationship between comic books and youth violence grew, in part, in response to the changing nature of their content—focusing more and more on crime and horror—and in part in response to their increased popularity: comic books reached a sales peak in 1953 and 1954, "by which time a staggering 75 million 10-cent copies were being bought and traded" each month (Springhall, 1998, p. 124).

Indeed, it was the immense popularity of these crime and horror comics that provided the fodder for the claims of psychiatrist Frederic Wertham, whose 1954 book, *Seduction of the Innocent*, put forth the unsubstantiated claim that such comics were a direct "contributing factor" in the perceived rise of juvenile delinquency. A psychiatrist counseling youth offenders, Wertham took on the role of moral crusader and offered as evidence the fact that the majority of youth with whom he worked were avid readers of comic books. Wertham himself conducted no controlled studies systematically isolating what, if any, influence such comics had on "normal" youth, and instead relied solely on his interviews with youth in treatment for various psychological, social, and criminal problems (Gilbert, 1986). By the time the book had been condensed in *Reader's Digest*, a publication that made his claims more accessible to the general public, these claims had created "an exaggerated fear among American parents of what was lurking behind the covers of the comic books read so avidly by their children" (Springhall, 1998, p. 125). While it's easy to look back now and dismiss Wertham's conclusions based on lack of concrete evidence, it is important to understand the climate of the U.S. in the 1950s, described by Springhall (1998) as characterized by "McCarthyism, intellectual hostility to mass culture, and the cult of domesticity" (p. 121), making it easy for parents, politicians, educators, clergy, and others to be easily convinced by the "reductionist causal link between comic books and crime" (p. 125) made by such a respected youth expert as Dr. Wertham.[1] As a result, a moral panic "amplified by the mass media and politicians, lent support to Wertham's unsubstantiated allegation" (Springhall, 1998, p. 135) relating comic books to juvenile delinquency.

It was within this cultural and political climate that the Senate Subcommittee to Investigate Juvenile Delinquency was formed in 1953. While charged with investigating a range of potential causes of juvenile delinquency including substandard schools and families, "the mass media held center stage [as a potential cause] from 1954 through 1956" (Gilbert, 1986, p. 143). Indeed, between 1953 and 1955, the committee received more than fifteen thousand unsolicited letters from citizens, some 75% of which expressed concerns about the link between juvenile delinquency and mass media (Springhall, 1998). During the course of these hearings, numerous representatives from various media industries, including comic-book publishers (notably EC Comics's Bill Gaines), as well as so-called violence experts, testified for or against the belief that comic books were harmful.

When the political and media circus was over, the subcommittee rejected "Wertham's monocausal model of juvenile delinquency" (Springhall, 1998, p. 139), opting instead to identify comic books as one factor in a greater social problem and choosing not to undertake any kind of federal government legislation against the medium, while at the same time warning that the industry should undertake responsible self-regulatory means. At the same time, however, in eighteen states, local ordinances restricting the sale of crime and horror comics were passed (Springhall, 1998). In response, a group of comic-book publishers formed the Comics Magazine Association of America in late 1954, a group responsible for creating and administering the newly created Comics Code. Based on the self-regulations imposed by the Comics Code, "all scenes of horror, excessive bloodshed, gory or gruesome crimes, depravity, lust, sadism, and masochism...walking dead, torture, vampires, ghouls, cannibalism and werewolfism" were forbidden, as were titles containing the words *horror* or *terror* (Springhall, 1998, p. 140). Publishers had to submit their books to code authorities who, if they approved, issued a seal of approval that would ensure distribution to retail outlets. The end result of the code was that numerous comic-book titles and publishers were forced out of business since they could not comply with code guidelines and still produce the content they had become known for. Without the code's endorsement, it was all but impossible to distribute and sell comic books.[2]

Popular Music in the 1980s

In the mid-1980s, the Parents' Music Resource Center (PMRC) was placed in the "expert" (moral crusader) role that Wertham occupied in the 1950s by leading the campaign against what some called "porn rock." Formed in May 1985 and headed by a group of prominent Washington, D.C., wives—Tipper Gore (wife of then-senator Al Gore), Susan Baker (wife of then-treasury secretary James Baker), and Peatsy Hollings (wife of then-senator Ernest Hollings), among others—the group got its start, in part, in response to Gore's concerns about Prince's *Darling Nikki*, a song referencing masturbation. Focusing primarily on heavy-metal rock, the PMRC advocated for warning labels and/or printed lyrics on controversial albums so as to warn parents that the content was inappropriate for children. Using as an example a hit list of songs they identified as "The Filthy Fifteen," (including songs by Sheena Easton, Judas Priest, Madonna, Prince, and Def Leppard, among others), they proposed a rating system somewhat akin to the motion picture ratings.

Beginning in September 1985, hearings were held before the Senate Commerce Technology and Transportation Committee featuring testimony by the PMRC on one side, and a strange-bedfellows mixture of musicians including Frank Zappa, Dee Snyder (Twisted Sister), and John Denver representing the music industry. The end result was a November 1985 agreement on the part of the Recording Industry Association of America (RIAA) to "encourage" its members (representing 85% of U.S. record companies) to place warning labels on controversial albums or to print the lyrics on the album cover (Chastagner, 1999; Heins, 1993). Between January 1986 and August 1989, 49 out of the 7,500 albums released contained a warning label, despite the fact that the PMRC had deemed 121 albums to be offensive (Chastagner, 1999).

But the closure of the hearings and the RIAA's agreement did not take the issue out of the public eye (Heins, 1993). In 1988, the PMRC created and marketed an inflammatory video for parents called *Rising to the Challenge: A Revealing Look at the Pied Pipers of Today's Rock 'n' Roll* (DeMoss & Norwood, 1988). Bob DeMoss of the fundamentalist group Focus on the Family (Chastagner, 1999) produced the video, marketed as "an eye-opening educational video for parents." The video, intended to warn parents about what their children were listening to and seeing on album covers and in music videos, offering graphic visual and lyrical evidence of what was categorized as the dangerous content of popular music, notably heavy metal. What is notable about the video is that it employed the same tactics used by the PMRC throughout its campaign. Like Wertham, they offered no scientific or controlled evidence that there was a link between the music and the resulting effects they warned about: adolescent drinking, drug use, sexual promiscuity, rape, and suicide. Contrary to their promotional claims, that this was "33 minutes of carefully documented evidence sure to change the way you and your children listen to music" (video case back cover), the evidence in the video was far from "carefully documented." Instead, the video offered a wealth of frightening and compelling statistics on such phenomena as the rise in youth violence, drinking, and suicide, which were then linked to music by focusing on the manifest content of various song lyrics. But the video presented no research evidence to document or support a cause-and-effect relationship between the music and any of these phenomena (DeMoss & Norwood, 1988). At a time when the country was undergoing a conservative and reactionary turn in the mid- to late-1980s, and when adult fears of youthful transgressions were again peaking, the video spoke to already existing fears.

By 1990, some eighteen states were considering legislation related either to music labeling or censorship (Heins, 1993), a fact that led the RIAA to follow a longstanding trend (seen, for example, in the creation of the Comics Code in the 1950s) for industry self-regulation to avoid the threat of government regulation. In 1990, the RIAA adopted the "Parental Advisory/ Explicit Lyrics" label we have all become so familiar with. Most of the major company members of the RIAA adopted the label, although, unlike in the case of the Comics Code seal, each individual company made the decision about which albums would carry the label. Neither centralized industry-wide guidelines nor a board overseeing the use of the label was established like in the case of the Comics Code or as there is in the case of the Motion Picture Association of America (MPAA) movie ratings. Yet, as in the case of the Comics Code, there was an effect on sales, although not to the same extreme, as some retailers, notably Wal-Mart, refused to carry stickered albums.[3]

Taking Aim at the Causes of School Shootings

Some fifty years after the juvenile delinquency/comic-book hearings, the arguments remained the same. The aftermath of the April 20, 1999, Columbine High School shootings, in which two male students, Dylan Klebold and Eric Harris, killed thirteen others at the school before taking their own lives, provides an example of the moral panic about youth violence in general, school shootings in particular, and the alleged role of mass culture in contributing to both.

While 71% of adults polled shortly after the incident believed "a school shooting was 'likely' to happen in their community," research conducted by the Justice Policy Institute found that a child's chance of being killed in school is a mere 1 in 2 million (Brooks, Schiraldi, & Zieden-berg, 2000, p. 6). This discrepancy, the report argues, is due, in part, to the media coverage of such shootings that results in American adults being "exponentially misinformed" (p. 30). The report goes on to call for an end to the "hyperbole that too often follows school shootings" and for the media to "add more context" to their coverage of such events (p. 30).

In looking at the post-Columbine news coverage, Giroux (2000) isolates how our culture's belief in childhood innocence comes into play in news coverage of youth. Specifically, he notes that childhood innocence is generally applied only to White, middle-class youth, a phenomenon that became painfully clear from such Columbine headlines as "If It Could Happen Here, Many Say, It Could Happen Anywhere" or questioning "How Could This Happen?" The implication being how could this happen *here* (that is, in White, middle-class suburbia)? Moreover, other articles quoted sources exclaiming, "They were good" (that is, White, middle-class suburban) "kids." Implicit in such statements is the belief that this kind of behavior is to be expected of urban, poor, and/or African–American and Latino youth, but that these kinds of things just don't happen in White suburbia. Giroux (2000) argues that "white middle-class children often are protected by the myth of innocence and are considered incapable of exhibiting at risk behav-ior" (p. 8). When they do exhibit such behavior, as in the case of Columbine, it is accompanied both by a wave of "soul searching" (p. 8) and the need to identify outside causes (for example, popular culture) "well removed from the spaces of 'whiteness' and affluence" (p. 8).

Indeed, in the ensuing moral panic and national soul searching, hundreds of articles were published addressing the "causes" of this tragedy, a significant proportion of which singled out media and popular culture. In their content analysis of Columbine coverage, Erica Scharrer, Lisa Weidman, and Kimberly Bissell (2003) document how the press "quickly came to focus on popular-culture and entertainment-media products as causal contributors to the massacre" (p. 81). It didn't take long—only until the next day, in fact—for the press to start looking for causes (Scharrer *et al.*, 2003). In this case, some of the most frequently mentioned causes were movies (for example, *The Matrix* and *The Basketball Diaries*), video games (*Doom* and *Quake*), the Internet, the goth subculture, and popular music (Marilyn Manson and the German band KMFDM). More than any other alleged cause, it was Manson who bore the brunt of attacks, prompting him to publish an eloquent response in *Rolling Stone* (1999) in which he wrote of the post-Columbine "witch hunt": "Man's greatest fear is chaos. It was unthinkable that these kids did not have a simple black-and-white reason for their actions. And so a scapegoat was needed" (Manson, 1999).

As in the case of other moral panics about youth culture, extensive media coverage was ac-companied by government hearings to investigate both the shootings in general and the role of media and popular culture in contributing to them. In this case, the hearings were held before the Senate Commerce Committee. As a well-respected scholar on video games (although not a supporter of the belief that video games cause youth violence), Henry Jenkins was called to testify along with others whom he describes as "anti-popular culture types, ranging from Joseph Lieberman to William Bennett" (Jenkins, 1999), and high-profile military psychologist and anti-video game crusader David Grossman, as well as industry spokespeople. Jenkins realized he "would be the only media scholar who did not come from the 'media effects' tradition and the only one who was not representing popular culture as a 'social problem,'" a fact he worried was a "setup" (Jenkins, 1999). In a reflection piece he posted on the Internet shortly after the hearings, Jenkins described the circuslike atmosphere of the hearings, which included displays consisting of "massive posters" of ads for "some of the most violent videogames on the market," "professional witnesses" with accompanying staffs, "props," "professionally-edited videos," and out-of-context clips from movies such as *The Basketball Diaries* (Jenkins, 1999). In the end, Jenkins likened the experience to a "national witch hunt" (Jenkins, 1999). According to Jenkins, both the senators and the press covering the hearing clearly had their minds made up in advance about the causes—popular culture such as video games, music, and the Internet—and he, as the only scholar speaking from outside of the media effects tradition, was attacked and dismissed. Clearly, according to Jenkins, the government and the press in this example had an agenda to deliver to the U.S. public, a particular message and a predesignated enemy—popular culture. Jenkins's views simply did not support the plan, so he was silenced.

The Media Landscape Changes

When I wrote the first edition of this chapter, I concluded with a 1999 quote from the above-mentioned Jenkins reflection piece arguing that we have become so caught up in our concerns about what media has been doing to kids that have failed to understand what "our children are doing with media." This failure is due in part because, according to Jenkins (1999), "We are afraid of our children. We are afraid of their reactions to digital media. And we suddenly can't avoid either." Adults fear new technologies and what youth will do with them, primarily because adults lack the knowledge and expertise to incorporate these technologies into their own lives, and youth culture has grown increasingly visible, making it harder than ever to ignore.

When Jenkins expressed these concerns, he was referring to how the young incorporate media and technology into their daily lives (see Chapter 16 for more details). He was not, however, advocating for a new panic about how young people use technologies. But in the interim, that is exactly what has transpired.

According to the Pew Research Center, 92% of U.S. teens report going online daily, most often from some mobile device including the 73% who have or have access to a smartphone (Lenhart, 2015). In a media landscape dominated by smartphones and social media, adults' overriding concern about the relationship between young people and media has shifted. Where earlier moral panics were, as Jenkins asserted, grounded in a fear about what the content of various technologies was *doing to* youth, now the panic centers on what youth are *doing with* these technologies—chatting with potential predators, divulging private information, cyberbullying, sexting, and more.

Current concerns about cyberbullying—"bullying carried out using newer forms of media such as text messaging and social media" (Ryalls, 2017)—and sexting—"the transfer of nude or semi-nude pictures or videos between mobile devices" (Draper, 2012, p. 221)—have dominated the public discourse about youth and media in recent years. It is a discourse grounded in technological determinism (boyd, 2014; Draper, 2012)—the "assumption that technology possesses intrinsic powers" (boyd, 2014, p. 15). While technological determinism can be either utopian or dystopian, it is the dystopian version—or "a focus on all of the terrible things that will happen because of the widespread adoption of a particular technology" (boyd, 2014, p. 15) which pervades the concerns about young people digital technologies at present.

Sternheimer (2015) describes the panic over sexting as "a crusaderless crusade" (p. 136) arguing that news "editors and producers looking for a 'hot topic'" (p. 136) first raised concerns. Similarly, there appears to be no distinct moral crusader active in the case of cyberbullying either (at least none emerges from reading Ryall's extensive analysis of the topic). In their research on news coverage of sexting and cyberbullying respectively, Draper (2012) and Ryalls (2017) expose the media's role in perpetuating a panic about how young people use the Internet and/or mobile phones. Moreover, both authors document how the news coverage and resulting public response has not, as in the case of earlier moral panics, demanded regulation of the technology itself. As Sternheimer (2015) notes, "twentieth century solutions no longer work in the digital age" (p. 146). Rather, the proffered solution now is for criminalization and/or increased surveillance of young people. For example, numerous localities have treated sexting as equivalent to child pornography and have prosecuted young people under such statutes (Draper, 2012; Sternheimer, 2015), while some states have proposed legislation to make sexting a crime but not equivalent to child pornography (Sternheimer, 2015). According to Sternheimer (2015), "sexting's legal gray area serves as a reminder of how quickly the technology landscape changes, and how these changes trigger fears of new media" (p. 140). Likewise, Ryalls reports fifty states currently have anti-bullying laws, twenty-three of which include cyberbullying specifically, and she documents multiple high profile cases where young people have been charged with various crimes such as those when someone else commits suicide allegedly as a result of cyberbullying.

Ryalls (2017), for example, "argues that the contemporary moral panic about how teens use technology to bully (i.e., cyberbullying) frames technology as a dangerous bullying tool and has led to responses to cyberbullying that potentially infringe on students' free speech rights (for instance, school officials monitoring students' social media)." (Refer to Chapter 18 for an extensive discussion of such legislation and policies as they relate to young people's rights in this digital age.)

Both Ryalls and Draper are careful to clarify they do not mean to trivialize or downplay the potentially serious issues raised by cyberbullying and sexting respectively. Rather, both set about to document the cultural discourse and increasing panic surrounding young people's use of technology in general—a discourse rooted in technological determinism and with the potential of infringing on young people's rights.

What's the Big Deal?

Why does it matter that as a culture we've devoted so many newspaper pages, government hearings, court cases, and sleepless nights to the relationship between youth and media/technology? One hallmark of moral panics is that they focus attention and direct resources toward simple solutions to complex problems and often serve as smokescreens enabling us as a society to ignore larger, more troubling problems. These misdirected panics take attention away from the real problems confronting youth in our society (Giroux, 2000; Lipsitz, 1998; Males, 1999; Sternheimer, 2015)—notably the dramatic decline in government funding of education, the reduction in social services for children, the disappearances of noncommercial public spaces for the young, and the increasing commercial and sexual exploitation of children, not to mention the epidemic of adult-perpetrated violence against children. But, as Sternheimer (2015) argues "crusades against popular culture are likely here to stay. They draw attention for their crusaders, play on existing concerns about both social change and media content, and allow us to express moral judgement about others in the public sphere" (p. 148).

Discussion Questions

1. Think about Sternheimer's assertions in the quote concluding this chapter. How did this play out in the 20th century examples discussed?

2. Think back to your years in middle and/or high school. What kind of surveillance of your media and technology use do you recall being carried out by your parents and/or schools?

3. When you were growing up, how did the warning labels on recorded music affect you? Did your parents forbid you to listen to music with a PAL Logo? Did the addition of the logo ever make you want to listen to the music more (the so-called "forbidden fruit" argument)?

Exercise

1. Find two fairly recent (2010-present) mainstream newspaper or magazine articles (at least 750 words each) or one TV news video story (at least 5 minutes long) about sexting. Analyze how the story constructs this topic by answering the following questions: (a) what *specific* problem is identified, (b) does the story use "scare" language to talk about the issue, (c) who is interviewed/quoted, (d) what solutions to the problem are offered? (NOTE: The assignment does not specify *teens* and sexting as the topic. Did anyone in the class happen to find a story about adults? If not, why do you think searching for stories on sexting in general yielded only stories about young people? If there were stories about adults, compare and contrast them with the stories about young people.)

Notes

1. Despite his legacy as a conservative, anti-comics, anti-popular culture crusader, recent books examining Wertham's writings and other works have revealed him to have been a progressive thinker whose ideas were appropriated by conservative social critics in support of the move to regulate the comic-book industry and mass culture in general (Beaty, 2005; Nyberg, 1998).
2. The Comics Code existed until 2011, although, as a result of new distribution outlets and the growth of underground comics, its influence was minimal for many years. For a compelling and detailed examination of the anti-comics movement and the Comics Code itself, see Nyberg (1998).
3. The PAL Mark, as it is now called, is still used by the RIAA although its wording now reads "Parental Advisory: Explicit Content" (RIAA, 2017b). The PAL Program has been revised over the years, but as of October 23, 2006 the RIAA's Standards include "uniform guidelines for determining whether a sound recording should use a PAL Mark" (RIAA, 2017a).

References

Austin, J., & Willard, M. N. (Eds.). (1998). Introduction: Angels of history, demons of culture. In J. Austin & M. N. Willard (Eds.), *Generations of youth: Youth cultures and history in twentieth-century America* (pp. 1–20). New York, NY: New York University Press.

Beaty, B. (2005). *Frederic Wertham and the critique of mass culture*. Jackson, MS: University Press of Mississippi.

boyd, d. (2014). *It's complicated: The social lives of networked teens*. New Haven, CT: Yale University Press.

Brooks, K., Schiraldi, V., & Ziedenberg, J. (2000). *School house hype: Two years later*. Washington, DC: Justice Policy Institute. Retrieved from http://www.prisonsucks.com/scans/jpi/shh2.pdf

Chastagner, C. (1999). The Parents' Music Resource Center: From information to censorship. *Popular Music, 18*(2), 179–192. doi:10.1017/S026114300000903X

Cohen, S. (1980). *Folk devils and moral panics: The creation of the mods and rockers.* New York, NY: St. Martin's.

DeMoss, R., Jr. (Executive Producer), & Norwood, J. (Writer). (1988). *Rising to the challenge: A revealing look at the pied pipers of today's rock 'n' roll* [videotape]. Arlington, VA: Parents Music Resource Center.

Draper, N. R. A. (2012). Is your teen at risk? Discourses of adolescent sexting in United States television news. *Journal of Children and Media, 6*(2), 221–236. doi:10.1080/17482798.2011.587147

Gilbert, J. (1986). *A cycle of outrage: America's reaction to the juvenile delinquent in the 1950s.* New York, NY: Oxford University Press.

Giroux, H. A. (1996). *Fugitive cultures: Race, violence, and youth.* New York, NY: Routledge.

Giroux, H. A. (2000). *Stealing innocence: Corporate culture's war on children.* New York, NY: Palgrave.

Hawes, J. M., & Hiner, N. R. (Eds.). (1985). *American childhood: A research guide and historical handbook.* Westport, CT: Greenwood.

Heins, M. (1993). *Sex, sin and blasphemy: A guide to America's censorship wars.* New York, NY: The New Press.

Hine, T. (1999, September). The rise and decline of the teenager. *American Heritage,* pp. 71–82. Retrieved from http://www.americanheritage.com/content/rise-and-decline-teenager

Jenkins, H. (1999). *Professor Jenkins goes to Washington.* Retrieved from http://web.mit.edu/21fms/www/faculty/henry3/profjenkins.html

Lenhart, A. (2015, April 9). *Teens, social media & technology overview 2015.* Retrieved from http://www.pewinternet.org/2015/04/09/teens-social-media-technology-2015/

Lipsitz, G. (1998). The hip hop hearings: Censorship, social memory, and intergenerational tensions among African Americans. In J. Austin & M. N. Willard (Eds.), *Generations of youth: Youth cultures and history in twentieth-century America* (pp. 395–411). New York, NY: New York University Press.

Males, M. (1999). *Framing youth: Ten myths about the next generation.* Monroe, ME: Common Courage Books.

Manson, M. (1999, May 28). Columbine: Whose fault is it? *Rolling Stone.* Retrieved from http://www.rollingstone.com/news/story/5923915/columbine_whose_fault_is_it

McRobbie, A. (1994). The moral panic in the age of the postmodern mass media. In A. McRobbie (Ed.), *Postmodernism and popular culture* (pp. 198–219). New York, NY: Routledge.

Nyberg, A. K. (1998). *Seal of approval: The history of the Comics Code.* Jackson, MS: University Press of Mississippi.

Palladino, G. (1996). *Teenagers: An American history.* New York, NY: Basic.

RIAA (2017a). *PAL standards.* Retrieved from https://www.riaa.com/resources-learning/pal-standards/

RIAA (2017b). *Parental advisory label.* Retrieved from https://www.riaa.com/resources-learning/parental-advisory-label/

Ryalls, E. D. (in press). *The culture of mean: Representing bullies and victims in popular culture.* New York, NY: Peter Lang.

Scharrer, E., Weidman, L. M., & Bissell, K. L. (2003). Pointing the finger of blame: News media coverage of popular culture culpability. *Journalism & Communication Monographs, 5*(2), 48–98. doi:10.1177/152263790300500201

Spigel, L. (1993). Seducing the innocent: Childhood and television in postwar America. In W. S. Solomon (Ed.), *Ruthless criticism: New perspectives in U.S. communication history* (pp. 259–290). Minneapolis, MN: University of Minnesota Press.

Springhall, J. (1998). *Youth, popular culture and moral panics: Penny gaffs to gangsta rap, 1830–1996.* New York, NY: St. Martin's.

Sternheimer, K. (2015). *Pop culture panics: How moral crusaders construct meanings of deviance and delinquency.* New York, NY: Routledge.

Wartella, E., & Mazzarella, S. (1990). A historical comparison of children's use of leisure time. In R. Butsch (Ed.), *For fun and profit: The transformation of leisure into consumption* (pp. 173–194). Philadelphia, PA: Temple University Press.

Wartella, E., & Reeves, B. (1985). Historical trends in research on children and the media, 1900–1960. *Journal of Communication, 35*(2), 118–133. doi:10.1111/j.1460-2466.1985.tb02238.x

CHAPTER 4

How Are the Needs of Children Considered in Children's Media?

Sherri Hope Culver

A popular YouTube video shows a young girl sitting on a sofa in her home while her little sister gives her a birthday present (YouTube, 2016). The present is a doll that has been retrofitted with a prosthetic leg. The video reveals that the girl also has a prosthetic leg, and records her emotional reaction when she realizes this isn't just any doll, it's a doll that looks "just like me." In seconds, her facial expression morphs from a simple smile at the gift of a doll, to hysterical tears when she realizes the doll looks just like her. Although this moment is prompted by a toy, it also conveys a central need when it comes to advocating for children's media content. Children are counting on adults to create media content that connects with who and where they really are and what matters most to them. When media content is able to do this, it can truly help children thrive.

The children's media industry is filled with people who care deeply about children and youth. They want children to laugh with friends, get hugs from loving families, and lead fulfilling lives. And they want to create content that helps to facilitate all of that. But sitting right beside those noble goals is an equally strong business imperative; to make money for the company for whom they work. Although this statement is true for all media companies, the children's media industry is unique in that it is targeting a young, impressionable audience. The people working at children's media companies are, at best, balancing their desire to create quality content that serves children in the best way possible, with the reality that one type of content or decision will yield more money for their company than another. It is for this reason that the organizations and individuals focused on advocating for the media-related needs of children and youth are so important.

The term "advocacy" or "advocate" may conjure up images of attorneys in formal legal environments, or helicopter-parents pushing forcefully on behalf of their children's needs, but in this chapter advocacy refers to a wide range of individuals and organizations that provide the research, the clout, and the passion necessary to assure that media content, media distribution and media platforms are mindful of their impact on children and youth, and make changes when that impact is found to be negative. The categories of organizations and groups advocating for healthy media for children include the following:

- Professional associations for educators (e.g., National Association for the Education of Young Children)
- Professional associations for librarians (e.g., American Association of School Librarians)
- Professional associations for medical professionals (e.g., American Academy of Pediatrics)
- Nonprofits focused on parents & children (e.g., National Fatherhood Initiative)
- Children's media companies (e.g., Nickelodeon, PBS, YouTube Kids)
- Rating system providers (e.g., Motion Picture Association of America, Common Sense Media)
- Government agencies (e.g., Federal Communications Commission, Federal Trade Commission)
- Research Centers (e.g., Center on Media and Child Health at Boston Children's Hospital)

In order to address the role of these various organizations, this chapter begins with a brief history of the organizations and people that have stood at the forefront of advocating for children's media rights since television first took over the central spot in many family living rooms. Next, the chapter discusses approaches to advocacy, from both within organizations and within children's media companies. The chapter concludes by considering current issues affecting children and media, the challenges facing the field, and the actions that could create bridges to improvements.

The Early Years

Many scholars acknowledge that advocacy for children's media came into its own in 1968 when Peggy Charren started Action for Children's Television (ACT) (Weber, 2015). Charren was a mother of two who ran a business that held book fairs for children, and she was frustrated with the abundance of commercials and cartoons flooding the TV programs her children were watching. ACT was an outgrowth of her single-minded concern for children's growing consumption of television. ACT wasn't the first to be concerned about the wildly popular television content children were consuming in ever-increasing minutes, but it was the first to lobby the government for a specific agenda of required changes to that content and the environment in which it was consumed. Her recommendations were eventually backed by a range of parents, educators and some in the medical community. ACT's earliest success was getting the Federal Communications Commission (FCC) to issue a Children's Television Policy statement in 1974, which was meant to encourage broadcasters to air educational and informational programming. But, this policy was not formal legislation and was, therefore, easily rescinded by subsequent administrations. By the mid-1980s, children's television advocates were once again fighting for basic policies and legislation.

ACT's greatest success came in 1990 when it was instrumental in getting the FCC to pass the Children's Television Act (CTA) after decades of lobbying. Prior to the passage of the CTA,

Charren and ACT had limited success in getting broadcasters and legislators to acknowledge the unique needs of children regarding television consumption. She argued fiercely that the needs of children should not be left to the marketplace where audiences are seen as consumers and where advertisers want to reach influential viewers. Charren said "Children's television can never be profitable because most of the people who watch it are very short, very young and have very small allowances" (Weber, 2015).

It is worth noting that no other comprehensive children's media legislation has been passed since the Children's Television Act of 1990, nor was any comprehensive children's media legislation passed before 1990. Consider the weight of that statement. Since the 1950s, television has been a popular mass medium for children. Over the decades it has continued to grow in popularity and offerings. Specialized children's media content is now available through 24-hour children's cable networks, online websites with original children's programming, and thousands of interactive digital media options. Despite countless parents, pediatricians, educators, elected officials, even presidents advocating for children as a vulnerable population, and decades of research showing the influence of media content on children, there are very few requirements or restrictions for media companies creating and providing media content for children and youth. (See Chapter 2 for a discussion of the regulation of children's media.) Those actions and protections that do exist are often a direct result of the pressure that comes from child advocates, or industry self-regulations, such as the movie ratings provided through the Motion Picture Association of America (MPAA).

Approaches to Advocacy

There are many organizations and groups whose major focus is the influence of media on children and youth including, but not limited to the following:

- American Academy of Pediatrics
- Campaign for a Commercial Free Childhood
- Center for Children and Technology
- Center for Media and Information Literacy
- Center for Media Literacy
- Children and Screens: Institute of Digital Media and Child Development
- Children's Digital Media Center at Georgetown University
- Children's Media Association
- Children Now
- Common Sense Media (CSM)
- DML Research Hub
- Family Online Safety Institute
- Geena Davis Institute on Gender in Media
- Joan Ganz Cooney Center
- Media Education Lab
- National Association for Media Literacy Education (NAMLE)
- Project Look Sharp
- The Fred Rogers Center
- The LAMP

Although advocates listed above and in the previous section focus on the needs of children and media, their approaches, actions, and strategies are often quite different, and sometimes even in opposition. Some organizations focus on the potential dangers when children interact with media. Their advocacy often focuses on shielding children and youth, on the passing of legal regulations, censorship, and restrictions on media use employing a protectionist view to advocacy. An example of this is "Screen Free Week", an outreach event sponsored by the Campaign for a Commercial Free Childhood (CCFC) in which children and families are encouraged to turn off all screen media in order to become more aware of their over-reliance on media (CCFC, n.d.). Other organizations focus on developing ways to empower children and youth when they interact with media. These organizations tend to focus on education, audience responsibility, curriculum development, and critical analysis using an empowerment view to advocacy. An example of this is the Media Breaker/Studios tool from The LAMP organization (The LAMP, n.d.). Media Breaker/Studio is an online learning platform in which educators and students edit, reconfigure and create commercials, music videos, and news clips and then use those media segments to engage in active inquiry and critical media analysis.

Other strategies or approaches to advocacy include:

- Advocating for media industry accountability (e.g., Children's Advertising Review Unit)
- Advocating for information to parents (e.g., Family Online Safety Institute)
- Advocating for media literacy (e.g., Media Literacy Now)
- Advocating for research (e.g., Pew Research Center)
- Advocating for kids media creation (e.g., Reel Girls)

Advocacy Organizations

At the heart of many concerns about children's media consumption is the concept of media literacy. Simply put, media literacy is the ability to think critically about media and create effective communication using media. It is an expanded definition of literacy that takes into account the myriad of ways in which children and youth share, consume and create information today. (For a detailed discussion of media literacy, see Chapter 5.) The National Association for Media Literacy Education (NAMLE) advocates for children and youth (and their teachers) to gain the skills necessary to thoughtfully consider their decisions about media consumption (NAMLE, n.d.).[1] NAMLE advocates for media literacy education to be included in all education environments. In 2015, NAMLE spearheaded the formation of US Media Literacy Week to bring attention to this need and galvanize others to take action so that critical analysis and creation of media is brought into formal and informal education environments nationwide. In addition, NAMLE holds a biennial conference and publishes research, scholarship and the pedagogy of media literacy education in the *Journal of Media Literacy Education*.

A nonprofit organization at the forefront of "helping kids thrive in a world of media and technology" is Common Sense Media (CSM). CSM aims to help families make smart media choices (Common Sense Media, n.d.). It does this by providing comprehensive ratings for thousands of television shows, movies, apps and video games made for children and youth. The ratings were the core of its work when the organization started in 2003. Today, its knowledge base and resources go much deeper and its actions, more broad. CSM provides research reports on targeted issues affecting parents, children and youth; its education division, Common Sense

Media Education, provides digital literacy and digital citizenship tools for teachers and school communities; and Common Sense Kids Action focuses on advocacy and works with policy makers, business leaders and other advocates to drive policies that support a range of education and media needs for children and youth. For example, researchers followed the media practices of specific children from lower-income, African-American and Latino families as a window into their moment-by-moment choices regarding media (Konopasky & Williams, 2016).

Is the name Joan Ganz Cooney familiar to you? If you're interested in children's media it should be! She led the team that created Sesame Street in 1966, and she spent a lifetime advocating for children. Her legacy continues through the Joan Ganz Cooney Center founded in 2007 with the mission is to "advance children's literacy skills and foster innovation in children's learning through digital media" (Joan Ganz Cooney Center, n.d.). The Cooney Center conducts research on trending topics in children's literacy in which media and technology are a central component. For example, researchers analyzed literacy-focused apps for children 0–8 years which shed light on the proliferation of apps claiming they are educational, often with little-to-no research to back up the claims (Vaala, Ly, & Levine, 2015).

Note that all of the organizations highlighted in this chapter focus on a mission of learning and education and its connection to media for children and youth. Certainly children's media content should also be entertaining, compelling, and fun, but there is no shortage of companies focusing on those needs. Advocacy focuses on the actions needed to help children and youth develop into happy, well-adjusted adults.

Advocacy from Within Children's Media Companies

In addition to independent (and often nonprofit) organizations highlighted above, there are sometimes divisions *within* children's media companies designed to provide advocacy or research that can inform the field, as well as inform the content and practices of that company. When advocacy initiatives are developed within a media company they come under the umbrella term Corporate Social Responsibility (CSR). CSR emphasizes a business model in which companies aim to do good, while doing well. Companies implementing CSR engage in business initiatives that aspire to benefit their audience or society-at-large, and balance that goal with the needs of their stockholders or other stakeholders (Carroll, 2015).

Companies engage in CSR for a variety of reasons:

Philanthropic: "We want to give back."
Defensive: "Our customers are angry at us so we're doing something positive to change their view."
Promotional: "Look at this great thing we're doing."
Strategic: "We've embarked on this effort because it connects to our company goals."
Transformative: "We think it's the right thing to do."

Two examples of CSR campaigns are Cartoon Network's "Stop Bullying Speak Up" campaign and Toca Boca's "Stand For Play" campaign.

In 2010, Cartoon Network learned that a major concern in the lives of its target audience (boys 8–11) was bullying. Under the guidance of CSR executive, Alice Cahn, an advisory team determined the materials and resources necessary to help youth deal with this problem. The network devoted airtime for special program presentations and created a campaign-specific website (www.stopbullyingspeakup.com). In 2012, the campaign went global, launching on

Cartoon Network channels across the UK, Europe and Latin America reflecting the network's ongoing commitment to the issue.

In 2016, the app company Toca Boca unveiled its' "Stand For Play" campaign to encourage play that is "open-ended, unstructured, free-from-rules-and-goals" (www.tocaboca.com/standforplay). The campaign shared research and play ideas. Additionally, the campaign asked parents and kids to draw a "Take a stand for play" poster and share a photo of it on social media. The overall goal was to get more parents and kids talking about play, and increasing the moments in their life when play can happen.

The Role of Research in Advocacy

What issue gets you riled up, or passionately concerned? It's not unusual to feel strongly about an issue and want to see changes made. It's quite another to convince those with the power to make those changes that there is value in doing so. The key to successful advocacy is this second point. The difference between feeling strongly about an issue and the satisfaction that can come from effective action often relies on *research*. Research can provide objective data and/or preeminent expertise to what otherwise might be seen as simply unsubstantiated opinion. While opinion may have a home on social media where personal expression rules, it is not effective when lobbying on behalf of issues affecting children and youth, especially if the outcome one seeks is legislative.

Consider the advocacy position of the American Academy of Pediatrics (AAP) when it released a report advocating new guidelines on children and screens. In 2016, the AAP released guidelines updating their prior recommendations for children's media use based on a new research study. Prior guidelines basically recommended no screen time for children under 2, and one hour of screen time for children under 5. When those guidelines were released in 2012, they were met with concern from those who felt it was unrealistic to tell parents they should not allow their youngest children any time with media or, at most, one hour a day. At the time the AAP held firm, stating that research showed children were negatively influenced by early media use. But in 2016, the guidelines were revised.

One of the reasons for the revision was due to changes in the technologies used by children, as well as research on these new screens. Earlier guidelines were "based on research on TV and videos" prior to 2011. The report cites new research on repeated viewing, parasocial relationships, and new types of screen use, including touch screens and video chatting (Council on Communications and Media, 2016a).

The revised guidelines were detailed over three documents of varying lengths and focus; (1) *Media and Young Minds*, a policy statement focusing on the media needs of children from infant through pre-school (Council on Communications and Media, 2016a), (2) *Media Use in School Aged Children and Adolescents*, a policy statement focusing on the media needs of children age 5–18 (Council on Communications and Media, 2016b), and (3) a comprehensive report, *Children, Adolescents, and Digital Media*, providing more detailed data for children from infant through age 18, and including additional recommendations (Chassiakos, Radesky, Christakis, Moreno, & Cross, 2016). News organizations reported on the shift in the recommendations. Social media pundits provided opinion. And advocacy organizations evaluated what the changes meant to their constituency, highlighting benefits, as well as concerns.

AAP research and recommendations are highly respected by those involved in children's issues. But it is the distribution and subsequent interpretation of that research across different types of advocacy organizations that influences the strategy used by those organizations.

Current Issues

This section briefly explores some of the issues currently being addressed by those advocating for children, youth and media.

Screen Time

The issue of how much screen time is too much is one that continues to be reviewed and revised. There is greater consensus than ever among educators, parents, researchers and others that media use is ubiquitous, even for children. As such, the conversation has slowly shifted from a focus on *hours* of screen time, to *content* of screen time.

In addition, because children are recognized as a vulnerable group, and because so many people have this vulnerable group in their own home, it can seem as if everyone has an anecdote about what worked with *their* children, *their* teen, or those of their friends, relatives and colleagues. With new research studies being released several times a year, often with conflicting advice, and personal experience that may or may not align with those research outcomes, this issue remains a concern.

Privacy

Advancements in technology have made it possible to bring customization to media content in ever more personal ways. Apps and games are able to learn details about their user and adjust the story or difficulty-level to that specific person (Family Online Safety Institute, 2016). But in order to execute that personalization, the app or game needs to retain information about the user, in this case a child. Who has access to that information? For what purpose? When used in educational settings will children be tracked into some courses of study and out of others at a younger age? Privacy concerns have increased with the growth of customized content. Adults routinely provide personal information in order to access media content for free, rarely considering the privacy implications. Should one expect different behavior from children? Understanding how a child's personal data is used, stored, and monetized is increasing in importance, and yet decreasing in understanding for users and their caregivers.

Empathy

An issue that has grown in importance as children's school and community environments have become more diverse is empathy. In 2016, Sesame Workshop unveiled data from a new survey in which parents and teachers share their feeling that instances of *un*kindness are on the rise, and 70% of parents worry that the world is an unkind place for children.[2] Several popular children's television programs have integrated *pro-social behaviors,* such as empathy, into their scripts and characters for years, including *Dora the Explorer, Arthur,* and *Doc McStuffins.*

Unfortunately, there is little-to-no backlash for content creators who choose not to include pro-social issues in their content. Advocates often seek ways to convince the creators of children's media content to recognize the impact of the content they create and make changes where appropriate, but this continues to be a challenge.

Media Effects

Several issues have been on the minds and in the actions of child advocates for many years. These issues are often categorized as focusing on media dangers and the effects from those perceived dangers. These media effects issues include drug messaging, violence, gender stereotyping, racial/ethnic representation, body image, consumerism, and food marketing.

There is an ongoing need for advocacy on these issues since the issues themselves are constantly evolving. Some recent examples include:

- The American Psychological Association Task Force assessment of violent video games. (Calvert *et al.*, 2017)
- Research on gender stereotyping as influenced by the film *The Hunger Games* by the Geena Davis Institute on Gender in Media (Heldman, 2016)
- Research on television food advertising conducted by the Rudd Center for Food Policy and Obesity. (Fleming-Milici & Harris, 2016)

Media Literacy

Due to the openness of the Internet and the massive ease with which news can be digitally shared, the proliferation of what's been deemed "fake news" continues to rise. Recent reports confirm that middle school and high school students lack the skills to separate reputable news stories (i.e. stories from credible sources) from fake news stories (i.e. stories that have not been fact-checked, or include misinformation) (Wineburg, McGrew, Breakstone, & Ortega, 2016). Analyzing media content requires critical thinking/media literacy skills, as advocated for by the Center for Media and Information Literacy, among other media literacy organizations. Helping children gain the skills to critically analyze news and information is vitally important to their ability to grow into responsible citizens.

Integrating Advocacy into Media Content

A commonly referenced old African proverb states "it takes a village to raise a child", and the same is true when it comes to considering the impact of media on a child. The influence of media isn't solely dependent on choices a parent makes for their child, or how an educator uses media in the classroom, or the point-of-view of a religious institution. A child's media use and understanding of media is influenced by *all* of this, including media creators and media institutions.

Content creators have been known to rely on the refrain, "if you don't like the media, turn it off", as a way to hold on to their right to create content however they choose. While this statement is true, the action of simply turning off their television or mobile device does not help the child.

Media consumption is a part of most children's lives in the United States. In addition to providing information and educational content, children like to use media because it is fun. It connects them to their friends. It helps them express their creativity. Omitting media from a child's life is not always a viable option (protectionist advocacy). A stronger option is helping children gain the knowledge they need to make wise choices in their media use, with greater consideration of its impact (empowerment advocacy).

Creators of children's media content need not worry that children will walk away from media once they gain an ability to critically analyze it. A deeper understanding of media may help children become more discerning and more selective. That may lead them to make different choices, but not to reject the experience and overall enjoyment from media. It can be challenging for advocacy organizations to convince media creators to remove a potentially negatively-influencing element or add an educational element while at the same time convey the message that media consumption for children is OK, and they can have a great time doing it. But that is the goal.

From Roadblocks to Bridges

If there is agreement that children's media use has a powerful influence on children's lives, why isn't there more effective advocacy on the topic? What roadblocks and challenges hold back improvement? How can actions move beyond flagging problems to a focus on building bridges?

Challenges facing advocacy on children's media use fall into three categories:

- Challenges *building consensus* about a pressing need
- Challenges *adopting* best practices
- Challenges *funding* the actions

Building Consensus about a Pressing Need

The needs of children often receive less financial support from government and large funding institutions than those issues affecting adults and adult-related issues. Additionally, the influence of media on children may be seen as less of a priority than other issues affecting children, such as pediatric diseases or violence against children. However, children's ubiquitous use of media ultimately affects many of these other issues since children learn about socialization, conflict resolution, culture, news, healthcare, nutrition and more when engaging with media, especially digital media.

Stakeholders must perceive the issue of children's media use as a pressing need before they will prioritize it over other issues and take action. They must see children's media use as an issue that, without attention, will be severely damaging to children's health, education and well-being, as well as impacting adults and adult jobs, parental support, research funding, even political campaigns. Many of the organizations noted in this chapter have been at the forefront of making this case to stakeholders. Successful advocacy on children's media use seems to occur most often when a single specific issue becomes a trending focus of news reports in popular media or among parents and educators. This happened in the early 2000s with cyber-bullying and in 2016 with attention on the proliferation of fake news. In these two examples, consensus on a common need was built organically; in other words, the focus grew out of children's actual experiences, teacher feedback, and parental observations.

Adopting Best Practices

Research has been conducted on a wide range of topics affecting children and media yielding specific recommendations and best practices. But adoption of those best practices from people making day-to-day decisions about children's media use remains challenging. For example, research has shown a negative impact on a child's health and wellbeing when a television or other digital media is placed in a child's bedroom, but many parents ignore this recommendation. Parents are known to rely on the histories and habits of their own upbringing when considering decisions about their children.

Media creators may be equally reluctant. For decades, media creators have heard about research proclaiming the dangers of children watching too much TV or playing too many hours of video games, leading to a belief that the goal of many media studies is to confirm that children should consume less media. Why would any media creator adopt a best practice seeming to intend to diminish their audience?

Encouraging adoption of best practices is a daunting goal. Parents are understandably sensitive about recommendations that seem to criticize their parenting decisions. Some recommendations aimed at parents have little regard for the realities of two-parent working families, single parent households, economic realities or media access. Recommendations about best practices are not always shared among researchers, depending on their area of expertise or focus. New technologies may negate prior research that aimed to provide a recommendation for all forms of media. But this challenge must be acknowledged and tackled if the goal of improving children's media use is to be achieved.

Funding the Actions

As with many social issues, children's media use needs a steady influx of funding to support solid, well-documented research, the dissemination of that information, and the creation of materials that support the sharing of best practices. Without funding (or with minimal funding), issues get little-to-no attention, research focus, or comprehensive distribution. Additionally, funding is one of those areas that builds upon itself. When a prominent funder or corporate sponsor or philanthropist shows a commitment to a topic that very action brings attention to the issue and encourages other funders to pay attention to the same issue and consider supporting it as well. Unfortunately, children's media has very few dedicated funding sources. Years ago, the Kaiser Family Foundation had a funding priority connected to children's media that lead to many years of excellent research and dissemination. But in the late 2000s the foundation shifted its funding priorities and stopping funding children's media research. Large foundations, such as the Knight Foundation, Gates Foundation, MacArthur Foundation and others have specific programs that offer limited funding to media-related projects and research, but not a specific focus on children's media.

Conclusion: How Can Bridges to Greater Advocacy Be Built?

There has perhaps never been a stronger moment in time in which the full cadre of concerned stakeholders could be rallied effectively around the media needs of children and youth. The simultaneous influences on children of social media, the Internet, lower cost technology, free public WIFI, age-specific content development from infants through teens, mobile media, and ubiquitous access has created a media storm of influence. This storm is not a dangerous thunderstorm of destruction, for there are many elements of children's lives that are enhanced and improved through media. But it does create a powerful opportunity, even necessity, that consideration of the influence of media on children and youth be fully considered and direct action taken. For example, there are a wide range of opportunities for advocacy and partnerships including:

- Build relationships with specific news organizations to help build understanding about children's issues, trends, and research reports.
- Lobby the larger private and public foundations to make children's media use one of their funding priorities.
- Cultivate relationships with elected officials at the local, state, and federal level, as well as those appointed to high level positions in government (e.g., U.S. Department of Education and the Federal Communications Commission) so they understand how media is intertwined with many of the other concerns for children on which they focus.
- Consider the ways in which other countries have supported children's media through legislation, research and funding.
- Work with news outlets to highlight a specific issue facing children's media use on a consistently occurring basis (e.g., weekly).
- Use the annual Media Literacy Week event as an opportunity to shine a light on a specific children's media issue.
- Gather children's media advocates on a regular basis to discuss the issues and come to agreement on an annual issue on which to focus.
- Encourage academic journals to highlight a specific children's media topic in a single journal issue, among several articles.
- Coordinate best practice information more effectively across stakeholder groups. For example, encouraging more pediatricians to include media use as one of the topics discussed in a child's annual checkup with parents.
- Seek opportunities to shift the rhetoric that (a particular) media is bad, to one that focuses on media consumption as a media literacy skill, focused on critical thinking.

The influence of media on children and youth cannot be categorized as simply a parental concern, educators' concern, a concern only for people creating media content, or any other group or individual with a direct relationship to children. The influence of media on children and youth must be advocated as a concern for all when the goal is providing children with the opportunity to grow up happy and healthy.

Discussion Questions

1. Is there one stakeholder group that you feel should be held ultimately responsible for the media content consumed by children and youth? Why?

2. Many other countries have stricter rules about media content for children and youth and the advertising placed around that media. What are the pros and cons of having stricter rules? What are the pros and cons of having a more market-driven system as reflected in the US?

3. Do children's media content providers have a responsibility for the influence of their content? What if the content may be influencing children in a negative way?

4. Evaluate the CSR example of Toca Boca's "Take a stand for play". Is this a strong topic for a CSR campaign? Why or why not? How might it be improved?

Exercises

1. Select a current topic affecting children and media where there has been a recently reported change. Gather information from at least four sources that covered the topic. Write an analysis on how the research was reported vs. how what the research actually stated.

2. Create a scenario in which students role-play the stakeholders at various points in a particular issue. For example, a scenario in which Congress is being lobbied to make changes to the COPPA legislation. Students could take on the roles of FCC Commissioner, parent, executive director of a child advocacy organization, producer from a top children's TV network, teacher, state Department of Education commissioner, app developer, pediatrician, researcher, etc. Each stakeholder has five minutes (more/less) to make their case about why this legislation should or should not be adopted.

3. Select an issue currently impacting children or youth. How has that issue been addressed in children's media content? Discuss specific programs and episodes. How has it been addressed by specific child advocacy groups with a media focus? Discuss actions that have been taken and whether or not they have been successful.

4. Play "Walk the Line". Create a line on the floor with tape that runs the length or width of the room. One person (instructor) serves as the facilitator. The facilitator makes an opinion statement, such as "Ultimately, children are the responsibility of their parents and parents should be held accountable for the media their children consume." Students in agreement with the statement stand to the right of the line. Students in disagreement stand to the left of the line. (Discourage center-standers. Push students to select one response or the other, agreement or disagreement.) Discuss what made a person stand in a particular spot. What would have changed their position?

Notes

1. The author served as president of NAMLE from 2007–2015.
2. Results from this Sesame Workshop study are available at http://kindness.sesamestreet.org/view-the-results/

References

Calvert, S., Appelbaum, M., Dodge, K., Graham, S., Nagayama, H., Gordon C., … Hedges, L. (2017). The American Psychological Association Task Force assessment of violent video games: Science in the service of public interest. *American Psychologist, 72*(2), 126–143.

Campaign for a Commercial Free Childhood. (n.d.) Retrieved from http://www.screenfree.org/

Carroll, A. (2015). Corporate social responsibility: The centerpiece of competing and complementary frameworks. *Organizational Dynamics, 44*(2), 87–96.

Chassiakos, Y., Radesky, J., Christakis, D., Moreno, M., Cross, C. (2016). Children and adolescents and digital media. *Pediatrics, 138*(5). Council on Communications and Media. Retrieved from http://pediatrics. aappublications.org/content/early/2016/10/19/peds.2016-2593

Common Sense Media. (n.d.) *About Us*. Retrieved from https://www.commonsensemedia.org/about-us/our-mission#

Council on Communications and Media. (2016a). Media and young minds. *Pediatrics, 138*(5). American Academy of Pediatrics. Retrieved from http://pediatrics.aappublications.org/content/early/2016/10/19/peds.2016-2591

Council on Communications and Media. (2016b). Media use in school-aged children and adolescents. *Pediatrics, 138*(5). American Academy of Pediatrics. Retrieved from http://pediatrics.aappublications.org/content/early/2016/10/19/peds.2016-2592

Family Online Safety Institute. (2016). *Kids and the connected home: Privacy in the age of connected dolls, talking dinosaurs, and battling robots*. Retrieved from https://www.fosi.org/policy-research/kids-connected-home-privacy-age-connected-dolls-talking-dinosaurs-and-battling-robots/

Fleming-Milici, F., & Harris, J. L. (2016). Television food advertising viewed by preschoolers, children and adolescents: Contributors to differences in exposure for black and white youth in the United States. *Pediatric Obesity*. doi:10.1111/ijpo.12203

Heldman, C. (2016). *Hitting the Bullseye: Reel girl archers inspire real girl archers*. Geena Davis Institute on Gender in Media. Retrieved from https://seejane.org/wp-content/uploads/hitting-the-bullseye-reel-girl-archers-inspire-real-girl-archers-short.pdf

Joan Ganz Cooney Center. (n.d.). *About Us*. Retrieved from http://www.joanganzcooneycenter.org/about-us/

Konopasky, A., & Williams, A. (2016). *Connection and control: Case studies of media use among lower-income minority youth and parents*. San Francisco, CA: Common Sense Media.

The LAMP. (n.d.). *Media breaker*. Retrieved from http://thelamp.org/portfolio/media-breaker/

National Association for Media Literacy Education (n.d.) Media Literacy Week. Retrieved from https://medialiteracyweek.us/

Vaala, S., Ly, A., & Levine, L. (2015). *Getting a read on the app stores: A market scan and analysis of children's literacy apps*. Joan Ganz Cooney Center, New York, NY. Retrieved from http://www.joanganzcooneycenter.org/wp-ontent/uploads/2015/12/jgcc_gettingaread.pdf

Weber, B. (2015, January 22). Peggy Charren, Children's TV Crusader. *New York Times*. Retrieved from http://www.nytimes.com/2015/01/23/arts/peggy-charren-childrens-tv-crusader-is-dead-at-86.html?_r=0

Wineburg, S., & McGrew, S., & Breakstone, J., & Ortega, T. (2016). *Evaluating information: The cornerstone of civic online reasoning*. Stanford Digital Repository. Retrieved from http://purl.stanford.edu/fv751yt5934

YouTube. (2016). *Little girl cries tears of joy after getting doll with a prosthetic leg*. Retrieved from https://www.youtube.com/watch?v=FGhAcBwwpo0

CHAPTER 5

What Is Media Literacy Education?

Renee Hobbs

Perhaps when you were growing up, you got a bit of media literacy education in school. Did you ever critically analyze a television commercial about alcohol in a health class, looking at how beer ads are constructed? Perhaps you noticed how it uses children and animals to connect beer across the generations, as in the Budweiser ad from Superbowl XVII that featured an interaction between a puppy and a Clydesdale horse. Or you may have had a history teacher who invited discussion about current events by playing news clips and discussing how the media constructs social reality by the strategic selection of local, national and international events. Did your librarian or your social studies teacher demonstrate how to select primary and secondary sources and evaluate the quality of a website? You may even have had a "Media Literacy" class where you had the opportunity to critically analyze entertainment films, consider gender and racial stereotypes in the media, learn about media industries, or debate the effects of social media on people's attention and social relationships. Perhaps you got the opportunity to compose videos yourself, working with a small team to create a short documentary or a public service announcement, for example. It's possible that you have had many different types of media literacy learning experiences during your elementary and secondary school career. And you may also be currently having a media literacy learning experience in college, if you're enrolled in a course that's exploring the topic of children and the media.

Sadly, it's also possible that you *never* had a media literacy experience. Because American public education is decentralized, with each of the 15,000 school districts making independent decisions about curriculum and instruction, we can't easily measure the extent to which American students have had exposure to media literacy education.

Media literacy education is a multidisciplinary education reform movement that aims to improve education by connecting the classroom to contemporary culture (Thoman & Jolls, 2004). The formal study of media, popular culture and digital technology and the practice of media literacy pedagogy increases the relevance of learning and builds knowledge and skills that help people become informed citizens of a democracy (Bennett, 2008). Since Texas included media literacy competencies within the framework of language arts instruction in 2001, there has been steady national growth in the use of both media analysis and media production in K-12 classrooms. Media literacy in K-12 environments generally feature activities which, minimally, invite students to:

- reflect on and analyze their own media consumption habits;
- identify the author, purpose and point of view in films, commercials, television and radio programs, magazine and newspaper editorials, and online media;
- identify the range of production techniques that are used to communicate point of view and shape audience response;
- identify and evaluate the quality of media's representation of the world by examining patterns of representation, stereotyping, emphasis and omission in print and television news and other media;
- appreciate the economic underpinnings of mass media industries, making distinctions between those media which sell audiences to advertisers and those which do not;
- gain familiarity and experience in creating media for both personal expression and for purposes of social and political advocacy (Hobbs, 2006).

When people think about the role of media and technology in the lives of children and youth, they generally have two competing ideas recognizing that children need *protection* from potentially harmful media while at the same time recognizing the *empowerment* that comes from media used as a tool for learning, information and self-advocacy. These perspectives have long been identified as the two overarching themes in the media literacy education community, reflecting a tension between those who see media literacy education as a means to address the complexities and challenges of growing up in a media- and technology-saturated cultural environment and those who see media literacy as a tool for personal, social, cultural and political empowerment (Hobbs, 1998).

In this chapter, you will learn about the history of media literacy education in relation to its changing meanings and definitions. We'll see how media literacy is expanding to include digital literacy as a result of the rise of the Internet and social media. You will learn about media literacy interventions designed to mitigate the potentially harmful effects of media. Specific examples of media literacy education in the context of elementary and secondary schools will help you visualize the kind of instructional practices that are becoming more common in schools around the country. Finally, we'll look briefly at the rise of global media literacy education around the world.

Definitions of Media Literacy

The generally accepted definition of media literacy was created by a group of scholars and activists nearly twenty-five years ago at the National Leadership Conference on Media Literacy, noting that "a media literate person can decode, evaluate, analyze and produce both print and electronic media" (Aufderheide & Firestone, 1993, p. 1). Stakeholders in media literacy education include parents, teachers, librarians, media professionals, and school leaders. Media literacy education may occur in the home, in formal education, or in afterschool or informal education that occurs in libraries, museums and non-profit cultural organizations. In any context, however, educators consider the *production process* (looking at how media texts are created and the institutional constraints that shape production), the *text* (looking at the content and form of the message), the *audience* (looking at the ways in which people construct meaning as they use or interact with the media) and the *culture* (looking at the social, political and economic context in which media messages circulate (Buckingham, 2003a).

Another way of defining media literacy comes from Hoeschmann and Poyntz (2012):

> Media literacy is a set of competencies that enable us to interpret media texts and institutions, to make media of our own, and to recognize and engage with the social and political influence on media in everyday life. (p. 1)

Here we see the definition places emphasis on personal interpretation, creation of media, and understanding the role of media within the larger society. In deepening the idea of engaging with media as a form of citizenship, I define the competencies of digital and media literacy that are needed for full participation in contemporary civic life, emphasizing five elements:

> *Access.* Finding and sharing appropriate and relevant information and use media texts and technology tools well.
> *Analyze.* Using critical thinking to analyze message purpose, target audience, quality, veracity, credibility, point of view and potential effects or consequences of messages.
> *Create.* Composing or generating content using creativity and confidence in self-expression, with awareness of purpose, audience and composition techniques.
> *Reflect.* Considering the impact of media messages and technology tools upon our thinking and actions in daily life and applying social responsibility and ethical principles to our own identity, communication behavior and conduct.
> *Act.* Working individually and collaboratively to share knowledge and solve problems in the family, the workplace, and the community, and participating as a member of a community at local, regional, national and international levels. (Hobbs, 2011a, p. 12)

To embody the practice of critical analysis, media literacy education involves a pedagogy of "asking questions about what you watch see and read" and involves responding to media texts through collaborative dialogue. Because there is a "widening gap between young people's worlds outside school and their experiences in the classroom" (Buckingham, 2003b, p. 311), teachers are using popular culture texts such as television, magazines, film, video games, and music to engage students in critical conversations. Media literacy expands on traditional literacy practices by adding film, television, radio, newspapers, video games, advertisements, music, and pop culture in addition to learning about media industries (Hart & Hicks, 2002; Lemke, 2006).

Critical Questions and Key Concepts

Learners can analyze texts they experience at home or in school by focusing on five major questions:

1. Who is sending the message and what is the author's purpose?
2. What techniques are used to attract and hold attention?
3. What lifestyles, values, and points of view are represented in this message?
4. How might different people interpret this message differently?
5. What is omitted from this message? (Hobbs, 2006)

These critical questions are relevant to many forms of media, including websites, podcasts, YouTube videos, and even traditional course content, including novels, textbooks and primary sources (Rheingold, 2008). Media literacy educators aim to help learners of all ages internalize these questions as they encounter information, entertainment and persuasion.

The National Association for Media Literacy Education (NAMLE, 2012) has identified five key concepts of media literacy: (1) All media messages are constructed; (2) Each medium has different characteristics, strengths and a unique "language"; (3) media messages are produced for particular purposes; (4) people use their individual skills, beliefs and experiences to construct their own meaning from media messages; and (5) media can influence the beliefs, attitudes, values and behaviors and the democratic process. These ideas represent a synthesis of fifty years of practice and theory of media literacy education in the United States. Core principles represent ideas about media literacy education that are widely shared among members of the professional community.

Media literacy education requires active inquiry and critical thinking about the messages we receive and create; it expands the concept of literacy to include all forms of media; it builds and reinforces skills for learners of all ages. Like print literacy, those skills necessitate integrated, interactive, and repeated practice. Media literacy education develops informed, reflective and engaged participants essential for a democratic society, recognizing that media are a part of culture and function as agents of socialization. Finally, media literacy education affirms that people use their individual skills, beliefs and experiences to construct their own meanings from media messages (NAMLE, 2012).

New Media Literacy

Although the term media literacy has been historically aligned with both the literature on *media effects* (Austin & Johnson, 1997; Austin & Meili, 1995; Singer, Zuckerman, & Singer, 1980) and the instructional practices of *literacy learning* (Hart & Hicks, 2002; Lemke, 2006; Miller & McVee, 2012; Postman, 1970) over the past few decades, the inquiry-focused approach to media literacy education, has grown to include two new approaches.

One is focused on *digital literacy* primarily in informal out-of-school or online contexts, as a means to promote increased student motivation and engagement in school through the use of digital technologies (Digital Literacy, 2011; Gurak, 2001; Lankshear & Knobel, 2008). The increasingly availability of in-school wireless broadband, tablets, mobile media, and social media for teaching and learning is creating new opportunities for digital and media literacy education in the context of elementary and secondary education. The easy availability of digital media production tools has brought digital and media literacy closer together through digital composition practices (Miller & McVee, 2012). Burn and Durran (2007) propose strategies for the holistic assessment of learning progression in media literacy, as students advance the ability to be more strategic and intentional in their work as media critics and producers.

Another strand conceptualizes a new media literacy that is rooted in the changing nature of *participatory culture*. Scholars have identified habits of mind that enable people to experience both personal and civic empowerment as a result of engaging with digital media and technologies. For example, Jenkins, Ito, and boyd (2015, p. viii) note that user-generated content, "crowdsourcing, peer production and Web 2.0 are moving from geek culture to a more globalized mainstream." Among the new media literacy skills required for participatory culture are:

Play: The capacity to experiment with one's surroundings as a form of problem-solving.

Performance: The ability to adopt alternative identities for the purpose of improvisation and discovery.

Simulation: The ability to interpret and construct dynamic models of real-world processes.

Appropriation: The ability to meaningfully sample and remix media content.

Multitasking: The ability to scan one's environment and shift focus as needed to salient details.

Distributed cognition: The ability to interact meaningfully with tools that expand mental capacities.

Collective intelligence: The ability to pool knowledge and compare notes with others toward a common goal.

Judgment: The ability to evaluate the reliability and credibility of different information sources.

Transmedia navigation: The ability to follow the flow of stories and information across multiple modalities.

Networking: The ability to search for, synthesize, and disseminate information.

Negotiation: The ability to travel across diverse communities, discerning and respecting multiple perspectives, and grasping and following alternative norms.

Visualization: The ability to interpret and create data representations for the purposes of expressing ideas, finding patterns, and identifying trends. (Jenkins, Clinton, Purushotma, Robison, & Weigel, 2006)

Different nuances exist in the definitions of media literacy because there are a variety of different motivations, learning outcomes and goals for the practice of media literacy education. A teacher's approach to teaching media literacy in the elementary grades may focus on empowerment or protection. For example, a teacher may encourage a child to learn to use an iPad app for composing a story (if the teacher believes this has value for the child) or she may involve children in critical discussions of media stereotypes of Disney princesses (if the teacher believes that such representations are potentially damaging to the development of gender stereotypes). Naturally, these vary depending on the needs of the learner and the context of the learning environment. For example, a college student may learn media literacy competencies through academic assignments that involve learning about the political economy of the media industry, the practice of filmmaking, by participating in a university-school partnership exploring how to teach students about media violence (Scharrer, 2005, 2006).

Media literacy education takes different forms in different places. Unlike in other nations, the U.S. has no national curriculum and this means that media literacy may be integrated into existing curriculum in English language arts, social studies or health education or exist as a stand-alone elective course or subject taught by a specialist teacher. Those educators who are concerned about issues of media ownership or representation will perhaps be troubled by "less critical" perspectives that seems to celebrate the mere use or simple enjoyment of media. Because of this diversity, media literacy educators sometimes argue and debate about the relative merit of different instructional approaches (Hobbs, 1998, 2011b; Potter, 2010).

Media Literacy and English Education

The term "media awareness" was used in the early 1970s alongside the term "media literacy" to describe its importance to English educators, who were influenced by the work of Neil Postman, who urged the National Council of Teachers of English (NCTE) to include media literacy as part of English education. In 1970, Postman had written that an essential feature of becoming well-educated was learning the fine art of "crap detection." He explained that through critical thinking about culture and values, students can learn to recognize the faults in our tribes and affiliations and able to see how symbol systems indoctrinate, manipulate, distort and create prejudice.

These educators took seriously the belief that media—not just print—ought to be a fundamental part of the English language arts curriculum. For example, as early as 1970, the members of this professional organization acknowledged that non-print media had already "become a major means of transmitting information, entertainment, values and ideal of our culture" (NCTE, 1970). The NCTE stated that understanding the new media and using them constructively and creativity "required developing a new form of literacy—new critical abilities in reading, listening, viewing and thinking" that would enable students to deal with "multisensory tactics of persuasion and new technology-based art forms." The organization emphasized the need for teacher education programs and cooperation with teachers of journalism, the social sciences and speech communication "to promote the understanding and develop the insights students need to evaluate critically the messages disseminated by the mass media" (NCTE, 1975, p. 1).

Reflecting a conceptualization of literacy as consisting of both "reading" and "writing," some emphasize the instructional or pedagogical values associated with the habits of mind linked to critical analysis of mass media, digital media and popular culture, especially when combined with media composition activities involving visual, print, sound and digital media tools and technologies (Beach, 2007). Distinct set of pedagogical practices (including close analysis of media texts, cross-media comparison, keeping a media diary, role playing and multimedia composition) help learners build awareness of the constructedness of the media and technology environment. Through these activities, learners deploy strategies useful in the meaning-making process, understand the economic, political and historical context in which media messages circulate, and appreciate the ways messages influence attitudes and behavior (Wilson, Grizzle, Tuazon, Akyempong, & Cheung, 2011). That is why in 1996, the NCTE endorsed a resolution that "viewing and visually representing are a part of our growing consciousness of how people gather and share information. ... Teachers should guide students in constructing meaning through creating and viewing nonprint texts." Teachers aim to introduce students to concepts including *authors and audiences, messages and meanings, and representation and reality*, which can be used to analyze all forms of media (Hobbs, 2006). To illustrate these concepts, let's look at some representative examples in elementary and secondary education to visualize the nature and the diversity of media literacy learning experiences.

Elementary

Young children can develop precursor skills of media literacy through activities that involve describing and naming the characteristics of the media and technology they use at home (Hobbs & RobbGrieco, 2012). Kindergarten and Grade 1 children learned how to recognize the constructed nature of the photograph, noticing "what's inside and what's outside" the frame. Working with a horizontal cardboard square, children learned that the photographer makes choices of where to point the camera, and this affects what the viewer sees. In another activity, children created their own paper laptops and used them to have a conversation with each other, simulating the experience of "talking" through social media and understanding the many different types of communication activities that occur online (Hobbs & Moore, 2013). Some teachers ask children to draw pictures of a paper laptop or tablet and then talk about the different forms of communication that occur using laptops. Mertala (2016) asked preschool children to describe how they would like to use digital media for learning and discovered that media production was the second most often referred activity by the children in this study (after playing digital media games). Because digital cameras are such easy to use tools for children, media production by young children can be an effective tool for self-expression, communication, documentation and evaluation in early childhood education (Friesem, 2015).

Intermediate students can develop critical perspectives on media stereotypes. Fourth and fifth grade U.S. students engaged in a class project on stereotypes in toy marketing. Michele Hatchell (2016), an art and social studies teacher, designed the learning experience to explore how LEGO toys represented gender and cultural diversity. Children activated math skills by counting the characters from over 600 LEGO sets, finding that most Lego sets were marketed almost exclusively to boys and included very few female figures. Among the exceptions were the "Friends" and "Princess" sets which were almost exclusively marketed to girls, which included few male figures and lots of gender stereotypes. As one 4th grader put it, "Lego Friends has too much pink and purple." Students also found that, in a sample of 407 human mini-figures, only 27 represented non-European cultures.

As part of the curriculum, children wrote letters to the CEO of Lego and, inspired by Lego's famous 1981 "What it is is beautiful" ad, they decided to create their own versions of the print ads to remind LEGO that "diversity is perfect" and all children can play with LEGOs. "This project is lovely because it gives the kids a voice as they talk about this and communicate via art, writing and research," Hatchell said. When the CEO of Lego responded to the children, students learned about the concept of representation and discovered the power of communication and information to make a difference in the world (Hatchell, 2016).

Middle School

At middle schools, teachers often explore advertising in the context of examining persuasion. For example, Cuff and Statz (2010) used the clips from *Consuming Kids*, a documentary about advertising to children, with their middle schools students. After viewing, students responded to these questions: What stands out for you from the video clip? What do you agree with? What do you disagree with? Students wrote for several minutes and then shared their ideas. Teachers wrote: "As we listened, we were pleased to see how excited they were to discuss the world of advertising and how media targets young people" (Cuff & Statz, 2010, p. 28).

Teachers observed the responses of children who, as part of classroom instruction, gained awareness of how brand loyalty is taught at an early age. They observed that, in the context of classroom dialogue, children could challenge assertions made in the video, including the claim that children are more obese today than in years past. To synthesize ideas, students were asked to write some reflections after their reading and viewing activities. Students were free to select the genre of expression, and some chose poetry, diary entries, fiction, memoir, and even science fiction. The teachers observe that "Because students take this bombardment of ads and rampant consumerism as a given, they may not give it the critical attention it deserves. Meaning-making matters, and English teachers must provide students with the language to question their visual culture and form their own opinions" (Cuff & Statz, 2010, p. 31).

High School

Media literacy education includes the practice of creating media, which uses project-based learning pedagogies to promote intense experiential learning. Twelfth grade students worked on a documentary project focused on immigration, with support from the media teacher, the

English teacher; and the history teacher. Parker (2013, p. 669) notes that for these students to take a stance within the immigrant documentary, they needed to be "both distant and close to their subjects" to discover how to tell the story in a way that would be comprehensible for an audience. This kind of learning can be highly personal and potentially transformative.

Students were then required to produce a documentary on immigration and interview an immigrant (preferably from Latin America), using photography to present a coherent narrative of his or her life through film. The guiding questions for this unit were: (1) What are the major benefits and drawbacks of living in the United States for Latino immigrants, and (2) What factors affect their success or ability to succeed in U.S. society? As part of the learning experience, students read texts such as T.C. Boyle's *The Tortilla Curtain*, the motion picture *Babel* and the documentary *Made in L.A.* They also looked at photographs taken at the U.S.—Mexico border and explored examples of Chicano art.

When students began to interview their subjects, they encountered some ethical tensions in the filmmaker–subject relationship, as students had to promote trust in order for the subjects to openly discuss their personal and emotional immigration experiences. For one student who learned what it was like for someone to come to the United States as a 6-year-old and grow up as an undocumented person, the opportunity to appreciate the constant fear that her family could be deported at any time intensified feelings of empathy. It took considerable trust to talk freely about her life experience as she had been told her whole life not to talk about being an immigrant. As Parker notes, "being able to represent the other relied on a reciprocity of a shared story: A filmmaker had to trust that her subject had a story to tell, and the subject then had to trust that the filmmaker would respectfully and ethically represent this story" (2013, p. 674).

Media Literacy Interventions

Media literacy has found to be effective in a wide variety of contexts and learning environments. There have been a number of empirical investigations of media literacy interventions by social science researchers from the disciplines of psychology, communication or public health (Jeong, Cho, & Hwang, 2012; Martens, 2010). Some programs consist of only one or two sessions and other programs are a semester length or longer. Some focus on one issue (violence, advertising, alcohol) while others address many different topics. Important initiatives have examined educational programs that explore the representation of alcohol (Austin & Johnson, 1997; Austin & Meili, 1995; Austin, Pinkleton, Hust, & Cohen, 2005); tobacco advertising (Banerjee & Greene, 2006, 2007); sexuality (Pinkleton, Austin, Cohen, Chen, & Fitzgerald, 2008); media violence (Byrne, 2009); and advertising and consumer culture (Livingstone & Helsper, 2006).

Rooted in the spirit of protecting young people from potentially harmful media use, sometimes media literacy interventions tend to frame up media exposure as the problem and media literacy as a solution. For example, a program for children ages 9–14 who were involved in the juvenile justice system asked them to consider and reflect critically upon their exposure to media violence and to evaluate the unrealistic representations of substance abuse (Moore, DeChillo, Nicholson, Genovese, & Sladen, 2000). Researchers tested whether children's fears about terrorism could be mitigated with a three-session media literacy program targeting their mothers, who learned about how news is constructed as a means to help them calm children who might witness violence on television news (Comer, Furr, Beidas, Weiner, & Kendall, 2008).

One program even explicitly used media literacy education on the theme of media violence as a means to reduce the amount of exposure to television and other media. The program's goal was to get kids ages 6–10 to watch less television. The intervention essentially persuaded children to have critical attitudes concerning television violence and the program was successful in decreasing the amount of time children watched media violence, an effect that lasted up to eight months (Rosenkoetter, Rosenkoetter, & Acock, 2009). Such approaches to media literacy have been criticized as essentially coercive and not truly embodying the core principles of media literacy education, which respect the autonomy of the individual viewer to make independent and well-informed choices (Hobbs, 2011b).

Conclusion

The United States is not alone in advancing media literacy through formal and information education. Countries including Austria, Brazil, Spain, South Korea, Finland, Argentina, Turkey and other nations have begun to develop media literacy education programs (Frau-Meigs & Torrent, 2009). Worldwide momentum for media literacy has been increasingly evident since the European Commission made media literacy a priority in 2009. At the Education, Youth and Culture meeting held in Brussels in 2009, the Council of the European Union formally adopted a policy on a European approach to media literacy in the digital environment, "embedded in a package of measures to ensure an effective European single market for emerging audiovisual media services" (O'Neill, 2010, p. 328). Recognizing the increased competitive environment of the audiovisual sector that results from an inclusive knowledge society, the Council noted that the education system must better support people's ability to access, understand, evaluate, create and communicate media content as part of lifelong learning. They noted, "The responsible and informed use of new technologies and new media requires citizens to be aware of risks and to respect relevant legal provisions, but most literacy policies should address such questions in the context of a generally positive message" (Council of Europe, 2007, p. 2). The Council recommended the progressive development of criteria to assess the levels of media literacy in member states, beginning in 2011, a task that has been initiated by a number of federal agencies with support from key European scholars.

In a refreshing sign of the maturing of the field, media literacy education initiatives are moving away from the "inflated promotional language and overbroad generalizations" about the transformative power of media literacy education (Cappello, Felini, & Hobbs, 2011, p. 67). Over time, the global research community of media literacy scholars has paid more attention to transdsciplinary theoretical framing, careful description of practices, clarity in identifying outcome measures and precision and integrity in reporting program results, impacts, and consequences (Livingstone & Haddon, 2009; Ranieri, 2016). Over time, we can anticipate that media literacy will take on many shapes and forms as it is implemented in countries around the world.

Exercises

1. Make a list of five things that you think every teacher should know about media literacy after reading this chapter. Create your own example of a media literacy activity for students of a specific age group, including a description of the activity and your learning goals for the activity.

2. Document your own life history as a media maker. What are your earliest memories of creating media by taking photographs, using a video camera, creating a blog or posting to social media? Were these individual or collaborative projects? What kinds of media productions did you create in and out of school? How might the process of creating media have shaped your personal and social identity?

3. Interview an elementary or secondary teacher about their knowledge of media literacy education. How do they define it? Who should be responsible for teaching it? What are the benefits of helping students critically analyze and create media? What are the obstacles why media literacy education doesn't occur in every school or community?

References

Aufderheide, P., & Firestone, C. (1993). *Media literacy: A report of the national leadership conference on media literacy.* Queenstown, MD: Aspen Institute.

Austin, E. W., & Johnson, K. K. (1997). Effects of general and alcohol-specific media literacy training on children's decision making about alcohol. *Journal of Health Communication, 2*(1), 17–42. doi:10.1080/108107397127897

Austin, E. W., & Meili, H. K. (1995). Effects of interpretations of television alcohol portrayals on children's alcohol beliefs. *Journal of Broadcasting & Electronic Media, 39,* 417–435. doi:10.1080/08838159409364276

Austin, E. W., Pinkleton, B. E., Hust, S. J. T., & Cohen, M. (2005). Evaluation of an American Legacy Foundation/Washington State Department of Health media literacy pilot study. *Health Communication, 18*(1), 75–95. doi:10.1207/s15327027hc1801_4

Banerjee, S. C., & Greene, K. (2006). Analysis versus production: Adolescent cognitive and attitudinal responses to antismoking interventions. *Journal of Communication, 56*(4), 773–794. doi:10.1111/j.1460–2466.2006.00319.x

Banerjee, S. C., & Greene, K. (2007). Antismoking initiatives: Effects of analysis versus production media literacy interventions on smoking-related attitude, norm, and behavioral intention. *Health Communication, 22*(1), 37–48. doi:10.1080/10410230701310281

Beach, R. (2007). *Teaching media literacy.* Thousand Oaks, CA: Corwin/Sage.

Bennett, W. L. (2008). *Civic life online: Learning how digital media can engage youth.* John D. and Catherine T. MacArthur Foundation Series on Digital Media and Learning. Cambridge, MA: The MIT Press.

Buckingham, D. (2003a). *Media education: Literacy, learning and contemporary culture.* Cambridge: Polity Press.

Buckingham, D. (2003b). Media education and the end of the critical consumer. *Harvard Educational Review, 73*(3), 309–327. doi:10.17763/haer.73.3.c149w3g81t381p67

Burn, A., & Durran, J. (2007). *Media literacy in schools.* London: Paul Chapman.

Byrne, S. (2009). Media literacy interventions: What makes them boom or boomerang? *Communication Education, 58*(1), 1–14. doi:10.1080/03634520802226444

Cappello, G., Felini, D., & Hobbs, R. (2011). Reflections on global developments in media literacy education: Bridging theory and practice. *Journal of Media Literacy Education, 3*(2), 66–73. Retrieved from http://files.eric.ed.gov/fulltext/EJ985668.pdf

Comer, J. S., Furr, J. M., Beidas, R. S., Weiner, C. L., & Kendall, P. C. (2008). Children and terrorism-related news: Training parents in coping and media literacy. *Journal of Consulting and Clinical Psychology, 76*(4), 568–578. doi:10.1037/0022–006X.76.4.568

Council of Europe. (2007). *Recommendation CM/REC-2007–11 of the Committee of Ministers to Member States on Promoting Freedom of Expression and Information in the New Information and Communications Environment.* Strasbourg: Author. Retrieved from http://bit.ly/2qjzTd1

Cuff, S., & Statz, H. (2010). The story of stuff: Reading advertisements through critical eyes. *English Journal, 99*(3), 27–32.

Digital Literacy. (2011). *Digital literacy.* Retrieved from http://digitalliteracy.gov

Frau-Meigs, D., & Torrent, J. (2009). *Mapping media education policies in the world: Visions, programmes and challenges.* Paris: UNESCO.

Friesem, J. (2015). *On becoming a digital literacy mentor: Self-determination and media production in elementary education* (PhD dissertation, University of Rhode Island). Retrieved from http://digitalcommons.uri.edu/dissertations/AAI3738539/

Gurak, L. (2001). *Cyberliteracy: Navigating the Internet with awareness.* New Haven, CT: Yale University Press.

Hart, A., & Hicks, A. (2002). *Teaching media in the English curriculum.* Stoke on Trent: Trentham Books.

Hatchell, M. (2016). *What it is is Beautiful*. Retrieved from http://www.whatitisisbeautiful.com/

Hobbs, R. (1998). The seven great debates in the media literacy movement. *Journal of Communication, 48*(1), 16–32. doi:10.1111/j.1460–2466.1998.tb02734.x

Hobbs, R. (2006). Multiple visions of multimedia literacy: Emerging areas of synthesis. In M. McKenna, L. Labbo, R. Kiefer, & D. Reinking (Eds.), *International handbook of literacy and technology, Volume II* (pp. 15–28). Mahwah, NJ: Lawrence Erlbaum Associates.

Hobbs, R. (2011a). *Digital and media literacy: Connecting culture to classroom*. Thousand Oaks, CA: Corwin/Sage.

Hobbs, R. (2011b). The state of media literacy: A response to Potter. *Journal of Broadcasting and Electronic Media, 55*(3), 419–430. doi:10.1080/08838151.2011.597594

Hobbs, R., & Moore, D. C. (2013). *Discovering media literacy*. Thousand Oaks, CA: Corwin Sage.

Hobbs, R., & RobbGrieco, M. (2012). African-American children's active reasoning about media texts as a precursor to media literacy. *Journal of Children and Media, 6*(4), 502–519. doi:10.1080/17482798.2012.740413

Hoeschmann, M., & Poyntz, S. (2012). *Media literacies*. Malden, MA: Blackwell.

Jenkins, H., Clinton, K., Purushotma, R., Robison, A., & Weigel, M. (2006). *Confronting the challenges of participatory culture: Media education for the 21ˢᵗ century*. Chicago, IL: The John D. and Catherine T. MacArthur Foundation.

Jenkins, H., Ito, M., & boyd, d. (2015). *Participatory culture in a networked era*. Cambridge: Polity Press.

Jeong, S-H., Cho, H., & Hwang, Y. (2012). Media literacy interventions: A meta-analytic review. *Journal of Communication, 62*(3), 454–472. doi:10.1111/j.1460–2466.2012.01643.x

Lankshear, C., & Knobel, M. (2008). *Digital literacies: Concepts, policies and practices*. New York, NY: Peter Lang.

Lemke, J. (2006). Toward critical multimedia literacy: Technology, research and politics. In M. McKenna, L. Labbo, R. Kiefer, & D. Reinking (Eds.), *International handbook of literacy and technology, Volume II* (pp. 3–14). Mahwah, NJ: Lawrence Erlbaum Associates

Livingstone, S., & Haddon, L. (Eds.). (2009). *Kids online: Opportunities and risks for children*. Bristol: Polity Press.

Livingstone, S., & Helsper, E. (2006). Does advertising literacy mediate the effects of advertising on children? A critical examination of two linked research literatures in relation to obesity and food choice. *Journal of Communication, 56*(3), 560–584. doi:10.1111/j.1460–2466.2006.00301.x

Martens, H. (2010). Evaluating media literacy education: Concepts, theories and future directions. *Journal of Media Literacy Education, 2*(1), 1–22.

Mertala, P. (2016). Fun and games: Finnish children's ideas for the use of digital media in preschool. *Nordic Journal of Digital Literacy, 11*(4), 207–226. doi:10.18261/issn.1891–943x-2016-04-01

Miller, S., & McVee, M. (2012). *Multimodal composing in classrooms: Learning and teaching for the digital world*. New York, NY: Routledge.

Moore, J., DeChillo, N., Nicholson, B., Genovese, A., & Sladen, S. (2000). Flashpoint: An innovative media literacy intervention for high-risk adolescents. *Juvenile and Family Court Journal, 51*(2), 23–34. doi:10.1111/j.1755–6988.2000.tb00019.x

National Association for Media Literacy Education. (2012). *Core principles of media literacy education in the United States*. Retrieved from https://namle.net/publications/core-principles

National Council of Teachers of English. (1970). *Resolution on media literacy*. Retrieved from http://www.ncte.org/positions/statements/medialiteracy

National Council of Teachers of English. (1975). *Resolution on promoting media literacy*. Retrieved from http://www.ncte.org/positions/statements/promotingmedialit

O'Neill, B. (2010). Media literacy and communication rights: Ethical individualism in the New Media environment. *International Communication Gazette, 72*(4–5), 323–338. doi:10.1177/1748048510362445

Parker, J. K. (2013). Critical literacy and the ethical responsibilities of student media production. *Journal of Adolescent and Adult Literacy, 56*(8), 668–676. doi:10.1002/JAAL.194

Pinkleton, B. E., Austin, E. W., Cohen, M., Chen, Y. C., & Fitzgerald, E. (2008). Effects of a peer-led media literacy curriculum on adolescents' knowledge and attitudes toward sexual behavior and media portrayals of sex. *Health Communication, 23*(5), 462–472. doi:10.1080/10410230802342135

Postman, N. (1970). The politics of reading. *Harvard Educational Review, 40*, 244–252. doi:10.17763/haer.40.2.b5j6417k71j34116

Potter, J. (2010). The state of media literacy. *Journal of Broadcasting & Electronic Media, 54*(4), 675–696. doi:10.1080/08838151.2011.521462

Ranieri, M. (2016). *Media education, populism and change: Challenging discrimination in contemporary societies*. New York, NY: Routledge.

Rheingold, H. (2008). Using participatory media and public voice to encourage civic engagement. In W. L. Bennett (Ed.), *Civic life online: Learning how digital media can engage youth* (pp. 97–118). The John D. and Catherine T. MacArthur Foundation Series on Digital Media and Learning. Cambridge, MA: MIT Press.

Rosenkoetter, L. I., Rosenkoetter, S. E., & Acock, A. C. (2009). Television violence: An intervention to reduce its impact on children. *Journal of Applied Developmental Psychology, 30*(4), 381–397. doi:10.1016/j.app-dev.2008.12.019

Scharrer, E. (2005). Sixth graders take on television: Media literacy and critical attitudes about television violence. *Communication Research Reports, 24*, 325–333. doi:10.1080/00036810500317714

Scharrer, E. (2006). "I noticed more violence:" The effects of a media literacy program on knowledge and attitudes about media violence. *Journal of Mass Media Ethics, 21*(1), 70–87. doi:10.1207/s15327728jmme2101_5

Singer, D. G., Zuckerman, D. M., & Singer, J. L. (1980). Helping elementary school children learn about TV. *Journal of Communication, 30*(3), 84–93. doi:10.1111/j.1460-2466.1980.tb01995.x

Thoman, E., & Jolls, T. (2004). Media literacy: A national priority for a changing world. *American Behavioral Scientist, 48*(1), 18–29. doi:10.1177/0002764204267246

Wilson, C., Grizzle, A., Tuazon, R., Akyempong, K., & Cheung, C. (2011). *Media and information literacy curriculum for educators.* Paris: UNESCO. Retrieved from http://unesdoc.unesco.org/images/0019/001929/192971e.pdf

CHAPTER 6

Piaget and Pokémon

What Can Theories of Developmental Psychology Tell Us about Children and Media?

Cyndy Scheibe

For more than fifty years, researchers have explored ways in which people use different forms of media, and how the media—primarily television, films, and video games—are likely to affect their beliefs, attitudes, emotional responses, and behaviors. Much of this research shows that children of different ages use and are affected by media differently (Scantlin, 2011; Wartella & Robb, 2011). The explosion of digital media technologies over the past decade (including apps, Internet sites, and social media) has led to a much more complex media diet beginning in early childhood as well as a dramatic increase in the amount of time children and teens spend using media, both in and outside of school (Common Sense Media, 2013; Rideout, Foehr, & Roberts, 2010). The debut of the iPad in 2010, in particular—with its touch screen technology and advanced interactive capabilities—caused a transformation in the nature of media use by young children, especially in terms of learning and education (Buckleitner, 2015; Vasquez & Felderman, 2013).

Media use by individuals of all ages, in fact, has become increasingly interactive and individualized. Favorite characters and programs can be viewed across multiple platforms at all times of the day and with running commentary on social media by children, teens and adults who view them. *Pokémon*, for example, debuted in the early 1990s as a video game and later as a popular anime TV show featuring Trainers who control pocket monsters with special powers. Its media franchise now includes more than 800 Pokémon characters appearing on trading cards, feature films, children's books, fandom sites, YouTube videos, Macy's parade floats and popular apps like Pokémon Go!. The impact of popular media like Pokémon on children, therefore, is much more complex than just the result of watching a TV show or movie, making research on the effects of media much more challenging.

Theories of developmental psychology can help us interpret this increasingly complex media world of children and teens by identifying potential mechanisms explaining why those effects may occur, and by guiding our predictions about who is most at risk for specific effects. They also help to explain how children make sense of media content, and how their understanding changes with age. Finally, in the absence of a credible mechanism or theoretical explanation for how two variables are related, developmental theories can help to separate real causal relationships from spurious ones.

Generally speaking, most developmental theories can be organized into three main categories: those that emphasize the development of acquired *behaviors*, those that emphasize the development of *cognition* (e.g., attention, learning, memory, understanding), and those that emphasize the development of *personality and emotions*. Theories of *moral development* (including moral reasoning and the development of a conscience) reflect a combination of those components, and are especially relevant to studying media effects.

Which theoretical approach you use to explain a given set of data or observations depends partly on your own view of human development and partly on the nature of the question under consideration. Theories differ in their emphasis on cognition, for example. If you are interested in how children understand (or misunderstand) what they see on television, then all of the cognitive theories will be applicable to that question; many other theories (e.g., behaviorism or Freud's psychosexual theory) have little to say about thinking or understanding. In addition, some developmental theories describe qualitative changes that occur during specific and predictable stages of development (e.g., Piaget's theory), whereas others portray a more gradual process of changes that occur with age (e.g., social learning and information-processing theories). Finally, some theories emphasize the importance of innate, biological, or unconscious influences ("nature"), while others stress the importance of environmental influences ("nurture"); the latter are most useful for studying children and media.

Developmental Theories and Children's Learning

One of the key issues of interest in the study of children and media has to do with learning: *how* children learn a given behavior, idea, or piece of information, and *what factors play a role* in whether a given child will be likely to learn something from a particular media example?

Generally speaking, there are four basic ways in which children can learn and "key issues" that affect the likelihood of learning for each.

1. *Direct experience.* This primarily reflects learning through *operant conditioning*, where the child actually *does* the behavior and experiences some consequence. If they are rewarded (reinforced), then they should be more likely to repeat the behavior again; if they are corrected or punished, then they should be *less* likely to repeat it. The key issue has to do with the nature of the reward or punishment—what will work for this particular individual? Effective reinforcers for young children are usually different from those that work for older children or teens. For example, young children are likely to be heavily influenced by praise or criticism from their parents and other family members, while teens might be more heavily influenced by feedback from their peers.

2. *Observational learning.* This involves learning by watching someone else do the behavior and then imitating them (or deciding *not* to imitate that behavior because of negative con-

sequences experienced by that person). Here the key issue involves the extent to which you identify with the person observed, see yourself as similar to them, and/or want to be like them; in other words, is that person a *role model*? Again, this is likely to vary for children of different ages (and different sexes); younger children typically identify with and look up to their same-sex parents and older siblings, while older children and teens often model their behavior after peers and figures from popular culture.

3. *Symbolic learning.* For older children, adolescents, and adults, most of our learning comes through written or spoken language; we are often told to do (or not to do) something, and why. Symbolic learning can also occur through visual symbols that convey a message (e.g., on traffic signs, websites, or apps). There are two key issues in this case: 1) the child's prior understanding and fluency with the language or symbols used to convey the information; and 2) the credibility of the source; how much do you trust them or believe that they are telling the truth?

4. *Cognitive learning.* In this case learning is based on information and cognitive skills that the child already has and their attempts to achieve a successful outcome or conclusion. With cognitive learning, there are a number of key issues that come into play, including developmental stage (age), cognitive abilities, prior information available, and educational experiences.

How do these four ways of learning relate to children and media? Until relatively recently, *learning through direct experience* had only limited application because traditional media (like television and films) didn't directly reinforce (reward or punish) children for their behaviors. The exception was video games, where active participation is coupled with rewards for successful actions; this can have strong educational benefits when the focus of the game involves skill development, but has also been shown to increase aggression and anti-social behavior when the game incorporates violence and a "first person shooter" component (Keil, 2014; Swing & Anderson, 2008). Today, however, with increasing use of interactive digital media (especially computer games and apps) beginning in early childhood, learning from direct experience plays an important role through immediate feedback designed to reinforce the child's actions or indicate that their strategies and actions were not successful (Robb & Lauricella, 2015). Furthermore, with complex media phenomena like Pokémon, children (and even adults) engage in direct experience learning as they capture, train and fight with Pokémon characters, sharing strategies and experiences with competitors and friends.

Even for traditional media, however, direct experience learning is reflected in the positive or negative responses from parents and/or peers to something a child does (or says) after learning it on TV, which might well influence the likelihood of it occurring again. Children are also influenced by whether the media characters they see are rewarded or punished for their actions; numerous content analyses have noted that violent actions often go unpunished or are even rewarded, making it more likely for children to conclude that aggression is a good thing (Bushman & Huesmann, 2001). Of course parents may also, intentionally or unintentionally, reward certain kinds of media use (for example, reading) and punish or set restrictions on other kinds (for example, "screen time").

Observational learning easily applies to media's influence on children, and is discussed in more detail in the section on social learning theories below. *Symbolic learning* and *cognitive learning* also apply, especially with respect to children's use of media for information, ideas, and skill development (e.g., through books, news, educational TV shows and apps). They also reflect developmental differences in children's interpretation of media messages and their understanding of the media in general. These theories apply to adolescents and adults too, of course, as reflected in recent concerns about the ability of social media users to be able to distinguish between actual (credible) news and "fake news" reports on social media sites (Stanford History Education Group, 2016), underscoring the importance of ongoing media literacy education.

All of these types of learning, therefore, can be viewed in the context of learning from and through mediated experiences. They also serve as important mediators in media effects and are reflected in the specific developmental theories discussed below.

Social Learning (Social Cognitive) Theories

Developed by Albert Bandura, *social learning theory* was initially grounded in behaviorism, emphasizing behaviors that children could and would imitate from observing role models in their social environment and a gradual, continuous process of developmental change (Bandura, 1977). Unlike traditional behavioral theorists, however, Bandura believed that behavior is due to more than just the influence of the environment; it also reflects children's observations and interpretations of what they see and the individuals (or characters) with whom they identify most strongly. Social learning theory predicts that children are more likely to imitate people they admire, those who are rewarded for their actions, and those similar to themselves.

Over time, Bandura increasingly emphasized the importance of cognition, including the roles of individual choice and interpretation in determining a person's modeled behaviors. Now called *social cognitive theory* (Bandura, 2002), it is not a stage theory of development (like Piaget's), although it does include the concept that social cognitive processes change with age. Role models for young children are not the same as those for adolescents, and while young children often directly and immediately imitate what they see, adolescents and adults are more likely to observe and remember a given behavior that can be demonstrated later if the appropriate situation arises. Both children and adults may also learn what *not* to do from observing the behaviors of others, especially by paying attention to the consequences of their actions in the situation observed.

Before television and movies, children's role models were limited to people they saw in their everyday lives (e.g., parents, older siblings, other family members, people in the neighborhood, teachers). Today, television and other audiovisual media provide a wide range of exciting and intriguing role models for children and teens, including real people, characters who are played by live actors, superheroes, and cartoon characters. Once television and movies became part of children's daily lives, the potential for social cognitive learning through observation and imitation of the behaviors of media characters skyrocketed.

But *would* children imitate mediated portrayals of behaviors in the same way they imitated behaviors they saw performed by real people in their own world? Bandura's earliest and most famous series of studies on this topic (Bandura, Ross, & Ross, 1963) demonstrated that they could and would imitate specific aggressive behaviors shown on television (for example, kicking a "bobo doll"), and that their imitation of a "cartoon" character (in this case, a person dressed as a cat) was almost as high as imitation of a real person. This is a particularly important finding, given children's frequent viewing of cartoons, and it has been supported by subsequent studies of imitation of cartoon violence (Bushman & Huesmann, 2001).

Social cognitive theory would also predict that children will learn prosocial behaviors from viewing media portrayals as well as antisocial behaviors, and indeed that is supported by research (Dorr, Rabin, & Irlen, 2002; Mares, Palmer, & Sullivan, 2011). It also means that children may learn what *not* to do from cartoons and other media. However, such learning may only be effective if there are realistic consequences shown for an action; if the Coyote is fine again after falling off a cliff or being hit on the head with an anvil in the *Looney Tunes* Road Runner cartoons, then children may well be drawing inaccurate conclusions.

An important tenet of social cognitive theory involves the relationship between the observer (child) and the observed (media character), especially how much the child identifies with the character and sees him or her as a role model. By the age of three or four, children have developed gender awareness and gender constancy (that is, understanding that gender is permanent regardless of changes in hair, clothing, or activities), after which gender is often an important mediator of social cognitive learning. Research has shown that boys are much more likely to choose role models who are male (especially powerful ones), while girls are more likely to select both male and female role models (Anderson & Cavallaro, 2002; Hust & Brown, 2011). The same studies have found that African-American and White children are most likely to pick role models of the same race as themselves, while Latino and Asian-American children are most likely to pick White role models (possibly because there are far fewer portrayals of Latino and Asian characters on children's television). Interestingly, while the Pokémon franchise is located in Japan, the Pokémon Trainers aren't identifiably Asian in appearance or speaking style, and while the main character (Ash Ketchum) is male, the Trainers include both males and females with different skin and hair colors, many with their own fandom sites.

Cognitive-Developmental Theories

While Swiss psychologist Jean Piaget actually died long before *Pokémon* debuted in the 1990s, his *cognitive-developmental theory* has important applications for the study of children's understanding of media, especially regarding the limitations in cognitive reasoning abilities of young children. Piaget's theory argues that children actively construct their understanding of the world through the ongoing processes of *assimilation* (incorporating new information into existing knowledge) and *accommodation* (reorganizing ways of understanding to take into account new information) (Arnett, 2012).

Unlike social cognitive theory, cognitive-developmental theories describe children's development as occurring in a series of stages, with dramatic and abrupt shifts in the quality of children's thinking as they move from one stage to the next. As children develop, their understanding of the world doesn't just gradually improve; it is qualitatively *different* than before. Piaget believed that this process unfolds naturally, with all children proceeding through these stages in the same order and at roughly the same ages. While his approach reflects many biological concepts of maturation, he did not believe that cognitive development was entirely genetically based. Instead he emphasized the child's own role in developing cognitive *schemes* (ways of knowing or action patterns) by actively exploring, manipulating, and making sense of his or her environment (Crain, 2011).

Piagetian theory includes four stages of cognitive development that always occur in the same sequence (Singer & Revenson, 1996), although the exact age at which children move from one stage to the next may vary:

1. The *sensori-motor stage* (birth to two years), in which infants and toddlers get information through their senses and manipulation of objects; by age two, children have developed an internal representation of schemes including the capability for deferred imitation, an understanding of object permanence, basic grasp of cause and effect, the beginnings of language, and self-awareness.

2. The *preoperational stage* (two to seven years), during which there is rapid growth and re-organization of understanding and symbolic thought, but the child's thinking is illogical and his or her approach to problem-solving is unsystematic; during the early part of this stage, the child's thinking is often *egocentric* (marked by an inability to take into account other perspectives than his or her own) and *animistic* (attributing human motivation and characteristics to inanimate objects), and they have difficulty distinguishing between fantasy and reality.

3. The *concrete operational stage* (seven to twelve years), in which children can demonstrate the ability to mentally manipulate objects and are able to consider more than one dimension of an object and different perspectives, but are still limited to applying this understanding to concrete (rather than abstract) examples.

4. The *formal operational stage* (twelve years and older), in which most adolescents can demonstrate abstract thinking, hypothetical-deductive reasoning, and systematic approaches to problem-solving.

Most of the media research using a Piagetian framework has focused on the cognitive limitations of preoperational thinking, especially for children under the age of four or five who have a difficult time fully grasping the nature of media and their content. One classic study showed that two- and three-year-old children often believe that the TV characters lived inside the TV set (Noble, 1975), while another found that three-year-old children interpreted a television image of a glass of water as more similar to real life (where the water would spill out if you turned it upside down) than to a photograph of a glass of water (where it wouldn't) (Flavell, Flavell, Green, & Korfmacher, 1990).

Research on children's understanding of fantasy versus reality indicates that while children as young as two or three can both engage in fantasy play and understand that it is only pretense, they are much more confused by whether something is real or make-believe on television (Davies, 1997). This has been explored in a number of important realms, including children's consumer behavior (Young, 2011) and the impact of media violence (Wilson, 2011). Research on media and children's fears shows that young children are most afraid of characters and scenes that *look* scary (like monsters and witches), while older children are more afraid of realistic scenes and situations could actually happen (Cantor, 2001).

Other preoperational limitations are reflected in the study of children's *theory of mind*— understanding their own mental processes and those of other people (Flavell, 2004). Preschoolers tend to believe that other people know and see what they know, and have difficulty understanding concepts like *false beliefs* (believing something that is not actually true) or *dreams* (which are often believed to be real). They also have difficulty with what is known as the *appearance-reality distinction* (understanding the difference between what something seems to be and what it actually is). It is not surprising, then, that young children are often confused by media storylines that emphasize secret knowledge or characters who appear to be good (or look nice on the outside) but are really bad, and vice versa.

Information Processing and Educational Theories

Information-processing theories focus primarily on memory and attention (using a computer-based model of data input/output, and storage), and while they do not predict unique ways of processing information by children of different ages, developmental studies have shown that younger children do attend to and remember information less well than older children. For example, young children are less likely to pay attention to the central or important information, instead attending to irrelevant or idiosyncratic aspects of a situation (Santrock, 2015). They are also less likely to be able to recall detailed information about something they have been taught or experienced.

Studies of children's attention to and comprehension of television confirm the importance of these developmental limitations (Barr, 2011). Young children often miss the salient information that's important for the story to make sense and may recall only unrelated pieces of information that were interesting to them rather than the main points of the story. They are also more likely to attend to unusual auditory or visual features (for example, special visual effects, funny voices, sound effects) even when they are unrelated to the main story.

Information-processing theories also emphasize the importance of information that is already available to the individual (from learning and prior experience) as a mediator of understanding and interpretation; using the computer model, an individual can only process information in the context of information she or he already has stored. Interpretation of a TV storyline, then, will be influenced by *explicit knowledge*: what the child already knows about the common structure of stories, the "formal features" of television (that is, the meaning of special visual or auditory effects), and the characters in the program. In the complex *Pokémon* stories, children familiar with the characters and premise may have a better understanding than children (or even adults) not familiar with the show. However, understanding will also be influenced by the child's *implicit knowledge*: knowledge about the real world and inferences drawn about interscene relationships and character motivations. It is this latter category that often puts children at a disadvantage (Collins, 1981; Condry, 1989).

Information processing also helps to explain how children develop beliefs and ideas (including erroneous ones) about a topic. Their beliefs are likely to be based on inaccurate sources such as advertising or fictional media stories; children are less likely to question fictional stories because they don't have the training or real-world knowledge to judge their credibility. This is similar to cultivation theory in communications (Gerbner, Gross, Morgan, & Signorielli, 1994), which predicts that heavy viewers who "mainstream" themselves into the world of television are more likely to incorporate information from television (even fictional television) into their beliefs about the real world. It is also reflective of cognitive script theory (Valkenburg, 2004), which deals with the ways children develop expectations about how to act in certain situations based on "scripts" they have seen in real life and the media.

Information-processing theory also helps to explain children's learning of educational content from television. Some children's television producers, such as Sesame Workshop, carefully base their program content on research about children's learning. The importance of reinforcing concepts and understanding by using explicit and concrete examples with sufficient repetition, for example, has been demonstrated by research on the effectiveness of programs like *Sesame Street* (Fisch & Truglio, 2001) and educational digital technologies (Vasquez & Felderman, 2013). These same techniques have been used in media literacy curricula aimed at improving children's understanding of the purpose of TV commercials and misleading messages about nutrition (Rogow & Scheibe, 2016), and a broader understanding of how media messages are constructed (Hobbs & Cooper Moore, 2013; Scheibe & Rogow, 2012).

Parents and early childhood educators have increasingly found that the new interactive digital technologies can support early literacy education (Guernsey & Levine, 2015; Vasquez & Felderman, 2013) and aid in children's learning across multiple disciplines (Donahue, 2015). Even Montessori approaches to early childhood education—which have traditionally viewed all media (except for books) as harmful for children's development—have begun to incorporate elements of digital technologies, concluding that the interactivity of apps and other educational digital media allow children to explore their worlds in ways that even Maria Montessori would likely appreciate (Buckleitner, 2015).

Theories of Moral Development

Piaget proposed stages of moral reasoning that are also relevant to the understanding of media effects (Crain, 2011). During the preoperational stage, children's reasoning reflects moral *heteronomy*, which is grounded in blind adherence to rules that are immutable, a sense of immanent justice (that is, that wrong-doers will always be caught and punished), and judgments of right and wrong that focus on the consequences of the action. Older children, especially after the age of ten, exhibit moral *autonomy*; they understand that rules can be changed and that wrong-doers might not be discovered, and base moral judgments more on the individual's *intentions* rather than the consequences of the action. Young children, then, may easily misinterpret the moral lessons found in media stories that are centered on judgments about an actor's intentions, or when someone breaks the rules in order to achieve a more positive and just outcome.

Lawrence Kohlberg's theory of moral reasoning is probably the most well-known theory of moral development (Crain, 2011; Keil, 2014). He laid out six stages of moral reasoning that gradually develop across childhood and adolescence, occurring in three levels:

- *Preconventional Reasoning*, where children's judgments of right and wrong relate solely to themselves, including fear of punishment (Stage 1, What will happen to me?) and achievement of rewards (Stage 2, What's in it for me?).
- *Conventional Reasoning*, where children's judgments of right and wrong are based on the conventions and expectations of their family, social group and society, including wanting to please others (Stage 3, What will people think of me?) and follow the rules (Stage 4, What if everyone did it?).
- *Postconventional Reasoning*, where children's judgments of right and wrong go beyond their own self-interest and expectations of others to weigh the costs and benefits of an action (Stage 5, What is best for the common good?) and to develop their own moral compass (Stage 6, What are my personal moral principles?). This high level of moral integrity and reasoning is sometimes associated with certain media characters, like Atticus Finch in *To Kill a Mockingbird* (Esquith, 2007).

Kohlberg's theory has been used to explore the impact of television (Rosenkoetter, 2001), especially with respect to moral dilemmas incorporated into programs aimed at children and teens. Much like social learning theory and social scripts described earlier, the moral lessons children are likely to take away from these shows will depend on the actions of the characters they most identify with (usually the "good guys" or main characters); if they lie, steal, cheat, or hurt people—even "bad guys"—to win or get what they want, then Stage 1 or 2 moral reasoning are reflected. If, on the other hand, media content reinforces empathy, fair play, and working to achieve a common goal, higher levels of moral reasoning will be supported.

With the rise of the Internet and social media, these moral issues take on even greater importance. Cyberbullying—harassing or humiliating someone through digital media like chat rooms or text messages with rumors, doctored photographs, and hateful comments—is growing among older children and teens, often with devastating consequences. The anonymity of the attacker(s) bypasses the feelings of guilt and empathy that may be triggered in a real-world encounter, and the potential for quickly reaching a wide audience of peers can serve to reward the cyberbully and further isolate their victims (Keil, 2014).

Summary and Conclusions

In 1978 former FCC commissioner Nicholas Johnson said, "All television is educational television. The question is: what is it teaching?" (Condry, 1989). Today, the same question can be posed regarding the wide range of media that are central to children's lives (Donahue, 2015; Swing & Anderson, 2008). Developmental theories are key to answering this question, emphasizing the age and unique nature of the child who is being taught. Unfortunately, with few exceptions (e.g., Arnett, 2012; Keil, 2014), developmental psychology textbooks still include surprisingly little content about issues related to media use and effects in relation to cognitive development and learning. The explosion of interactive digital media created for and used by young children is likely to change that, as well as the landscape of research on children and media in general.

Discussion Questions

1. Which developmental theories could be used to explain the influence of *Pokémon* on children's beliefs, attitudes, behaviors, and emotions, and what would each one predict? Would those same theories apply to the influence of educational children's TV programs (like *Sesame Street*) or movies (like *Frozen* or *Zootopia*)?

2. Think about another effect of media content on children's learning that you have heard about. Which of the four ways in which children learn would be most applicable to explaining this effect, and why? How would the "key issues" help determine whether a given child would be likely to learn that behavior or information from a particular media experience?

3. Based on the developmental theories presented in this chapter, what types of media might have the strongest impact on children's aggression and other behaviors? On their knowledge and beliefs? How will this vary depending on the child's age or gender?

4. How have new digital media formats (including apps, computer games, Internet sites, and social media) changed the ways in which children are affected by media, and which

developmental theories are most useful in explaining those impacts?

Exercises

1. Watch two half-hour children's TV shows, one that is educational or emphasizes pro-social lessons (on PBS, Disney Playhouse or Nick Jr.) and one that that features good guys vs. bad guys. Identify which characters might be role models for children, including whether they would be more appealing to boys or girls (or both), and/or children from a particular age group. What behaviors might children be likely to imitate from these programs, and why?

2. Watch several TV programs or movies aimed at children and young teens. Take notes on the gender messages that are included (including those in the commercials shown during the TV shows, if any). Based on the messages you saw, what kind of conclusions might children draw about what it means to be a boy or a girl?

3. Preview an educational video game, computer game or app that is designed for young children (ages 2–6). Identify ways in which the app or game is designed to appeal to children from this age group, and the techniques that are used to promote children's learning. Identify the developmental theories that would be reflected in children's use of the game or app, and the type(s) of learning that would occur as they use it.

References

Anderson, K. J., & Cavallaro, D. (2002). Parents or pop culture? Children's heroes and role models. *Childhood Education, 79*, 161–168. doi:10.1080/00094056.202.10522728

Arnett, J. (2012). *Human development: A cultural approach.* Boston, MA: Pearson.

Bandura, A. (1977). *Social learning theory.* Englewood Cliffs, NJ: Prentice-Hall.

Bandura, A. (2002). Social cognitive theory: An agentic perspective. *Annual Review of Psychology* (Vol. 52, pp. 1–26). Palo Alto, CA: Annual Reviews.

Bandura, A., Ross, D., & Ross, S. A. (1963). Imitation of film-mediated aggressive models. *Journal of Abnormal and Social Psychology, 63*(1), 3–11. doi:10.1037/h0045550

Barr, R. (2011). Attention and learning form media during infancy and early childhood. In S. Calvert & B. Wilson (Eds.), *Handbook of children, media and development* (pp. 141–165). Oxford: Blackwell.

Buckleitner, W. (2015). What would Maria Montessori say about the i-pad? Theoretical frameworks for children's interactive media. In C. Donohue (Ed.), *Technology and digital media in the early years: Tools for teaching and learning* (pp. 54–69). New York, NY: Routledge.

Bushman, B. J., & Huesmann, L. R. (2001). Effects of televised violence on aggression. In D. G. Singer & J. L. Singer (Eds.), *Handbook of children and the media* (pp. 223–254). Thousand Oaks, CA: Sage.

Cantor, J. (2001). The media and children's fears, anxieties and perceptions of danger. In D. G. Singer & J. L. Singer (Eds.), *Handbook of children and the media* (pp. 207–222). Thousand Oaks, CA: Sage.

Collins, W. A. (1981). Schemata for understanding television. In H. Kelly & H. Gardener (Eds.), *Viewing children through television* (pp. 31–45). San Francisco, CA: Jossey-Bass.

Common Sense Media. (2013). *Zero to eight: Children's media use in America 2013.* San Francisco, CA: Author.

Condry, J. (1989). *The psychology of television.* Hillsdale, NJ: Lawrence Erlbaum.

Crain, W. (2011). *Theories of development: Concepts and applications* (6ᵗʰ ed.). Boston, MA: Pearson.

Davies, M. M. (1997). *Fake, fact, and fantasy: Children's interpretations of television reality.* Mahwah, NJ: Lawrence Erlbaum.

Donahue, C. (2015). *Technology and digital media in the early years: Tools for teaching and learning.* New York, NY: Routledge.

Dorr, A., Rabin, B. E., & Irlen, S. (2002). Parents, children, and the media. In M. H. Bornstein (Ed.), *Handbook of parenting* (Vol. 5, 2nd ed.) (pp. 349–374). Mahwah, NJ: Lawrence Erlbaum.

Esquith, R. (2007). *Teach like your hair's on fire: The methods and madness inside room 56.* New York, NY: Penguin.

Fisch, S. M., & Truglio, R. T. (2001). Why children learn from *Sesame Street.* In S. M. Fisch & R. T. Truglio (Eds.), *"G" is for growing: Thirty years of research on children and Sesame Street* (pp. 233–244). Mahwah, NJ: Lawrence Erlbaum.

Flavell, J. H. (2004). Theory of mind development: Retrospect and prospect. *Merrill-Palmer Quarterly, 50*(3), 274–290. doi:10.1353/mpq.2004.0018

Flavell, J. H., Flavell, E. R., Green, F. L., & Korfmacher, J. E. (1990). Do young children think of television images as pictures or real objects? *Journal of Broadcasting & Electronic Media, 34*(4), 399–419. doi:10/1080/08838159009386752

Gerbner, G., Gross, L., Morgan, M., & Signorielli, N. (1994). Growing up with television: The cultivation perspective. In J. Bryant & D. Zillmann (Eds.), *Media effects: Advances in theory and research* (pp. 17–41). Hillsdale, NJ: Lawrence Erlbaum.

Guernsey, L., & Levine, M. H. (2015). Pioneering literacy in the digital age. In C. Donahue (Ed.), *Technology and digital media in the early years: Tools for teaching and learning* (pp. 104–114). New York, NY: Routledge.

Hobbs, R., & Cooper Moore, D. (2013). *Discovering media literacy: Teaching digital media and popular culture in elementary school.* Thousand Oaks, CA: Corwin/Sage.

Hust, S. J. T., & Brown, J. D. (2011). Gender, media use, and effects. In S. Calvert & B. Wilson (Eds.), *Handbook of children, media and development* (pp. 98–120). Oxford: Blackwell.

Keil, F. (2014). *Developmental psychology: The growth of mind and behavior.* New York, NY: Norton.

Mares, M. L., Palmer, E., & Sullivan, T. (2011). Prosocial effects of media exposure. In S. Calvert & B. Wilson (Eds.), *Handbook of children, media and development* (pp. 49–73). Oxford: Blackwell.

Noble, G. (1975). *Children in front of the small screen.* London: Constable.

Rideout, V., Foehr, U., & Roberts, D. (2010). *Generation M²: Media in the lives of 8-to-18-year-olds.* Menlo Park, CA: Kaiser Family Foundation.

Robb, M. B., & Lauricella, A. R. (2015). Connecting child development and technology: What we know and what it means. In C. Donohue (Ed.), *Technology and digital media in the early years: Tools for teaching and learning* (pp. 70–85). New York, NY: Routledge.

Rogow, F., & Scheibe, C. (2016). Sharing media literacy approaches with parents and families. In C. Donohue (Ed.), *Family engagement in the digital age: Early childhood educators as media mentors* (pp. 183–196). New York, NY: Routledge.

Rosenkoetter, L. (2001). Television and morality. In D. G. Singer & J. L. Singer (Eds.), *Handbook of children and the media* (pp. 463–473). Thousand Oaks, CA: Sage.

Santrock, J. W. (2015). *Life-span development* (15th ed.). Boston, MA: McGraw-Hill.

Scantlin, R. (2011). Media use across childhood: Access, time and content. In S. Calvert & B. Wilson (Eds.), *Handbook of children, media and development* (pp. 49–73). Oxford: Blackwell.

Scheibe, C., & Rogow, F. (2012). *The teacher's guide to media literacy: Critical thinking in a multi-media world.* Thousand Oaks, CA: Corwin/Sage.

Singer, D. G., & Revenson, T. A. (1996). *A Piaget primer: How a child thinks.* New York, NY: Plume.

Stanford History Education Group. (2016). *Evaluating information: The cornerstone of civic online reasoning.* Retrieved from https://sheg.stanford.edu/upload/V3LessonPlans/Executive%20Summary%2011.21.16.pdf

Swing, E. L., & Anderson, C. A. (2008). How and what do video games teach? In T. Willoughby & E. Wood (Eds.), *Children's learning in a digital world* (pp. 64–84). Oxford: Blackwell.

Valkenburg, P. M. (2004). *Children's responses to the screen: A media psychological approach.* Mahwah, NJ: Lawrence Erlbaum.

Vasquez, V. M., & Felderman, C. B. (2013). *Technology and critical literacy in early childhood.* New York, NY: Routledge.

Wartella, E., & Robb, M. (2011). Historical and recurring concerns about children's use of the mass media. In S. Calvert & B. Wilson (Eds.), *Handbook of children, media and development* (pp. 7–26). Oxford: Blackwell.

Wilson, B. (2011). Media violence and aggression in youth. In S. Calvert & B. Wilson (Eds.), *Handbook of children, media and development* (pp. 235–267). Oxford: Blackwell.

Young, B. (2011). Media and advertising effects. In S. Calvert & B. Wilson (Eds.), *Handbook of children, media and development* (pp. 407–431). Oxford: Blackwell.

CHAPTER 7

How Do Researchers Study Young People[1] and the Media?

Dafna Lemish

As researchers, parents, educators, legislators, producers, health professionals, and so on, we have many questions regarding children, youth, and the media. These questions are diverse, exciting, and challenging. But do we have adequate tools in our "kit" to investigate them? Often, the methods we choose for research are as important as the questions themselves, as they reveal a great deal about our perception of who children are, what they are capable of doing and willing to share with us, the value of our findings, and the interpretations we make of them.

Throughout the long history of research on children, youth, and media, a diverse array of methodologies have been applied. One reason for this is that a broad range of researchers from a variety of disciplinary homes have contributed to our knowledge base: media specialists; developmental psychologists; sociologists studying childhood and leisure; cultural studies scholars concerned with children's popular culture, identities, and globalization processes; educators working in the field of media literacy; health professionals specializing in children's physical and mental health; professionals engaged in the production of texts for children; and policymakers concerned about children's well-being. In fact, most of these perspectives are represented by the various chapters in this book. These various scholarly and applied populations have worked within the research traditions familiar to them; that is, those perceived as legitimate and "scientific" within their own epistemological[2] communities. As a result, a wide range of methodologies available for studying social and psychological phenomena have been applied to the study of children and media: experimental designs, surveys, big data analyses, field studies, ethnographies, interviews, life histories, artwork, and content and critical analyses.

The Challenges: Children as Unique Research Participants

While many of the methodological concerns raised in this chapter are shared by scholars across disciplines, several have discussed the unique challenges we face given our particular interest in children and media (Buckingham, 1993; Götz, Lemish, Aidman, & Moon, 2005; Lemish, 2015). In summarizing these concerns, we should recall that children are a very special group of people to study: they develop and change at a rate and intensity unparalleled in the human life cycle. As a result, what may be an appropriate method for studying adults (such as filling in a questionnaire) may be completely inappropriate for young children. For example, the use of language (such as the wording of specific questions) needs to be tailored differently for children even a few years apart. This makes studies that compare children of different ages particularly tricky. Furthermore, the study of young children raises a host of ethical concerns: the need to guarantee anonymity, not to exploit their naiveté and trust of adults, and to make them aware that their own words can be used against them.

The gap that exists between their abilities (that is, mental skills, knowledge, and comprehension) and their linguistic performance, too, means that young children's explanations may well be unsatisfactory, as we cannot assume that language is a clear indicator of the child's actual inner world. For example, in a study of kindergartners' understanding of television (Lemish, 1997), I found that the interviewees often failed to represent their understanding due to shyness. Indeed, one child resorted to producing strings of "I don't know" in response to various questions concerning his favorite cartoon. A less persistent or inexperienced interviewer might have concluded that the child "really doesn't know." However, later in the interview, when the child was involved in a different chain of thought, other stimuli prompted the same child to suddenly produce complicated and sophisticated responses referring directly to the issue previously avoided. In other cases, children produced more complicated talk than they were actually able to understand, using concepts and terms in a mistaken or irrelevant way. For example, in the aforementioned study one child used the term *audience* to refer to a specific person, most likely the director of a television show.

Children and media researchers are also required to pay particular attention to the social context in which their study is conducted, as from a very young age many children adapt to the social expectations of the environment and learn to behave in accordance with what they perceive to be both their social role (for example, a pupil at school or the family's "baby" at home) as well as their other roles, such as gender role (that is, in ways perceived by society as appropriate for boys or girls). For example, studies conducted in schools or with research assignments that require children to "think," "explain," and "write," often elicit a school-related behavior that may facilitate cognitive achievements but not necessarily spontaneous sharing of feelings and attitudes (Buckingham, 1993). Studies conducted at home may induce more free talk, but also anxieties due to "impression management"[3] of the family and their socioeconomic and class status. Similarly, the biological sex of the participants is often a central dimension of context, as children react differently in uni-sex situations in comparison with mixed groups. Further, this tendency takes different forms and shapes at different stages of their development, as their relationships with the opposite sex change.

As a result of all of the above, studying children and media often requires designing and employing creative research methods that engage children in pleasurable activities that can optimize their cooperation and facilitate a more valid understanding of their inner worlds.

Given this broad survey of the nature of the world of children and research, the purpose of this chapter is to present some of the central methodological approaches that have been applied to our field, to highlight their major advantages and disadvantages, and to raise questions about how knowledge of the world of young people is obtained by applying certain research methodologies. This chapter presents the two methodological traditions that are central in our field, discusses their underlying assumptions and the primary methodologies they utilize, and gives examples of the types of questions they have sought to answer in specific research projects. The chapter will conclude with a brief presentation of an emerging trend, in which various methods are combined to foster our understanding of the role media have in the lives of children and youth around the world.

The Grand Divide

The literature published in our field in academic journals and books is characterized by a binary discourse between what are most commonly referred to as "quantitative" and "qualitative" methods. Other names you might find in the literature contrast "positivist" studies with "ethnographic" ones; "American logical empiricism" with "European cultural studies"; and more. While these terms are unsatisfactory, they are widely used, and for lack of better terms, I will apply them here, too, in order to discuss the central concern of this chapter: How have these two methodological schools of thought been applied in the study of children and media?

The "Becoming" Child: The Quantitative Approach

Traditionally, studies of children and media that embrace developmental theories in cognitive psychology have centered on the individual child. (See Chapter 6 for a detailed explanation of the application of developmental psychology in the study of youth and media.) Accordingly, this approach views children as in the process of "becoming" an adult. Their abilities and skills are tested and measured in comparison to the ideal model of the adult thinker. This approach has been often named "the deficiency model", as it assumes that the child is "deficient" in comparison to the adult. Thus, for example, the development of children's ability to distinguish between fantasy and reality in media content has been studied from this perspective, as well as children's understanding of narrative, their moral judgments of characters on the screen, their computer-literacy skills, their naive trust of advertisements, their reckless mobile sexting and social media bullying; and their emotional reactions to disturbing news (Calvert & Wilson, 2008).

This approach has been advanced by a research paradigm with roots in various stimulus-response models in psychology, as well as effects studies in communication, whose main goal is to find how media affect child behavior, cognition, and emotions. They look for causal relationships between, for example, television violence and aggressive behavior (Bushman & Huesmann, 2012), heavy use of Internet pornography and distorted attitudes about sex and sexuality (Wright, Malamouth, & Donnerstein, 2012), and viewing of educational television and learning and prosocial behaviors (Fisch, 2004).

Research applying this approach has been conducted primarily through "quantitative" methods, such as experimental designs, where children are brought into a study setting and presented with various tasks. In most cases, such studies quantify predefined activities. Thus, for example, the researcher counts the number of times the child behaves in a specific manner in response to viewing television (for example, says something aloud, sings a song, imitates a behavior), or tests the child on specific skills acquired (for example, new vocabulary, a concept, a piece of information). The major strength of studies conducted in such a manner is that they can isolate and control the issues selected for study and place each child in a comparable situation. For example, they can control the kind of screen material to which the child is exposed during the experiment, the skills tested, and the toys available in the room. Researchers assume that such a context has a greater chance of attaining more specific information, as well as causal explanations. For example, they can determine that specific content in an educational program can elicit a certain behavior, while a violent program does not. There are many examples for this line of research: for example, researchers measure toddlers' learning of a specific behavior or new vocabulary after having been presented with screen content designed for that age group; follow children's strategies of surfing the net once provided with a specific task; or their choice of snack following exposure to different food commercials. (See Chapter 12 for a discussion of the research on the effectiveness of educational programs; Chapter 8 for a synthesis of fifty years of research into the effects of media violence on youth; and Chapter 14 for a discussion of the effects of children's advertising.)

Many questions can be raised regarding the type of activities selected for coding or the cognitive and behavioral skills measured. Most of the reservations, however, are made regarding the suitability of the unnatural experimental setting for studying children's media-related behaviors: Is the way children behave under unnatural research conditions indicative of their everyday behavior? Does the short-term effect measured in such a situation last beyond that particular time?

In correlation studies, another often-applied research format, everyday media-related behaviors are measured through responses to questionnaires and analyzed to examine associations (or correlations) between these behaviors and other variables such as cognitive skills, emotions, attitudes, and behaviors. For example, children's exposure to news in the various media is measured as well as their knowledge about the political and social world. The responses are correlated, suggesting, for example, that those who are heavier users of printed news media are better informed about current events than those more heavily dependent on television news. A different correlation study may correlate between young people's exposure to pornography in the media (viewing pornographic programs, playing pornographic computer and video games, surfing pornographic Web sites, reading pornographic magazines) and their self-reports of their attitudes toward women, intimacy, sexuality, and sexual crimes. Such a study might present evidence that adolescents who are heavy consumers of pornography in the media hold more stereotypical attitudes toward women and have a more callous attitude toward sexual crimes in comparison to those who are not exposed regularly to such content.

The major strength of this research method is its ability to examine long-term, accumulative influences of media use on a very large number of children and to offer insights that can be generalized to other situations. There are many variations on this method, including longitudinal studies that follow a group of children over time. Those might involve asking a question such as the following: Is heavy viewing of television in the early years related to lower achievement scores in school? Are heavy consumers of violent content more involved in aggressive incidents as young adults? While such longitudinal studies are few and far between, due to their costly nature and the difficulty to locate the children after long periods of time, they usually attract a great deal of attention and controversy. The central focus of concern here is the question of causality: Is it possible to infer from correlation studies a causal direction? Is it possible to suggest that behavior at a young age is indeed the reason for behavior at a later stage? Or could it be the other way around; that an early predisposition or tendency leads to the media-related behavior in the first place? For example, are children who consume a lot of violent content attracted to it in the first place for personal or social reasons? Is spending a lot of screen time causing obesity in young people or are children who have heavy weight tendencies more attracted to sedentary activities in the first place? Does heavy consumption of sexual content at a young age lead to early onset of sexual activity, or is an interest in sex at a young age motivating such youth to consume more sexual content prematurely? Naturally, different studies try to respond to these challenges in different ways.

The "Being" Child: The Qualitative Approach

The "qualitative" research tradition observes children in their own familiar settings as they express or articulate their inner worlds in their talk, play, drawings, collages, or other art forms, including producing media products themselves (such as YouTube videos, Web sites, Facebook pages, and blogs). These are usually small-scale studies that take place in the natural environments—homes, schools, playgrounds, as well as on the Internet—where children engage in and reveal the role of media in their lives spontaneously. Researchers who apply ethnographic methods (Lindlof & Taylor, 2011) observe, talk to children, and analyze their work, and try to make sense of what they do and say. They focus on seeing children as "beings" in their own right, at each individual stage of their development.

In studies conducted through the qualitative approach, children are presumed to act subjectively in meaningful ways that express their own perspectives, worldviews, and self-image. Researchers approach children as socially competent, autonomous individuals who actively make sense of—indeed, construct and express meanings for—the world around them as they interact with it. What is perceived as central or important in a medium or a text for adults is not necessarily so for children; thus the comparison with adults as a central criterion to evaluating children's cognitive, emotional, social, or behavioral worlds is perceived as unsatisfactory, even misleading. Such studies concentrate on "the meaning media have for children" rather than on "how children's comprehension of media is deficient in comparison to adults" and on "what children do with media," rather than on "what media do to children." A case in point is a study of how children understood the controversial issue of television violence and the pleasures they derived from it (Tobin, 2000); or the role media have in children's make believe worlds (Götz et al., 2005).

To understand how children evaluate characters, judge their morality, or identify with them requires understanding the social context of the child. The epistemological implications of this approach assume that the use of media, understanding of texts, and the pleasures derived from them, are by definition both individualized as well as contextualized experiences. Like adults, children, too, have a gender, a race, a social class, a religion, a culture, a political view. They live in very diverse cultures and conditions all over the world. Therefore, ethnographic studies investigate how children who live in different contexts comprehend media texts and develop different explanations and models of such comprehension. Such studies, for example, documented how children from various social classes and ethnicities interpreted television series differently (Buckingham, 1993); how South Asian immigrant girls in the United States used the media to construct their sexuality and diaspora identity (Durham, 2004); how children in different countries experience screen elicited fear differently (Lemish & Alon-Tirosh, 2014); or how girls around the world use the web to construct their identities (Mazzarella, 2010).

Given the assumptions and ambitions of this approach as well as the complexities involved in studying children, there is a need to design creative methods to complement traditional approaches to ethnography that are based on participant observation; for example, observing babies' behaviors around television in their homes (Lemish, 1987); observing children's free media-related play at home and in school playgrounds (Orr Vered, 2008); combining roles of teacher-researcher as a participant observer in schools or community centers (Seiter, 2005); and in-depth interviews with children, individually or in focus groups (Mazzarella & Pecora, 1999). There are many possibilities for applying creative methods: interpreting children's drawings and artwork; allowing them to videotape themselves as they go about their daily routines and to tell us about them; studying their bedroom possessions (including various media, wall posters, memorabilia, clothes, toys, and games); designing role-playing situations; having them, or their parents, fill in diaries; playing computer games with them; or friending them on social media. One study, for example, followed a class of students in London for an entire year, studying the role of media in their lives in school, in their homes, and within their peer groups (Livingstone & Sefton-Green, 2016). Others have worked over time with activist youth organizations employing media as an integrated part of their political and media engagement (Jenkins, Shersthova, Gamber-Thompson, Kligler-Vilenchik, & Zimmerman, 2016).

This research tradition has been enriched by the development of feminist scholarship (for example, hooks, 2000; Lemish, 2013), which understands gender as a social construction, and is particularly sensitive to the conditions of individual children and youth, diversified by race, class, sexual orientation, religion, ethnicity, and disability. Much of this form of research rejects binary oppositions such as public/private (for example, school versus home use of media), rational/emotional (for example, what children learn from media versus how they feel about it), and nature/culture (for example, what children bring with them genetically versus what they acquire socially and culturally). Rather, it shifts research interests to the previously devalued and ignored domains of the private sphere, the emotional realm, and the taboos surrounding bodily functions and sexuality. Its ethics are sensitive to individuality and diversity, and to the power hierarchies in the research situation, particularly those existing between the children studied and the privileged positions of the usually middle-class, well-educated researcher who is often from a majority ethnic group.

However, this approach is not without its own weaknesses. Such in-depth studies are almost always very limited in the number of children studied and therefore their findings cannot be generalized to larger populations of children. This, of course, is a thorny issue, as researchers would like to be able to make claims that enable us to speak about experiences and understandings that extend beyond a specific group of children. In addition, they do not claim to be able to provide causal explanations, as they nearly always posit that there are multiple individual qualities of children interacting with the multiple characteristics of any medium, thus it is almost impossible to make predictions about the ways media may be affecting their lives.

Epistemological Terms of the Debate

The debate between the two approaches in the social sciences, presented above succinctly, has been long, complicated, and not without serious implications for both research and researchers engaged in it. It is important to realize that this is not a trivial debate, as it is deeply rooted in the most central questions regarding what science and the production of knowledge are all about (consult, for example, the following resources: Deacon, Pickering, Godling, & Murdock, 2007; Keyton, 2015; Lindlof & Taylor, 2011; Wimmer & Dominick, 2016). These can be summarized, in a purist and oversimplified form, around the following four main issues as they become relevant to the study of children and media.

The goals of science. The first concern is for the goal of science and our research activities. "Quantitative" research sets out to confirm specific hypotheses[4] that have been deducted from a more general theory. Its goal is to be able to make predictions according to certain rules. For example: to make a prediction that children who are heavy players of violent computer games will become more violent in their everyday behaviors; or that girls who are heavy consumers of screen content depicting a particular thin-beauty model will be more prone to having low self-image and to develop eating disorders. As a result, this research tradition emphasizes the need for random sampling[5] that will reveal the unifying rules of social life and provide explanations for any deviations from them.

"Qualitative" research, on the other hand, is inductive. Being mainly concerned with understanding phenomena, it seeks to discover rather than to prove. Qualitative research dismisses representative sampling as representing a form of objectivity, as it argues that such sampling has a different built-in bias: it assumes that all children are similar, when in reality they are not. For example, it will try to understand the kinds of pleasures and meanings that boys get from playing violent computer games as they negotiate the meaning of masculinity, and not assume negative behavioral effects, or the processes of adoration or identification that girls engage in with their female role models as they explore the meaning of femininity and not necessarily try to prove effects on lowering their self-image.

The difference between the social and the physical worlds. The second central issue concerns the understandings of the difference between the social and physical worlds and, as a consequence, between the social and natural sciences. On the whole, "quantitative" researchers argue that "the scientific method"[6] as applied in the study of the physical/natural sciences should be emulated in studying the social world. Further, they argue that since the social sciences are relatively young in comparison to the natural ones, they have not as yet had the chance to develop accurate measures and methods for studying human phenomena, but that, with time, their sampling methods, research tools and measures, statistical programming, and applied mathematical models will be perfected. The difference between the social and natural sciences are mostly perceived as differences in degree, and not in kind. For example, while it is true that we are dependent on children's cooperation for examining their surfing behaviors on the Internet, we can design research tools that follow and map their movements in virtual reality and provide us with comprehensive accounts of all of their activities, and thus bypass the need to count on children's cooperation and subjective self-reporting. Similarly, rather than ask children about being aroused by pornography or stimulated by action-adventure programs, one can measure physical reactions in real time, such as their blood pressure, heart beat, and activation of glands.

In contrast, "qualitative" researchers assume that the differences between the two realms of inquiry are differences of kind and not of degree. Children, like all people, are unpredictable individuals, and their media-related behaviors, understandings, pleasures, and influences can be neither predicted nor generalized. Research in of itself is perceived to be a form of human activity and, like all forms of behaviors, it is dependent on the views, training, and experiences of individual researchers, academic institutions and fashions, and economical and political constraints. Therefore, the research orientation applied to study the social world requires a very different methodology. Accordingly, such researchers may have little interest in the sophisticated mapping of children's online activities, or big data analyses of media use, as they may argue that it does not help us unveil the meaning of these activities.

The subject-object distinction. In a related matter, "quantitative" research distinguishes clearly between the thinking, feeling "child-subject" and the media with which the child interacts, and tries to create objective knowledge that is independent of the child. For example, in studying children's reaction to news reporting of a major terror attack, researchers will assign meaning to that coverage (such as "scary", "incomprehensible", "inhuman"). They may design a survey or an experiment on children's attitudes and emotional reactions toward this news reporting. The survey will include a set of questions and clear instructions for the interviewer not to divert from the wording, not to express emotions or opinions, and not to interact with the child in any way that might influence responses. All children will be approached through the same research terms, asked the very same questions in the same manner, while the researcher is assumed to be uninvolved in the process or in the reality she or he is studying.

"Qualitative" research, on the other hand, assumes that there is no meaningful independent existence of the object outside of the child-subject that experiences it; that is to say, there is no one or universal meaning of the news reporting of the terror attack but only meaning constructed in the experience of the individual child viewing it. Furthermore, it dismisses the possibility of distinguishing between the researcher and that which is researched, as both are involved in the research interaction that affects both of them. Research, accordingly, can never be neutral or objective, in that it always stems from a point of view, an ideology, a perspective on life. As a result, "qualitative" research encourages researchers not to erase their subjective individuality but, on the contrary, to make use of it for digging deeper into understanding of the underlining meanings of the phenomenon studied.

The role of everyday experience. Finally, the fourth major difference relates to the way both traditions evaluate the role of our everyday knowledge and experiences. "Quantitative" research is based on the claim that researchers should not count on their own personal experiences and common sense or on those of the children they study since it is only in the symbolic realm of rational thought that it is possible to understand reality. Consequently, children's personal accounts of their media pleasures, for example, are not deemed "truthful" or "true to life," as they are not based on rational analysis of data we call "facts" and that different researchers can study and agree on the same findings (for example, the number of hours playing video games; list of Web sites accessed last night; type of emoticons used in texting).

"Qualitative" research, on the other hand, assigns great importance to those taken-for-granted, everyday experiences, including those happening in the private sphere of the child's own bedroom or those belonging to the world of emotion that reading comic books, listening to pop music, or posting favorite photos on Instagram evoke. It also supports the researcher's employment of his or her own everyday experience in making sense of these phenomena, such as a researcher using her mothering skills to interview a reluctant child, or to compare her own mobile phone use in an attempt to make sense of somebody else's.

Bridging the Divide?

Is it possible to bridge such differences? Can researchers from both traditions learn from each other, even cooperate? To date, those seeking to confront such dilemmas in relation to conducting research on children and media are working with two general approaches. Some researchers, from both traditions, believe that the two are so fundamentally and philosophically different, and that there is no way to bridge the gap or to compromise between them. You are either with "us" or with "them": you conduct research purely according to your chosen research tradition, you publish it in appropriate outlets, and you do not incorporate knowledge created within the opposing tradition in your own work. The opposite approach accepts that each research tradition has its advantages and disadvantages that each contributes to our accumulating knowledge in different ways, and that therefore both should be used according to the type of research question, the characteristics of the children studied, the different stage of the research, or even the personal preference and strength of the researcher.

Aside from various proclamations, it is also instructive to see how some research projects have attempted to combine methods from both traditions. For example, a study of children and their changing media environment in twelve European countries (Livingstone & Bovill, 2001) combined personal in-depth interviews with large-scale surveys. In this case, the data collected in the interviews preceded the distribution of the survey and provided insights into the building of the latter research tool. A different strategy was practiced in a study of the Internet in the lives of immigrant children in Israel: Participants completed structured questionnaires that provided the basis for the in-depth interviews that followed (Elias & Lemish, 2008). There are many possibilities for "mix and match," given that researchers find that they can bridge the underlying theoretical underpinnings of the two approaches and benefit from both.

Indeed, I would like to make a "proper disclosure" and suggest that my personal perspective is that these two approaches should be treated as complementary rather than competitive, and that we should seek to integrate the knowledge gained from both traditions into a fuller and more comprehensible understanding of the role of media in children's lives. In my view, it is possible to accept that children lack the skills and knowledge that adults have developed as they have matured, but at the same time to respect the meanings they produce from media as worthwhile in their own right. We can consider each child's individual development, but at the same time integrate our understanding of this development as embedded in complicated social contexts. We can seek to reach generalizations that will allow us to predict some of children's reactions, yet at the same time also pursue attaining in-depth understandings of individual and unique experiences that provide us with insights into larger phenomena. The particular path we choose to follow, as individual researchers, will say much about the questions we ask and the kind of knowledge we produce, but it will also say much about who we are as researchers.

Editors' Note

This book has been structured purposely to include both quantitative and qualitative scholars as well as those working to bridge the divide. Only by including a range of voices can we fully understand the topic of youth and media.

Discussion Questions

1. How does the kind of research method used affect the kind of knowledge it produces?

2. Do you have a preference for either one of the research traditions? Explain your reasoning. Is there anything in your particular academic education that may have influenced this preference? Courses you took? Professors that influenced you? An article you read?

3. Based on this chapter, what do you think are appropriate criteria for evaluating whether a study is a "good" one?

Exercises

1. Review a number of chapters in this book and make a list of methods used in the studies they discuss. Which categories, quantitative, qualitative, or mixed, do they fall into? Note for each study the main research question. Review your list: Is there anything in common among the research questions asked in each of the three categories?

2. Select two different studies described in various chapters in this book, one study from each of the two main research traditions: quantitative and qualitative. Suggest a complementary method for each from the second tradition that will investigate the same research question.

3. Check the *Journal of Children and Media* in your institution's library (if you have no access to it—look for other communication journals that publish work on children and media). Scan the pages of current issues. Can you find three studies that combine methods from different traditions? What did they study and how?

Notes

1. In this chapter, I use the phrase "young people" to refer to anyone under the age of 18.
2. Epistemology refers to the study of knowledge including how knowledge is produced, evaluated, organized, and re/presented.
3. "Impression management" describes the various forms of behavior of individuals who wish to convey a special impression of themselves (for example, the way they dress, move, and talk, their facial expressions, the accessories they use, and the like).
4. A hypothesis is an expectation based on some theory about particular phenomena or relationships between variables.
5. Random sampling is a procedure of selecting cases from a population to be studied in such a way that each case (here, a "case" is a child) has an equal and known chance of being included in the sample. As a result, the sample drawn for the purpose of the particular study is presumed to represent the entire population of interest (in this case children).
6. The scientific method refers to the various means scientists use in making claims, answering questions, and drawing conclusions.

References

Buckingham, D. (1993). *Children talking television: The making of television literacy.* London: Falmer.

Bushman, B. J., & Huesmann, L. R. (2012). Effects of violent media on aggression. In D. G. Singer & J. L. Singer (Eds.), *Handbook of children and the media* (pp. 231–248). Thousand Oaks, CA: Sage.

Calvert, S. L., & Wilson, B. J. (2008). *The handbook of children, media, and development.* Malden, MA: Blackwell.

Deacon, D., Pickering, M., Godling, P., & Murdock, G. (2007). *Researching communications: A practical guide to methods in media and cultural analysis* (2nd ed.). London: Bloomsbury Academic.

Durham, M. G. (2004). Constructing the "new ethnicities": Media, sexuality and diaspora identity in the lives of South Asian immigrant girls. *Critical Studies in Media Communication, 21*(2), 140–161. doi:10.1080/07393 180410001688047

Elias, N., & Lemish, D. (2008). The internet life of Former Soviet Union adolescents in Israel. In I. Rydin & U. Sjöberg (Eds.), *Mediated crossroads: Identity, youth culture and ethnicity – Theoretical and methodological challenges* (pp. 173–192). Göteborg: Nordicom, Göteborg University.

Fisch, S. (2004). *Children's learning from educational television: Sesame Street and beyond.* Mahwah, NJ: Lawrence Erlbaum.

Götz, M., Lemish, D., Aidman, A., & Moon, H. (2005). *Media and the make believe worlds of children: When Harry Potter met Pokémon in Disneyland.* Mahwah, NJ: Lawrence Erlbaum.

hooks, b. (2000). *Feminism is for everybody: Passionate politics.* Cambridge, MA: South End.

Jenkins, H., Shersthova, S., Gamber-Thompson, L., Kligler-Vilenchik, N., & Zimmerman, A. M. (2016). *By any media necessary: The new youth activism.* New York, NY: New York University Press.

Keyton, J. (2015). *Communication research: Asking questions, finding answers* (4th ed.). New York, NY: McGraw-Hill.

Lemish, D. (1987). Viewers in diapers: The early development of television viewing. In T. Lindlof (Ed.), *Natural audiences: Qualitative research of media uses and effects* (pp. 33–57). Norwood, NJ: Ablex.

Lemish, D. (1997). Kindergartners' understandings of television: A cross cultural comparison. *Communication Studies, 48*(2), 109–126. doi:10.1080/10510979709368495

Lemish, D. (2013). Feminist theory approaches to the study of children and media. In D. Lemish (Ed.), *The Routledge international handbook of children, adolescents and media* (pp. 68–74). New York, NY and Abingdon: Routledge.

Lemish, D. (2015). *Children and media: A global perspective.* Malden, MA: Wiley Blackwell.

Lemish, D., & Alon-Tirosh, M. (2014). "I was really scared": A cross-cultural comparison of reconstructing childhood fearful viewing experiences. In M. Moshe (Ed.), *The emotion industry* (pp. 137–157). New York, NY: Science Publishers.

Lindlof, T. R., & Taylor, B. C. (2011). *Qualitative communication research method* (3rd ed.). Thousand Oaks, CA: Sage.

Livingstone, S., & Bovill, M. (Eds.). (2001). *Children and their changing media environment: A European comparative study.* Mahwah, NJ: Lawrence Erlbaum.

Livingstone, S., & Sefton-Green, J. (2016). *The class: Living and learning in the digital age.* New York, NY: New York University Press.

Mazzarella, S. R. (Ed.). (2010). *Girl wide web 2.0: Revisiting girls, the internet, and the negotiation of identity.* New York, NY: Peter Lang.

Mazzarella, S. R., & Pecora, N. (Eds.). (1999). *Growing up girls: Popular culture and the construction of identity.* New York, NY: Peter Lang.

Orr Vered, K. (2008). *Children and media outside the home: Playing and learning in afterschool care.* New York, NY: Palgrave Macmillan.

Seiter, E. (2005). *The Internet playground: Children's access, entertainment, and miseducation.* New York, NY: Peter Lang.

Tobin, J. (2000). *"Good guys don't wear hats": Children's talk about the media.* New York, NY: Teachers College Press.

Wimmer, R. D., & Dominick, J. R. (2016). *Mass media research: An introduction* (10th ed.). Belmont, CA: Wadsworth.

Wright, P. J., Malamouth, N. M., & Donnerstein, E. (2012). Research on sex in the media: What do we know about effects on children and adolescents? In D. G. Singer & J. L. Singer (Eds.), *Handbook of children and the media* (pp. 249–272). Thousand Oaks, CA: Sage.

PART 2

The Concerns: Media Use, Content, & Effects

CHAPTER 8

Should We Be Concerned about Media Violence?

Erica Scharrer

As a media studies scholar, I have often found myself fielding this question: "So, you study media violence. Do you really think movies, TV shows, or video games make kids go out and shoot people?" My response is that the study of media violence is typically much broader and more complex. It is not usually about extreme and highly unusual violent copycat crimes, partly because they are impossible to study using social science techniques due to the fact that they have already occurred in "uncontrolled" circumstances in which cause and effect would be impossible to sort out, and partly because they are so unique and rare. Rather, the study of media violence effects is often concerned not just with individuals' behavior, but also with effects on thoughts and attitudes—how individuals think about various issues; the way they see themselves, others, and the world at large; the fears that they hold; and the things they think of as "normal" or appropriate, as right or wrong. If we think of the effects of media violence as restricted only to the dramatic direct imitation of violent scenes depicted in television, movies, and video games that occasionally makes news headlines, it is too easy to dismiss these effects as very uncommon, as occurring only for those who undoubtedly have some deep-seated psychological trauma, or as explained away by some other factor. By taking a more complex and encompassing view of potential effects we see that the influence of media violence on the thoughts, attitudes, and behavior of children and teens (as well as adults, although the focus here is on young people) cannot be so readily dismissed.

When we do study behavioral effects, most of the behaviors we study are more appropriately characterized as aggression than as violence, with the former term signifying a wider range of behaviors that varies from the relatively less severe (like pushing and shoving on the playground) to the more serious actions that would put a young person in trouble with the law instead of just in trouble with a parent or the principal. We also consider not just physical forms of aggression but also verbal and social forms, which include manifestations like bullying, yelling, name calling, spreading rumors, and purposely excluding others to cause distress. In addition to effects, we investigate media content and opinions and uses of media.

In writing this chapter, I attempt to address the broad question "Should we be concerned about media violence?" by asking a number of related subquestions, using the research on the topic to provide an answer. I begin with "How is violence portrayed in the media?" because there are a number of ways to show violence, and those variations in depictions can make a substantial difference in how audience members respond. In the next section, the question "Why is there violence in the media, and what explains its appeal?" is posed, so that we can understand why violent stories have enjoyed such a "starring role" in the media over time. Finally, I ask "What are the effects of media violence?" in order to illuminate the important issues brought up in this introduction and to directly answer the question posed by the chapter's title.

How Much Aggression Is There in the Media, and How Is It Portrayed?

Content analyses—studies that use definitions of concepts applied systematically to document and describe the messages that appear in media—have provided a great deal of knowledge about how much violence appears in various media forms, and how it is portrayed. With violence most often defined in these studies as one character using physical actions to purposefully attempt to harm or to actually harm another character, researchers have found that many types of media have a substantial amount of violence. When one adds to these tallies verbal and social or relational acts of aggression to include interactions that cause psychological rather than physical damage, the estimates swell. Content analyses have shown further that violence and aggression are sometimes depicted in a way that might encourage an effect on the audience.

Children's Television

The stories designed specifically for children via cartoons and live-action programs in kid-friendly television slots (like weekend mornings) typically contain more acts of violence and aggression than other types of television programs. The "violence profile" studies of George Gerbner and his associates have found between eighteen and thirty-two acts of violence per hour in Saturday-morning television, a time slot dominated by cartoons, over a span of more than thirty years (Gerbner, Gross, Morgan, & Signorielli, 1994). The most recent data available estimate an average of 16.7 acts of physical aggression per hour in Saturday morning children's programming (Signorielli, 2008). The National Television Violence Study (NTVS), a uniquely comprehensive content analysis, also gives cartoons the dubious distinction of containing one of the highest rates of violent acts per hour of any television programming type (Smith *et al.*, 1998).

More recently, Luther and Legg (2010) studied cartoons on Cartoon Network, Toon Disney, and Nickelodeon for the presence of aggression using hand-to-hand physical contact, aggression using weapons, verbal threats of physical harm, insulting or name-calling, and threatening social isolation (a form of social or relational aggression). Interactions meeting one of these criteria occurred at a rate of .88 acts per minute in the sample, and the vast majority of acts (over 83%) were physically rather than verbally or socially aggressive. Child and teen characters engaged in more aggression than adult characters. Thus, the characters with whom young audiences are most likely to relate provide frequent models of aggression.

A comparison of the depiction of violence in programs on television targeting children aged thirteen and younger to the depiction of violence in general audience programs showed that in children's television, long-term consequences for violence were more rare, violence was more frequently combined with humor, and unrealistically low levels of harm were more likely to occur (Smith *et al.*, 1998). (For low levels of harm, think of Tom being hit repeatedly by an iron frying pan, but showing no signs of stopping his pursuit of Jerry in the classic cartoon *Tom and Jerry*.) Among the 50 most popular programs for two to eleven-year-olds, Martins and Wilson (2012) found one act of social aggression—defined as acts meant to damage one's self-esteem or social status—occurred every 14 minutes, with social aggression more often presented humorously and as perpetrated by likeable characters than physical aggression.

Children's Films

Fumie Yokota and Kimberly Thompson (2000) studied all G-rated animated feature films from 1937 to 1999 that were available on videotape for the presence of intentional, physical acts with the potential to injure or harm. In a total of 74 films, every single film had at least one act meeting that definition of violence. Violent scenes took up an average of 9.5 minutes of screen time, on average, across the films. Approximately one third of the films (32%) contained an explicit message *against* violence. Yet 49% contained cheering or laughing about violence, thereby making light of violence. Just over half of all violent acts (55%) involved the "good" characters fighting against the "bad" characters, a scenario that may inspire identification and perhaps emulation. Sarah Coyne and Emily Whitehead (2008) also studied Disney films (a total of 47) and documented the depiction of social exclusion, malicious humor, making others feel guilty, and engaging in "indirect physical aggression" that included plotting against others, kidnapping them, and using spells against them. Just over 9 of these incidents occurred per hour in the films.

Additional studies examine changes over time. Amy Bleakley, Daniel Romer, and Patrick E. Jamieson (2014), for example, performed a content analysis of 390 top-grossing films from 1985 (when the PG 13 rating was introduced) to 2010. Defining violence as physical contact with the intent to cause or actually causing injury or harm, they found that in about 90% of the films one or more main character committed at least one act of violence; that percentage remained stable over time; and films with various ratings (G, PG, PG 13, or R) were not statistically different in their inclusion of such violence. Almost two thirds (65%) of G- and PG-rated films were found to be explicitly violent in nature, depicting the aftermath of violence rather than leaving it to viewers' imagination. When the authors performed a similar analysis across a wider period of time, examining 855 movies with top box office receipts from 1950 to 2006, they found that the proportion of main characters—both male and female—who either perpetrated or were targets of violence increased steadily over time (Bleakley, Jamieson, & Romer, 2012). In PG 13 movies, the rate of gun violence has been found to have tripled since the rating was introduced in 1985 (Bushman, Jamieson, Weitz, & Romer, 2013).

We can conclude, therefore, that when one takes a long historical view of movie content created for general audiences, there is evidence of increasing violence, whereas within relatively shorter time periods no such rise is apparent. And when one considers, especially, films that carry more lenient, family-friendly ratings, audiences should still expect to encounter physical aggression or violence among those characters most likely to capture viewer interest and involvement, the main characters in the film, and some of those acts will be explicit in nature.

General Audience Television

As children grow up they begin to watch programs created for general audiences more so than (or sometimes in addition to) animated films, cartoons, and content produced specifically for kids, and studies show these programs are a frequent source of exposure to violence, as well. A study done by Nancy Signorielli (2003) showed an average, between spring 1993 and fall 2001, of 4.5 acts of physical violence per program during primetime (8 to 11 p.m.), with six out of ten programs containing at least one violent act. About one third of the violent acts were presented as justified, meaning the character using violence had some ostensibly good reason to do so, like revenge, self-defense, or rescuing someone. This type of portrayal can send the message that violence is acceptable if you are provoked and therefore is seen as a negative way to depict violence. Almost two thirds of the violent acts were depicted without accompanying consequences, glossing over pain, harm, regret, or other penalties that might prevent an individual from using violence in real life. Signorielli's comparison of the latest data with those collected over the last thirty-odd years showed only small and sporadic peaks and valleys in an otherwise stable and consistent presence of violence in prime-time television, a finding supported by additional research, as well (Hetsroni, 2007). Although we can claim that changes have occurred over the years in *how* violence is shown on primetime, general audience television—generally becoming more realistic-looking and graphic in nature (Signorielli, 2003)—the data do not permit us to claim rising rates in *how much* violence is shown.

In the NTVS, a content analysis that documented violence in television programming in all but the wee hours of the night/early morning, it was found that 61% of all programs contained at least one violent act (Smith *et al.*, 1998). There was ample evidence that violence was commonly presented in a context that made it appear rather harmless or as an acceptable way to solve problems. For instance, only 16% of programs with violence portrayed long-term negative consequences that might realistically accompany violent actions (like jail time for perpetrators). Almost three quarters of scenes that contained violence depicted no remorse, regret, or "negative sanctions" against violence. About half of all violent interactions showed no pain associated with acts that would cause considerable physical injury in real life. Although in the minority of violent portrayals, 28% of all violent interactions stemmed from circumstances considered justifiable by the characters involved and 39% were perpetrated by appealing, attractive characters. Violence conducted by "good guys" is widely acknowledged to be more problematic than violence conducted by "bad guys," because young people tend to look up to the former.

Video Games

Violence often takes center stage in video games. Stacy Smith, Ken Lachlan, and Ron Tamborini (2003), in their study of the first ten minutes of game play in the twenty most widely sold games of 1999, found that 68% of the games had at least one violent act. Games rated for older audiences (T for teen, M for mature) contained more violence than games with less restrictive ratings, as would be expected. Nevertheless, a full 57% of games rated for children or all audiences contained violence. The majority of games, 61%, depicted little injury or pain in violent interactions, while 41% portrayed violence in a humorous context, which could minimize perceptions of the severity of violence. Kimberly Thompson and Kevin Haninger (2001) studied a sample of E-rated games (E signifies that the game has been rated as appropriate for "everyone") and found that in 60% it was necessary for one character to intentionally harm another character in order to progress. Almost half (44%) of the games that contained violence did not carry a "content descriptor" label warning of its presence.

In a content analysis of five minutes of recorded play, Tilo Hartman and colleagues (Hartman, Krakowiak, & Tsay-Vogel, 2014) found that in 88% of the games in their sample of popular first-person shooters, the main narrative was that an atrocity or violation had been committed by the opponents or "bad guys" that needed to be addressed. In just over two thirds of the recorded segments the researchers studied, consequences were shown to be distorted (through unrealistic or completely absent depictions of pain and suffering, for instance) and in just over half of segments (55%), the "enemy" was dehumanized through the use of such techniques as not showing faces or having "enemies" be rather indistinguishable. On the whole, the study showed that these widely circulating games tended to use a number of storytelling techniques that present violence as morally acceptable. To date, it seems no scholar has tracked whether video game content has gotten more (or less) violent over time, although clearly the games have gotten more and more realistic looking.

Who Are the "Bad Guys?"

As young people spend time with media content that contains violence and aggression, they are also receiving messages about gender, race and ethnicity, and other aspects of identity and the social world. Across many different forms and types of programming, there is a strong tendency in media content to associate violence and physical aggression with masculinity. Analyses find male characters are more frequently involved in physical violence—as both aggressors and recipients of aggression—on primetime television (Hetsroni, 2007), in televised crime dramas (Parrott & Titcomb Parrott, 2015), in films targeted toward teens (Coyne, Callister, & Robinson, 2010), and in video games (Dill & Thill, 2007) compared to female characters. Chief among the characterizations in video game play are muscular, aggressive male characters and sexualized and/or victimized female characters (Anderson, Gentile, & Dill, 2012). In cartoons, female characters have been determined to be more likely to use verbal and social forms of aggression and male characters physical forms (Luther & Legg, 2010). In Disney films, male characters engaged in more malicious humor than female characters, whereas female characters engaged in more guilt induction (Coyne & Whitehead, 2008), suggesting that even social or indirect forms of aggression can be presented in gender-stereotyped patterns.

Although there is some indication of more positive portrayals of Black and Latino characters on television over time, stereotypical associations of people of color with crime and violence remain in entertainment programming (Tukachinsky, Mastro, & Yarchi, 2015) as well as in the news (Dixon & Linz, 2000). According to analysis of video game ads, characters of color are largely absent in games, but when they are present, African-American characters, especially, appear most often as either athletes or as dangerous criminals (Burgess, Dill, Stermer, Burgess, & Brown, 2011). Thus, we see imbalances in power and stereotypes in who is presented as violent or aggressive in the media.

Why Is There Violence in the Media,
and What Explains Its Appeal?

Like all questions about why media producers create the content that they do, one important place to look for answers is the economic structure of the media industries. Although violent television programs are not usually the ones to draw the highest ratings, and violent films are not typically the highest grossing (Hamilton, 1998), they do attract audiences that are sizeable and that have characteristics appealing to advertisers. James Hamilton (1998) has determined that the largest audience for violent television and film is males eighteen to thirty-four, followed by females eighteen to thirty-four and males thirty-five to forty-nine. The younger groups are attractive to advertisers since people of this age begin to establish brand preferences that may carry through their lifetimes. So advertisers could encourage lifelong consumers through ads positioned during programs that people of this age are likely to see. Economic analyses have also determined that violent films and television shows are likely to bring in revenue through exportation to other countries (Gerbner *et al.*, 1994). Unlike comedy, which does not tend to translate well across language and cultural differences, violence is a universal plot device that is easily comprehended by all.

But this is a book about youth and media, so let's talk specifically about why there is violence in children's media. One explanation is that some children are interested in and drawn to television programs that contain violence. Members of media industries may think that because children tend to be rather impulsive and because they have so much physical energy, programs and games with action are the best way to attract them to the screen, and programs and games with action often contain violence. In fact, action is ranked highly by children when asked about characteristics of television programs that they like (Valkenburg & Janssen, 1999). There is additional research that demonstrates that among a sample of elementary-aged children, the presence of action in a television clip but not violence sparked expressions of liking of the clip among boys but not girls (Weaver, Jensen, Martins, Hurley, & Wilson, 2011). So, if media producers could present action without also presenting violence, it's likely that such content would be appealing to at least some kids.

Another explanation pertains to the long history of children's stories (in books, nursery rhymes, or the media) that use violence as a way to teach morals. The fate of the "bad guys" serves as a lesson to children, apparently, to be good, even in the face of continuing challenges from "evil." *Disposition theory* suggests that media audience members make moral judgments while attending to media and feel gratified when good things happen to characters they perceive to be good and when bad things happen to characters they perceive to be bad (Raney & Bryant, 2002). Since violent media tend to use the tropes of good versus evil in storytelling, this might help explain interest of young people in violent content, as well. Somewhat similarly, some children like to experience fear from exposure to media violence, because that experience shows them that they can *control their emotions*, and they enjoy the feeling of *reassurance* when everything works out alright in the plot in the end (Cantor & Nathanson, 1997).

There are also some important differences among young people that may make them more or less likely to enjoy violent media. *Gender differences* have been found in the research, for instance, with boys having been found to be more likely to prefer violent video games (Shibuya, Sakamoto, Ihori, & Yukawa, 2008), violent television and movie content (Weaver, 2011), and fright-inducing media (Hoffner & Levine, 2005). A range of personality variables also come into play. For example, children with higher *aggressive tendencies* are generally found to seek out and enjoy violent media more often than those with lower such tendencies (Cantor & Nathanson, 1997; Hoffner & Levine, 2005; Weaver, 2011). Another personality variable that predicts preference for violent and fright-inducing media is *sensation seeking* (Hoffner & Levine, 2005), defined as enjoyment of the thrill that stems from taking risks and engaging in adrenaline-producing experiences. Those scoring low on measures of *empathy* are also more likely to like violent and frightening media (Hoffner & Levine, 2005). Finally, the presence of labels and ratings warning that media content is appropriate only for older audiences can trigger a *"forbidden fruit" effect* that (ironically!) increases the appeal of that content to the child (Bijvank, Konijn, Bushman, & Roelofsma, 2009), particularly after the age of eleven and especially among boys (Bushman & Cantor, 2003).

What Are the Effects of Media Violence?

Keeping in mind the broad conceptualization of media impact discussed in the introduction to this chapter, research over the last few decades has pointed to three main effects of violent media: learning aggression, desensitization, and fear (or the mean-world syndrome) (Smith *et al.*, 1998). *Learning aggression* encompasses not only exhibiting aggressive or violent physical behavior but also having aggressive thoughts and expressing attitudes toward aggression that consider it "normal," acceptable, favorable, or inevitable. This has been the subject, by far, of the majority of the research on media violence effects, and therefore I'll devote the most attention to aggressive effects in this chapter, as well. *Desensitization* means becoming so used to seeing violence in the media that you no longer have the same reaction to it (for example, being alarmed, upset, concerned, or anxious). Finally, *fear* effects are rather self-explanatory—experiencing fright from exposure to violence or other content in the news, in movies, or in other media forms—whereas *mean-world syndrome* effects occur when heavy television exposure shapes an individual's view of the "real world" so that it seems more dangerous, violent, and scary. Since the mean world syndrome is not studied that much among children and adolescents, I'll limit the discussion in this chapter of that final category of effects to fear.

Learning Aggression

Among the first social science research examinations conducted on whether media violence exposure can lead to aggression in children were those published by Albert Bandura and his colleagues (Bandura, Ross, & Ross, 1963a, 1963b). They performed experiments in a research laboratory that found that aggressive behavior in preschool-aged children—as measured by interactions with a bobo doll (a rubberized inflated figure that pops back up when you whack it) and other toys—was triggered by exposure to a filmed model engaging in aggressive play.

Many laboratory-based and survey research studies have since been conducted and have generally shown increases in aggression among those exposed to violence in the media (Anderson *et al.*, 2010). Yet, the real-world meaning of the studies in this area has been called into question given the validity of some of the ways that aggression has been measured, given the relatively modest size of the statistical association between media use and aggression (especially in comparison to other causal contributors to violent behavior), and given the fact that, for the most part, rates of violent crime have been declining despite the steady presence of violence in the media (Ferguson, 2013). In this review, there's not enough space to get into the nuances of all of these existing studies. Rather, I'll focus on a subset of existing studies that feature children or adolescents as research participants and I'll rely on meta-analyses, which are articles that take a whole bunch of studies on the same topic and aggregate them to form a numerical conclusion about the relationships between the main variables.

Television and Film. Laura A. Daly and Linda M. Perez (2009) studied the daily exposure of a sample of three- to five-year-olds to television programs and films containing violence and then observed the children during free play at preschool. Children with higher rates of violence viewing among the shows listed as favorites by parents and caregivers (a list that included a number of Disney movies in addition to content featuring superheroes like Batman and Superman) exhibited higher levels of both verbal and physical forms of aggression in play compared to those children with lower levels of such media exposure.

Marina Krcmar and Stephen Curtis (2003) assigned 121 five- to fourteen-year-olds to one of three experimental conditions: viewing a fantasy violence television program with a physically violent ending to a conflict, viewing the same program that featured a peaceful conflict resolution, or not viewing anything at all. The young people who saw the violent ending judged scenarios of justified violence presented to them in subsequent stories as more morally acceptable and used less advanced moral reasoning strategies when explaining their answers compared to those in the other groups. The implication is that viewing media violence can shape young people's sense of whether violence is right and wrong under particular circumstances.

Coyne, Archer, and Eslea (2004) analyzed the impact of exposure to a filmed story featuring direct aggression (depicting yelling, purposely bumping into, and slapping of one character by another), indirect aggression (depicting purposely damaging a romantic relationship, spreading rumors, and posting embarrassing photos of one character by another) compared to non-viewing control group participation among British adolescents (aged eleven to fourteen). They found that, compared to the control group, those teens who viewed either aggressive video evaluated a person who had insulted them in the context of the experiment regarding their performance on a seemingly unrelated task more harshly, an indication that levels of hostility were provoked. When presented with story vignettes asking what they would do in particular scenarios that might trigger aggression, those who viewed the indirect aggression in the clips chose indirectly aggressive responses and those who saw the direct aggression chose directly aggressive responses compared to those in the other two groups.

In each of these three examples, then, we see short-term effects of media exposure on aggressive thoughts and intentions (as in the Coyne and colleagues study), attitudes toward aggression (as in the Krcmar and Curtis study), and aggressive behavior (as in the Daley and Perez study). If we compare these results to the conclusions drawn from a meta-analysis conducted by Haejung Paik and George Comstock (1994), we see that these three studies match the overall pattern found across dozens of prior studies with children and teens, as well. When studies with all participants regardless of age are aggregated in the meta-analysis, the general pattern is that the size of the television or film violence exposure influence gets smaller—but still significant—when the outcome measure of aggression is seriously violent or criminal in nature. So, televised violence appears to have a stronger effect on more minor expressions of aggression than it does on extremely antisocial violent behavior.

Video Games. A growing number of studies have been conducted to determine whether playing violent video games can impact the aggression of young people. Many studies have, indeed, found such associations among adolescents in such locations as the U.S., Japan, Belgium, and Germany (e.g., Anderson *et al.*, 2008; Exelmans, Custers, & van den Bulck, 2015; Krahé, Bushing, & Möller, 2012), using measures of aggression that include (but are not limited to) self-reports of aggressive responses to story vignettes, teacher or peer ratings of aggression, and even self-reports of serious behaviors meeting the definition of "delinquency." Yet, in other studies when the outcome variable is limited to forms of behavior that would be characterized as "serious violent behavior" or as "delinquent" (e.g., stealing, damaging property, assaulting someone), no connection with violent video game exposure has been shown among youth (Ferguson & Olson, 2014; Ybarra *et al.*, 2008). We can tentatively conclude, then, just as we had with television and film, that the size of the video game influence is generally reduced when the aggressive behavior in question is extremely serious or illegal in nature.

There is also some indication that the ways that violence is portrayed contextually in games—whether it is rewarded, justified, accompanied by humor, graphic, etc.—might be more important for potential effects on young people's aggression than how much time they spend playing games with violence (Shibuya *et al.*, 2008). Just as we saw was the case in a study of television violence, there is indication that one potential effect of exposure to video game violence is that it can shape *moral reasoning* in young people (Vieira & Krcmar, 2011). Recent research with German adolescents also showed long-term implications of violent video game use for a concept known as *interpersonal trust* (Rothmund, Gollwitzer, Bender, & Klimmt, 2015). In that study, amount of exposure to games containing violence was a negative predictor of responses to items such as "Most people are basically good and kind," or "Most people are trustworthy" 12 months later.

A recent meta-analysis covering 136 prior studies on video game violence exposure and aggression with research participants young and old finds a relatively small but significant relationship between video game violence exposure and aggressive thoughts, attitudes, and behavior (Anderson *et al.*, 2010). Youth are not analyzed separately, but the authors note that every one of the longitudinal studies (those studies in which prior video game use is tested for whether it predicts later aggression) included in the meta-analysis used participants no older than age sixteen. Among just that subset of studies (of which there were fourteen), the data once again show a small but significant link between violent video game use and later levels of aggression.

Desensitization

Desensitization has been measured in many different ways, including through physiological evidence of becoming used to violence (for example, initially the subject's heart rate quickens when shown media violence but with repeated exposure it slows again; or different regions of the brain are activated among those with heavy or light media violence exposure), lack of empathy for victims of violence, becoming progressively more reluctant to label horror films or other media as "violent" or "disturbing," and willingness or speed with which an individual responds to an aggressive situation. Each of these measures of desensitization indicates a tendency to perceive violence as no big deal, which is a good way to define this effect.

In classic research with youth participants, even a single exposure to media violence has been shown to lead to an immediate drop in concern or sympathy about aggressive acts perpetrated by others (Drabman & Thomas, 1974a, 1974b). More recently, violent video game use has been linked to low scores on empathy among fourth and fifth graders (Funk, Baldacci, Pasold, & Baumgardner, 2004) and violent television exposure was seen to lead to a delay among child research participants in seeking help when a physical fight was believed to have occurred (Molitor & Hirsch, 1994). Parents, too, appear to be susceptible to the desensitization phenomenon. Daniel Romer and colleagues (2014) found that upon showing a series of movie clips containing sexual and violent content, parents got progressively more permissive in terms of what they said they'd let their child watch and what age they thought was appropriate for viewing the content.

Fear

Children may also experience fear responses from violent media exposure. In a survey of a randomly drawn sample of parents from across the U.S., Douglas Gentile and David Walsh (1999) found that 62% of parents reported that their child had expressed fear that something witnessed in a television program or movie might happen to them. In another study, 75% of preschoolers and elementary-school-aged children said they had become frightened by something seen on TV or in the movies (Wilson, Hoffner, & Cantor, 1987). More recently, 75% of a sample of five- and six-year-olds in Finland indicated that they had become fearful from something encountered on television (Korhonen & Lahikainen, 2008).

Fear is not necessarily a fleeting response, and its effects can be debilitating. In fact, the memory of a fear response to media can endure for quite some time. In studies, nearly all college-aged and older adults were able to remember in vivid detail being frightened as a child by something in the media (Hoekstra, Harris, & Helmick, 1999), with common consequences including sleep disturbances (reluctance to sleep alone, needing a nightlight or lights on, not being able to sleep, having nightmares), eating disturbances (such as loss of appetite), as well as generalized feelings of anxiety. A recent meta analysis of 31 studies examined links between exposure to scary television and film and worry, anxiety, depression, fear, and sadness (collectively known as "internalizing emotions") among research participants under the age of eighteen (Pearce & Field, 2016). Across the studies, the researchers found a "modest" but significant statistical relationship between scary television and film (fictional or non) and such outcomes, and the relationship was stronger for children under the age of ten compared to older children and adolescents. The good news is that research has also shown that parents and caregivers explaining things to kids and reassuring them can reduce the impact on fear, worry, and anxiety, especially among younger children (Buijzen, Van Der Molen, & Sondij, 2007).

So, Should We Be Concerned about Media Violence?

The research evidence brings us unambiguously to an answer to the question posed in the title of this chapter. Yes, media violence is a cause for concern. Although there are some studies that show findings to the contrary and although the size of the media effect can be relatively small compared to other influences, the bulk of the evidence does, indeed, point to a concerning link between violent television, film, and video game exposure and the learning and expression of aggression, as well as to experiencing desensitization or fear. We have seen that physical, verbal, and social/relational aggression have long been pervasive themes in media content of various types and forms. Children's media stands out as being particularly full of physically aggressive acts, with a rate of such acts per hour that is about four times as large as that found in prime-time television. Violence can be depicted in a way that, according to research, makes negative effects more likely, such as being accompanied by rewards or lack of punishment, occurring with few consequences, being perpetrated by likeable characters that have a justifiable reason for being violent, and being shown in a humorous context that can trivialize violence.

We have also seen that media industries enjoy economic gains that accrue from the characteristics of audience members for violent programming that attract advertisers and through exportation of content that contains violence. Yet, in response to scrutiny from politicians, interest groups, and others, media industries are sometimes pressured to put into place regulations, such as the inclusion of ratings for violence and other potentially objectionable forms of content (V for violence, S for sex, etc.) that now appear at the start of a television program. In addition to using labels and ratings to make informed decisions, two other ways to counter media violence also show promise, media literacy in schools and parental mediation. The former involves showing young people how to use media (for example, by encouraging them to create their own video projects) as well as how to critically analyze media content, effects, and production and distribution processes. (See Chapter 5 for more information on media literacy.) The latter encompasses the ways in which parents and caregivers set and explain rules for media use, discuss media depictions and potential effects while co-viewing (or watching video game play) with children, and generally encourage critical thinking about media. Recent media violence research has attested to the effectiveness of media literacy and parental mediation in creating knowledge and awareness about media violence and, in some cases, reducing the likelihood of experiencing one or more of the three effects.

Discussion Questions

1. How well do you think the labels for television programs work to alert viewers to violence, sex, and other forms of content that might cause concern? How about the ratings and labels for video games?

2. Do you think media content will get less violent in the future? Why or why not?

3. Is it the government's responsibility to regulate media violence?

4. Besides violent media exposure, what are other causes of aggression and violence? Which causes do you think are more or less impactful?

5. Do you think that other media that may contain violence, like the Internet and popular music, influence aggression, desensitization, or fear? Why or why not?

Exercises

1. Compare and contrast the experience of playing video games that are violent and watching television programs that are violent. On a sheet of paper, create two columns, one labeled "similarities" and one labeled "differences." Think carefully about how and why individuals use the two media forms. When you have finished filling in the two columns, discuss the implications of the two experiences (playing violent games and watching violent programs) for the possibility of each of the three effects (learning aggression, desensitization,

and fear).

2. Perform your own content analysis of the depiction of violence in your choice of media. First, decide on a type of content, such as television, news websites, movie trailers, or promotional materials for video games. Gather a small set of that content for your analysis. (If you were doing a full-fledged study, you'd want a large sample, but since this is just an exercise, a smaller sample will do.) Now, you need to come up with your coding scheme. What will you look for? How will you know it when you see it? If you are counting violent acts, come up with a clear definition of a violent act so that you can recognize them consistently. In addition to documenting how much violence there is, think about assessing how violence is presented. Is it rewarded? Done by likeable characters? Justified? For each of these characteristics of violent portrayals, you'll need careful and precise definitions in order to catalogue their presence in your sample.

3. Do you like media violence? If so, why do you find it appealing? If not, why not? Write a one-paragraph essay describing your own attraction (or lack thereof) to violent television programs, movies, and games, as well as your careful and considered assessment of the reasons for that attraction.

References

Anderson, C. A., Gentile, D. A., & Dill, K. E. (2012). Prosocial, antisocial, and other effects of recreational video games. In D. G. Singer & J. L. Singer (Eds.), *Handbook of children and the media* (2nd ed., pp. 249–272). Thousand Oaks, CA: Sage.

Anderson, C. A., Sakamoto, A., Gentile, D., Ihori, N., Shibuya, A., Yukawa, S., … Kobayashi K. (2008). Longitudinal effects of violent video games on aggression in Japan and the United States. *Pediatrics, 122*(5), e1067–e1072. doi:10.1542/peds.2008-1425

Anderson, C. A., Shibuya, A., Ihori, N., Swing, E. L., Bushman, B. J., Sakamoto, A., … Saleem, M. (2010). Violent video game effects on aggression, empathy, and prosocial behavior in Eastern and Western countries: A meta-analytic review. *Psychological Bulletin, 136*(2), 151–173. doi:10.1037/a0018251

Bandura, A., Ross, D., & Ross, S. A. (1963a). Imitation of film-mediated aggressive models. *Journal of Abnormal and Social Psychology, 66*(1), 3–11.

Bandura, A., Ross, D., & Ross, S. A. (1963b). Vicarious reinforcement and imitative learning. *Journal of Abnormal and Social Psychology, 67*, 601–607.

Bijvank, M., Konijn, E., Bushman, B. J., & Roelofsma, P. (2009). Age and violent-content labels make video games forbidden fruits for youth. *Pediatrics, 123*(3), 870–876. doi:10.1542/peds.2008–0601

Bleakley, A., Jamieson, P. E., & Romer, D. (2012). Trends in sexual and violent content by gender in top-grossing U.S. films, 1950–2006. *Journal of Adolescent Health, 51*(1), 73–79. doi:10.1016/j.jadohealth.2012.02.006

Bleakley, A., Romer, D., & Jamieson, P. E. (2014). Violent film characters' portrayal of alcohol, sex, and tobacco-related behaviors. *Pediatrics, 133*(1), 171–177. doi:10.1542/peds.2013–1922

Buijzen, M., Van Der Molen, J. H., & Sondij, P. (2007). Parental mediation of children's responses to a violent news event. *Communication Research, 34*(2), 212–230. doi:10.1177/0093650206298070

Burgess, M. E., Dill, K. E., Stermer, S. P., Burgess, S. R., & Brown, B. P. (2011). Playing with prejudice: The prevalence and consequences of racial stereotypes in video games. *Media Psychology, 14*(3), 289–311. doi:10.1080/15213269.2011.596467

Bushman, B. J., & Cantor, J. (2003). Media ratings for violence and sex: Implications for policymakers and parents. *American Psychologist, 58*(2), 130–141. doi:10.1037/0003–066X.58.2.130

Bushman, B. J., Jamieson, P. E., Weitz, I., & Romer, D. (2013). Gun violence trends in movies. *Pediatrics, 132*(6), 1014–1018. doi:10.1542/peds.2013–1600

Cantor, J., & Nathanson, A. I. (1997). Predictors of children's interest in violent television programs. *Journal of Broadcasting & Electronic Media, 41*(2), 155–168.

Coyne, S. M., Archer, J., & Eslea, M. (2004). Cruel intentions on television and in real life: Can viewing indirect aggression increase viewers' subsequent indirect aggression? *Journal of Experimental Child Psychology, 88*(3), 234–253. doi:10.1016/j.jecp.2004.03.001

Coyne, S. M., Callister, M., & Robinson, T. (2010). Yes, another teen movie. *Journal of Children and Media, 4*(4), 387–401. doi:10.1080/17482798.2010.510006

Coyne, S. M., & Whitehead, E. (2008). Indirect aggression in animated Disney films. *Journal of Communication, 58*(2), 382–395. doi:10.1111/j.1460–2466.2008.00390.x

Daly, L. A., & Perez, L. M. (2009). Exposure to media violence and other correlates of aggressive behavior in preschool children. *Early Childhood Research and Practice, 11*(2). Retrieved from http://www.comminit.com/early-child/content/exposure-media-violence-and-other-correlates-aggressive-behavior-preschool-children

Dill, K. E., & Thill, K. P. (2007). Video game characters and the socialization of gender roles: Young people's perceptions mirror sexist media depictions. *Sex Roles, 57*(11/12), 851–864. doi:10.1007/s11199-007-9278-1

Dixon, T., & Linz, D. (2000). Overrepresentation and underrepresentation of Blacks and Latinos as lawbreakers on television news. *Journal of Communication, 50*(2), 131–154. doi:10.1111/j.1460–2466.2000.tb02845.x

Drabman, R. S., & Thomas, M. H. (1974a). Does media violence increase children's toleration of real-life aggression? *Developmental Psychology, 10*(3), 418–421.

Drabman, R. S., & Thomas, M. H. (1974b). Exposure to filmed violence and children's toleration of real-life aggression. *Personality and Social Psychology Bulletin, 1*, 198–199.

Exelmans, L., Custers, K., & van den Bulck, J. (2015). Violent video games and risk factors in adolescents: A risk factors perspective. *Aggressive Behavior, 41*(3), 267–279. doi:10.1002/ab.21587

Ferguson, C. J. (2013). Violent video games and the Supreme Court: Lessons for the scientific community in the wake of Brown vs. Entertainment Merchants Association. *American Psychologist, 68*(2), 57–74. doi:10.1037/a0030597

Ferguson, C. J., & Olson, C. K. (2014). Video game violence use among "vulnerable populations:" The impact of violent video games on delinquency and bullying among children with clinically elevated depression or attention deficit symptoms. *Journal of Youth and Adolescence, 43*(1), 127–136. doi:10.1007/s10964-013–9986-5

Funk, J. B., Baldacci, H. B., Pasold, T., & Baumgardner, J. (2004). Violence exposure in real-life, video games, television, movies, and the Internet. Is there desensitization? *Journal of Adolescence, 27*(1), 23–39. doi:10.1016/j.adolescence.2003.10.005

Gentile, D. A., & Walsh, D. A. (1999). *MediaQuotient™: National survey of family media habits, knowledge, and attitudes.* Minneapolis, MN: National Institute on Media and the Family.

Gerbner, G., Gross, L., Morgan, M., & Signorielli, N. (1994). Growing up with television: The cultivation perspective. In J. Bryant & D. Zillmann (Eds.), *Media effects: Advances in theory and research* (pp. 17–41). Hillsdale, NJ: Erlbaum.

Hamilton, J. T. (1998). *Channeling violence.* Princeton, NJ: Princeton University Press.

Hartman, T., Krakowiak, K. M., & Tsay-Vogel, M. (2014). How violent video games communicate violence: A literature review and content analysis of moral disengagement factors. *Communication Monographs, 81*(3), 310–332. doi:10.1080/03637751.2014.922206

Hetsroni, A. (2007). Four decades of violent content on network prime-time television: A longitudinal meta-analytic review. *Journal of Communication, 57*(4), 759–784. doi:10.1111/j.1460–2466.2007.00367.x

Hoekstra, S. J., Harris, R. J., & Helmick, A. L. (1999). Autobiographical memories about the experience of seeing frightening movies in childhood. *Media Psychology, 1*, 117–140.

Hoffner, C. A., & Levine, K. J. (2005). Enjoyment of mediated fright and violence: A meta-analysis. *Media Psychology, 7*(2), 207–237. doi:10.1207/S1532785XMEP0702_5

Korhonen, P., & Lahikainen, A. R. (2008). Recent trends in young children's television-induced fears in Finland. *Journal of Children and Media, 2*(2), 147–162. doi:10.1080/17482790802078664

Krahé, B., Busching, R., & Möller, I. (2012). Media violence use and aggression among German adolescents: Associations and trajectories of change in a three-wave longitudinal study. *Psychology of Popular Media Culture, 1*(3), 152–166. doi:10.1037/a0028663

Krcmar, M., & Curtis, S. (2003). Mental models: Understanding the impact of fantasy violence on children. *Journal of Communication, 53*(3), 460–478. doi:10.1111/j.1460–2466.2003.tb02602.x

Luther, C. A., & Legg, J. R. (2010). Gender differences in depictions of social and physical aggression in children's television commercials in the U.S. *Journal of Children and Media, 4*(2), 191–205. doi:10.1080/17482791003629651

Martins, M., & Wilson, B. J. (2012). Mean on the screen: Social aggression on programs popular with children. *Journal of Communication, 62*(6), 991–1009. doi:10.1111/j.14602466.2011.01599.x

Molitor, F., & Hirsch, K. W. (1994). Children's toleration of real-life aggression after exposure to media violence: A replication of the Drabman and Thomas studies. *Child Study Journal, 24*(3), 191–208.

Paik, H., & Comstock, G. (1994). The effects of television violence on antisocial behavior: A meta analysis. *Communication Research, 21*(4), 516–547.

Parrott, S., & Titcomb Parrott, C. (2015). U.S. television's "mean world" for White women: The portrayal of gender and race on fictional crime dramas. *Sex Roles, 73*(1/2), 70–82. doi:10.1007/s11199-015–0505-x

Pearce, L. P., & Field, A. J. (2016). The impact of "scary" TV and film on children's internalizing emotions: A meta analysis. *Human Communication Research, 42*(1), 98–121. doi:10.1111/hcre.12069

Raney, A. A., & Bryant, J. (2002). Moral judgment and crime drama: An integrated theory of enjoyment. *Journal of Communication, 52*(2), 402–415. doi:10.1111/j.1460–2466.2002.tb02552.x

Romer, D., Jamieson, P. E., Bushman, B. J., Bleakley, A., Wang, A., Langleben, D., & Jamieson, K. H. (2014). Parental desensitization to violence and sex in movies. *Pediatrics, 134*(5), 877–884. doi:10.1542/peds.2014–1167

Rothmund, T., Gollwitzer, M., Bender, J., & Klimmt, C. (2015). Short- and long-term effects of video game violence on interpersonal trust. *Media Psychology, 18*(1), 106–133. doi:10.1080/15213269.2013.841526

Shibuya, A., Sakamoto, A., Ihori, N., & Yukawa, S. (2008). The effects of the presence and contexts of video game violence on children: A longitudinal study in Japan. *Simulation & Gaming, 39*(4), 528–539. doi:10.1177/1046878107306670

Signorielli, N. (2003). Prime-time violence, 1993–2001: Has the picture really changed? *Journal of Broadcasting & Electronic Media, 47*(1), 36–58.

Signorielli, N. (2008, November). *Children's programs in 2007: Basic demography and violence.* Paper presented at the annual meeting of the National Communication Association, San Diego, CA.

Smith, S. L., Lachlan, K., & Tamborini, R. (2003). Popular video games: Quantifying the presentation of violence and its context. *Journal of Broadcasting & Electronic Media, 47*(1), 58–76.

Smith, S. L., Wilson, B. J., Kunkel, D., Linz, D., Potter, W. J., Colvin, C. M., & Donnerstein, E. (1998). *National television violence study* (Vol. 3). Santa Barbara, CA: Center for Communication and Social Policy, University of California.

Thompson, K. M., & Haninger, K. (2001). Violence in E-rated video games. *JAMA, 286*(5), 591–598, 920.

Tukachinsky, R., Mastro, D., & Yarchi, M. (2015). Documenting portrayals on primetime television over a 20-year span and their association with national level racial and ethnic attitudes. *Journal of Social Issues, 71*(1), 17–38. doi:10.1111/josi.12094

Valkenburg, P. M., & Janssen, S. (1999). What do children value in entertainment programs? A cross-cultural investigation. *Journal of Communication, 49*(2), 3–21.

Vieira, E. T., & Krcmar, M. (2011). The influences of video gaming on U.S. children's moral reasoning about violence. *Journal of Children and Media, 5*(2), 113–131. doi:10.1080/17482798.2011.558258

Weaver, A. J. (2011). A meta-analytical review of selective exposure to and enjoyment of media violence. *Journal of Broadcasting & Electronic Media, 55*(2), 232–250. doi:10.1080/08838151.2011.570826

Weaver, A. J., Jensen, J. D., Martins, M., Hurley, R. J., & Wilson, B. J. (2011). Liking violence and action: An examination of gender differences in children's processing of animated content. *Media Psychology, 14*(1), 49–70. doi:10.1080/15213269.2010.547829

Wilson, B. J., Hoffner, C., & Cantor, J. (1987). Children's perceptions of the effectiveness of techniques to reduce fear from mass media. *Journal of Applied Developmental Psychology, 8*(1), 39–52.

Ybarra, M., Diener-West, M., Markow, D., Leaf, P., Hamburger, M., & Boxer, P. (2008). Linkages between internet and other media violence with seriously violent behavior by youth. *Pediatrics, 122*(5), 929–937. doi:10.1542/peds.2007–3377

Yokota, F., & Thompson, K. M. (2000). Violence in G-rated animated films. *JAMA, 283*(20), 2716–2720.

CHAPTER 9

Is Media Use Really Risky for Young People?

Sahara Byrne

Research is so funny. As you will probably gather by the time you finish this book, the answer any respectable social scientist will give to a yes or no question like this one is probably something like "*…uhhhmm, maybe, I guess…probably…sometimes?*" Think about your own life. You know, based on your own experience, that a lot of good things come out of your time spent with media! And many of you would not like to admit that anything ever goes wrong. Some of you, however, have had terrible experiences.

The research tells us there is truth to both sides, and everything in between. In this chapter, we will go over some of the behaviors having to do with media that would be deemed by many as risky or harmful for youth, and will take a deeper look at a recent study or two for each providing evidence that the effects can happen. Much of the most recent research looks at the Internet and social media, but more traditional media like music, TV, and movies are still a major part of the youth media diet. All of the behaviors below have a recently active line of research with evidence that the media do have a role to play in risky behavior. Be careful though! This evidence should be taken with a scientific grain of salt, because as you will see both from other chapters and your own deeper inquiries, there are many sides to the story and, without question, positive behaviors can also result from media use. It can be so confusing! This chapter is designed to introduce you to some of the most recently investigated risky elements of young people's use of the media and set you off on a path of exploring these topics more in-depth.

Identity Development

Can Media Use Negatively Affect Youth's General State of Simply Being?

While "being" might not be the most effortful behavior, the answer is, yes! A lot of work goes into figuring out who you are when you are young. Think of how many times you've talked to a friend about the TV shows you have binged, used music preferences to test if someone you just met is similar to you, or agreed on how you think Facebook is for mainly for parents nowadays. It turns out that developing one's identity and self-concept through media use can sometimes be an unhealthy experience. For example, Wu, Kirk, Ohinmaa, and Veugelers (2016) surveyed almost 5,000 Canadian youth, discovering that time spent watching TV or playing video games was associated self-esteem problems. Youth in their sample who watched TV for more than 5 hours per day were almost 70% more likely to feel unhappy or worried in their lives! Similarly, Lee and Chae (2007) surveyed 314 middle and high school students about what their phones and social media accounts mean to them, and 25% reported that they feel like they are "nothing" without their cell phone. Another researcher argued that as African American youth are exposed to negative TV portrayals of Black characters, and with a lack of positive portrayals, they may develop lower self-worth and an unhealthy racial identity (Martin, 2008).

Why Are Youth so Mean to Each Other Online?

One reason is that they are mean to each other offline too (Lazuras, Barkoukis, & Tsorbatzoudis, 2017). However, one of the key recent findings is that youth often participate in online harassment in the role of both a victim and a perpetrator (Festl, Vogelgesang, Scharkow, & Quandt, 2017). Part of the issue is that youth are able to reach one another unwatched and uncensored. A parent-child "matched pair" study found that private access to the Internet is associated with a rise in being bullied online without parents ever knowing about it (Byrne, Katz, Lee, Linz, & McIlrath, 2014). One of the saddest and most dangerous factors surrounding online harassment is that it is a risk factor for suicide, which is the top cause of death for teenagers (Messias, Kindrick, & Castro, 2014).

Can Young People Be Recruited for Criminal Activity Through Media?

Entities that rely on youth members to survive are using the Internet and social media as new-found successful recruitment channels, possibly because of the overlap between the desired age of new recruits and a typically savvy level of technical knowledge. Pyrooz, Decker, and Moule (2015) investigated this possibility while interviewing 585 youth and young adults at five city sites where street gang involvement was known to be high. They found that while gang members are using the Internet more than youth who are not in gangs, they use it for many of the same social activities as non-gang affiliated youth. While there is little evidence of highly organized online criminal efforts, they do use the Internet in a "low-tech" manner to sell drugs, coordinate assaults, and upload deviant videos. Younger gang members were more likely to identify the Internet as a useful recruitment tool compared to older members, suggesting a generational shift in media use for recruitment (Pyrooz et al., 2015).

But street gangs are not the only group using the Internet to find members. In fact, one could easily see how socially undesirable or even dangerous groups who rely on youth membership would turn to the Internet for recruitment. Lisa Blaker's (2015) article in Military Cyber

Affairs casts a stark warning about the processes by which terrorist organizations recruit young people all over the world. In February of 2015, three London schoolgirls ran away from home for Syria to join ISIS. Their families believe they were radicalized at a very early age and early access to smartphone technology contributed to their transformation. The Internet has allowed ISIS to connect to the thousands of youth from western nations who have joined ISIS, and potentially many more may be radicalized and remain within their home country. The ISIS propaganda effort produces high quality videos designed to specifically target westernized youth (Blaker, 2015). Jon Greenberg (2015) estimated that as many as 200,000 pro-ISIS tweets are posted per day. Haque, Choi, Phillips, and Bursztajn (2015) argue that ISIS is keenly able to articulate a match between the public offerings of joining their group with some of the more basic and well known developmental issues happening to teens at a time typically awash with identity crises.

Sharing and Seeking Information

Are Young People Exposed to Unsavory Content Online?

You bet they are. As soon as youth have gained unmonitored access to the media, some will use that newfound freedom to search for content such as sexually explicit images (Flood, 2009; Vandenbosch & Peter, 2016). Unfortunately, exposure to some types of sexual content may change how young people think about sex and gender norms (Walker, Temple-Smith, Higgs, & Sanci, 2015) and sexual behaviors (Hald, Kuyper, Adam, & de Wit, 2013).

Similarly, youth can accidently come across content they are not quite ready to see. Mistyping search terms or landing on the wrong channel at the wrong moment can have a strong emotional impact on young people (Flood, 2009). One study found that 23% of youth reported an unwanted exposure to Internet pornography (Jones, Mitchell, & Finkelhor, 2012). Pop-up ads containing click bait with links to pornography can appear to anyone, at any age (Walker *et al.*, 2015). Early exposure to sexually explicit material, purposefully or accidentally, can lower sexual satisfaction in later real-life intimate experiences (Flood, 2009; Stulhofer, Busko, & Landripet, 2010). But sex isn't the only thing kids can see with troubling effects. Exposure to scary images and violence also has consequences, as discussed below.

Is Sharing Personal Information through Media Common for Young People?

One of the sleeping giants of risky behaviors is when youth give up seemingly mundane personal information online. In the USA, online entities are not supposed to collect identifying information from kids under 13 due to the Children's Online Privacy Protection Act (COPPA), which is why many member-based social media sites do not allow youth to create profiles until that age. (See Chapter 2 for more information on COPPA.) Millions of youth, however, find a way around it, primarily by lying about their age (boyd, Hargittai, Schultz, & Palfrey, 2011). It turns out that parents are contributing to the problem, both by letting their children lie and by sharing deeply personal information and imagery about their own children's lives on social media (Ammari, Kumar, Lampe, & Schoenebeck, 2015). Researchers have found that problems can occur as a result from all of this posting and sharing on social media, especially heightened anxiety (Lee, 2014).

Do Young People Lack the Skills Required to Make Good Decisions about What to Publically Post?

Yes, and so do many adults! By sharing a certain version of oneself online, it solidifies the idea that a particular trait is part of one's identity (Gonzales & Hancock, 2008). Bryce and Fraser (2014) worked with youth age 9–19 in 18 different focus group to address the question of how youth decide what to post in online public interactions. It turned out that kids were pretty nuanced in their selection of what to post, avoiding information such as their home address, but offering photos and hobbies. Young people use media as a way to "try on" character traits and see how others will react (Craig & McInroy, 2014) and unfortunately these moments can sometimes lead to harassment (Jones, Mitchell, & Finkelhor, 2012). Additionally, the teenage years are a time of sexual development and exploration, and much of this exploration can happen online (Baumgartner, Valkenburg, & Peter, 2010), for example, in the form of sexting, "the transfer of nude or semi-nude pictures or videos between mobile devices" (Draper, 2012, p. 221). While many argue that sexting is within the bounds of productive behavior (Bond, 2011) and is unfairly gendered in who gets to do it and who doesn't (Albury, 2015), others have studied its negative effects. Ouytsel, Gool, Walrave, Ponnet, and Peeters (2016) conducted 11 focus groups in Belgium to explore exactly this issue. It turns out that girls send sexually explicit pictures of themselves mainly out of fear that they will lose their boyfriends. The youth in their study provided evidence for three consequences associated with sexting; the pictures can be used to blackmail, passed around to get back at each other during a breakup, or could be shared to friends who are gloating about receiving the picture (Ouytsel *et al.*, 2016). Recently, attention has been given to the legal controversy surrounding the criminal act of distributing what some consider child pornography and questions of consent (McGovern, Crofts, Lee, & Milivojevic, 2016). Sometimes, pictures are distributed consensually (as when a boyfriend willingly sends a pic of himself to a girlfriend) and other times, without consent (as when that girl later distributes the picture to the entire school for revenge when he breaks up with her). The unique situational variability, combined with nuances around age and sexual development, further complicate an already complex issue (Crofts & Lee, 2013). To deepen the gravity of the problem, many teens do not understand that they may be legally held accountable for distributing sexually explicit content, including being placed on Registered Sex Offender lists for the duration of their lives (Strohmaier, Murphy, & DeMatteo, 2014).

Are Online Predators Really a Thing?

Every parent's nightmare is that their child goes missing after a stranger solicitation by an online predator and, sadly, some children have fallen victim to this horrible circumstance. Three researchers from the Crimes Against Children Research Center in the U.S. conducted three separate phone surveys of 1,500 youth in 2000, 2005, and 2010, and found that across the ten year period, unwanted sexual solicitations actually declined steadily among youth by 50% (Jones *et al.*, 2012). However, youth who struggle in their lives due to previous maltreatment are at a greater risk for engaging with such solicitations (Noll, Shenk, Barnes, & Haralson, 2013). Though the issue may be portrayed as more frequent in the media than it actually is in real life (Brown, 2013), online predators do exist, and they possess a sophisticated grooming process by which they gain access their victims (Barber & Bettez, 2014; Winters, Kaylor, & Jeglic, 2017).

Developing Risky Financial Habits

Does Media Marketing Train Kids to Buy Things
They Don't Need and Spend Money They Don't Have?

Researchers in New Zealand conducted survey interviews and selection tasks with 73 parent-child dyads, discovering that pre-schoolers who see more advertising on TV tend to have higher recognition of common brands (Watkins, Aitken, Robertson, Thyne, & Williams, 2016). The researchers asked the children to select what makes them happiest from a wide array of pictorial cards depicting images of toys, clothes, money, sports, the beach, birthday parties, people, and pets. Pre-schoolers with higher brand recognition skills signaled preliminary evidence of also having a preference for material objects over alternatives such as relationships and activities. Ho, Shin, and Lwin (2017) found evidence for a fascinating idea—that high "consumption-oriented" social media use, such as interacting with friends and marketers about products, leads to more materialistic values. The research team argued that this effect occurs because these youth overestimate their own peers' level of spending. (See Chapters 14 and 15 for more information on the relationship between young people and consumer messages.)

Do Kids Really Use Media to Gamble?

It's certainly a growing concern. Televised sporting events often carry ads for online gaming opportunities, which increase youth intentions to partake in further gambling activities (Hing, Vitartas, Lamont, & Fink, 2014). In the past several decades, youth have seen enormous growth in the opportunity to access free gambling simulation games online, which may also lead to problematic gambling behaviors in adulthood when the money becomes real (King & Delfabbro, 2016). Participation in simulated gambling exposes youth to potentially addictive reward-based systems as well as promotions and incentives for gambling with real money (King, Delfabbro, Kaptsis, & Zwaans, 2014). To get a bigger picture of the problem, researchers in Canada surveyed 2,336 adolescents in Ontario. More than half reported partaking in gambling behaviors, with about 10% being at-risk or problematic gamblers. At that time, only about 3% reported gambling online, with the more popular activities being lottery, cards, and sports (Hardoon, Derevensky, & Gupta, 2002). About a decade later, in a survey of over 10,000 Canadian youth across three provinces, that figure grew to 41%, with almost 10% having gambled in the past three months and half of those activities were related to sports (Elton-Marshall, Leatherdale, & Turner, 2016). That percentage is consistent with a similar study in Greece (Tsitsika, Critselis, Janikian, Kormas, & Kafetzis, 2011). Considering this evidence, sports and Internet gambling are a growing global concern, as young people who gamble are at risk of becoming adults who risk their livelihoods for the thrill of a bet (King & Delfabbro, 2016).

Personal Health and Well-Being

Is There a Relationship Between Childhood Obesity and Media Use?

Media can be a double-edged sword when it comes to nutrition. While some recent work has focused on risks associated with using media to promote disordered eating behaviors (e.g., anorexia) and lack of nutrients (Perloff, 2014), others have focused on overeating and obesity (Kenney & Gortmaker, 2016). Jordan and Robinson (2008) point out four mechanisms that have been hypothesized as the way through which television viewing may lead children to be overweight: 1) lower resting energy expenditure, 2) displacement of physical activity, 3) food advertising leading to greater energy intake, and 4) eating while viewing leading to greater energy intake. Large scale survey studies have demonstrated a link between looking at screens and body mass and/or sedentary activity (Kenney & Gortmaker, 2016; Koezuka *et al.*, 2006). One study of school age kids in the United Kingdom showed that kid who watch a lot of TV tend to live in households where energy-dense (junk) food is available as snacks, which in turn is associated with increased consumption of these foods (Pearson *et al.*, 2014). One common thread among kids around the world is that those who access screens from their bedroom tend to engage in more sedentary behaviors (LeBlanc *et al.*, 2015), a risk factor that is likely compounded by the increase in advertisements they see.

Does Media Encourage Youth to Engage in Substance Use?

Exposure to certain types of media content can be associated with increase in usage of alcohol, drugs, and tobacco. Results from the U.S. National Youth Tobacco Survey indicated that susceptibility to use tobacco is predicted by exposure to ads, TV, and movies (Fulmer *et al.*, 2015). Exposure to e-cigarette advertising also increases youth's desire to try such products (Farrelly *et al.*, 2015). Media exposure also affects alcohol use. A German research institute performed a longitudinal study of 2,346 adolescents across 6 countries. At the start of the study, all of the youth reported never drinking and zero intention to drink in the next 12 months. About a year later, the youth in their sample who were heavily exposed to alcohol portrayals in movies were more likely to be among the 40% who had tried alcohol (Hanewinkel *et al.*, 2014). Along with seeing alcohol portrayals in narrative media, exposure to ads is a big problem. A comprehensive review of twelve studies on this topic concluded that exposure to alcohol marketing is clearly associated with problematic drinking (Jernigan, Noel, Landon, Thornton, & Lobstein, 2017). As social media takes over television as the primary source of reaching teenagers with ads (Winpenny, Marteau, & Nolte, 2014), there is very little in the way of barriers between youth and ads for risky products.

Can Media and Online Technology Encourage
Young People to Harm Themselves?

Media use is related to suicide and self-harm in a couple of ways. Youth look up to celebrities, and when their struggles are vividly portrayed in the news, copycat behaviors may occur. In 2005, after a famous young Korean actress named Lee Eun-ju committed suicide, an increase in same-method suicides occurred in subgroups with similar characteristics to the actress (Ji, Lee, Noh, & Yip, 2014). In addition, the endless pool of information found online may provide unhealthy solutions to problems young people face in their daily lives, even offering support for unhealthy behaviors such as disordered eating (Haas, Irr, Jennings, & Wagner, 2010). Among the most frightening of these offerings, exposure to pro-suicide websites is a high-risk factor for attempting suicidal behaviors (Durkee, Hadlaczky, Westerlund, & Carli, 2011). Oktan (2015) recently surveyed 736 high school students in Turkey, and found that problematic Internet use and self-injurious (harm to the self without intending suicide) behaviors are related. In the United Kingdom, youth who visited encouraging self-harm and suicide sites were seven times more likely to report they had thought about killing themselves (Mitchell, Wells, Priebe, & Ybarra, 2014).

Conclusion

Wow! After that long list of potential risks, you might be wondering why anyone would ever allow their child to engage with the media. Well, there are some very good reasons, not the least of which is that KIDS LOVE IT. For many youth, watching TV with family, going to movies with friends, connecting with peers over social media, laughing at YouTube videos, and sharing photos is the very definition of being a child or a teen. As exemplified by other chapters in this book, there are numerous studies that have documented the pro-social effects of media use (see, for example, Chapter 13) and another long line of research examining ways to help kids get the most out of their media experiences in a positive way (see Chapter 5). The goal of this book as a whole is to answer some questions related to young people and media, and to raise other questions that encourage you to explore these topics further. The answers may not always be clear but with continued research and experience, we can learn more about the complex issues facing youth and media.

Discussion Questions

1. Which of the topics discussed in this chapter do you think is most compelling to study and why?

2. Much of the recent research discussed in this chapter focuses on risky behaviors related to the Internet and social media, but young people still use music, TV, movies and other more "traditional" media. What is it about the relationship between young people and the Internet that generates so much research and interest?

3. As discussed in the conclusion, some researchers study the positive effects media can have on young people. But why do you think that the body of research on risky behaviors is significantly larger than that on positive effects?

Exercises

1. Select a study from this chapter that you find interesting. By searching online, obtain a copy of the study itself. Then search to see if you can find a study with the opposite findings of one mentioned here? Read both studies and consider why it might be that the authors came up with different findings. Think about 1) samples studied; 2) methods used; 3) specific medium studied; 4) other potential explanations for the different findings?

2. Compare the topics discussed in this chapter with the government & industry regulations discussed in Chapter 2. Which types of risky behaviors/effects are most likely to generate regulations? What kind of regulations have been instituted for which types of risks?

References

Albury, K. (2015). Selfies, sexts, and sneaky hats: Young people's understandings of gendered practices of self-representation. *International Journal of Communication, 9*(2015), 1734–1745.

Ammari, T., Kumar, P., Lampe, C., & Schoenebeck, S. (2015). Managing children's online identities: How parents decide what to disclose about their children online. *Proceedings of the 33rd annual ACM conference on Human factors in computing systems* (pp. 1895–1904), Seoul, Korea. Retrieved from http://dl.acm.org/citation.cfm?id=2702325

Barber, C., & Bettez, S. (2014). Deconstructing the online grooming of youth: Toward improved information systems for detection of online sexual predators. *ICIS 2014 Proceedings*. Retrieved from http://aisel.aisnet.org/icis2014/proceedings/ConferenceTheme/14

Baumgartner, S. E., Valkenburg, P. M., & Peter, J. (2010). Assessing causality in the relationship between adolescents' risky sexual online behavior and their perceptions of this behavior. *Journal of Youth and Adolescence, 39*(10), 1226–1239. doi:10.1007/s10964-010-9512-y

Blaker, L. (2015). The Islamic state's use of online social media. *Military Cyber Affairs, 1*(1). doi:10.5038/2378-0789.1.1.1004

Bond, E. (2011). The mobile phone – bike shed? Children, sex and mobile phones. *New Media & Society, 13*(4), 587–604. doi:10.1177/1461444810377919

boyd, D., Hargittai, E., Schultz, J., & Palfrey, J. (2011). Why parents help their children lie to Facebook about age: Unintended consequences of the 'Children's Online Privacy Protection Act'. *First Monday, 16*(11). Retrieved from http://journals.uic.edu/ojs/index.php/fm/article/view/3850

Brown, P. (2013). *"They're flooding the internet": A cross-national analysis of newspaper representations of the "internet predator" in Australia, Canada, the UK and USA* (PhD thesis, Cardiff University, Cardiff). Retrieved from http://orca.cf.ac.uk/46894/

Bryce, J., & Fraser, J. (2014). The role of disclosure of personal information in the evaluation of risk and trust in young peoples' online interactions. *Computers in Human Behavior, 30*, 299–306. doi:10.1016/j.chb.2013.09.012

Byrne, S., Katz, S. J., Lee, T., Linz, D., & McIlrath, M. (2014). Peers, predators, and porn: Predicting parental underestimation of children's risky online experiences. *Journal of Computer-Mediated Communication, 19*(2), 215–231. doi:10.1111/jcc4.12040

Craig, S. L., & McInroy, L. (2014). You can form a part of yourself online: The influence of new media on identity development and coming out for LGBTQ youth. *Journal of Gay & Lesbian Mental Health, 18*(1), 95–109. doi:10.1080/19359705.2013.777007

Crofts, T., & Lee, M. (2013). Sexting, children and child pornography. *Sydney Law Review, 35*(1), 85–106.

Draper, N. R. A. (2012). Is your teen at risk? Discourses of adolescent sexting in United States television news. *Journal of Children and Media, 6*(2), 221–236. doi:10.1080/17482798.2011.587147

Durkee, T., Hadlaczky, G., Westerlund, M., & Carli, V. (2011). Internet pathways in suicidality: A review of the evidence. *International Journal of Environmental Research and Public Health, 8*(10), 3938–3952. doi:10.3390/ijerph8103938

Elton-Marshall, T., Leatherdale, S. T., & Turner, N. E. (2016). An examination of internet and land-based gambling among adolescents in three Canadian provinces: Results from the youth gambling survey (YGS). *BMC Public Health, 16*(1), 277. doi:10.1186/s12889-016-2933-0

Farrelly, M. C., Duke, J. C., Crankshaw, E. C., Eggers, M. E., Lee, Y. O., Nonnemaker, J. M., … Porter, L. (2015). A randomized trial of the effect of e-cigarette TV advertisements on intentions to use e-cigarettes. *American Journal of Preventive Medicine, 49*(5), 686–693. doi:10.1016/j.amepre.2015.05.010

Festl, R., Vogelgesang, J., Scharkow, M., & Quandt, T. (2017). Longitudinal patterns of involvement in cyberbullying: Results from a Latent Transition Analysis. *Computers in Human Behavior, 66*, 7–15. doi:10.1016/j.chb.2016.09.027

Flood, M. (2009). The harms of pornography exposure among children and young people. *Child Abuse Review, 18*(6), 384–400. doi:10.1002/car.1092

Fulmer, E. B., Neilands, T. B., Dube, S. R., Kuiper, N. M., Arrazola, R. A., & Glantz, S. A. (2015). Protobacco media exposure and youth susceptibility to smoking cigarettes, cigarette experimentation, and current tobacco use among US youth. *PLoS One, 10*(8), e0134734. doi:10.1371/journal.pone.0134734

Gonzales, A. L., & Hancock, J. T. (2008). Identity shift in computer-mediated environments. *Media Psychology, 11*(2), 167–185. doi:10.1080/15213260802023433

Greenberg, J. (2015). *Does the Islamic State post 90,000 social media messages each day?* Retrieved from http://www.politifact.com/punditfact/statements/2015/feb/19/hillary-mann-leverett/cnn-expert-islamic-state-posts-90000-social-media-/

Haas, S. M., Irr, M. E., Jennings, N. A., & Wagner, L. M. (2010). Online negative enabling support groups. *New Media & Society, 13*(1), 40–57. doi:10.1177/1461444810363910

Hald, G. M., Kuyper, L., Adam, P. C. G., & de Wit, J. B. F. (2013). Does viewing explain doing? Assessing the association between sexually explicit materials use and sexual behaviors in a large sample of Dutch adolescents and young adults. *The Journal of Sexual Medicine, 10*(12), 2986–2995. doi:10.1111/jsm.12157

Hanewinkel, R., Sargent, J. D., Hunt, K., Sweeting, H., Engels, R. C. M. E., Scholte, R. H. J., ... Morgenstern, M. (2014). Portrayal of alcohol consumption in movies and drinking initiation in low-risk adolescents. *Pediatrics, 133*(6), 973–982. doi:10.1542/peds.2013–3880

Haque, O. S., Choi, J., Philips, T., & Bursztajn, H. (2015). Why are young Westerners drawn to terrorist organizations like ISIS? *Network, 13*, 14. Retrieved from http://www.psychiatrictimes.com/trauma-and-violence/why-are-young-westerners-drawn-terrorist-organizations-isis

Hardoon, K. K., Derevensky, J. L., & Gupta, R. (2002). *An examination of the influence of a familial, emotional, conduct, and cognitive problems, and hyperactivity upon youth risk-taking and adolescent gambling problems: Report to the Ontario Problem Gambling Research Centre.* R & G Child Development Consultants, Incorporated. Retrieved from http://youthgambling.mcgill.ca/en/PDF/OPGRC.pdf

Hing, N., Vitartas, P., Lamont, M., & Fink, E. (2014). Adolescent exposure to gambling promotions during televised sport: An exploratory study of links with gambling intentions. *International Gambling Studies, 14*(3), 374–393. doi:10.1080/14459795.2014.902489

Ho, H., Shin, W., & Lwin, M. O. (2017). Social networking site use and materialistic values among youth: The safeguarding role of the parent-child relationship and self-regulation. *Communication Research.* Advance online publication. doi:10.1177/0093650216683775

Jernigan, D., Noel, J., Landon, J., Thornton, N., & Lobstein, T. (2017). Alcohol marketing and youth alcohol consumption: A systematic review of longitudinal studies published since 2008. *Addiction, 112*(Suppl 1), 7–20. doi:10.1111/add.13591

Ji, N. J., Lee, W. Y., Noh, M. S., & Yip, P. S. F. (2014). The impact of indiscriminate media coverage of a celebrity suicide on a society with a high suicide rate: Epidemiological findings on copycat suicides from South Korea. *Journal of Affective Disorders, 156*, 56–61. doi:10.1016/j.jad.2013.11.015

Jones, L. M., Mitchell, K. J., & Finkelhor, D. (2012). Trends in youth Internet victimization: Findings from three youth Internet safety surveys 2000–2010. *Journal of Adolescent Health, 50*(2), 179–186. doi:10.1016/j.jadohealth.2011.09.015

Jordan, A. B., & Robinson, T. N. (2008). Children, television viewing, and weight status: Summary and recommendations from an expert panel meeting. *The ANNALS of the American Academy of Political and Social Science, 615*(1), 119–132. doi:10.1177/0002716207308681

Kenney, E. L., & Gortmaker, S. L. (2016). United States adolescents' television, computer, videogame, smartphone, and tablet use: Associations with sugary drinks, sleep, physical activity, and obesity. *The Journal of Pediatrics.* doi:10.1016/j.jpeds.2016.11.015

King, D. L., & Delfabbro, P. H. (2016). Early exposure to digital simulated gambling: A review and conceptual model. *Computers in Human Behavior, 55*(Pt. A), 198–206. doi:10.1016/j.chb.2015.09.012

King, D. L., Delfabbro, P. H., Kaptsis, D., & Zwaans, T. (2014). Adolescent simulated gambling via digital and social media: An emerging problem. *Computers in Human Behavior, 31*, 305–313. doi:10.1016/j.chb.2013.10.048

Koezuka, N., Koo, M., Allison, K. R., Adlaf, E. M., Dwyer, J. J. M., Faulkner, G., & Goodman, J. (2006). The relationship between sedentary activities and physical inactivity among adolescents: Results from the Canadian community health survey. *Journal of Adolescent Health, 39*(4), 515–522. doi:10.1016/j.jadohealth.2006.02.005

Lazuras, L., Barkoukis, V., & Tsorbatzoudis, H. (2017). Face-to-face bullying and cyberbullying in adolescents: Trans-contextual effects and role overlap. *Technology in Society, 48*, 97–101. doi:10.1016/j.techsoc.2016.12.001

LeBlanc, A. G., Katzmarzyk, P. T., Barreira, T. V., Broyles, S. T., Chaput, J.-P., Church, T. S., ... Group, I. R. (2015). Correlates of total sedentary time and screen time in 9–11 year-old children around the world: The international study of childhood obesity, lifestyle and the environment. *PLoS One, 10*(6), e0129622. doi:10.1371/journal.pone.0129622

Lee, E. B. (2014). Facebook use and texting among African American and Hispanic teenagers: An implication for academic performance. *Journal of Black Studies, 45*(2), 83–101. doi:10.1177/0021934713519819

Lee, S.-J., & Chae, Y.-G. (2007). Children's Internet use in a family context: Influence on family relationships and parental mediation. *CyberPsychology & Behavior, 10*(5), 640–644. doi:10.1089/cpb.2007.9975

Martin, A. C. (2008). Television media as a potential negative factor in the racial identity development of African American youth. *Academic Psychiatry, 32*(4), 338–342.

McGovern, A., Crofts, T., Lee, M., & Milivojevic, S. (2016). Media, legal and young people's discourses around sexting. *Global Studies of Childhood, 6*(4), 428–441. doi:10.1177/2043610616676028

Messias, E., Kindrick, K., & Castro, J. (2014). School bullying, cyberbullying, or both: Correlates of teen suicidality in the 2011 CDC youth risk behavior survey. *Comprehensive Psychiatry, 55*(5), 1063–1068. doi:10.1016/j.comppsych.2014.02.005

Mitchell, K. J., Wells, M., Priebe, G., & Ybarra, M. L. (2014). Exposure to websites that encourage self-harm and suicide: Prevalence rates and association with actual thoughts of self-harm and thoughts of suicide in the United States. *Journal of Adolescence, 37*(8), 1335–1344. doi:10.1016/j.adolescence.2014.09.011

Noll, J. G., Shenk, C. E., Barnes, J. E., & Haralson, K. J. (2013). Association of maltreatment with high-risk internet behaviors and offline encounters. *Pediatrics, 131*(2), e510–e517. doi:10.1542/peds.2012–1281

Oktan, V. (2015). An investigation of problematic internet use among adolescents in terms of self-injurious and risk-taking behavior. *Children and Youth Services Review, 52*, 63–67. doi:10.1016/j.childyouth.2015.03.009

Ouytsel, J. V., Gool, E. V., Walrave, M., Ponnet, K., & Peeters, E. (2016). Sexting: Adolescents' perceptions of the applications used for, motives for, and consequences of sexting. *Journal of Youth Studies, 20*(4), 446–470. doi: 10.1080/13676261.2016.1241865

Pearson, N., Biddle, S. J., Williams, L., Worsley, A., Crawford, D., & Ball, K. (2014). Adolescent television viewing and unhealthy snack food consumption: The mediating role of home availability of unhealthy snack foods. *Public Health Nutrition, 17*(2), 317–323. doi:10.1017/S1368980012005204

Perloff, R. M. (2014). Social media effects on young women's body image concerns: Theoretical perspectives and an agenda for research. *Sex Roles, 71*(11–12), 363–377. doi:10.1007/s11199-014–0384-6

Pyrooz, D. C., Decker, S. H., & Moule Jr., R. K. (2015). Criminal and routine activities in online settings: Gangs, offenders, and the Internet. *Justice Quarterly, 32*(3), 471–499. doi:10.1080/07418825.2013.778326

Strohmaier, H., Murphy, M., & DeMatteo, D. (2014). Youth sexting: Prevalence rates, driving motivations, and the deterrent effect of legal consequences. *Sexuality Research and Social Policy, 11*(3), 245–255. doi:10.1007/s13178-014–0162-9

Stulhofer, A., Busko, V., & Landripet, I. (2010). Pornography, sexual socialization, and satisfaction among young men. *Archives of Sexual Behavior, 39*(1), 168–178. doi:10.1007/s10508-008–9387-0

Tsitsika, A., Critselis, E., Janikian, M., Kormas, G., & Kafetzis, D. A. (2011). Association between Internet gambling and problematic Internet use among adolescents. *Journal of Gambling Studies, 27*(3), 389–400. doi:10.1007/s10899-010–9223-z

Vandenbosch, L., & Peter, J. (2016). Antecedents of the initiation of watching sexually explicit Internet material: A longitudinal study among adolescents. *Mass Communication and Society, 19*(4), 499–521. doi:10.1080/15 205436.2016.1148171

Walker, S., Temple-Smith, M., Higgs, P., & Sanci, L. (2015). 'It's always just there in your face': Young people's views on porn. *Sexual Health, 12*(3), 200–206. doi:10.1071/SH14225

Watkins, L., Aitken, R., Robertson, K., Thyne, M., & Williams, J. (2016). Advertising's impact on pre-schoolers' brand knowledge and materialism. *International Journal of Consumer Studies, 40*(5), 583–591. doi:10.1111/ijcs.12303

Winpenny, E. M., Marteau, T. M., & Nolte, E. (2014). Exposure of children and adolescents to alcohol marketing on social media websites. *Alcohol and Alcoholism, 49*(2), 154–159. doi:10.1093/alcalc/agt174

Winters, G. M., Kaylor, L. E., & Jeglic, E. L. (2017). Sexual offenders contacting children online: An examination of transcripts of sexual grooming. *Journal of Sexual Aggression, 23*(1), 62–76. doi:10.1080/13552600.2016.1 271146

Wu, X., Kirk, S. F. L., Ohinmaa, A., & Veugelers, P. (2016). Health behaviours, body weight and self-esteem among grade five students in Canada. *SpringerPlus, 5*(1), 1099. doi:10.1186/s40064-016–2744-x

CHAPTER 10

Why Do Kids Think Dora the Explorer Is Their Friend?

Nancy A. Jennings

H ave you ever seen a child sing along with a character on TV? Do you ever imagine what it would be like to have dinner with your favorite celebrity? Have you ever felt embarrassed for your favorite newscaster when she made a mistake? If you answered yes to any of these questions, you have witnessed or experienced phenomena known as parasocial interactions and parasocial relationships. There, you just experienced another one when you read that sentence because I am reaching out past the page to address you directly! We experience relationships with media personae (e.g., authors, characters, singers, reality television personalities, etc.) on many different levels and in many different media platforms, and so do children. This chapter explores how children and youth engage with characters at different stages of their development and examines how media characters and personae have reached out to the hearts and minds of viewers through the years.

What Are Key Terms to Know about Parasocial Concepts?

The concepts of parasocial interactions (PSI) and parasocial relationships (PSR) were first introduced by Horton and Wohl in 1956. While often used interchangeably, there are key distinctions between the two that are important to know and remember. First, let's look at PSI. A PSI is a simulation of conversational give and take in which the on-screen personality (live or animated) uses the camera as a portal to reach directly to the audience through eye-gaze, nonverbal movements, and verbal utterances. As such, the on-screen personality and the audience share a sense of mutual awareness and mutual attention to each other as if in a normal face-to-face encounter (Dibble, Hartmann, & Rosaen, 2016; Hartmann & Goldhoorn, 2011).

Traditionally, television has been considered as a form of one-way communication from the screen to the audience. A PSI, then, suggests two-way communication and acknowledges that there is an audience watching in which the audience perceives exchange and reciprocity with the media personae. Many television programs for preschoolers use this technique in many different ways. For example, *Sesame Street* starts each show by welcoming the audience to the street and subsequently the show. Some preschool shows rely on exchange and response from the viewers to teach lessons and advance the story by finding on-screen objects, answering questions, and following commands such as *Blue's Clues, Dora the Explorer,* and *Super WHY!* As such, these PSIs teach young viewers about communication exchange through simulation of conversation.

A PSR can be built with on-screen personalities and can lead to a sense of friendship and companionship. As such, a PSR is defined as a one-sided interpersonal relationship that resembles real-world relationships, particularly in terms of social support (Hartmann, Stuke, & Daschmann, 2008). PSRs are constructed similarly to the way real-life relationships are made, both actively such as talking about characters with other real-life people, and passively by observing the on-screen personality and learning about their thoughts, behaviors, and values (Perse & Rubin, 1989). In fact, social relationships and PSRs are based on similar constructs such as uncertainty reduction which suggests that relationships develop as people learn more about each other and can predict the other's behavior (Perse & Rubin, 1989). This is particularly important for children on a number of levels. First, in terms of viewing behaviors, children, particularly young children, often watch the same episode of a television show over and over again. With each viewing, the child's knowledge about the on-screen personality grows and is reinforced through repeated viewings thereby increasing the predictability and stability of that character's personality. Second, unlike in person interactions with others, on-screen characters and personalities are always the same in prerecorded shows. They behave the same way the first time the child sees the show and the next time, and the next. Unlike in-person interactions, the on-screen character is consistently reducing uncertainty as to what to expect from encounters. Depending on different circumstances, people in face to face interactions may respond differently, but that is not the case with the stable, pre-recorded on-screen character. This need for stability is further reflected through the requirements/instructions a character's creator/producer sets for 1) how that character may be used in different settings (e.g., which products or activities that character can be affiliated with) and 2) how to portray that character when in costume. For example, guidelines are provided for how costumed characters such as Disney princesses are supposed to behave and act in character at all times in order to "make sure nothing shatters the illusion that characters stepped right out of the movies" (Pedicini, 2015).

Parasocial relationships serve as a foundation for the development of fans and fandoms. Jenkins (1992) suggests that the early understanding of a "fan" was of unbridled and excessive enthusiasm, initially likened to followers of professional sports teams (particularly baseball), but eventually broadened to include people with an affinity for theater, television shows, movies, and celebrities. These fans were often associated with negative traits, and Jenkins (1992) submits that early news reports of fans characterized them as "psychopaths whose frustrated fantasies of intimate relationships with stars…take violent and antisocial forms" (p. 13). As such, fans were ostracized and marginalized, and the early fan studies focused on fan activities and practices such as conventions, fanfiction writing, and letter-writing campaigns. However, this academic construction ignored fans who love a show, watch every episode, love to talk about it, and form PSRs with characters, but who do not engage in any other fan practices. Gray, Sandvoss, and

Harrington (2007) suggest that this more subdued behavior is "fandom in one of its most common forms" (p. 4). Indeed, with a shift from broadcasting to narrowcasting, fans as a specialized and devoted consumer have become cherished by the industry and serve as a "centerpiece of media industries' marketing strategies" (Gray *et al.*, 2007, p. 4). Traditionally, research on fans and fandoms has been focused on adults, however, with the rise of YouTube stars and marketing activities around television characters, children and teens may also be considered fans and members of fandoms such as the Phandom (fans of YouTube stars Dan Howell and Phil Lester) or Potterheads (fans of Harry Potter).

What Makes Up a PSR for Children?

Children's PSRs are constructed from a variety of different elements. Recent research of parents of preschoolers identified three primary dimensions of PSR in preschool children: 1) Attachment, 2) Character personification, and 3) Social realism (Bond & Calvert, 2014a). *Attachment* refers to children's sense of comfort and security obtained by proximity to others, and begins during infancy with their attachment to their mother (Bowlby, 1969). *Character personification* is important for development of attachment. Personification suggests that person-like qualities and characteristics can be assigned to media characters. For children, these include such things as believing the character has wants or needs, or that the character has thoughts and emotions (Bond & Calvert, 2014a). This directly relates to the third dimension of *social realism*. When a character is perceived to be able to exist in the real world, that character embodies social realism. This is particularly relevant when considering children's understanding of media representations. Media figures may be shown as real people such as show hosts or presenters, while other figures may be fictional creations portrayed by actors and, particularly in the case of children's media, through animation or puppetry. Younger children have greater difficulty distinguishing between what is real and unreal (Wright, Huston, Reitz, & Piemyat, 1994). Older children tend to choose more realistic characters as their favorite characters and more realistic characters have higher PSI (Rosaen & Dibble, 2008). This raises another dimension of liking and attraction to characters.

The majority of research on children's PSI and PSR has focused on characters that children will like. Indeed, most researchers ask children to identify their favorite character and then answer questions about that character. If the characters are liked, PSRs can result in the formation of perceived friendships with them, which has been a primary focus of PSR research with children. The perceived friendship may lead to creation of fans of characters or shows and hence participation in fandoms. If on-screen personalities are not liked, relationships can still be established, but more in the sense of the character that "you love to hate" rather than as a friend and the PSR is expected to be lower than for liked characters. Jennings and Alper (2016) examined liked and disliked characters for children ages six to seven years. As expected, boys were more likely to choose same-sex characters as their friends than girls. For disliked characters, far more male characters were identified by the children as disliked than female characters. Children expressed that they disliked characters because of the way they behaved ("he is trying to hurt my friend") or because of the disposition of the character ("he's mean"). Boys were more likely to pick same-sex characters as being disliked than girls, similar to liked characters.

What Types of Shows Have PSI for Children?

Parasocial interactions and relationships have been a key element of children's programming from the very beginning. Hosted by "Big Brother" Bob Emery, the classic 1950s television program *Small Fry Club* opened with Emery singing the program's theme song on his ukulele while looking at the television camera and speaking directly to his audience. He offered to send his viewers the show's coloring book and asked them to send pictures and letters to the show's New York City address (Paley Center for Media, 2017). As we know, much of the children's programming in the 1950s was produced at the local level with live local programming (See Chapter 1). From coast to coast, local stations featured live shows for children with a host to direct the action and talk to the viewing audience directly through the camera, inviting the audience to play along.

Two early program formats integrating PSIs with the host were even franchised: *Romper Room* and *Bozo the Clown*. Developed by Bert and Nancy Claster, *Romper Room* created a televised kindergarten classroom complete with a teacher who interacted directly with the viewing audience. Nancy Claster trained each host teacher for the stations, and every element of the show was under the complete control of the Clasters. One such element which is an ideal PSI experience was the "Magic Mirror" in which the host teacher would hold an empty hand-mirror frame in front of her face and addressing the camera, she would say, "I see Mary and Bobby, and Tommy, and Donnie…" which were names of the show's fans who had sent in fan mail to the show (Hollis, 2001, p. 15). The second most successful franchised show was *Bozo the Clown*. The Bozo franchise focused more on entertainment and a wider range of ages for the child audience than *Romper Room*. Each station produced their own version of *Bozo the Clown* ranging from real-life circus acts to low-budget children's games with a live audience (Hollis, 2001). Locally produced children's shows began to fade in the 1960s but the use of PSI and PSR continued in new ways.

With the rise of cartoons in the next few decades, the manifestation of PSRs with television characters become evident in the close ties established between toy manufacturers and television producers. The rise of "program-length commercials" provided a path to increase sales of children's toys and merchandise that featured characters from the shows. As such, the strength of a PSR with a character (or as often was the case multiple characters such as *Smurfs, Care Bears,* and *My Little Pony*) served as the basis for the child's desire to bring a part of that show home through toys and merchandise. Repeated viewing increased the ties with the characters and thus raised the quest for toys and merchandise. (See Chapter 14.)

Educational shows for children continued to be a place where PSIs were directly incorporated into the show, often as a teaching technique. Starting with the very first episode, *Sesame Street* uses PSIs in a variety of ways to bring the child viewing audience into the show to enhance learning. One way this is done is through asking the viewer to play a game with an on-screen character. In the first episode, Susan performs in a sketch in which she shows the audience a display with four items on it (three images of the number "2" and one image of the letter "W"). The audience is asked to identify which object doesn't belong with the rest of the group as Susan sings "One of These Things." By the end of the episode, another character, Gordon, invites the viewers to come back again soon to Sesame Street, in other words, come back to see the next episode. All types of characters engage with the child audience including humans, Muppets, puppets, and animations. Many of these shows were directed to a younger audience and characters that talk to the screen became a key element in very successful preschool shows. (Refer to Chapter 12 for more on educational television.)

Parasocial interactions took a new step in the 1990s beginning with the success of *Blue's Clues* which launched in September, 1996. Todd Kessler, one of the show's creators, submits, "We want to integrate the viewer as one of the protagonists" (Moore, 1998), and that's exactly what makes *Blue's Clues* a unique trend-setter. We've seen uses of PSIs in other educational shows, but never before has "viewer as protagonist" and PSIs been at the core of the narrative development. This was a critical element to the success of *Blue's Clues* and set the stage for the development of other shows such as *Dora the Explorer*, *Go! Diego! Go!*, and later *Super WHY!* and *Mickey Mouse Clubhouse* where child viewer responses seemingly direct the show.

Finally, it is important to note that even now, children's programs are hosted by television characters and personae, both in the United States and abroad. Show hosts also known as presenters speak directly to the camera similar to a newscaster. For example, many of the nature shows in contemporary educational and informational shows on U.S. broadcast stations feature a real-life human host to introduce new animals, settings, or scientific information such as ABC's *Outback Adventures with Tim Faulkner*, or NBC's *The Voyager with Josh Garcia*. Sprout, a 24-hour preschool premium channel, features blocks of programs that are hosted by media personae such as a puppet named Chica on *Sunny Side Up*, and Nina (human) and Star (puppet) on *The Good Night Show*. Presenters in other countries have included Reuben (human), and Bosco (puppet) on RTÉ and RTÉJr in Ireland; Catherine "Cat" Sandion (human), and Alex Winters (human) on CBeebies in the UK; and Gesa Dankwerth (human) and Willi Weitzel (human) in Germany.

What Kind of Responses Do Children Have to Media Characters?

Given the amount of PSIs present in preschool programming, it should come as no surprise that the vast majority of research on children's PSIs and PSRs has been conducted with children (and their parents) younger than eight years. Some research has been conducted with children in middle childhood (between the ages of eight to twelve years), and far less is known about how adolescents respond to media characters. We will explore what is known about children and media characters and personae to date, looking at with which characters children form PSRs, how they respond to PSIs, and what are some of the effects of having PSRs on learning and consumer behavior.

Toddlers

Beginning with toddlers, research has demonstrated that even young children establish and can benefit from PSRs with media characters on television. In a set of experiments involving a familiar character (Elmo from *Sesame Street*) with an unfamiliar character (DoDo from a famous Taiwanese children's television show), PSRs with the character played a key factor in how well children learned from the televised character. Results indicated that children who watched Elmo (a socially meaningful and familiar character with which children had PSR) outperformed those who viewed DoDo, suggesting that an emotional attachment with the characters can have a positive impact on learning (Lauricella, Howard Gola, & Calvert, 2011). Another experiment with DoDo tests this even further by familiarizing young children with DoDo. In this case, 18-month-old toddlers were given a DoDo plush toy and had three months to play with the plush toy and watch DoDo videos. While 3 months may not have been long enough to form a deep relationship for the toddlers, this study does demonstrate the ability of play with toys to increase familiarity and subsequent PSRs with characters thus increasing the transfer potential of learning from a two-dimensional screen experience to a three-dimensional living space (Howard Gola, Richards, Lauricella, & Calvert, 2013). Interestingly, when examining PSRs and source credibility by toddlers on a touchscreen tablet (iPad), children as young as 24-months use the accuracy of the information provided by characters more than their PSRs with the character to assess source credibility. In this study, children played an app in which they were asked to pick the correct word or label for different kinds of fruit that were labeled correctly by DoDo (unfamiliar character) or Elmo (familiar character). In this case, children did not let the familiarity or PSR with the character cloud their judgement on which character held the correct label (Richards & Calvert, 2015). This suggests that when it comes to touchscreen technology and accuracy judgements, PSRs may play less of an important role in an interactive setting than in observed learning from television. However, the PSR may drive children to play educational games that feature familiar characters on touchscreen devices.

Preschool

With the tremendous growth in preschool shows in the late 1990s and rise of 24-hour preschool programming channels including Sprout and Playhouse Disney, it should come as no surprise that a substantial amount of research in children's media has been focused on preschool children. In terms of character traits and identification, biological sex seems to play an important role in PSRs for preschool children. Preschool boys chose same-sex characters as their favorite more frequently than did girls, and girls had a stronger desire to be like their favorite character than did boys (Wilson & Drogos, 2007). Similarly, Calvert, Strong, Jacobs, and Conger (2007) found that girls identified with the Hispanic female character (Dora) more than boys, and benefited more from interactions with Dora. As such, sex does seem to have implications on preschool PSRs, particularly for girls.

As with the research on toddlers and parasocial concepts in media, much of the work with preschoolers has focused on the effects of PSIs and PSRs with media characters on children's learning outcomes. Early research focused on NickJr.'s *Blue's Clues* which found that children do interact with the characters both verbally and nonverbally (Crawley, Anderson, Wilder, Williams, & Santomero, 1999) and, moreover, that with repeated exposure to the program, children's interactions with the educational portions of the program increase (Crawley *et al.*, 1999). Similarly, experimental research on Nick Jr.'s show *Dora the Explorer* found that preschoolers who responded verbally and physically to Dora's requests learned more about the plot-related material than those who did not interact (Calvert *et al.*, 2007). However, the PSIs did not seem to help children learn the educational content of the program, except in situations where children were familiar (PSRs) with the program and characters (Piotrowski, 2014). Moreover, trust of characters as a credible source of information has been found to be a contributing factor to comprehension and transfer of knowledge from television characters in preschoolers (Schlesinger, Flynn, & Richert, 2016). Combined this research suggests that while PSIs alone may not lead to higher learning outcomes, they may help to familiarize the viewer with the character and the learning expectations within the show, increase engagement with the character and subsequent educational content, and may serve as a means to encourage repeated viewing which also has educational benefits. Trusted characters and familiar characters are also important for positive educational outcomes for preschool viewers.

While these shows can provide educational benefits, the established relationship with the character may also lead to other unintended outcomes, particularly in relationship to food advertising. Use of spokespeople (celebrities or popular characters) has been a technique used in advertising practices for children and adults. With the rise in childhood obesity, more attention has been paid to the contributing factors to this phenomenon. As a result, the advertising techniques associated with food products have been under scrutiny. In one study, preschoolers preferred foods paired with *Sesame Street* characters than with the unfamiliar characters. Moreover, a "fan effect" was found for sugary and salty snacks. That is, children who were strong fans of *Sesame Street* were more likely to choose a food associated with a *Sesame Street* character than children who were low-medium fans. Moreover, in a taste test, children were also more likely to taste healthy foods associated with Elmo from *Sesame Street* than with no character or an unfamiliar red character (Kotler, Schiffman, & Hanson, 2012). Similar results were found with three- to six-year-olds in Guatemala. Despite the fact that the same food was in both packages, the children were more likely to indicate a preference for the food packaged with a character (SpongeBob SquarePants or the Pink Panther) than without a character, particularly younger children (Letona, Chacon, Roberto, & Barnoya, 2014).

Finally, as preschoolers grow up, they tend to begin to watch other shows and leave their preschool shows and characters behind. As such, they experience what is known as parasocial breakup or a dissolution of a PSR (Bond & Calvert, 2014b). Often, this breakup usually occurs for adults when a character or actor dies or a show ends or is cancelled. However, for children, this breakup is more likely to occur as their interests move from their favorite preschool shows to more age-appropriate programming as they grow older. School-age children become "too old" to watch preschool shows, and they begin to develop new relationships with other characters and celebrities. Preschool parents also report that preschoolers experience a breakup when they become interested in a new character or show from another preschool show or through habituation, that is, they lose interest in a character after overexposure to the same content through repeated viewing (Bond & Calvert, 2014b). According to the parents, preschoolers experienced parasocial breakup on average at the age of three years, and the strength of stereotypical gender attributes increases with their new favorite characters following the breakup. That is, the masculinity of boys' favorite characters increased as the boys aged, and the femininity of girls' favorite characters increase for girls as well (Bond & Calvert, 2014b). This suggests an impact of prior PSRs on children's new relationships with different characters which has implications for children as they grow and develop.

School-age Children

Interestingly, the research on PSR and PSI with school-age children focuses less on the effects of these relationships and becomes more targeted on the PSR by examining who and how children are attracted to and why. One of the most well cited studies of this kind was conducted by Cynthia Hoffner whose work serves as a cornerstone of research in parasocial concepts with children. With children ages seven to twelve years, Hoffner (1996) found that, similar to preschoolers, boys were more likely to select same-sex characters as their favorite character than girls. Moreover, girls had a higher PSI for same-sex characters than boys. In other words, girls had a strong connection with female characters than male characters even though both were selected as favorite characters. The favorite female characters were also adored more by the girls than were the favorite male characters.

When examining what traits were important for the school-aged children, physical attributes, character traits, and social realism were all relevant. Regarding physical traits, self-identification was an important factor in selection of preferred hosts. In a large study of children from 27 different countries, children were asked to identify their ideal physical traits of presenters (Holler, Götz, & Alper, 2016). Results indicate that children of both sexes prefer a same-sex presenter, and this preference grows stronger with age. Moreover, children seem to prefer lighter-skinned hosts, particularly children who self-reported having light-skin themselves, and slimmer children prefer a slimmer host while heavier children prefer a heavier host. Concerning character traits, some sex differences were observed (Hoffner, 1996). For favorite male characters, attractiveness and intelligence of the character predicted PSI for both girls and boys. Strength was also an important predictor of PSI of male characters, but for boys only. However, for favorite female characters, attractiveness was the only predictor of PSI for girls (Hoffner, 1996), and girls tended to prefer a host who had a slimmer body shape than their own (Holler et al., 2016). It is important to note that children ranked characters higher on PSI and wishful identification that were regarded as kinder, more helpful, more caring, less mean, and less selfish (Hoffner, 1996). Finally, in order to tie theoretical models of PSR with character traits, Rosaen and Dibble (2008) examined children's beliefs of social realism and PSR. Results indicate that as children age, social realism becomes increasingly important. Older children chose characters as their favorite who are higher in social realism than did younger children, and stronger PSI is associated with more realistic characters (Rosaen & Dibble, 2008). These are important findings as it contributes to our understanding of what traits are appealing to children. Moreover, this research has implications for the type of characters and presenters children would like to see and which representations may be missing from their screens, particularly for marginalized youth.

Adolescents

For tweens and teens, the PSR research often turns more to the fandom side, with interest on how youth relate to celebrities in the media as role models. Cohen (1999) suggests that teens may be particularly susceptible to effects of relationships with media personae since identity work is major focus of teen development, and teens often turn to peers and media as sources of information rather than relying on their parents or teachers. Compared with younger children, teens put more value on the physical attractiveness of characters and are more likely to choose opposite-sex characters as their favorite than their younger counterparts, suggesting developmental differences in viewer involvement with characters (Cohen, 1999). Teens' preference for opposite-sex, same-age characters suggests a parasocial fantasized romance (Cohen, 1999). While we may expect teens to be more similar to adults than children in their responses to characters, research suggests that this is not necessarily the case. In terms of parasocial breakup, teens expect to be more upset by a parasocial breakup than adults (Cohen, 2003). Perhaps this is related to the previous findings about fantasized romance with media characters such that breaking up a romance may seem more disturbing for a teen than an adult. Interestingly, when teen girls were asked to identify a favorite same-sex character, they were more likely to select older females rather than same-age characters, suggesting a quest for a female role model rather than a peer which may be more useful in their identity work—finding a female to look up to rather than a peer (Theran, Newberg, & Gleason, 2010).

While traditionally PSRs have been conceptualized as a one-sided relationship, social media has allowed for opportunities to break the wall and suggest a two-sided relationship when characters and celebrities interact with their fans. Teens are avid users of social media sites, with 89% of U.S. teens reporting using at least one social media site (Lenhart, 2015). Following and interacting with celebrities on social media may provide a means to enhance PSR in new ways. Indeed, Bond (2016) discovered that surveilling celebrities on Twitter strengthened PSR for teens, although such behaviors on other social media sites such as Instagram and Facebook did not have a significant effect on PSR. Moreover, teens who had been retweeted or responded to by a media celebrity on Twitter had stronger PSRs than those who had not had such a computer-mediated communication experience (Bond, 2016). As such, Twitter provides a means for teens (and adults) to feel more connected with media celebrities and enhance their PSRs, thus altering the one-sided relationship. Moreover, teens are able to connect with celebrities in ways different than younger children who may express their connection by nurturing their celebrity toys.

Conclusion

Children and youth grow up in a parasocial world with media characters, personae, and celebrities all around. They develop relationships with television and movie characters both animated and live-action, sports stars and music performers, and more recently YouTubers and bloggers. Children and youth express their PSRs through different forms of engagement including taking care of their celebrity toys, wearing celebrity images on their shirts, subscribing to a personae's YouTube channel, and following a celebrity's social media profile. These relationships can lead to positive outcomes for children such as eating healthy foods endorsed by beloved characters or choosing an educational television show because they will get to spend time with their favorite mediated friends. However, sometimes these relationships can turn on them when their favorite show is cancelled or they simply outgrow their preschool media friends. Moreover, they can lead to tensions when these relationships become overwhelming and distracting from healthy habits.

We all have fond memories of favorite childhood characters—some from cartoons, others from video games, and some from movies and even books or comic books. Now you know more about those relationships that you built, and the ways in which they changed as you grew. Perhaps you even know why you still smile when you see them again years later—because they were and always will be your friends.

Discussion Questions

1. Suppose you were asked to create a preschool show with characters who engage in PSIs with the audience. What type of characters would you suggest? What kinds of attributes would they have? What would make them successful?

2. This chapter identifies several children's shows that use PSI as a production technique. Can you think of other shows that also do this? How are they similar or different than the ones mentioned in the chapter? What are some of the similarities and differences in PSIs across shows that appeal to different age groups?

3. Characters have been associated with and have endorsed many different kinds of food

products. Is that ethical, even for healthy products? Why or why not? How is use of a media character to promote a food the same or different than trade characters?

Exercises

1. Do a content analysis of a children's program that specifically uses PSIs. Which characters (male or female; live humans, animated, or puppets; peers or adults) are doing the PSIs? How often are PSIs used within the show? What types of PSIs are used (asking questions vs. giving commands)? What type of content is used with the PSI (educational, narrative development, entertainment)?

2. Follow a teen celebrity or a youth media character on social media. Examples of teen celebrities include Jennifer Lawrence, Taylor Swift, Harry Styles, and Sheldon Cooper. Other examples include Cookie Monster (@MeCookieMonster), Kermit the Frog (@KermitTheFrog), *The Fosters* (@TheFostersTV), *Pretty Little Liars* (@PLLTVSeries), or Phil Lester (@AmazingPhil). Describe this experience. Is fan fiction or fan art displayed or encouraged? What types of pictures or messages are tweeted/posted? How do the fans react to different posts? Who are these social media profiles targeting?

References

Bond, B. J. (2016). Following your "friend": Social media and the strength of adolescents' parasocial relationships with media personae. *Cyberpsychology, Behavior, and Social Networking, 19*(11), 656–660. doi:10.1089/cyber.2016.0355

Bond, B. J., & Calvert, S. L. (2014a). A model and measure of US parents' perceptions of young children's parasocial relationships. *Journal of Children and Media, 8*(3), 286–304. doi:10.1080/17482798.2014.890948

Bond, B. J., & Calvert, S. L. (2014b). Parasocial breakup among young children in the United States. *Journal of Children and Media, 8*(4), 474–490. doi:10.1080/17482798.2014.953559

Bowlby, J. (1969). *Attachment and loss: Vol. 1. Attachment.* New York, NY: Basic Books.

Calvert, S. L., Strong, B. L., Jacobs, E. L., & Conger, E. E. (2007). Interaction and participation for young Hispanic and Caucasian girls' and boys' learning of media content. *Media Psychology, 9*(2), 431–445. doi:10.1080/15213260701291379

Cohen, J. (1999). Favorite characters of teenage viewers of Israeli serials. *Journal of Broadcasting & Electronic Media, 43*(3), 327–345. doi:10.1080/08838159909364495

Cohen, J. (2003). Parasocial breakups: Measuring individual differences in responses to the dissolution of parasocial relationships. *Mass Communication & Society, 6*(2), 191–202. doi:10.1207/S15327825MCS0602_5

Crawley, A. M., Anderson, D. R., Wilder, A., Williams, M., & Santomero, A. (1999). Effects of repeated exposures to a single episode of the television program *Blue's Clues* on the viewing behaviors and comprehension of preschool children. *Journal of Educational Psychology, 91*(4), 630–637. doi:10.1037/0022-0663.91.4.630

Dibble, J. L., Hartmann, T., & Rosaen, S. F. (2016). Parasocial interaction and parasocial relationship: Conceptual clarification and a critical assessment of measures. *Human Communication Research, 42*(1), 21–44. doi:10.1111/hcre.12063

Gray, J., Sandvoss, C., & Harrington, C. L. (2007). Introduction: Why study fans? In J. Gray, C. Sandvoss, & C. L. Harrington (Eds.), *Fandom: Identities and communities in a mediated world* (pp. 1–18). New York, NY: New York University Press.

Hartmann, T., & Goldhoorn, C. (2011). Horton and Wohl revisited: Exploring viewers' experience of parasocial interaction. *Journal of Communication, 61*(6), 1104–1121. doi:10.1111/j.1460-2466.2011.01595.x

Hartmann, T., Stuke, D., & Daschmann, G. (2008). Positive parasocial relationships with drivers affect suspense in racing sport spectators. *Journal of Media Psychology, 20*(1), 24–34. doi:10.1027/1864-1105.20.1.24

Hoffner, C. (1996). Children's wishful identification and parasocial interaction with favorite television characters. *Journal of Broadcasting & Electronic Media, 40*(3), 389–402. doi:10.1080/08838159609364360

Holler, A., Götz, M., & Alper, M. (2016). Children's preferences for TV show hosts: An international perspective on learning from television. *Journal of Children and Media, 10*(4), 497–507. doi:10.1080/17482798.2016.1203804

Hollis, T. (2001). *Hi there, boys and girls!: America's local children's TV programs.* Jackson, MS: University Press of Mississippi.

Horton, D., & Wohl, R. R. (1956). Mass communication and para-social interaction: Observations on intimacy at a distance. *Psychiatry, 19*(3), 215–229. doi:10.1080/00332747.1956.11023049

Howard Gola, A. A., Richards, M. N., Lauricella, A. R., & Calvert, S. L. (2013). Building meaningful parasocial relationships between toddlers and media characters to teach early mathematical skills. *Media Psychology, 16*(4), 390–411. doi:10.1080/15213269.2013.783774

Jenkins, H. (1992). *Textual poachers: Television fans and participatory culture.* New York, NY: Routledge.

Jennings, N., & Alper, M. (2016). Young children's positive and negative parasocial relationships with media characters. *Communication Research Reports, 33*(2), 96–102. doi:10.1080/08824096.2016.1154833

Kotler, J. A., Schiffman, J. M., & Hanson, K. G. (2012). The influence of media characters on children's food choices. *Journal of Health Communication, 17*(8), 886–898. doi:10.1080/10810730.2011.650822

Lauricella, A. R., Howard Gola, A. A., & Calvert, S. L. (2011). Toddlers' learning from socially meaningful video characters. *Media Psychology, 14*(2), 216–232. doi:10.1080/15213269.2011.573465

Lenhart, A. (2015). *Teens, social media, and technology overview 2015.* Retrieved from http://www.pewinternet.org/2015/04/09/teens-social-media-technology-2015/

Letona, P., Chacon, V., Roberto, C., & Barnoya, J. (2014). Effects of licensed characters on children's taste and snack preferences in Guatemala, a low/middle income country. *International Journal of Obesity, 38*(11), 1466–1469. doi:10.1038/ijo.2014.38

Moore, F. (1998, June 13). Series for preschoolers lets them help solve adult problem. *St. Louis Post-Dispatch*, p. 4 (Entertainment).

Paley Center for Media. (2017). *Small Fry Club, The {Segment} (TV).* Retrieved from https://www.paleycenter.org/collection/item/?q=Small+Fry+Club&p=1&item=B:12187

Pedicini, S. (2015, June 4). *Disney policy requiring character confidentiality comes under fire.* Orlando Sentinel. Retrieved from http://www.orlandosentinel.com/business/os-disney-characters-20150604-story.html

Perse, E. M., & Rubin, R. B. (1989). Attribution in social and parasocial relationships. *Communication Research, 16*(1), 59–77. doi:10.1177/009365089016001003

Piotrowski, J. T. (2014). Participatory cues and program familiarity predict young children's learning from educational television. *Media Psychology, 17*(3), 311–331. doi:10.1080/15213269.2014.932288

Richards, M. N., & Calvert, S. L. (2015). Toddlers' judgments of media character source credibility on touchscreens. *American Behavioral Scientist, 59*(14), 1755–1775. doi:10.1177/0002764215596551

Rosaen, S. F., & Dibble, J. L. (2008). Investigating the relationships among child's age, parasocial interactions, and the social realism of favorite television characters. *Communication Research Reports, 25*(2), 145–154. doi:10.1080/08824090802021806

Schlesinger, M. A., Flynn, R. M., & Richert, R. A. (2016). US preschoolers' trust of and learning from media characters. *Journal of Children and Media, 10*(3), 321–340. doi:10.1080/17482798.2016.1162184

Theran, S. A., Newberg, E. M., & Gleason, T. R. (2010). Adolescent girls' parasocial interactions with media figures. *The Journal of Genetic Psychology, 171*(3), 270–277. doi:10.1080/00221325.2010.483700

Wilson, B. J., & Drogos, K. L. (2007). *Preschoolers' attraction to media characters.* Presented at the National Communication Association, Chicago, IL.

Wright, J. C., Huston, A. C., Reitz, S., & Piemyat, S. (1994). Young children's perceptions of television reality: Determinants and developmental differences. *Developmental Psychology, 30*, 229–239. doi:10.1037/0012–1649.30.2.229

CHAPTER 11

What Do Television and Film Teach Kids about Gender?

Rebecca C. Hains and Kyra Hunting

To answer the question posed in the title, we would like to begin by making an assumption explicit: The media have a socializing function in our society. As social cognitive theory (Bandura, 2009) suggests, when we watch television, we learn about social systems. The type of media we watch influences us, shaping our (mis)conceptions about sex roles, gender, and other social categories—thereby also shaping our personal goals and worldview and informing our own production of social systems (Bandura, 2009). As gender role theory (Shen, Ratan, Cai, & Leavitt, 2016) explains, parenting, peer groups, the educational system, and media alike reinforce gender stereotypes, encouraging males and females to occupy different roles in society. Through patterns in mediated characters' gender representations, then, viewers learn about the statuses of boys, girls, men, and women in society, including the possibilities and limitations that are culturally proscribed for people according to their sex. For this reason, the answer to our question—"What do television & film teach kids about gender?"—matters.

But what is gender, anyway? Contrary to popular usage, "sex" and "gender" are not synonymous. Sex refers to biological sex, while gender is a cultural construct, a product of discourses about what is considered appropriate for women, girls, men, and boys (Lemish, 2010). Gender relates to whether one identifies as masculine, feminine, or has adopted a genderqueer or non-binary gender identity. The traits we associate with a specific gender are socially constructed through cultural practices, and as these practices constantly evolve (Mesoudi, 2011), societies' perceptions of which characteristics are appropriate for which gender change. An individual can also embrace or eschew attributes from multiple gender categories at a time, but their choices may or may not be regarded as acceptable by the society in which they are living at that specific time.

One cultural institution from which people learn about gender roles and expectations is the media. Although adults often assume ourselves immune to media influence, this is a misconception (Perloff, 2009). For example, LGBT+ rights' recent acceptance has been attributed to positive news media coverage and on-screen portrayals of fictional LGBT+ characters (Garretson, 2009; Levina, Waldo, & Fitzgerald, 2000). Similarly, media can influence children's attitudes and behaviors. For example, one study of male and female preschoolers found an association between significant consumption of Disney princess media and behaviors and attitudes consistent with female gender stereotypes (Coyne, Linder, Rasmussen, Nelson, & Birbeck, 2016). Meanwhile, high levels of superhero viewing promoted male stereotypical and weapons play in both boy and girl preschoolers (Coyne, Linder, Rasmussen, Nelson, & Collier, 2014). The media's potential to affect our beliefs and assumptions, including gender norms and stereotypes (Ward, 2005), makes understanding who the media represents, and how, particularly important.

To this end, in this chapter, we discuss what television and films teach children about gender. First, we discuss the comparative representation levels of boys and girls in children's television and films. Then, we examine the gender stereotypes commonly found in these on-screen representations. Finally, we make a call for more diverse, intersectional representations of gender in children's media.

Who's on Screen?

Children's media consistently over-represent boys. Even though women outnumber men in the U.S., male characters outnumber females 2 to 1 on children's television and cable channels (Gerding & Signorielli, 2014; Hentges & Case, 2013). Children's films have a wider gap, with male-to-female ratios of 2.57 to 1 reported (Smith, Pieper, Granados, & Choueiti, 2010). Men are overrepresented as main characters in children's favorite TV programs (Aubrey & Harrison, 2004); in Pixar films (Wooden & Gillam, 2014); as superheroes (Baker & Raney, 2007); as monsters and creatures (Hentges & Case, 2013); as animals (Gotz & Lemish, 2012); and as comedians (Hentges & Case, 2013). Similar patterns have been found in global studies of children's television (Gotz & Lemish, 2012).

By persistently minimizing and decentering girls, the media teach viewers that boys' stories are more important than girls'. Genres and channels targeting girl viewers tend to be more balanced, however: While boy-oriented Cartoon Network has a greater than 2-to-1 male-female ratio, girl-oriented Disney Channel is more balanced (Hentges & Case, 2013). The same pattern occurs in male-oriented genres: males outnumber females at 4 to 1 in adventure cartoons (Leaper, Breed, Hoffman, & Perlman, 2002), 3 to 1 in action-adventure programs (Gerding & Signorielli, 2014), and 2 to 1 in comedies (Leaper et al., 2002), while girl-oriented, school-and-relationship centered "teen scene" programs offer a nearly 1 to 1 ratio (Gerding & Signorielli, 2014). These patterns teach boys and girls that while boys' stories can be of general interest, girls' stories are for female communities only.

Gender Representations in Children's Media

In addition to unequal representation levels, children's media peddle unrealistic gender stereotypes. They present masculinity and femininity as oppositional—separate but rarely equal, with masculinity inherently superior. This is accomplished by gendered patterns of representation in two key areas: physical appearance and behavior.

What the Media Teach Kids about Gender and Physical Appearance

As Western society favors attractive people, physical appearance matters for both sexes. For example, physical appearance influences how children treat peers (Harriger, Calogero, Witherington, & Smith, 2010). Attractiveness is highly gendered, however. Idealized (White, Western) feminine physical beauty is narrowly defined: light-skinned, long hair, a round face dominated by large eyes, and an extremely thin-but-curvaceous body well below a typical healthy weight (Engeln-Maddox, 2006). In contrast, a large, hyper-muscular body often denotes a masculine ideal, which is also unhealthy (Baker & Raney, 2007). These opposite physical types inaccurately imply the human sexes are dimorphic, or naturally easy to visually identify as "male" or "female."

Male characters are much less frequently muscle-bound than female characters are extremely thin (Gotz & Herche, 2012) and are less likely to be restricted to a narrow image of attractiveness. More than 72% of children's animated films sampled in one study *emphasized* female characters' physical attractiveness (Herbozo, Tantleff-Dunn, Gokee-Larose, & Thompson, 2004), reflecting a real-life pattern: Girls and women of all ages and educational levels—but not their male counterparts—find their physical appearances constantly evaluated (Darlow & Lobel, 2010) and held to a mostly unattainable standard. Unfortunately, those who internalize these beauty ideals and self-surveil or compare themselves to others are at higher risk for eating disorders, body disturbances, and other consequences (Manago, Ward, Lemm, & Seabrook, 2014; Tylka & Sabik, 2010).

By normalizing and highlighting female characters' successful performance of beauty standards, the media suggest feminine beauty is compulsory (Donaghue & Clemitshaw, 2012; Hains, 2012, 2014), a prerequisite to render traits like intelligence palatable (Hains, 2007). Storylines showing normatively beautiful girls and women reaping social rewards reinforce this. One study found 84% of children's animated films sampled associated a woman's good looks with her kindness, happiness, or success, and suggested men love women primarily for their physical appearances (Herbozo *et al.*, 2004).

What the Media Teach Kids about Gender and Behavior

Scholars and feminists have long criticized the media's limiting range of female gender roles. Romantic relationships' representations offer problematic ideas about heterosexual relationships, and tropes like the "damsel in distress" paint female characters as helpless prizes to be won. Mediated girls are also too often emotional, passive or submissive (England, Descartes, & Collier-Meek, 2011). Promisingly, however, female characters are increasingly portrayed as intelligent and assertive. These shifting representations may help broaden the range of behaviors and interests considered appropriate for girls. In order to better understand these patterns, let's consider which traits typically distinguish feminine characters from masculine characters, and which traits they share.

Portraying femininity in children's media. As discussed above, female characters are significantly more likely than male characters to focus on appearance (Gerding & Signorielli, 2014; Hentges & Case, 2013), exemplified by the "make-over" storyline. For example, Smith and Cook (2008) found that across 13 G-rated films, one-third of female characters overhauled their appearances, reinforcing "the idea that females are most important in their function as adornments" (p. 17). However, closer examinations reveal complexities: Smith and Cook's (2008) study included *Mulan*, in which the title character overhauls her appearance not to become more feminine, but to disguise herself as a man and succeed in war as a heroic soldier. Therefore, the contexts of such storylines are important.

Female characters are not necessarily centrally defined by their interest in their physical appearances. Although Hentges and Case (2013) found female characters were twice as likely as male characters to be interested in appearance, this was true of only 4% of female characters sampled. More female characters rescued someone, displayed aggression, showed affection, helped another, or demonstrated authority than fixated on physical appearance. In another study, while Disney Princesses sampled "tended to their physical appearances" 20 times more often than did princes, they were more likely to be athletic, troublesome, fearful, assertive and affectionate than appearance-oriented (England *et al.*, 2011, p. 559). The lessons the media teach children about physical appearance and femininity are thus complex: Female characters can be many things—assertive, aggressive, heroic—but they need to be attractive, too (Hains, 2007).

The media also teach children that women are other- and relationship-oriented. Compared with male characters, they are more likely to be defined by relationships (Hentges & Case, 2013; Smith *et al.*, 2010), more likely to be part of a team, and less likely to be independent (Gotz & Lemish, 2012). Female characters are also more affectionate, domestic, emotionally expressive, and likely to ask questions than to answer them (Baker & Raney, 2007). Children's media portray female characters as responsible for emotional labor (Hentges & Case, 2013) and relationship maintenance. These patterns are not universal, though: One study found both male and female characters were assertive and expressed opinions (Aubrey & Harrison, 2004), and another ranked assertiveness as a top-five trait among Disney princesses and princes alike (England *et al.*, 2011).

Just as male and female characters' representation levels vary by genre and target audience, their gendered behaviors also vary. Female characters are less likely to be domestic or emotional in boy-oriented adventure cartoons than in girls' media (Thompson & Zerbinos, 1995), and in superhero cartoons, male and female characters often reject traits like affection (Baker & Raney, 2007). These findings are consistent with studies that indicate boys will watch programs with female protagonists, but only if those characters do not act stereotypically feminine (Calvert, Kotler, Zehnder, & Shockney, 2003). Female characters may have more counter-stereotypical traits in these genres to fit male audiences' preferences. Conversely, male characters are more likely to express affection or emotion in girls' media than in boys' (Thompson & Zerbinos, 1995). On the Disney Channel, male characters are more likely than girls to display affection (Hentges & Case, 2013); and in Disney films, although Princesses are most likely to display affection, affection is a top-five trait among prince and princess characters alike (England *et al.*, 2011). Therefore, while girl viewers are more likely to see their own sex modeling affection, listening, or emotional openness, they are also more likely to see models of *male* affectionateness and emotion than boy viewers are.

Newer trends in girls' representations directly counter gender stereotypes, which Jane (2015) argues can complicate our ideas about gender. Newer media frequently portray female characters as intelligent (Smith *et al.*, 2010), academically goal-oriented and successful in school (Hunting, Grumbein, & Cahill, 2016), and exceptionally technically skilled (Gerding & Signorielli, 2014). The hero's gender in children's media is also changing. Past studies found male characters are most likely to rescue others (Thompson & Zerbinos, 1995), but now, in channels targeting boys, female and male characters rescue others at the same rate (Gerding & Signorielli,

2014; Hentges & Case, 2013). Likewise, Disney princesses rescue others as frequently as male characters (England *et al.*, 2011), and in recent Disney films like *Moana, Frozen, Merida,* and *Tangled,* beautiful princess lead characters accomplished the films' pivotal rescues. This change is consistent with ideas mainstreamed by girl power in the 2000s decade: While maintaining the prerequisite conventionally attractive appearance, girl power superheroes routinely rescued male and female characters alike, defeated a wide array of villains, and embraced some stereotypically masculine behaviors and interests (Hains, 2004, 2007, 2012).

Note that stereotypical and counter-stereotypical behaviors can work in concert within any character. One study found most Disney princesses and princes individually embodied feminine and masculine characteristics: being affectionate, assertive, and athletic were among the top 5 characteristics of both sexes. However, these characters still perpetuated stereotypes that girls are fearful and boys physically strong (England *et al.*, 2011). Modern Disney princesses and princes share more commonalities than did their predecessors—reflecting the societal truth that boys and girls share many characteristics across gender lines.

Portraying masculinity in children's media. While society has historically given boys great agency, their behavior has nonetheless been policed, with sanctions for interests and behaviors perceived as feminine. As such, today's boys are growing up in an active, rough-and-tumble, building-oriented world that seems miles away from girls' frilly, pink, image-oriented world (Paoletti, 2012). While many media depictions present boys' and girls' lives as essentially different, in reality, our social images of masculinity and femininity are mutually constituting and deeply intertwined. Therefore, it is essential to account for the popular discourses around boyhood and the representations of boyhood in the media (Wannamaker, 2011).

One of the main lessons boys learn from society, reinforced by media representations, is: *Don't be feminine.* Media often make this argument by presenting villains who are less traditionally masculine than the heroes who oppose them (Wooden & Gillam, 2014), and while there is no universal requirement that male characters be "attractive" in a narrowly defined way, being small can be a source of derision or humor. Animated films often cue "villainy" in male characters, like Scar in *Lion King* or Jafar in *Aladdin,* with stereotypically feminine features (like small waists, high cheek bones and small chins), physical gestures (like a "prim" walk), and/or objects (very ornamental costumes or spaces with flowers and mirrors) (Li-Vollmer & LaPointe, 2003). By associating traits of feminine appearance or behavior with villainy, and consequently failure, children's media may inculcate homophobia, since these markers are associated with homophobic stereotypes. Simultaneously, studies have found roughly half of five- to six-year-old boys reject anything they consider girlish (Halim, Ruble, Tamis-LeMonda, & Shrout, 2013; Paoletti, 2012), ranging from toys and household items featuring the color pink (Hains, 2014), to films and television shows featuring female protagonists.

In children's media, the traits most consistently associated with male characters are physical aggression (Luther & Legg, 2010; Thompson & Zerbinos, 1995) and physical strength (England *et al.*, 2011; Smith *et al.*, 2010), often depicted through storylines as the best solution to a problem. While some Pixar films focus on solving problems via intelligence, cooperation, and perseverance (Hentges & Case, 2013; Wooden & Gillam, 2014), these are far outnumbered by storylines in which violence is the solution.

Beyond physical aggression, studies have identified additional attributes commonly associated with masculinity. These include achieving a goal (Aubrey & Harrison, 2004); displaying power (Tanner, Haddock, Zimmerman, & Lund, 2003); demonstrating technical skills (Thompson & Zerbinos, 1995); and helping others (Hentges & Case, 2013). These attributes vary with genre and source. For example, physical aggression is more common in programming and channels targeted at boys than in girl-oriented programming (Hentges & Case, 2013). This means children—especially boys—learn that masculine men are inherently aggressive, and that violence is the appropriate response to "bad" guys. Even in films or franchises that posit alternative masculinities or depict masculinity as socially constructed, achieving a masculinity rooted in status and power is framed as the marker of maturation and success (Serrato, 2011). Masculine status and power further is often achieved in media texts at the expense of less masculine males (Wooden & Gillam, 2014) or female characters (Serrato, 2011) who are often cast as villains to be fought or victims to be saved.

When these texts circulate to girl viewers, girls likewise learn to accept aggression as an essential masculine feature. The popular male superhero genre exemplifies this messaging about physical aggression. When children see superheroes rewarded for fighting villains, they learn that fighting is an appropriately masculine solution (Bandura, 2009). Although some scholars disagree that violence in children's media should warrant concern (e.g., Freedman, 2002), a 2010 report in *Pediatrics* presented it as a problem on par with cigarette smoking: not impacting everyone who consumes it, but significant nevertheless (Strasburger, Jordan, & Donnerstein, 2010, p. 759).

For this reason, we pause when publications celebrate the increase in girl superheroes (Hopkins, 2002) without interrogating the problematic privileging of aggression and masculine values. To what extent do such shifts devalue traditionally feminine characteristics, like affection or nurturing? Hendershot (1998) rightly critiqued the ubiquity and intensity of these features in product-based programming targeted at girls, but it is rarely a concern that these features are underrepresented in male characters' personalities and in boys' media.

Masculinity is not a monolith, however. Despite the stereotypical association of masculinity and stoicism, children's films and television increasingly depict male characters as displaying emotion (Hentges & Case, 2013). Some films, like *Chicken Little* and *Cloudy with a Chance of Meatballs*, make counter-stereotypical behavior development pivotal to characters' evolution. For example, storylines portray fathers and sons as improving their relationships via displays of affection, emotional expression, and listening (Åström, 2015). We have only just begun to understand how patterns in masculine representations may differ when we compare channels, genres, and mediums.

(Hetero)sexual relationships in children's media. The norms of masculinity and femininity represented in children's media invariably impact the models of relationships presented in these texts. Taboos around meaningful, substantive discussion of sex and sexuality on children's television limit what is available to children (Lemish, 2010). As a result, compulsory heterosexuality continues to be the norm in most children's television. LGBT+ characters (especially children) remain extremely underrepresented and controversial. Some programs, notably *Steven Universe*, have begun to challenge this norm, but young children's media lag behind genres such as teen dramas in non-heterosexual representations. Given the potential educational and social value of substantive age-appropriate sexual health messages (Ward, Day, & Epstein, 2006), this absence is notable—particularly in relation to the simultaneous circulation of problematic heterosexual

scripts, or narratives about men and women's behaviors in romantic or sexual contexts (Hust, Brown, & Ladin L'Engle, 2008).

These narratives are more common in teen media, where explicit depictions of dating and sex are pervasive (Van Damme, 2010); but younger children's television heterosexual scripts, while less explicit, still create norms of gendered behavior. For example, one study of children's programs on Nick and Disney found boys frequently depicted as commenting on or valuing girls for their attractiveness and making the first move, while relegating girls to passive roles: flattering boys, dressing to impress them, and flirting passively (Kirsch & Murnen, 2015). These stereotypically gendered heterosexual scripts send problematic messages about dating-related behavioral norms to children just when they are beginning to imagine and experiment with romantic relationships.

Diversity within Gender: Intersectionality and Children's Gender Representation

We have mostly discussed gender as if an isolated characteristic, using "female characters" and "male characters" as catch-alls without considering differences in race, class, religion, and more. We have also treated gender representation through a male-female binary lens. To some extent, this reflects children's television norms, which with few exceptions (Jane, 2015) marks gender for humans, animals, and anthropomorphized objects alike (Birthisel, 2014). This pattern fails to account for the variety of gender orientations that children and their loved ones may inhabit, however. While children may begin to express a transgender identity as early as 3 or 4, the slow increase in trans representation rarely extends to programs for children or teens, and the few trans images available are rarely positive or accurate (Jennings, 2016). As shows such as *Annedroids* are beginning to depict nonbinary characters, potentially encouraging more flexible attitudes about gender in child viewers (Beck, Hains, & Russo, forthcoming), more work on spaces for gender queer or trans representation in children's media and on how children understand media in these ways is warranted.

The existing research on gender in children's media also largely fails to account for race. Race can be tricky in children's media, as characters are often racially ambiguous or non-human. Nonetheless, in a study of tween television, researchers found 84% of characters were racially classifiable: 68% were white, 7% were black, 4% were Asian, 1% were Latino, and 4% were characterized as "other" (Gerding & Signorielli, 2014). Another study of global children's television found female characters were more likely than males to be non-White (Gotz & Lemish, 2012). While diversity is positive, the researchers argued that this pattern reflects a problematic tendency of producers to "find an easy way out by having both marginalized groups in one character" (p. 32), doubly marginalizing them.

Race is a crucial variable that can affect gender representation. For example, according to one study of television commercials featuring children, White boys were more likely than boys of color to be shown in scenes containing aggression (Larson, 2003). Meanwhile, Lacroix (2004) argued Disney's non-White heroines from the 1990s were sexualized and framed as the "orientalized" exotic other—particularly via representations as objects of male characters' love and lust (Lacroix, 2004). These studies suggested an intersectional approach to research is important, and scholars are beginning to explore intersectionality's role in children's gendered media representations.

A study of *Doc McStuffins* and *Dora the Explorer* provides a useful model for approaching intersectionality in children's media. Keys (2016) explores how the shows' title characters' appearances, homes, and uses of language provide messages about their relationship to their racial identities and their class positions. She also considers how counter-stereotypical gendered behavior, like Doc's role as a doctor, expert, and leader, can work against racial and gender stereotypes—even while Doc's stereotypical gendered behavior, like her role as a nurturer, has stereotypical resonance via the historical lens of the Black "mammy" (Keys, 2016). Scholars have identified a similar dynamic with *Dora the Explorer*. On the one hand, *Dora's* ethnic representation reinforced a problematic universalized image of the Latinidades that erased national and racial specificity (Guidotti-Hernández, 2007) and traded on stereotypicalized "tropicalizing tropes" (Harewood & Valdivia, 2005) that cast Latina/os as the "other." On the other hand, *Dora's* role as an explorer, cartographer and teacher is potentially a valuable counter-stereotypical gender model (Guidotti-Hernández, 2007). To fully understand media representations' complexity, we need to consider how male and female characters' representations fit stereotypical models of visibility, appearance, and behavior, as well as how those representations intersect with race and class. Intersectional research on gender representation in children's media is urgently needed to address this question: What are children learning about the relationship between race and gender from media culture?

Conclusion

In this chapter, we do not mean to imply that all girls and all boys learn problematic, regressive lessons about gender from the media at all times. According to active audience theory, viewers are not simply passive dupes who accept the media's messages. As Projansky (2014) has argued, girls are often critical of female characters' depictions, rejecting the characteristics associated with a given gender; and as Hains (2012) reported, the African-American girls in her study of girl power were highly critical of how children's media and merchandise represented female characters of color.

Nevertheless, even though audience members are active viewers, the media serve a socializing function in our society and can constrain children's inner worlds (Lemish, 2010). It is promising that representations of gendered behaviors are shifting, with (for example) more masculine characters portrayed as in touch with their emotions, and more feminine characters portrayed as technologically savvy. Unfortunately, however, with children's media's increasing segmentation, progressive changes may not reach all children. Counter-stereotypical images of girls seem to be directed at boys, and vice-versa, but we believe both sexes would benefit from expanded ideas about what masculinity, femininity, and nonbinary gender identity may encompass. The content differences found between channels and genres indicate greater-than-expected complexity in lessons children learn about gender, but it is hard to gauge whether any child viewer is actually receiving more diverse and counter-stereotypical gender representations. In general, scripts of masculinity that emphasize aggression and violence still limit boys, just as scripts emphasizing appearance still limit girls.

In this rapidly changing context, how can we answer our main question? What *do* television and films teach kids about gender? Historically, the media have taught children that boys are more important than girls; that girls should be physically attractive, but that boys don't necessarily have to be; that only heterosexual relationships are valued; and that while it can be okay for girls to embrace boys' interests, boys should avoid the feminine at all costs. Children are often taught that if they fail to conform to the stereotypes associated with their sex, there will be consequences. However, these messages can be complex, with Disney Princesses appearing as both rescuer and relationship centered or male characters appearing as both aggressive and affectionate. We hope future research will explore the degree to which children learn and/or resist the lessons being taught by the media, particularly from an intersectional perspective.

Discussion Questions

1. When you were growing up, did you believe there were "girls' TV shows" and "boys' TV shows"? What do you think gave you this impression? Did you ever watch shows you believed were intended for the opposite sex? Why or why not?

2. When you were a child, do you recall identifying strongly with a television or movie character of the opposite sex? Who was it, and why did you identify with them?

3. Studies of gender representation often assume people identify with characters of their own sex. Is that true for you today? What factors might complicate this for viewers of various backgrounds?

4. What behaviors or other elements of representation haven't been accounted for in this chapter? Why do you think they should be?

Exercise

1. Visit the toy department of a large department store. At least one section is likely to be segregated into boys' toys and girls' toys, many of which are based on characters from children's media. Take careful notes on what you see, then analyze what messages about gender you saw in the toy department. Be descriptive and specific. Questions to consider include, but are not limited to, the following: What types of toys have been categorized as boys' toys? What types have been categorized as girls' toys? How can you tell the difference? Which categorizations surprised you, and why? Which did not—and why not? Did you find anything problematic about these categorizations?

References

Åström, B. (2015). Postfeminist fatherhood in the animated feature films *Chicken Little* and *Cloudy with a Chance of Meatballs*. *Journal of Children and Media, 9*(3), 294–307. doi:10.1080/17482798.2015.1048145

Aubrey, J. S., & Harrison, K. (2004). The gender role content of children's favorite television programs and its links to their gender-related perceptions. *Media Psychology, 6*(2), 111–146. doi:10.1207/s1532785xmep0602_1

Baker, K., & Raney, A. A. (2007). Equally super? Gender-role stereotyping of superheroes in children's animated programs. *Mass Communication and Society, 10*(1), 25–41. doi:10.1080/15205430709337003

Bandura, A. (2009). Social cognitive theory of mass communication. In J. Bryant & M. B. Oliver (Eds.), *Media effects: Advances in theory and research* (pp. 94–124). New York, NY: Routledge.

Beck, S. L., Hains, R. C., & Johnson, C. R. (forthcoming). "PAL can just be themself": Children respond to *Annedroids'* genderless TV character. In M. Gotz & D. Lemish (Eds.), *Beyond the stereotypes: Boys, girls, and their images*. Gothenburg: The International Clearinghouse on Children, Youth and Media, Nordicom.

Birthisel, J. (2014). How body, heterosexuality and patriarchal entanglements mark non-human characters as male in CGI-animated children's films. *Journal of Children and Media, 8*(4), 336–352. doi:10.1080/17482798.2014.960435

Calvert, S. L., Kotler, J. A., Zehnder, S., & Shockney, E. (2003). Gender-stereotyping in children's reports about educational and informational television programs. *Media Psychology, 5*(2), 139–162. doi:10/1207/S1532785X-MEP0502_2

Coyne, S. M., Linder, J. R., Rasmussen, E. E., Nelson, D. A., & Birbeck, V. (2016). Pretty as a princess: Longitudinal effects of engagement with Disney princesses on gender stereotypes, body esteem, and prosocial behavior in children. *Child Development, 87*(6), 1909–1925. doi:10.1111/cdev.12569

Coyne, S. M., Linder, J. R., Rasmussen, E. E., Nelson, D. A., & Collier K. M. (2014). It's a bird! It's a plane! It's a gender stereotype!: Longitudinal associations between superhero viewing and gender stereotyped play. *Sex Roles, 70*(9), 416–430. doi:10.1007/s11199-014-0374-8

Darlow, S., & Lobel, M. (2010). Who is beholding my beauty? Thinness ideals, weight, and women's responses to appearance evaluation. *Sex Roles, 63*(11–12), 833–843. doi:10.1007/s11199-010-9845-8

Donaghue, N., & Clemitshaw, A. (2012). "I'm totally smart and a feminist…and yet I want to be a waif": Exploring ambivalence towards the thin ideal within the fat acceptance movement. *Women's Studies International Forum, 35*(6), 415–425. doi:10.1016/j.wsif.2012.07.005

Engeln-Maddox, R. (2006). Buying a beauty standard or dreaming of a new life? Expectations associated with media ideals. *Psychology of Women Quarterly, 30*, 258–266. doi:10.1111/j.1471–6402.2006.00294.x

England, D. E., Descartes, L., & Collier-Meek, M. A. (2011). Gender role portrayal and the Disney princesses. *Sex Roles, 64*(7), 555–567. doi:10.1007/s11199-011-9930-7

Freedman, J. L. (2002). *Media violence and its effect on aggression: Assessing the scientific evidence.* Toronto: University of Toronto Press.

Garretson, J. (2009). *Changing media, changing minds: The lesbian and gay movement, television, and public opinion* (Doctoral dissertation). Nashville, TN: Vanderbilt University.

Gerding, A., & Signorielli, N. (2014). Gender roles in tween television programming: A content analysis of two genres. *Sex Roles, 70*(1), 43–56. doi:10.1007/s11199-013-0330-z

Gotz, M., & Herche, M. (2012). "Wasp waists and V-shape torso": Measuring the body of the "global" girl and boy in animated children's programs. In M. Gotz & D. Lemish (Eds.), *Sexy girls, heroes and funny losers: Gender representations in children's TV around the world.* New York, NY: Peter Lang.

Gotz, M., & Lemish, D. (Eds.). (2012). *Sexy girls, heroes and funny losers: Gender representations in children's TV around the world.* New York, NY: Peter Lang.

Guidotti-Hernández, N. (2007). *Dora The Explorer,* constructing "LATINIDADES" and the politics of global citizenship. *Latino Studies, 5*(2), 209–232. doi:10.1057/palgrave.lst.8600254

Hains, R. C. (2004). The problematics of reclaiming the girlish: *The Powerpuff Girls* and girl power. *Femspec, 5*(2), 1–39.

Hains, R. C. (2007). Pretty smart: Subversive intelligence in girl power cartoons. In S. A. Inness (Ed.), *Geek chic: Smart women in popular culture* (pp. 65–84). New York, NY: Palgrave Macmillan.

Hains, R. C. (2012). *Growing up with girl power: Girlhood on screen and in everyday life.* New York, NY: Peter Lang.

Hains, R. C. (2014). *The princess problem: Guiding our girls through the princess-obsessed years.* Naperville, IL: Sourcebooks.

Halim, M. L., Ruble, D., Tamis-LeMonda, C., & Shrout, P. (2013). Rigidity in gender-typed behaviors in early childhood: A longitudinal study of ethnic minority children. *Child Development, 84*(4), 1269–1284. doi:10.1111/cdev.12057

Harewood, S. J., & Valdivia, A. (2005). Exploring Dora: Re-embedded Latinidad on the web. In S. Mazzarella (Ed.), *Girl Wide Web: Girls, the Internet and the negotiation of identity* (pp. 85–104). New York, NY: Peter Lang.

Harriger, J. A., Calogero, R. M., Witherington, D. C., & Smith, J. E. (2010). Body size stereotyping and internalization of the thin ideal in preschool girls. *Sex Roles, 63*(9–10), 609–620. doi:10.1007/s11199-010-9868-1

Hendershot, H. (1998). *Saturday morning censors: Television regulation before the V-Chip.* Durham, NC: Duke University Press.

Hentges, B., & Case, K. (2013). Gender representations on Disney Channel, Cartoon Network and Nickelodeon broadcasts in the United States. *Journal of Children and Media, 7*(3), 319–333. doi:10.1080/17482798.2012.729150

Herbozo, S., Tantleff-Dunn, S., Gokee-Larose, J., & Thompson, J. K. (2004). Beauty and thinness messages in children's media: A content analysis. *Eating Disorders, 12*(1), 21–34. doi:10.1080/10640260490267742

Hopkins, S. (2002). *Girl heroes: The new force in popular culture.* London: Pluto.

Hunting, K., Grumbein, A., & Cahill, M. (2016, July). *Schooled! Gender and education on children's television.* Leicester, UK: International Association for Media and Communication Research.

Hust, S., Brown J. D., & Ladin L'Engle, K. (2008). Boys will be boys and girls better be prepared: An analysis of the rare sexual health messages in young adolescents' media. *Mass Communication & Society, 11*(1), 3–23. doi:10.1080/15205430701668139

Jane, E. A. (2015). "Gunter's a woman?!" – Doing and undoing gender in Cartoon Network's *Adventure Time*. *Journal of Children and Media, 9*(5), 231–247. doi:10.1080/17482798.2015.1024002

Jennings, N. (2016). I am who I am: Media, identity, and transgender youth. *Televizion, 29*, 33–35. Retrieved from http://www.br-online.de/jugend/izi/english/publication/televizion/29_2016_E/Jennings-I_am_who_I_am.pdf

Keys, J. (2016). *Doc McStuffins* and *Dora the Explorer:* Representations of gender, race, and class in US animation. *Journal of Children and Media, 10*(3), 355–368. doi:10.1080/17482798.2015.1127835

Kirsch, A. C., & Murnen, S. K. (2015). "Hot girls and "cool dudes": Examining the prevalence of the heterosexual script in American children's television media. *Psychology of Popular Media Culture, 4*(1), 18–30. doi:10/1037/ppm0000017

Lacroix, C. (2004). Images of animated others: The orientalization of Disney's cartoon heroines from the Little Mermaid to the Hunchback of Notre Dame. *Popular Communication, 2*(4), 213–229. doi:10.1207/s15405710pc0204_2

Larson, M. S. (2003). Gender, race and aggression in television commercials that feature children. *Sex Roles, 48*(1), 67–75. doi:10.1023/A:1022396729398

Leaper, C., Breed, L., Hoffman, L., & Perlman, C. (2002). Variations in the gender-stereotyped content of children's television cartoons across genres. *Journal of Applied Social Psychology, 32*(8), 1653–1662. doi:10.1111/j.1559–1816.2002.tb02767.x

Lemish, D. (2010). *Screening gender on children's television: The views of producers around the world.* New York, NY: Routledge.

Levina, M., Waldo, C. R., & Fitzgerald, L. F. (2000). We're here, we're queer, we're on TV: The effects of visual media on heterosexuals' attitudes toward gay men and lesbians. *Journal of Applied Psychology, 30*(4), 738–758. doi:10.1111/j.1559–1816.2000.tb02821.x

Li-Vollmer, M., & LaPointe, M. E. (2003). Gender transgression and villainy in animated film. *Popular Communication: The International Journal of Media and Culture, 1*(2), 89–109. doi:10.1207/S15405710PC0102_2

Luther, C. A., & Legg Jr., J. R. (2010). Gender differences in depictions of social and physical aggression in children's television cartoons in the US. *Journal of Children and Media, 4*(10), 191–205. doi:10.1080/17482791003629651

Manago, A. M., Ward, L. M., Lemm, K. M., Reed, L., & Seabrook, R. (2014). Facebook involvement, objectified body consciousness, body shame, and sexual assertiveness in college women and men. *Sex Roles, 72*(1), 1–14. doi:10.1007/s11199-014–0441-1

Mesoudi, A. (2011). *Cultural evolution: How Darwinian theory can explain human culture and synthesize the social sciences.* Chicago, IL: University of Chicago Press.

Paoletti, J. (2012). *Pink and blue: Telling the boys from the girls in America.* Bloomington, IN: Indiana University Press.

Perloff, R. M. (2009). The third person effect: A critical review and synthesis. *Media Psychology, 1*(4), 353–378. doi:10.1207/s1532785xmep0104_4

Projansky, S. (2014). *Spectacular girls: Media fascination and celebrity culture.* New York, NY: New York University Press.

Serrato, P. (2011). From "booger breath" to "the guy": Juni Cortez grows up in Robert Rodriguez's *Spy Kids* trilogy. In A. Wannamaker (Ed.), *Mediated boyhoods: Boys, teens, and young men in popular media and culture* (pp. 81–96). New York, NY: Peter Lang.

Shen, C., Ratan, R., Cai, Y. D., & Leavitt, A. (2016). Do men advance faster than women? Debunking the gender performance gap in two massively multiplayer online games. *Journal of Computer-Mediated Communication, 21*(4), 312–329. doi:10.1111/jcc4.12159

Smith, S. L., & Cook, C. A. (2008). *Gender stereotypes: An analysis of popular films and TV.* Los Angeles, CA: The Geena Davis Institute for Gender and Media. Retrieved from https://seejane.org/wp-content/uploads/GDIGM_Gender_Stereotypes.pdf

Smith, S. L., Pieper, K. M., Granados, A., & Choueiti, M. (2010). Assessing gender-related portrayals in top-gross G-rated films. *Sex Roles, 62*(11), 774–786. doi:10.1007/s11199-009–9736-z

Strasburger, V. C., Jordan, A., & Donnerstein, E. (2010). Health effects of media on children and adolescents. *Pediatrics, 125*(4), 756–767. doi:10.1542/peds.2009–2563

Tanner, L. R., Haddock, S. A., Zimmerman, T. S., & Lund, L. K. (2003). Images of couples and families in Disney feature-length animated films. *The American Journal of Family Therapy, 31*(5), 355–373. doi:10.1080/01926180390223987

Thompson, T. L., & Zerbinos, E. (1995). Gender roles in animated cartoons: Has the picture changed in 20 years? *Sex Roles, 32*(9/10), 651–673. doi:10.1007/BF01544217

Tylka, T. L., & Sabik, N. J. (2010). Integrating social comparison theory and self-esteem within objectification theory to predict women's disordered eating. *Sex Roles, 63*, 18–31. doi:10.1007/s11199-010–9785-3

Van Damme, E. (2010). Gender and sexual scripts in popular US teen series: A study on the gender discourses in *One Tree Hill* and *Gossip Girl*. *Catalan Journal of Communication & Cultural Studies, 2*(1), 77–92. doi:10.1386/cjcs.2.1.77_1

Wannamaker, A. (2011). Introduction: "Media bout boys, for boys and by boys". In A. Wannamaker (Ed.), *Mediated boyhoods: Boys, teens, and young men in popular media and culture* (pp. 1–14). New York, NY: Peter Lang.

Ward, L. M. (2005). Children, adolescents, and the media: The molding of minds, bodies, and deeds. *New Directions for Child and Adolescent Development, 109*, 63–71. doi:10.1002/cd.138

Ward, L. M., Day, K. M., & Epstein, M. (2006). Uncommonly good: Exploring how mass media may be a positive influence on young women's sexual health and development. *New Directions for Child and Adolescent Development, 112*, 57–70. doi:10.1002/cd.162

Wooden, S., & Gillam, K. (2014). *Pixar's boy stories: Masculinity in a postmodern age.* Lanham, MD: Rowman and Littlefield.

CHAPTER 12

Is Educational Media
an Oxymoron?

Jessica Taylor Piotrowski

In his now classic 1998 piece, Daniel Anderson, one of the leading academicians of youth and media research, posed the question—"is educational television an oxymoron?" At the time, children's educational television—defined as television explicitly designed with the intention to support the academic or social skills of its viewers—was receiving increased attention with American shows such as *Sesame Street* and *Mister Roger's Neighborhood* making their mark in young children's lives. Yet, at the same time, these and other similar shows were coming under increased criticism from individuals who believed that, rather than support children's healthy development, this content was "inimical to the intellectual development of children" (Anderson, 1998, p. 25). Indeed, in two popular trade books of the time (*The Plug-In Drug* and *Unplugging the Plug-In Drug*), Marie Winn argued that television was problematic for young viewers and a detriment to children's healthy cognitive development (Winn, 1985, 1987). She argued that television's (particularly *Sesame Street's*) constant movement and scene changes induced a form of addiction which ultimately would induce passivity and produced shortened attention spans among young viewers. These concerns, and others like them, were similarly echoed in other trade publications of the time including *Four Arguments for the Elimination of Television* (Mander, 1978), *Growing Up on Television* (Moody, 1980), *Amusing Ourselves to Death* (Postman, 2006), and *Endangered Minds: Why Our Children Don't Think* (Healy, 1990). Healy's book, in particular, provided a rather damning attack against *Sesame Street*—arguing that television provides experiences inappropriate for healthy brain development during the formative years and, as a result, the language skills of the so-called "TV generation" had deteriorated along with children's ability to follow or produce argumentation (Anderson, 1998).

Anderson, in his 1998 article, questioned the sentiment that television was uniformly harmful for children not only because such argumentation was based largely on anecdotal data, but because his scholarship and the work of others suggested an alternative view. Rather than showing that children were cognitively-inactive television zombies, his work and other emerging scholarship demonstrated that young children are "intellectually active when they watch television; they selectively attend to aspects of the program content that they find potentially comprehensible and interesting, ignoring those parts of programs that are uninteresting" (p. 28). Moreover, Anderson highlighted a bulk of empirical evidence showing that young children who consumed a diet of *Sesame Street* and other similar programs performed *better* on school readiness and vocabulary assessments than children who watched other kinds of television content. In other words, contrary to the fearful rhetoric propagated by Healy and others, Anderson argued that children are active television viewers who, when confronted with well-designed developmentally-appropriate educational television, can experience both cognitive and social-emotional benefits. Far from an oxymoron, his review demonstrated that educational television may be, as Linebarger and Wainwright (2007) suggest, a "dream come true" wherein the highly-popular entertainment medium of television can be successfully harnessed to support children's healthy development.

Anderson's piece focused specifically on educational television, particularly on *Sesame Street*. At its time, this focus was a reasonable one as television was amongst the only media form available for children. Video-on-demand services, computers, touchscreen technology, video chat, social media, interactive toys, and other developments from the digital revolution were just beginning to enter the media sphere, and there was certainly little (if any) research on their potential for educational outcomes. Yet today we are working in a far different space. While television continues to reign supreme, there have been significant advancements in the quality and format of this media content. The television landscape is a cluttered one with options far exceeding those of the 1990s. Alongside this, children not only have access to this media content on-demand, but they also have access to a host of games that can played on the family computer or on their (parents') iPads or iPhones. And through all of this change, educational media has evolved too. It is no longer limited to a host of publicly-funded television shows, but instead can be found across today's diverse media landscape in a range of formats and styles for a range of audiences. With such change, it seems high time to revisit Anderson's original question, focusing not only on television but the wide array of media content now available.

As such, the aim of this chapter is to answer the question *is educational* **media** *an oxymoron?* To answer the question, the chapter takes a three-fold approach beginning with a brief history. It then summarizes two key theories used to explain how educational media effects occur, followed by the review of key findings on educational media effects. Following Anderson, this chapter defines educational media as that which has been developed with the *explicit intent* to support the academic or social development of children. Moreover, this chapter focuses on the use of such media in the home context as a tool for informal learning.

The Historical Landscape

Educational media secured its place in history with the arrival of *Sesame Street* in 1969. At its time revolutionary, *Sesame Street* was developed to help prepare young children for school by focusing on developmentally-appropriate academic and social-emotional curricula. While there were other educational programs available for children at the time, *Sesame*'s reliance on empirical research throughout the production process helped distinguish it from other programs. Specifically, throughout the design process, developers relied on the input of experts who understand children's developmental and pedagogical needs. Rather than separating creatives from child development experts, these individuals work together to develop content—testing this content throughout its development (formative research) and after its completion (summative research) in order to ensure that the content meets its intended goals (see also Fisch & Truglio, 2001). To this day, *Sesame Street* continues to rely on this approach and has become one of the leading exemplars of how to effectively bridge research with practice.

The popularity and success of *Sesame Street* and other similar shows (e.g., *Mister Roger's Neighborhood, Barney & Friends*) began to create quite a stir by the late 1990s, particularly in the United States. Not only were these programs experiencing reasonable financial success, but they were regarded positively by parents, teachers, and practitioners, enjoyed by children, and most excitingly, empirical research was converging to support the short *and* long-term benefits of well-developed educational media (namely, educational television). As a result, this approach of embedding academic and social-emotional curricula into media content began to catch on and, by 1996, educational media (specifically, television) was not only a mainstay in the children's media landscape but became a public mandate, at least in the United States. Specifically, in 1996, the Children's Television Act (CTA) in the United States was launched—a law that the Federal Communication Commission (FCC) implemented requiring broadcast stations to air three hours of Educational/Information (E/I) children's programming weekly. (See Chapter 2 for more details.) And while the CTA often lead to efforts which met the letter more than the spirit of the law (Jordan, 2004), the fact that public policy was encouraging the proliferation of children's educational television made a clear statement that children can and do benefit from such content (Anderson, 1998).

Today, educational media are firmly entrenched in children's media diets. Estimates show that American children between two and ten years of age spend about an hour per day with educational media—with similar estimates in other industrialized countries around the world (Rideout, 2014; Szybist, 2011). And, more than ever before, even the youngest "diaper demographic" is getting in on the action with the littlest eyes using screen media (primarily educational screen media) for nearly one hour per day (Wartella, Rideout, Lauricella, & Connell, 2013). Yet, this use tends to be unequally distributed with nearly 78% of children two to four years of age using educational media daily compared with only 27% of eight to ten year olds (Rideout, 2014).

While some argue these differences may reflect the fact that as children enter formal schooling they have less discretionary time for media use, the more likely argument is that there are fewer educational media options for children as they get older. Thanks in part to the regulatory climate, a growth in niche media, and a realization that educational media can make money, the educational media market for young children is a crowded one (Hendershot, 2004; Lemish, 1987; Piotrowski, 2014b; Valkenburg & Vroone, 2004). This is particularly true for the very youngest demographic. Yet, at the same time, the available options for children in middle childhood and adolescence are markedly smaller, and when available, tend to fall into the category of "chocolate-covered broccoli" (i.e., they are interpreted as *too* educational and not sufficiently entertaining by the intended audience). This trend highlights a missed opportunity as well as the challenges that developers face in creating content which is equally entertaining *and* educational for an audience that is increasingly critical of media content. Related to this downtrend in use, it is equally possible that this change reflects the "spinach syndrome"—a period of time starting around five years of age when children begin to reject anything that is supposed to be good for them (Valkenburg & Piotrowski, 2017). Nonetheless, it is clear that educational media continues to find its way into children's everyday lives.

The Theoretical Landscape

Of course, knowing that educational media is accessible and used by young people is only a first step in answering the question as to whether educational media is any oxymoron. It is also necessary to understand how educational media are expected to teach. Several scholars have attempted to explain educational media effects, most notably Albert Bandura with his social cognitive theory and Shalom Fisch with his capacity model.

Social Cognitive Theory

Social cognitive theory (SCT) (Bandura, 2009) is one of the most commonly used theories to explain why and how media can influence the behavior of children (also see Chapter 6). Often referred to as observational learning theory, SCT goes beyond mere imitation and instead argues that, by observing behavior, audiences learn more abstract rules about behavior which can then be applied in future situations.

In order to learn these abstract rules, Bandura posits that four cognitive processes must occur. First, *attention* to the model and the model's behavior is critical. Different characteristics of models can elicit differing levels of attention. In the case of educational television, for example, television characters such as *Dora the Explorer's* Boots (an animated monkey) have distinctive and engaging features which easily attract attention (e.g., animation, animal, wacky voice). Attention is also influenced by characteristics of the child, such as their own needs and interests. As such, SCT predicts that that most effective educational content will be content that attracts and sustains attention to the key lessons in the content *while* mapping onto the child's own needs and interests.

Once a child attends to the educational content, SCT argues the next step is *retention*. In terms of educational media, it is often the case that there is a significant time lag between media exposure and the performance of the behavior. For example, children may be watching a television program that aims to teach inclusivity, yet it may be a significant period of time until the child is faced with a situation in which s/he is called upon to use this information in practice. SCT acknowledges that the observer can only model the behavior if s/he has retained the information. While such retention is difficult to guarantee, retention is generally superior when it connects well to the background knowledge of the audience and when it is repeated frequently, giving the user time to encode the content in his/her knowledge structures.

Assuming the observer has retained the information, SCT explains that the child must then be able to engage in *motoric reproduction*. In other words, the child must be able to convert the stored information into behaviors that s/he can actually do. Thus, the messages that children receive in educational media must be ones that they can actually enact. Finally, even if the observer is able to do the behavior, s/he needs to be *motivated* to do so. While children's own motivation helps here, this motivation can also come from external reinforcement in his/her environment. This is where adult caregivers can play a role in helping ensure that children are motivated to use what they have learned.

Capacity Model

The capacity model (CM) (Fisch, 2004), with its roots in information processing research, is a model designed to explain how children extract and comprehend educational content from educational television. Central to the model is the supposition that working memory is limited and, for content to be processed effectively, the demands of the viewing task cannot exceed the resources available in the working memory. The CM focuses on children's allocation of cognitive resources during television viewing, with specific attention to the degree to which working memory resources are allocated to the narrative versus educational content.

Narrative content is defined as content which presents the story in the program whereas educational content is the underlying concept or message which the program is intended to convey. For example, in an episode of *Dora the Explorer*, a character (Benny the Bull) experiences distress as his hot air balloon develops a hole and, without help, he will soon crash into Crocodile River. During the narrative, Benny's friends (Dora and Boots) set out to rescue Benny before he crashes. In order to rescue Benny, Dora and Boots must navigate several tricky situations, all of which require numeracy and color recognition skills to solve (the educational content embedded within the narrative).

According to the CM, cognitive demands are said to come from three basic elements: (1) processing the narrative, (2) processing the educational content, and (3) the distance between the two. Distance refers to the relationship between the narrative and educational content. The CM predicts that educational media will be most effective when the distance between content types is minimized so that, rather than being seemingly unrelated to one another, the narrative and educational content are so complementary that neither can exist on their own. The CM further predicts that factors that allow for improved processing of either content type will reduce cognitive resources and subsequently increase comprehension. These factors may be viewer characteristics (e.g., story understanding can improve narrative comprehension, resulting in greater resources for educational content; Piotrowski, 2014b) or programmatic characteristics (e.g., participatory cues can encourage greater engagement with educational television content; Piotrowski, 2014a).

In total, the capacity model predicts five ways that learning from educational media can be increased: (a) by increasing the total amount of working memory resources devoted to understanding the television program as a whole, (b) by reducing the demands of processing the narrative, (c) by reducing the demands of the educational content, (d) by minimizing the distance between narrative and educational content in the program, and (e) via viewers' voluntary allocation of a greater proportion of working memory resources to the processing of educational content. While evidence to support the CM is not as robust as that of SCT, recently, researchers have demonstrated the accuracy of these predictions with young children's learning from educational television (e.g., Piotrowski, 2014a, 2014b).

Importantly, however, one must acknowledge that this capacity model was developed explicitly for television. While researchers (e.g., Kirkorian & Anderson, 2009) do argue it can easily be applied to other educational media as well (e.g., videogames), it remains unclear at this time how well this application works. In response to the new educational media environment Fisch has introduced the Capacity Model 2.0, a model designed to understand learning from educational games (Fisch, 2016). Like its predecessor, the model pays careful attention to the relationship between narrative and educational content in determining allocation of working memory. However, the 2.0 version also notes that the *gameplay* (i.e., defined as usability, game design, and player characteristics) of digital-based educational media *also* influences working memory allocation. This new model highlights the importance of ensuring minimal distance between educational content and gameplay so that gaming elements work to support educational content rather than drain valuable cognitive resources. While as of this writing there exists no empirical evaluation of the CM 2.0, it is certainly an important theoretical advancement to help explain how children can learn from educational media in the 21st century.

The Empirical Landscape

Guided by predictions of theories such as SCT and the CM, researchers have been conducting investigations to evaluate whether, when, and if educational media meets its intended goals. This work has primarily focused on television, although in recent years there has been influx of empirical studies on digital content as well. Importantly, there are key developmental trends in the availability of empirical scholarship on educational media. In particular, work with children under two takes on a decidedly different tone and focus than work with older children.

Infants and Toddlers

For the very youngest children (under the age of two), the great majority of existing scholarship has focused on whether they can learn academic skills from media and how this learning compares to learning from adult role models (Courage & Setliff, 2009). All told, there is robust evidence to suggest that very young children are better able to learn from adult role models compared to media models (a phenomenon often referred to as a "video-deficit"). However, this does not mean they do not benefit from educational media. In fact, they do. Not only can very young children learn from media, but this video deficit can be reduced or even neutralized when the educational content is repeated (Barr, Muentener, Garcia, Fujimoto, & Chávez, 2007), when the child is familiar with media models delivering the content (Lauricella, Gola, & Calvert, 2011), or when parents discuss this content during and beyond the media experience (often referred to as scaffolding; Linebarger & Vaala, 2010).

The question as to whether children under two years of age learn from media has emerged in response to a long-standing debate as to whether screen media should even be a part of very young children's lives. Initially, many public policy organizations suggested that children under two should not be exposed to any screen media content because of the potential detrimental effects on development (see, for example, American Academy of Pediatrics Committee on Public Education, 2001). These statements were more of a cautionary tale, however, as there was limited evidence to support this recommendation. Recent recommendations have softened this stance. For example, the AAP now suggests that, for very young children (under 18 months), screen media use should be avoided except in the case of video-chatting (Reid Chassiakos *et al.*, 2016). Starting around 18 months of age, the AAP supports the occasional use of developmentally-appropriate high-quality media content, particularly when co-viewed or co-played with parents, while continuing to emphasize the importance of media-free time (e.g. during dinner, driving, or playtime) and media-free locations (e.g., bedrooms). This revised stance has been informed by newer scholarship which suggests that, rather than passive experiences, well-developed media (particularly digital games and apps) can provide very young children with experiences that echo traditional active play patterns and, in doing so, promote rather than hinder development (Christakis, 2014; see also Kirkorian, Choi, & Pempek, 2016).

Preschoolers and Older Children

The majority of existing research on educational media has concentrated on early to middle children (three to ten years of age), with only a handful of studies looking at the effects of such media during the (pre-) teen years. These studies have generally clustered around the effects of educational media on academic skills and social-emotional skills.

Academic Skills. Evidence in support of educational media on academic skills is substantial. More than 1,000 studies, for example, have examined the influence of *Sesame Street* on children's early academic skills, with the vast majority demonstrating its ability to support young children's learning (Fisch, 2004). The longest-ranging evidence for the impact of *Sesame Street* comes from a longitudinal study in which researchers found that children who watched the program as a youngster spent more time reading and in educational activities during childhood, and impressively, these effects seemed to carry over to school performance in adolescence (Anderson, Huston, Schmitt, Linebarger, & Wright, 2001). Moreover, just recently, scholars evaluated data from what they referred to as a "natural experiment" in which American children with access to *Sesame Street* during the preschool years were compared with peers who did not have such access. Results indicated that children with access performed better in school than their counterparts without access, particularly among boys, non-Hispanic Black children, and children growing up in low-economic environments (Kearney & Levine, 2015). Importantly, these findings are not relegated to the American context. A recent meta-analysis on the effects of the international co-productions of *Sesame Street* in 15 countries revealed significant positive effects of the program on children's school readiness skills (Mares & Pan, 2013).

Sesame Street is not the only program that has been shown to support early academic skills. Experimental research with *Super Why!*, an animated literacy-based television show, also found that children aged three to six outperformed their non-viewing peers on nearly all literacy outcomes (Linebarger, 2015) while experimental research with the literacy program *Between the Lions* demonstrated similar literacy gains for children six-to-eight years of age (particularly among those moderately at-risk for literacy deficits) (Linebarger, Kosanic, Greenwood, & Doku, 2004). Moreover, programs such as *Barney and Friends, Dragon Tales, Blue's Clues,* and *Pinky Dinky Doo* (Fisch, 2004) and, more recently literacy-focused educational apps (Neuman, 2015), have also been linked with positive gains.

The few studies investing the effects of educational media on the academic skills of older children and teens have also found positive effects. Experimental research with the math-focused program *Cyberchase*, for example, showed that viewers of the program demonstrated improved problem-solving skills after only four weeks of viewing of the show (Fisch, 2003). These findings were particularly robust when the program content was combined with the ancillary website content (Fisch, Lesh, Motoki, Crespo, & Melfi, 2010). Similarly, evaluations of *Bill Nye the Science Guy* and *The Magic School Bus* (i.e., science programs targeting older children) showed that viewers had improved understanding of scientific concepts and the process of scientific discovery when compared to non-viewers (Fisch, 2004).

Social-emotional skills. When people use the term "educational media," it is common to think of content that supports traditional academic skills. However, as the founders of *Sesame Street* noted in the 1970s, academic skills are only one portion of the lessons that media can teach. Educational media are equally suited to teach social-emotional skills. That said, research on this topic is more limited, particularly amongst young children, and has thus far focused primarily on prosocial behavior, self-regulation, and emotion recognition.

Prosocial behavior refers to a range of positive behaviors including positive interactions, altruism, and behaviors that reduce stereotypes (Mares, Palmer, & Sullivan, 2011; see also Chapter 13). More than thirty studies have been conducted to identify whether and how pro-social media content (primarily television) might contribute to children's prosocial behavior. A 2007 meta-analysis of this work revealed that children who watched more prosocial television do indeed exhibit more prosocial behavior, particularly when prosocial behaviors were explic-itly modeled in the shows (Mares & Woodard, 2007). Moreover, children's age influenced this relationship. The effects of prosocial media seem to increase sharply during early childhood, peak in middle childhood (age seven), and then decline throughout the tween and teen years.

Mares and Woodard (2007) believe that the peak around age seven implies that younger children may not yet fully understand the prosocial content on television, and may especially have difficulty extracting the prosocial messages from media content. However, why would the effect decline during the tween and teen years? A possible explanation might be that the pro-grams included in the meta-analysis were less appealing to older children. If more age appropri-ate and appealing programs were available, the effects of might have held equally among older children. Several newer studies confirm that appealing developmentally-appropriate prosocial content can lead to prosocial behavior among older children and teens. For example, tweens' and teens' who watched of an episode of a teen-targeted news program featuring prosocial action for UNICEF were more likely to donate to UNICEF than watching an episode without proso-cial action modeled (de Leeuw, Kleemans, Rozendaal, Anschütz, & Buijzen, 2015). Similarly, Gentile and colleagues found robust evidence to support the argument that playing video games in which characters model prosocial behavior increases players' short and long-term prosocial behaviors (Gentile *et al.*, 2009).

While prosocial behavior is perhaps the most frequently studied in the context of social-emotional benefits of educational media, there are other expressions of social-emotional learning which media may also support. Indeed, in recent years we have seen an influx of media content designed to support other aspects of social-emotional development. For example, there are numerous apps which purport to teach children about emotions (e.g., *Daniel Tiger's Grr-ific Feelings, Inside Out: Storybook Deluxe*) or even empathy (e.g., *Peppy Pals*). New television shows have also been added to the children's television landscape which focus on emotional develop-ment (e.g., *Daniel Tiger's Neighborhood*), and we have seen Disney opt to focus on emotions in its movie *Inside Out*—an animated film focusing on a young girl's emotions as she moves with her parents across the country. And, in recent years, we have seen the American version of *Sesame Street* place a key emphasis on the development of self-regulatory skills (Season 44) and kindness (Season 47).

Although empirical work is limited to support these initiatives, early findings are promis-ing. For example, an experimental study investigated whether *Sesame Street's* efforts to teach self-regulation via the loveable Cookie Monster (a poster child for teaching self-regulation!) were effective. Using the classic marshmallow task to assess gratification delay, results showed that viewers of the Cookie Monster content were able to wait on average nearly four minutes longer than non-viewers before enjoying their marshmallow treat (Linebarger, 2014). Simi-larly, Rasmussen and colleagues, in their experimental study, investigated the effects of *Daniel Tiger's Neighborhood* on a range of social-emotional outcomes. Results revealed that viewers of the program who are accustomed to active parental media mediation, compared to their non-viewing peers, exhibited higher levels of empathy, self-efficacy, and emotional recognition

(Rasmussen *et al.*, 2016). And, more generally, researchers have found that a media diet which consists primarily of prosocial media content led to increased social and emotional competence for children three to five years old (Christakis *et al.*, 2013).

Is Educational Media an Oxymoron?

So, is educational media an oxymoron? When Dan Anderson wrote his 1998 manuscript, he was confronting a myriad of publications which suggested that television was harmful for children. He countered this rhetoric by showing that children are active television consumers (not passive zombies!) and that developmentally-appropriate television content designed with the explicit intent to support academic or social-emotional outcomes exists. Rather than an oxymoron, he demonstrated that educational television is a powerful tool that can support healthy development of youngsters. Nearly two decades later, the naysayers still abound. We increasingly hear arguments that the new media environment is making all of us, children included, mentally lazier and leading to what some call *digital dementia* (Spitzer, 2012). We hear commentators lament that media is making children more violent, sexualizing them too soon, and increasing their narcissism. And while it is absolutely fair to assert that some media does have negative consequences for its users, this is not true of all media. As this chapter shows, developmentally-appropriate media designed with the explicit intent to support academic and social-emotional skills exists. This does not mean that all educational media is equally effective for all users. Instead, as the predictions of both SCT and the CM make clear, these effects are dependent on the successful merging of content and audience characteristics. Creating developmentally-appropriate educational media content is not easy. Finding the sweet spot between entertainment and educational content is complicated, and this is made only more complicated when factoring in individual audience differences. But it is possible to create media content, whether it be analogue or digital, that supports children's academic and social-emotional development. Far from being an oxymoron, educational media is a promising and powerful educational opportunity for millions of children worldwide.

Discussion Questions

1. Reflect on the age findings in the meta-analysis by Mares & Woodard related to prosocial media content. Are these findings (or the interpretations of these findings) in line with either of the theories discussed in this chapter? Explain.

2. The chapter concludes by noting that educational media is not easy to create. Why? Consider your answer within the context of "chocolate-covered broccoli" and "spinach-syndrome".

3. Is educational media an oxymoron? Why or why not?

Exercises

1. Find and download an educational app that targets a child under the age of five from the AppStore. Along with this, download the document "Best Practices: Designing Touch Tablet Experiences for Preschoolers" created by Sesame Workshop <http://bit.ly/SesameTabletBestPractices>. Analyze the app within the context of this document. Which aspects of the app do you think, based on these best practices, are effective? What could be improved, and how?

2. Visit YouTube and watch recent episode from Sesame Street's Season 47 (kindness). Design a study to test whether this kindness curriculum will work. What will your design look like? Who is your audience? What will you measure? How will you measure it?

3. You have been asked to develop a new television show to encourage empathy skills in teens. Reflecting on what you know from Social Cognitive Theory and the Capacity Model, as well as what you know about the importance of bridging entertaining and educational content, what should this content look like? What should be avoided?

4. You have been asked by a local news media organization to write a 300 word article, for parents, on the potential benefits of media and provide them advice on selecting media for their child(ren). Your article should be succinct, clear, and accessibly written (jargon-free).

References

American Academy of Pediatrics Committee on Public Education. (2001). Children, adolescents, and television. *Pediatrics, 107*(2), 423–426.

Anderson, D. R. (1998). Educational television is not an oxymoron. *Annals of the American Academy of Political and Social Science, 557*(1), 24–38. doi:10.1177/0002716298557000003

Anderson, D. R., Huston, A. C., Schmitt, K. L., Linebarger, D. L., & Wright, J. C. (2001). Early childhood television viewing and adolescent behavior: The recontact study. *Monographs of the Society for Research in Child Development, 66*(1), 1–143.

Bandura, A. (2009). Social cognitive theory of mass communication. In J. Bryant & M. B. Oliver (Eds.), *Media effects: Advances in theory and research* (pp. 94–124). New York, NY: Routledge.

Barr, R., Muentener, P., Garcia, A., Fujimoto, M., & Chávez, V. (2007). The effect of repetition on imitation from television during infancy. *Developmental Psychobiology, 49*(2), 196–207. doi:10.1002/dev.20208

Christakis, D. A. (2014). Infants and interactive media use – Reply. *JAMA Pediatrics, 168*(10), 969–970. doi:10.1001/jamapediatrics.2014.748

Christakis, D. A., Garrison, M. M., Herrenkohl, T., Haggerty, K., Rivara, F. P., Zhou, C., & Liekweg, K. (2013). Modifying media content for preschool children: A randomized controlled trial. *Pediatrics, 131*(3), 431–438. doi:10.1542/peds.2012–1493

Courage, M. L., & Setliff, A. E. (2009). Debating the impact of television and video material on very young children: Attention, learning, and the developing brain. *Child Development Perspectives, 3*(1), 72–78. doi:10.1111/j.1750–8606.2008.00080.x

de Leeuw, R. N. H., Kleemans, M., Rozendaal, E., Anschütz, D. J., & Buijzen, M. (2015). The impact of prosocial television news on children's prosocial behavior: An experimental study in the Netherlands. *Journal of Children and Media, 9*(4), 419–434. doi:10.1080/17482798.2015.1089297

Fisch, S. M. (2003). *The impact of cyberchase on children's mathematical problem solving.* Teaneck, NJ: MediaKidz Research & Consulting. Retrieved from http://www-tc.pbskids.org/cyberchase/parentsteachers/show/pdf/Fisch_executivesummaryFINAL.pdf

Fisch, S. M. (2004). *Children's learning from educational television.* Mahwah, NJ: Lawrence Erlbaum.

Fisch, S. M. (2016). *The capacity model 2.0: Cognitive processing in children's comprehension of educational games*. Paper presented at the Society for Research in Children's Development: Special Topics Media on Technology and Children's Development, Irvine, CA.

Fisch, S. M., Lesh, R., Motoki, E., Crespo, S., & Melfi, V. (2010). *Children's learning from multiple media in informal mathematics education*. Retrieved from http://www-tc.pbskids.org/cyberchase//parentsteachers/show/pdf/ExecSumm_Cyberchase_MultMedia.pdf

Fisch, S. M., & Truglio, R. T. (Eds.). (2001). *"G" is for growing: Thirty years of research on children and Sesame Street*. Mahwah, NJ: Lawrence Erlbaum Associates.

Gentile, D. A., Anderson, C. A., Yukawa, S., Ihori, N., Saleem, M., Lim Kam Ming, … Sakamoto, A. (2009). The effects of prosocial video games on prosocial behaviors: International evidence from correlational, longitudinal, and experimental studies. *Personality and Social Psychology Bulletin, 35*(6), 752–763. doi:10.1177/0146167209333045

Healy, J. (1990). *Endangered minds: Why our children don't think*. New York, NY: Simon & Schuster.

Hendershot, H. (2004). *Nickelodeon Nation: The history, politics, and economics of America's only TV channel for kids*. New York, NY: New York University Press.

Jordan, A. B. (2004). The three-hour rule and educational television for children. *Popular Communication, 2*(2), 103–118. doi:10.1207/s15405710pc0202_3

Kearney, M. S., & Levine, P. B. (2015). Early childhood education by MOOC: Lessons from Sesame Street. *The National Bureau of Economic Research* (NBER Working Paper No. w21229). doi:10.3386/w21229

Kirkorian, H. L., & Anderson, D. R. (2009). Learning from educational media. In S. L. Calvert & B. Wilson (Eds.), *The handbook of children, media, and development* (pp. 188–213). Oxford: Blackwell Publishing.

Kirkorian, H. L., Choi, K., & Pempek, T. A. (2016). Toddlers' word learning from contingent and non-contingent video on touchscreens. *Child Development, 87*(2), 405–413. doi:10.1111/cdev.12508

Lauricella, A. R., Gola, A. A., & Calvert, S. L. (2011). Toddlers' learning from socially meaningful video characters. *Media Psychology, 14*(2), 216–232. doi:10.1080/15213269.2011.573465

Lemish, D. (1987). Viewings in diapers: The early development of television viewing. In T. R. Lindlof (Ed.), *Natural audiences: Qualitative research of media uses and effects* (pp. 33–57). Norwood, NJ: Ablex Publishing.

Linebarger, D. L. (2014). *Lessons from Cookie Monster: Educational television, preschoolers, and executive function*. Iowa City, IA: University of Iowa. Retrieved from http://downloads.cdn.sesame.org/sw/SWorg/documents/U_of_Iowa_Exec_Function_Study.pdf

Linebarger, D. L. (2015). Super Why! to the rescue: Can preschoolers learn early literacy skills from educational television? *International Journal of Cross-Disciplinary Subjects in Education, 6*(1), 2060–2068.

Linebarger, D. L., Kosanic, A. Z., Greenwood, C. R., & Doku, N. S. (2004). Effects of viewing the television program *Between the Lions* on the emergent literacy skills of young children. *Journal of Educational Psychology, 96*(2), 297–308. doi:10.1037/0022–0663.96.2.297

Linebarger, D. L., & Vaala, S. E. (2010). Screen media and language development in infants and toddlers: An ecological perspective. *Developmental Review, 30*(2), 176–202. doi:10.1016/j.dr.2010.03.006

Linebarger, D. L., & Wainwright, D. K. (2007). Learning while viewing: Urban myth or dream come true? In S. R. Mazzarella (Ed.), *20 Questions about youth and the media* (pp. 179–196). New York, NY: Peter Lang.

Mander, J. (1978). *Four arguments for the elimination of television*. New York, NY: Quill.

Mares, M.-L., Palmer, E. L., & Sullivan, T. (2011). Prosocial effects of media exposure. In S. L. Calvert & B. J. Wilson (Eds.), *The handbook of children, media, and development* (pp. 268–289). West Sussex: Wiley-Blackwell.

Mares, M.-L., & Pan, Z. D. (2013). Effects of Sesame Street: A meta-analysis of children's learning in 15 countries. *Journal of Applied Developmental Psychology, 34*(3), 140–151. doi:10.1016/j.appdev.2013.01.001

Mares, M.-L., & Woodard, E. (2007). Positive effects of television on children's social interaction: A meta-analysis. In R. W. Preiss, B. M. Gayle, N. Burrell, M. Allen, & J. Bryant (Eds.), *Mass media effects research: Advances through meta-analysis* (pp. 281–300). Mahwah, NJ: Lawrence Erlbaum.

Moody, K. (1980). *A report to parents: Growing up on television: The TV Effect*: New York, NY: Times Books.

Neuman, S. B. (2015). *Closing the app gap: Improving children's phonological skills*. New York, NY: Author. Retrieved from https://learnwithhomer.com/Closing-the-App-Gap.pdf

Piotrowski, J. T. (2014a). Participatory cues and program familiarity predict young children's learning from educational television. *Media Psychology, 17*(3), 311–331. doi:10.1080/15213269.2014.932288

Piotrowski, J. T. (2014b). The relationship between narrative processing demands and young American children's comprehension of educational television. *Journal of Children and Media, 8*(3), 267–285. doi:10.1080/17482798.2013.878740

Postman, N. (2006). *Amusing ourselves to death: Public discourse in the age of show business*. New York, NY: Penguin.

Rasmussen, E. E., Shafer, A., Colwell, M. J., White, S., Punyanunt-Carter, N., Densley, R. L., & Wright, H. (2016). Relation between active mediation, exposure to Daniel Tiger's Neighborhood, and US preschoolers'

social and emotional development. *Journal of Children and Media, 10*(4), 443–461. doi:10.1080/17482798.
2016.1203806

Reid Chassiakos, Y., Radesky, J., Christakis, D., Moreno, M. A., Cross, C., Hill, D., … Swanson, W. S. (2016).
Children and adolescents and digital media. *Pediatrics, 138*(5). doi:10.1542/peds.2016–2593

Rideout, V. (2014). *Learning at home: Families' educational media use in America.* A report of the Families and
Media Project. New York, NY: Joan Ganz Cooney Center at Sesame Workshop. Retrieved from http://www.
joanganzcooneycenter.org/wp-content/uploads/2014/01/jgcc_learningathome.pdf

Spitzer, M. (2012). *Digitale Demenz: Wie wir uns und unsere Kinder um den Verstand bringen.* München, Germany:
Droemer.

Szybist, J. (2011). Is TV on the decrease? *Televizion, 24*, 26.

Valkenburg, P. M., & Piotrowski, J. T. (2017). *Plugged in: How media attract and affect youth.* New Haven, CT: Yale
University Press.

Valkenburg, P. M., & Vroone, M. (2004). Developmental changes in infants' and toddlers' attention to television
entertainment. *Communication Research, 31*(3), 288–311. doi:10.1177/0093650204263435

Wartella, E. A., Rideout, V. J., Lauricella, A. R., & Connell, S. L. (2013). *Parenting in the age of digital technology:
A national survey.* Evanston, IL: School of Communication, Northwestern University.

Winn, M. (1985). *The plug-in drug.* New York, NY: Penguin Books.

Winn, M. (1987). *Unplugging the plug-in drug.* New York, NY: Penguin Books.

CHAPTER 13

Can Media Contribute to Happiness in Children and Adolescents?

Rebecca N. H. de Leeuw and Moniek Buijzen

Most parents wish their children to be happy (Diener & Lucas, 2004). Striving for happiness seems to be a fulfilling purpose as happiness has been found to be related to many benefits in life, such as academic success and fulfilled social relationships (Holder, 2012; Hoyt, Chase-Lansdale, McDade, & Adam, 2012; Lyubomirsky, King, & Diener, 2005). Improving happiness is not only valuable for humans involved but also for society at large, because happiness is related to having good health and longevity (Lyubomirsky *et al.*, 2005; Seligman & Csikszentmihalyi, 2000) and is found to be contagious (Fowler & Christakis, 2008). Although the study of happiness has received a magnificent boost from the start of the field of positive psychology (Seligman & Csikszentmihalyi, 2000), the amount of research on the potential positive effects of media is in sharp contrast with research on negative media effects.

It is, of course, crucial to examine whether the rise in media technology contributes to, for instance, increases in narcissism (Twenge & Foster, 2010) and declines in empathic concern and perspective taking (Konrath, O'Brien, & Hsing, 2011). However, it is equally crucial to investigate positive media effects. Article 17 of the Convention on the Rights of the Child (United Nations, 1989) states that:

> States Parties recognize the important function performed by the mass media and shall ensure that the child has access to information and material from a diversity of national and international sources, especially those aimed at the promotion of his or her social, spiritual and moral well-being and physical and mental health. (p. 5)

Therefore, it is important to know not only what should be discouraged, but also what should be encouraged when it comes to children and adolescents' media consumption. In this chapter, we summarize existing work on this topic while also highlighting gaps in the literature.

What Is Known and How Do Media Contribute to Happiness?

To understand the causes of happiness, it is essential that researchers first define it. In her seminal book from 2007, happiness researcher Sonja Lyubomirsky described happiness—a term that is often used interchangeably with subjective well-being—as "the experience of joy, contentment, or positive well-being, combined with a sense that one's life is good, meaningful, and worthwhile" (p. 31). We can distinguish two ways in which media can contribute to happiness. First, media can nurture happy feelings in a direct way. For instance, watching movies can lead to positive emotions, such as happiness, which subsequently can even create an upward spiral of continuous growth and flourishing (Cohn & Fredrickson, 2006; Fredrickson, 2001, 2003). Second, media can contribute to happiness in an indirect way, by affecting precursors of happiness. Capturing all precursors of happiness would result in a book instead of a chapter, therefore, in this chapter we focus on one of the most important precursors of happiness, that is, humanity. Humanity includes strengths that manifest in caring social relationships (Peterson & Seligman, 2004). Findings from comprehensive longitudinal studies on happiness indicated that close relationships early in life are essential for well-being in late life (Waldinger, 2015; Waldinger & Schulz, 2016). Similarly, Lyubomirsky *et al.* (2005) demonstrated in their review that happy people are more likely to have fulfilling social relationships than less happy people, but that this also can be explained in the opposite direction with happy people to be better able to acquire fulfilling social relations.

An important strength contributing to humanity is kindness, which is being compassionate and concerned about others—doing favors for them, performing good deeds, and taking care of them (Peterson & Seligman, 2004). Findings on kindness and happiness are in line with the work on social relationships and happiness, demonstrating that people who are kind tend to be happier and, vice versa, people who are happy tend to be kinder (Lyubomirsky *et al.*, 2005; Peterson & Seligman, 2004). Findings among children illustrated that being kind is related to being liked more, having more close friends, and being happy later in life (Cillessen & Rose, 2005; Clark & Ladd, 2000; Hastings, Utendale, & Sullivan, 2007; Holder & Coleman, 2008; Östberg, 2003). Even toddlers are found to be happier after giving to others than when they receive treats themselves, suggesting that humans have evolved to find kindness rewarding (Aknin, Hamlin, & Dunn, 2012). In addition, research revealed that happiness can be enhanced by encouraging acts of kindness (Layous, Nelson, Oberle, Schonert-Reichl, & Lyubomirsky, 2012; Sin & Lyubomirsky, 2009). Therefore, in this chapter research findings are described that link media use to happiness directly, but also indirectly, by means of strengths of humanity. The findings are summarized for the three most popular media activities among children and adolescents: (1) watching television and (short) movies, (2) social media, and (3) gaming (ChildWise, 2016; Lenhart, 2015; Rideout, Foehr, & Roberts, 2010; Rideout, Vandewater, & Wartella, 2003).

The Benefits of Watching Television and (Short) Movies

While watching television, children are exposed to a large number of altruistic portrayals, such as helping and sharing (Smith *et al.*, 2006). Despite this high prevalence, only a minority of studies have focused on the effects of these portrayals on children's behavior (Mares & Woodard, 2005, 2012), contrasting sharply with the vast amount of studies on the effects of violent television (Paik & Comstock, 1994). Nevertheless, there is accumulating evidence that children's prosocial behaviors—involving voluntary behaviors intended to benefit others, such as kindness (Eisenberg, Fabes, & Spinrad, 2007; Padilla-Walker, Coyne, Fraser, & Stockdale, 2013)—can be encouraged by exposure to prosocial television programming (Mares & Woodard, 2005). For instance, the television series *Dragon Tales* was found to encourage children between two and six years old to play, to share and cooperate with others (Rust, 2001). Similarly, *Daniel Tiger's Neighborhood* was found to contribute to children's levels of empathy and emotion recognition (Rasmussen *et al.*, 2016). In addition to these short-term effects, long-term effects were found, indicating that watching prosocial television content was negatively related to aggressive behavior two years later (Padilla-Walker, Coyne, Collier, & Nielson, 2015). Interestingly, when parents were assisted in showing high-quality prosocial and educational television programming instead of aggression-laden programming, improvements in their children's social competence and a decrease in externalizing behaviors were found (Christakis *et al.*, 2013). In the United States, for example, the Children's Television Act of 1990 (CTA) was designed to increase the amount of educational children's programming on U.S. television. Research has since found that of all U.S. "educational and informational" (E/I) programming, 67% is now addressing basic social-emotional lessons (Wilson, Kunkel, & Drogos, 2008). In addition, Sesame's current mission is to help parents and teachers to instill kindness and empathy in children (Sesame Workshop, 2016). Based on the current state of knowledge, one might argue that such initiatives indeed are good ways to help children to thrive and flourish.

When it comes to watching movies, Disney's animated movies are of particular interest, given the findings of a content analysis that these movies hold a substantial amount of prosocial behavior portrayals (Padilla-Walker *et al.*, 2013), almost seven times higher than children's average television programming (*cf.* Smith *et al.*, 2006). The occurrence of aggression in Disney movies also has been found to be quite low (Coyne & Whitehead, 2008; Padilla-Walker *et al.*, 2013). Ward (1996, 2002) has argued that Disney is an important moral educator with (mythic) narratives fostering values such as honesty and openness. Combined with its popularity, this makes Disney a particularly fascinating phenomenon to examine. Disney's popularity is reflected not only from topping the worldwide ranking of the most powerful brands (Brand Finance, 2016), but also from the fact that children often watch Disney's animated movies over and over again (Dreier, 2007). Moreover, parents identify Disney as quality family entertainment (Buckingham, 1997; Forgacs, 1992), which increases the likelihood of children being allowed to watch Disney. Empirical studies on the effects of watching Disney movies are, however, scarce. In an experimental study on the effects of Disney movies, de Leeuw and van der Laan (2017) examined whether Disney movies could inspire children to help their friends. After being exposed to a helping Disney character, children were more likely to help than children who watched a neutral Disney fragment, indicating that children can be inspired to help by watching helping Disney characters.

The pioneering work from Oliver and Raney's research group on meaningful entertainment among adults might also give useful information for how watching audiovisual media can contribute to well-being in children and adolescents. Adults are found not to only use media entertainment for experiencing enjoyment, but also as a source of grappling with questions concerning life's purpose and meaningfulness (Oliver & Raney, 2011). The question is whether children and adolescents can see movies as meaningful as well, and whether they can be inspired by such movies in a comparable way as adults. For instance, adults are found to experience moral elevation, defined as a warm, uplifting feeling when witnessing unexpected acts of human compassion or virtue (Haidt, 2000), also when they see this on screen (Oliver, Hartmann, & Woolley, 2012). After experiencing moral elevation, people are often more motivated to connect with and help others. A study by Janicke and Oliver (2015) demonstrated that meaningful movies can enhance experiences of connectedness to the transcendent, which eventually can enhance concern about the welfare of others, and motivation to be more caring even to strangers. Another study among young adults revealed that an online video could elicit feelings of elevation, and greater affinity and less prejudice toward diverse racial and ethnic groups (Oliver *et al.*, 2015). Among younger people, this kind of research has not yet been conducted. However, there are preliminary findings among adolescents indicating that, similar to adults, they are also able to experience moral elevation and a desire to connect to family and friends upon watching a short movie clip in which people express gratitude toward beloved ones (Rosen, 2015).

The "inspire and rewire" hypothesis, offered by Haidt (2003), describes that momentary experiences can cause permanent moral transformation. Even though this has not yet been investigated among children or adolescents, it is conceivable that (short) movies may act as such "mental reset button" in young people, feeding them with feelings of love, hope, and moral inspiration. As yet, the question remains whether young people's images of humanity are different for the ones who often consume inspiring media compared to the ones who merely consume "just" entertaining media. Although research largely supports the idea that television cultivates higher levels of cynicism and distrust about other human beings—generally referred to as the "mean world syndrome" (Gerbner, Gross, Morgan, Signorielli, & Shanahan, 2002), research on elevation implies that portrayals in media have the potential to do the reverse—to construct perceptions of a "kind world" with positive perspectives on humanity (Oliver, Ash, & Woolley, 2013).

The Benefits of Social Media

Young people use social media and various ways of messaging to keep in touch with friends from their offline lives (Subrahmanyam & Greenfield, 2008). Almost half of U.S. teenagers believe that the Internet improved their friendships (Lenhart, Rainie, & Lewis, 2001). A survey study by Valkenburg and Peter (2007) found support for this belief by demonstrating that online communication was positively related to the closeness of friendships among (pre)adolescents. As young people appear to be inclined to share predominantly positive events (Sas, Dix, Hart, & Su, 2009), social network sites provide an excellent platform to nurture positive emotions, such as reliving good times but also re-experiencing others' positive events. Humans often turn to others to share good news, a process called capitalization (Langston, 1994). Sharing positive events with others, for instance by communicating about them or celebrating them, is related to well-being, above and beyond the influence of the event itself. When reactions by others are perceived as enthusiastic, the effects on well-being are even stronger (Gable & Reis, 2010; Gable, Reis, Impett, & Asher, 2004). This effect also occurs in the online world, as the received feedback on social networking profiles was found to affect adolescents' self-esteem, which was subsequently related to well-being (Valkenburg, Peter, & Schouten, 2006). More specifically, positive feedback was found to enhance self-esteem and a negative tone was found to diminish it. Fortunately, most adolescents indicated they always or predominantly received positive feedback. Another study found that an increasing number of status updates reduced loneliness, due to deepened feelings of being connected to friends on a daily basis (Deters & Mehl, 2012).

Although social media seem to be a good place for positive interactions (Wright & Li, 2011), it is important to note that almost two-thirds of teenagers studied feel that the Internet takes away time they would spend with their families (Lenhart *et al.*, 2001). Moreover, the use of Facebook has also been found related to lower levels of well-being (Kross *et al.*, 2013; Sagioglou & Greitemeyer, 2014; Verduyn *et al.*, 2015) and taking a break from Facebook for a week has been found to improve well-being among young adults (Tromholt, 2016). Interestingly, the adverse effects seem to be stronger for heavy users, for the ones who use it passively compared to actively, and for people who have the tendency to envy others on Facebook, which indicates that when examining the effects of social networking sites it is important to take into account *how* exactly social media are used.

Moreover, social networking sites are a fascinating phenomenon to examine given their functionality of posting audiovisual materials. On Instagram alone, almost 85 million short videos and photos are uploaded every day (Lowe, 2016). Preliminary findings indicate that smartphone photography can boost positive affect (Chen, Mark, & Ali, 2016). Diving deeper into the positive psychology of photography, Diehl, Zauberman, and Barasch (2016) indicated that taking pictures indeed could enhance enjoyment of an experience; however, the researchers noted some important caveats. Photo taking was less likely to enhance engagement with the experience when the experience is already highly engaging, or when photo taking actually hindered the experience. Furthermore, enhanced enjoyment only occurred for taking pictures of positive experiences. In line with these results, Kurtz and Lyubomirsky (2013) found that mindful photography could help students to capture meaningful or positive things in their lives to enhance their happiness and appreciation of one's life in general.

The Benefits of Gaming

The vast majority of research on the effects of gaming has also focused on adverse effects; for instance, concerning aggression, addiction, and depression (e.g., Anderson *et al.*, 2010; Ferguson, 2013; Lemola *et al.*, 2011). However, a review study by Granic, Lobel, and Engels (2014) revealed that video games hold immense potential for acquiring new behaviors that can promote well-being, such as social skills and prosocial behaviors. More specifically, playing prosocial games appear to have short-term effects on helping behaviors. Longitudinal effects were also found, indicating that children who played prosocial games often at the beginning of the school year were more likely to be helpful later that year. Interestingly, where prosocial games are found to increase prosocial behaviors, violent games are just as likely to foster prosocial behaviors. A critical point appeared to be that these games should encourage cooperative rather than competitive play. Playing violent games that encourage cooperative play are found to increase helping online as well as offline. In addition to encouraging helping, gaming often leads to positive experiences that may promote well-being. For instance, gamers often report to experience a state of *flow*—a state which is characterized by being fully immersed in what one does, which has been repeatedly associated with a host of positive outcomes such as commitment and achievement at school (Csikszentmihalyi, 1990; Granic *et al.*, 2014).

Furthermore, superhero games might also be related to happiness. Although this has not been investigated for video games specifically, there is evidence to suggest that priming students with superheroes not only increases spontaneous helping behavior, but also future volunteering (Nelson & Norton, 2004). Moreover, in an innovative virtual reality study by Rosenberg, Baughman, and Bailenson (2013), participants were given the feeling they either possessed the power of flight (like a superhero) or were a passenger in a helicopter (more human-like) while helping to find a missing child. After the virtual experience, participants who were given the power of flight were more likely to help picking up "accidently" dropped pens, compared to those who were virtually in the helicopter. These findings are promising as apparently having the "superpower" of flight in a virtual game increases real-world helping behavior.

Food for Thought

In sum, answering the question in this chapter's title, the research literature shows that media can increase happiness in young people, directly as well as indirectly via humanity. Research also shows that young people's media environment contains numerous instances of altruistic behaviors toward others, having short-term as well as long term effects. Considering these conclusions from the perspective of cultivation theory, the question arises whether media exposure could evoke a "kind world syndrome" rather than "mean world syndrome" (cf. Gerbner et al., 2002; Oliver et al., 2013). In this respect, it is important to take into account the "dose-response" effect, involving the amount of time children and adolescents are involved with media. Previous findings demonstrated that the total time of watching television is negatively related to children's prosocial behavior (Mares & Woodard, 2012), implying that children can be inspired to be more kind, but only if they watch not too often in general. For social media, findings appear to be comparable, with heavy users scoring lower on well-being (Kross et al., 2013; Sagioglou & Greitemeyer, 2014; Verduyn et al., 2015). Research on the overall relation between digital-screen time and well-being among adolescents demonstrated that heavy media use is associated with lower happiness (Przybylski & Weinstein, 2017; Foerster & Röösli, 2017). Moreover, research revealed that children who were being deprived of media use and spent five days at an overnight nature camp, improved their skills of recognizing nonverbal emotion cues compared to children who experienced their normal media exposure (Uhls et al., 2014). Taken together, research evidence does not indicate a straightforward positive dose-response effect, and even indicate that caution is warranted regarding heavy screen time. Thus, when considering the positive impact of media on children and adolescents' happiness, it is crucial to acknowledge the complexity and conditions of this relationship.

Discussion Questions

1. How do you think young people should use social media in order to foster well-being instead of undermining it? Pretend that you are a parent of a teenager, how would you encourage your child(ren) to use it? Would you have rules on the amount of time spent on social media? Discuss your ideas with fellow students.

2. Still pretending to be a parent, what would you do when it comes to gaming? Discuss these ideas with fellow students.

Exercises

1. Read article 17 from the Convention on the Rights of the Child (United Nations, 1989) and describe in which ways media can be used specifically to realize these rights. Discuss your ideas with your fellow students.

2. Find an inspiring movie clip that gives you the experience of moral elevation and examine whether it also elicits uplifted and inspired feelings among your family, friends, and/or fellow-students. Examine this in the same way as Oliver *et al.* (2012) did in their study.

3. The final challenge: set up a study on positive media psychology for children and adolescents and describe why it is innovative, what the current state of knowledge is, and how you exactly will examine your research question(s).

References

Aknin, L. B., Hamlin, J. K., & Dunn, E. W. (2012). Giving leads to happiness in young children. *PLoS One, 7,* e39211. doi:10.1371/journal.pone.0039211

Anderson, C. A., Shibuya, A., Ihori, N., Swing, E. L., Bushman, B. J., Sakamoto, A., & Saleem, M. (2010). Violent video game effects on aggression, empathy, and prosocial behavior in Eastern and Western countries: A meta-analytic review. *Psychological Bulletin, 136,* 151–173. doi:10.1037/a0018251

Brand Finance. (2016). *The world's most powerful brands.* Retrieved from http://brandfinance.com/press-releases/global-500-2016-star-wars-sends-disneys-brand-into-hyperdrive/

Buckingham, D. (1997). Dissin' Disney: Critical perspectives on children's media culture. *Media, Culture & Society, 19,* 285–293. doi:10.1177/016344397019002010

Chen, Y., Mark, G., & Ali, S. (2016). Promoting positive affect through smartphone photography. *Psychology of Well-Being, 6,* 1–16. doi:10.1186/s13612-016-0044-4

ChildWise. (2016). *The monitor report 2016: Children's media use and purchasing.* ChildWise, Norwich.

Christakis, D. A., Garrison, M. M., Herrenkohl, T., Haggerty, K., Rivara, F. P., Zhou, C., & Liekweg, K. (2013). Modifying media content for preschool children: A randomized controlled trial. *Pediatrics, 131,* 431–438. doi:10.1542/peds.2012–1493

Cillessen, A. H. N., & Rose, A. J. (2005). Understanding popularity in the peer system. *Current Directions in Psychological Science, 14,* 102–105.

Clark, K. E., & Ladd, G. W. (2000). Connectedness and autonomy support in parent-child relationships: Links to children's socioemotional orientation and peer relationships. *Developmental Psychology, 36,* 485–498.

Cohn, M. A., & Fredrickson, B. L. (2006). Beyond the moment, beyond the self: Shared ground between selective investment theory and the broaden-and-build theory of positive emotions. *Psychological Inquiry, 17,* 39–44. doi:10.1207/s15327965pli1701_02

Coyne, S. M., &Whitehead, E. (2008). Indirect aggression in animated Disney films. *Journal of Communication, 58,* 382–395. doi:10.1111/j.1460–2466.2008.00390.x

Csikszentmihalyi, M. (1990). *Flow: The psychology of optimal experience.* New York, NY: Harper & Row.

de Leeuw, R. N. H., & van der Laan, C. A. (2017, May). *Exposure to prosocial Disney content and children's helping behavior: An experimental study.* Presented at the 67th annual conference of the International Communication Association. San Diego, CA.

Deters, F. G., & Mehl, M. R. (2012). Does posting Facebook status updates increase or decrease loneliness? An online social networking experiment. *Social Psychological and Personality Science, 4,* 579–586. doi:10.1177/1948550612469233

Diehl, K., Zauberman, G., & Barasch, A. (2016). How taking photos increases enjoyment of experiences. *Journal of Personality and Social Psychology, 111,* 119–140. doi:10.1037/pspa0000055

Diener, M. L., & Lucas, R. E. (2004). Adults' desires for children's emotions across 48 countries. *Journal of Cross-Cultural Psychology, 35,* 525–547. doi:10.1177/0022022104268387

Dreier, H. (2007). Disney. In J. J. Arnett (Ed.), *Encyclopedia of children, adolescents, and the media* (Vol. 1, pp. 242–245). Thousand Oaks, CA: Sage.

Eisenberg, N., Fabes, R. A., & Spinrad, T. (2007). Prosocial development. In N. Eisenberg & W. Damon (Eds.), *Handbook of child psychology, Volume 3, Social, Emotional, and Personality Development* (6th ed., pp. 646–718). New York, NY: John Wiley & Sons.

Ferguson, C. J. (2013). Violent video games and the Supreme Court. *American Psychologist, 68,* 57–74. doi:10.1037/a0030597

Foerster, M., & Röösli, M. (2017). A latent class analysis on adolescents media use and associations with health related quality of life. *Computers in Human Behavior, 71,* 266–274. doi:10.1016/j.chb.2017.02.015

Forgacs, D. (1992). Disney animation and the business of childhood. *Screen, 33,* 361–373. doi:10.1093/screen/33.4.361

Fowler, J. H., & Christakis, N. A. (2008). Dynamic spread of happiness in a large social network: Longitudinal analysis over 20 years in the Framingham Heart Study. *British Medical Journal, 337*, a2338. doi:10.1136/bmj.a2338

Fredrickson, B. L. (2001). The role of positive emotions in positive psychology: The broaden-and-build theory of positive emotions. *American Psychologist, 56*, 218–226.

Fredrickson, B. L. (2003). The value of positive emotions: The emerging science of positive psychology is coming to understand why it's good to feel good. *American Scientist, 91*, 330–335. doi:10.1511/2003.4.330

Gable, S. L., & Reis, H. T. (2010). Good news! Capitalizing on positive events in an interpersonal context. In M. P. Zanna (Ed.), *Advances in experimental social psychology* (Vol. 42, pp. 195–257). San Diego, CA: Elsevier Academic Press. doi:10.1016/S0065-2601(10)42004-3

Gable, S. L., Reis, H. T., Impett, E. A., & Asher, E. R. (2004). What do you do when things go right? The intrapersonal and interpersonal benefits of sharing positive events. *Journal of Personality and Social Psychology, 87*, 228–245. doi:10.1037/0022-3514.87.2.228

Gerbner, G., Gross, L., Morgan, M., Signorielli, N., & Shanahan, J. (2002). Growing up with television: Cultivation processes. In J. Bryant & D. Zillmann (Eds.), *Media effects: Advances in theory and research* (pp. 43–67). Mahwah, NJ: Lawrence Erlbaum Associates.

Granic, I., Lobel, A., & Engels, R. C. (2014). The benefits of playing video games. *American Psychologist, 69*, 66–78. doi:10.1037/a0034857

Haidt, J. (2000). The positive emotion of elevation. *Prevention and Treatment, 3*, 1–5. doi:10.1037/1522-3736.3.1.33c

Haidt, J. (2003). Elevation and the positive psychology of morality. In C. L. M. Keyes & J. Haidt (Eds.), *Flourishing: Positive psychology and the life well-lived* (pp. 275–289). Washington, DC: American Psychological Association. doi:10.1037/10594–012

Hastings, P. D., Utendale, W. T., & Sullivan, C. (2007). The socialization of prosocial development. In J. E. Grusec & P. D. Hastings (Eds.), *Handbook of socialization: Theory and research* (pp. 638–664). New York, NY: The Guilford Press.

Holder, M. D. (2012). *Happiness in children: Measurement, correlated, and enhancement of positive subjective well-being.* New York, NY: Springer.

Holder, M. D., & Coleman, B. (2008). The contribution of temperament, popularity, and physical appearance to children's happiness. *Journal of Happiness Studies, 9*, 279–302.

Hoyt, L. T., Chase-Lansdale, P. L., McDade, T. W., & Adam, E. K. (2012). Positive youth, healthy adults: Does positive wellbeing in adolescence predict better perceived health and fewer risky health behaviours in young adulthood? *Journal of Adolescent Health, 50*, 66–73. doi:10.1016/j.jadohealth.2011.05.002

Janicke, S. H., & Oliver, M. B. (2015). The relationship between elevation, connectedness, and compassionate love in meaningful films. *Psychology of Popular Media Culture.* (Advance online publication). doi:10.1037/ppm0000105

Konrath, S. H., O'Brien, E. H., & Hsing, C. (2011). Changes in dispositional empathy in American college students over time: A meta-analysis. *Personality and Social Psychology Review, 15*, 180–198. doi:10.1177/1088868310377395

Kross, E., Verduyn, P., Demiralp, E., Park, J., Lee, D. S., Lin, N., … Ybarra, O. (2013). Facebook use predicts declines in subjective well-being in young adults. *PLoS One, 8*, 1–6. doi:10.1371/journal.pone.0069841

Kurtz, J. L., & Lyubomirsky, S. (2013). Happiness promotion: Using mindful photography to increase positive emotion and appreciation. In J. J. Froh & A. C. Parks (Eds.), *Activities for teaching positive psychology: A guide for instructors* (pp. 133–136). Washington, DC: American Psychological Association.

Langston, C. A. (1994). Capitalizing on and coping with daily-life events: Expressive responses to positive events. *Journal of Personality and Social Psychology, 67*, 1112–1125.

Layous, K., Nelson, S. K., Oberle, E., Schonert-Reichl, K. A., & Lyubomirsky, S. (2012). Kindness counts: Prompting prosocial behavior in preadolescents boosts peer acceptance and well-being. *PLoS One, 7*, e51380. doi:10.1371/journal.pone.0051380

Lemola, S., Brand, S., Vogler, N., Perkinson-Gloor, N., Allemand, M., & Grob, A. (2011). Habitual computer game playing at night is related to depressive symptoms. *Personality and Individual Differences, 51*, 117–122. doi:10.1016/j.paid.2011.03.024

Lenhart, A. (2015). *Teen, social media and technology overview 2015.* Pew Research Center, DC: Washington.

Lenhart, A., Rainie, L., & Lewis, O. (2001). *Teenage life online: The rise of the instant-message generation and the Internet's impact on friendships and family relationships.* Washington, DC: Pew Internet & American Life Project.

Lowe, L. (2016). *125 Amazing social media statistics you should know in 2016.* Retrieved from https://socialpilot.co/blog/125-amazing-social-media-statistics-know-2016/

Lyubomirsky, S. (2007). *The how of happiness: A scientific approach to getting the life you want.* New York, NY: Penguin Press.

Lyubomirsky, S., King, L., & Diener, E. (2005). The benefits of frequent positive affect: Does happiness lead to success? *Psychological Bulletin, 131*, 803–855. doi:10.1037/0033–2909.131.6.803

Mares, M. L., & Woodard, E. (2005). Positive effects of television on children's social interactions: A meta-analysis. *Media Psychology, 7*, 301–322. doi:10.1207/S1532785XMEP0703_4

Mares, M. L., & Woodard, E. (2012). Effects of prosocial media content on children's social interactions. In D. G. Singer & J. L. Singer (Eds.), *Handbook of children and the media* (2nd ed., pp. 197–214). Thousand Oaks, CA: Sage Publications.

Nelson, L. D., & Norton, M. I. (2004). From student to superhero: Situational primes shape future helping. *Journal of Experimental Social Psychology, 41*, 423–430. doi:10.1016/j.jesp.2004.08.003

Oliver, M. B., Ash, E., & Woolley, J. K. (2013). The experience of elevation: Responses to media portrayals of moral beauty. In R. C. Tamborini (Ed.), *Media and the moral mind* (pp. 93–108). New York, NY: Routledge.

Oliver, M. B., Hartmann, T., & Woolley, J. K. (2012). Elevation in response to entertainment portrayals of moral virtue. *Human Communication Research, 38*, 360–378. doi:10.1111/j.1468–2958.2012.01427.x

Oliver, M. B., Kim, K., Hoewe, J., Chung, M., Ash, E., Woolley, J. K., Shade, D. D. (2015). Media-induced elevation as a means of enhancing feelings of intergroup connectedness. *Journal of Social Issues, 71*, 106–122. doi:10.1111/josi.12099

Oliver, M. B., & Raney, A. A. (2011). Entertainment as pleasurable and meaningful: Identifying hedonic and eudaimonic motivations for entertainment consumption. *Journal of Communication, 61*, 984–1004. doi:10.1111/j.1460–2466.2011.01585.x

Östberg, V. (2003). Children in classrooms: Peer status, status distribution and mental well-being. *Social Science & Medicine, 56*, 17–29.

Padilla-Walker, L. M., Coyne, S. M., Collier, K. M., & Nielson, M. G. (2015). Longitudinal relations between prosocial television content and adolescents' prosocial and aggressive behavior: The mediating role of empathic concern and self-regulation. *Developmental psychology, 51*, 1317–1328. doi:10.1037/a0039488

Padilla-Walker, L. M., Coyne, S. M., Fraser, A. M., & Stockdale, L. A. (2013). Is Disney the nicest place on earth? A content analysis of prosocial behavior in animated Disney films. *Journal of Communication, 63*, 393–412. doi:10.1111/jcom.12022

Paik, H., & Comstock, G. (1994). The effects of television violence on antisocial behavior: A meta-analysis. *Communication Research, 21*, 516–546.

Peterson, C., & Seligman, M. E. P. (2004). *Character strengths and virtues: A handbook and classification*. Oxford: Oxford University Press.

Przybylski, A. K., & Weinstein, N. (2017). A large-scale test of the Goldilocks hypothesis: Quantifying the relations between digital-screen use and the mental well-being of adolescents. *Psychological Science, 28*(2), 1–12. doi:10.1177/0956797616678438

Rasmussen, E. E., Shafer, A., Colwell, M. J., White, S., Punyanunt-Carter, N., Densley, R. L., & Wright, H. (2016). Relation between active mediation, exposure to Daniel Tiger's Neighborhood, and US preschoolers' social and emotional development. *Journal of Children and Media, 10*, 443–461. doi:10.1080/17482798.2016.1203806

Rideout, V. J., Foehr, U. G., & Roberts, D. F. (2010). *Generation M2: Media in the lives of 8–18 year-olds*. Menlo Park, CA: The Henry Kaiser Family Foundation.

Rideout, V. J., Vandewater, E. A., & Wartella, E. A. (2003). *Zero to six: Electronic media in the lives of infants, toddlers and preschoolers*. Menlo Park, CA: The Henry Kaiser Family Foundation.

Rosen, Y. (2015). *Raising happiness with a movie clip in adolescents: Inspiring gratitude and broadening thought-action repertoires* (Unpublished Master thesis, Radboud University, Nijmegen, The Netherlands).

Rosenberg, R. S., Baughman, S. L., & Bailenson, J. N. (2013). Virtual superheroes: Using superpowers in virtual reality to encourage prosocial behavior. *PLoS One, 8*, e55003. doi:10.1371/journal.pone.0055003

Rust, L. W. (2001). *Summative evaluation of Dragon Tales*. New York, NY: Sesame Workshop.

Sagioglou, C., & Greitemeyer, T. (2014). Facebook's emotional consequences: Why Facebook causes a decrease in mood and why people still use it. *Computers in Human Behavior 2014, 35*, 359–363.

Sas, C., Dix, A., Hart, J., & Su, R. (2009). Dramaturgical capitalization of positive emotions: The answer for Facebook success? *Proceedings of the 23rd British HCI Group annual conference on People and computers: Celebrating people and technology* (pp. 120–129). British Computer Society.

Seligman, M., & Csikszentmihalyi, M. (2000). Positive psychology: An introduction. *American Psychologist, 55*, 5–14. doi:10.1037/0003–066X.55.1.5

Sesame Workshop. (2016). *About the kindness survey*. Retrieved from http://kindness.sesamestreet.org/about-the-survey/

Sin, N. L., & Lyubomirsky, S. (2009). Enhancing wellbeing and alleviating depressive symptoms with positive psychology interventions: A practice-friendly meta-analysis. *Journal of Clinical Psychology, 65*, 467–487. doi:10.1002/jclp.20593

Smith, S. W., Smith, S. L., Pieper, K. M., Yoo, J. H., Ferris, A. L., Downs, E., & Bowden, B. (2006). Altruism on American television: Examining the amount of, and context surrounding, acts of helping and sharing. *Journal of Communication, 56*, 707–727. doi:10.1111/j.1460–2466.2006.00316.x

Subrahmanyam, K., & Greenfield, P. (2008). Communicating online: Adolescent relationships and the media. *The Future of Children: Children and Media Technology, 18*, 119–146.

Tromholt, M. (2016). The Facebook experiment: Quitting Facebook leads to higher levels of well-being. *Cyberpsychology, Behavior, and Social Networking, 19*, 661–666. doi:10.1089/cyber.2016.0259

Twenge, J. M., & Foster, J. D. (2010). Birth cohort increases in narcissistic personality traits among American college students, 1982–2009. *Social Psychological and Personality Science, 1*, 99–106. doi:10.1177/1948550609355719

Uhls, Y. T., Michikyan, M., Morris, J., Garcia, D., Small, G. W., Zgourou, E., & Greenfield, P. M. (2014). Five days at outdoor education camp without screens improves preteen skills with nonverbal emotion cues. *Computers in Human Behavior, 39*, 387–392. doi:10.1016/j.chb.2014.05.036

United Nations. (1989). *Convention on the rights of the child.* Retrieved from http://www.ohchr.org/en/professionalinterest/pages/crc.aspx

Valkenburg, P. M., & Peter, J. (2007). Preadolescents' and adolescents' online communication and their closeness to friends. *Developmental Psychology, 43*, 267–277. doi:10.1037/0012–1649.43.2.267

Valkenburg, P. M., Peter, J., & Schouten, A. P. (2006). Friend networking sites and their relationship to adolescents' well-being and social self-esteem. *CyberPsychology & Behavior, 9*, 584–590. doi:10.1089/cpb.2006.9.584

Verduyn, P., Lee, D. S., Park, J., Shablack, H., Orvell, A., Bayer, J., Ybarra, O., Jonides, J., & Kross, E. (2015). Passive Facebook usage undermines affective well-being: Experimental and longitudinal evidence. *Journal of Experimental Psychology: General, 144*, 480–488.

Waldinger, R. J. (2015). *What makes a good life? Lessons from the longest study on happiness.* Retrieved from http://www.ted.com/talks/robert_waldinger_what_makes_a_good_life_lessons_from_the_longest_study_on_happiness?language=en

Waldinger, R. J., & Schulz, M. S. (2016). The long reach of nurturing family environments: Links with midlife emotion-regulatory styles and late-life security in intimate relationships. *Psychological Science, 27*(11), 1443–1450. doi:10.1177/0956797616661556

Ward, A. R. (1996). The Lion King's mythic narrative: Disney as moral educator. *Journal of Popular Film and Television, 23*, 171–178. doi:10.1080/01956051.1996.9943703

Ward, A. R. (2002). *Mouse morality: The rhetoric of Disney animated film.* Austin, TX: University of Texas Press.

Wilson, B. J., Kunkel, D., & Drogos, K. L. (2008). *Educationally/insufficient? An analysis of the availability & educational quality of children's E/I programming.* Oakland, CA: Children Now.

Wright, M. F., & Li, Y. (2011). The associations between young adults' face-to-face prosocial behaviors and their online prosocial behaviors. *Computers in Human Behavior, 27*, 1959–1962. doi:10.1016/j.chb.2011.04.019

CHAPTER 14

Are Children Buying What Marketers Are Selling?[1]

Matthew A. Lapierre and Chelsie Akers

While the promotion of goods and services had been part of human existence for millennia; advertising, as today's consumer might recognize it, got its start at the end of the 19th century (Cross, 2002). Brought on by the mass production of goods made available by the industrial revolution and a growing working/middle class, manufacturers needed a way to ensure that these new consumers knew about the products available to them that were accumulating in warehouses. At first, advertisers were uniquely focused on "the man of the house" and only eventually moved to marketing products to women with advertising to children coming significantly later (Cross, 2002, 2004). However, children were often used as "bait" in advertising directed towards adults as marketing messages would appeal to parental desires to provide for their child (Cross, 2004).

Yet, it was not until the early-to-middle part of the 20th century where children became a specific target of marketer appeals (Cross, 2004). By the start of the 1920s, advertisers were beginning to focus their energies on reaching the youngest consumers, as magazines like *American Boy* and mail campaigns made direct appeals to kids. Furthermore, with the increasing availability of radios, advertisers had a direct opportunity to "talk" to children. One particularly popular practice was for companies to form radio clubs for their young audiences. For example, Ovaltine, the sponsor of the *Little Orphan Annie* radio show, offered listeners a decoder pin if they consumed enough of their product. Children who sent in the requisite number of Ovaltine labels would get their pin and could decode "secret" messages asking that the child to drink more Ovaltine.

The technology that supercharged the practice of advertising to children was the television, as the ability to reach children with dynamic audio and visual appeals made it easy for children to process these messages (Kline, 1993). Television also furthered the practice of creating "kid only" spaces to both entertain and market to this audience with shows like the *Mickey Mouse Club* in the 1950s. While the format of the show would likely be viewed as antiquated by children growing up today, the show did help generate the "Kids Rule!" ethic that dominates nearly all of children's cultural and consumer outposts today (i.e., the belief that children's cultural and consumer power is greater than adults; Banet-Weiser, 2007). More importantly, the show demonstrated that appealing directly to children could be a boon to toy manufacturers as they sought ways to encourage product purchases from young viewers. For example, the toy maker Mattel began aggressively courting the child market in the late 1950s by appealing directly to children on a daily basis and saw their sales increase from $6 million/year in 1955 to $25 million by the end of the decade (Cross, 2004).

The practice of advertising to children only grew more sophisticated in the years following the *Mickey Mouse Club*. One major change was that children's programming became more segregated from adult focused content, as Saturday morning and after-school programming were increasingly reserved for child audiences meaning that marketers had pockets of time to engage children directly (Mittell, 2003). In addition, marketers and content creators began to realize that they could benefit one another by matching television programs to the products advertised. For example, the toy maker Mattel produced a half-hour long show for children based on their *Hot Wheels* line of miniature toys in the late 1960s, and while there was some initial resistance regarding this practice of airing what were essentially long-form commercials, by the 1980s this practice became commonplace and continues to this day (Kunkel & Wilcox, 2012).

The next major shift in advertising to children was the creation of entire channels dedicated to the child viewer. Specifically, with the rise in prominence of specialized cable channels, particularly Nickelodeon, these isolated pockets soon turned into large swaths of time for marketers to appeal to young people (Banet-Weiser, 2007). More importantly, channels like Nickelodeon (and to a lesser extent the "commercial free" Disney Channel) helped to build a consumer culture among children that empowered children to be bold in their consumer choices (Banet-Weiser, 2007).

The current consumer landscape for children has grown even denser in the last two decades. Specifically, with the improvement of interactive media and social networking platforms, the ways that marketers can reach children has increased dramatically. For example, if a child is watching Nickelodeon and sees a commercial for Froot Loops they can go to the product's website and play a game featuring Toucan Sam, or they can go on Froot Loop's Facebook page, or they can find videos on YouTube about the cereal (Knorr, 2014).

Children's Exposure to Advertising and Their Power as Consumers

Considering the scope of children's consumer landscape, it is important to note just how much marketers pay to reach this audience and what that means in subsequent advertising exposure for children. The best available estimates for television marketing expenditures towards children are over a decade old, but in 2004 that amount was estimated to be $15 billion (Institute of Medicine, 2006), which does not account for the amount that is spent in online environments (Calvert, 2008). With regard to exposure, recent research suggests that the average American child sees 25,600 advertisements per year on television (Rideout, 2014a). Yet, it is important to take a step back and understand where else children encounter advertising messages in the current landscape, as children can expect to find commercial messages nearly everywhere. Commercial messages targeting children will be found in educational settings, console video games, movies, outdoors, and in online and/or social networking outlets.

Unfortunately, it has become quite difficult for researchers to assess the level of exposure in these different formats (Rideout, 2014a). For example, one particular type of advertising that has grown more popular in recent years is guerilla marketing (Serazio, 2013). Guerilla marketing is marketing that does not look or sound like traditional marketing: it is a friend talking up a brand surreptitiously as a brand ambassador or a relative posting about their favorite ice cream on Facebook. As such, it is incredibly hard to quantify how much exposure there is, and research by Moore and Rideout (2007) shows that children are, in fact, exposed to such appeals.

Why do marketers find children to be such a valuable audience? There are three key reasons why marketers target children. First, children represent a valuable audience in their own right as young people purchase billions of consumer goods each year (Calvert, 2008). Second, marketers hope that the brand connections that make with young children turns into a connection that will last for years (McNeal, 2007). Finally, children hold a tremendous amount of sway in the home via influencing parent/family purchases.

This last aspect of children's consumer power is where children have the greatest economic power. Estimates by the Institute of Medicine in 2006 noted that children influenced $500 billion worth of family purchases (Institute of Medicine, 2006), and there are some indications that this amount has increased to approximately $1 trillion dollars/year in more recent estimates (White, 2013). Children influence their parents to purchase a wide variety of goods. These products include ordinary consumer goods (e.g., groceries, games) but also "big-ticket" consumer goods, like vacation locales and automobiles (Buijzen, Schuurman, & Bomhof, 2008).

Effects of Advertising on Children

The reason why marketers target children is that they want to encourage purchasing behaviors or engender favorable attitudes towards their products from young consumers. In this regard, advertising/marketing to children does seem to be effective. Research on children and exposure to advertising suggests that increased exposure to commercial messages is indeed linked to consumer behavior. In a study by Chamberlain, Wang, and Robinson (2006), the researchers assessed children's screen media exposure and their food/drink requests. They found that children's exposure to screen media was significantly linked to their purchase requests over a year-and-a-half later. Another study with pre-school aged children found that after just a 30-second exposure to a commercial message children were significantly more likely to want the advertised product over non-advertised products (Borzekowski & Robinson, 2001).

The power of advertising is particularly concerning when considering the food products that are regularly advertised to children. As public health and medical researchers have noted, child obesity has increased 300–400% over the last few decades with numerous secondary health issues associated with obesity (Ogden, Carroll, Kit, & Flegal, 2014). Research examining the types of food advertised to children place cereal, candy/snacks, and restaurants as the three most frequently advertised while fruits, vegetables, and whole grains are virtually non-existent (Gantz, Schwartz, Angelini, & Rideout, 2007). Moreover, when looking at the actual nutritional quality of these foods, nearly three-quarters of the food advertised to children is of poor nutritional quality (Kunkel, Castonguay, & Filer, 2015). Lastly, young people's exposure to both alcohol and nicotine products (via exposure to advertisements for adult programing) is associated with favorable attitudes towards these products (Anderson, de Bruijn, Angus, Gordon, & Hastings, 2009; Duke *et al.*, 2014).

There are also concerns that advertising exposure affects children's family life and well-being. As noted above, children have a powerful influence on purchasing decisions in the home, but this can come at a cost. For example, research on children's purchase requests have found that increased advertising exposure leads to increased purchase requests which then leads to increased parent child conflict (Buijzen & Valkenburg, 2003). Moreover, as reported by Henry and Borzekowski (2011), this conflict can lead to significant anxiety among parents. Other research has shown that increased exposure to advertising influences children's attitudes regarding materialism (i.e., focusing on the importance of obtaining material goods) as children's exposure to advertising later predicted increased feelings of materialism (Opree, Buijzen, & Valkenburg, 2012). Finally, there are serious issues related to advertising exposure among young people and body dissatisfaction, particularly girls and young women. In a review of research on the subject of advertising exposure and body satisfaction, the authors found that those young people who saw more advertisements featuring very thin fashion models or celebrities were more likely to express significant dissatisfaction for their own bodies (Grabe, Ward, & Hyde, 2008).

Ethical and Legal Issues Related to Children and Advertising

Development and Advertising

One of the most pressing issues regarding advertising to children, particularly when considering the issues noted above, is whether children represent a vulnerable audience and, if so, whether anything can be done to buffer the effects of advertising. In fact, the question of whether children possess the cognitive and emotional competencies to effectively protect themselves from commercial appeals has been at the center of this field of research since the very beginning (e.g., Ward, Wackman, & Wartella, 1977), as children's developing cognitive/emotional abilities makes process marketing messages more difficult than it is for adults.

There are three primary concerns related to children's development and their understanding/processing of advertisements. The first of these is whether children are able to differentiate program content (e.g., actual television shows) from commercial content (Oates, Blades, & Gunter, 2002). The second is whether young children are capable of understanding that persuasive messages are designed to persuade their audience and/or advocate for a specific behavioral response (i.e., purchasing the product advertised; Kunkel, 2010). The last of these is whether child audiences have the necessary cognitive and emotional maturity to control their responses to engaging commercial messages (Rozendaal, Lapierre, van Reijmersdal, & Buijzen, 2011).

Regarding this first issue, research has consistently shown that toddlers and pre-school aged children are unable to tell the difference between commercial content and program content. In other words, a child around the age of three is not likely able to say definitively whether what they just watched was a television program (e.g., *SpongeBob SquarePants*) or a commercial for Lucky Charms cereal. Conversely, a child over the age of five is able to make this distinction without much of a challenge (John, 1999). This ability is important for children to develop as being able to tell the difference between commercial and program content represents the first step in being able to carefully consider how to respond to persuasive appeals.

The second of these, when children develop the awareness that commercial messages are designed to persuade their audience, appears later in childhood although the approximate age has been somewhat disputed. The consensus view has traditionally been that children develop this ability around the age of eight (Kunkel *et al.*, 2004), although some research has shown that this ability develops earlier (Donohue, Henke, & Donohue, 1980) while others have shown that it develops later (Oates *et al.*, 2002). More recent research, however, suggests that this milestone is less connected to a specific age and, instead, is linked to children's neurological maturation (Lapierre, 2015; Moses & Baldwin, 2005). Specifically, the part of the brain known as the *pre-frontal cortex*, which develops rapidly during childhood, is responsible for aiding in both complex thought and considering the mental states of others, must sufficiently mature before children can understand advertising messages (Moses & Baldwin, 2005).

Developing this competency is vital for children if they are to carefully evaluate commercial appeals. Specifically, children who believe that commercials are un-biased will be more likely to believe that things asserted in the commercial are truthful and are simply informing audiences about how great their product is. Conversely, children who are aware that these messages are designed to encourage certain behaviors/attitudes and are likely to employ bias will be more likely to evaluate these messages more critically.

Regarding the last developmental competency, as anyone who has spent time with children of varying ages can likely attest, children's ability to control their emotions/thoughts improves as they age. For example, while it is not uncommon to see a three or four-year-old child throw a tantrum, that behavior typically becomes less frequent as that same child enters grade school and is exceedingly rare as that child reaches adolescence. This ability to control emotion/thought is, like the ability to understand the persuasive intent of commercials, linked to children's maturation of the pre-frontal cortex (Rozendaal *et al.*, 2011) and does not approach adult levels of processing until adolescence (Best & Miller, 2010). Moreover, children who are better able to regulate their emotions (Lapierre, 2016a) and control their thoughts (Lapierre, 2016b) are less likely to ask their parents for consumer goods.

Developing this ability represents a significant milestone for children's capability to consider marketing messages. Specifically, even if children are aware that they are watching a commercial and know that the message is showing them biased information, if they are unable to control their excitement when encountering the message, they will not be able to reasonably consider the appeal. As such, while recognizing that a message is persuasive in nature is important, having the cognitive/emotional ability to engage the message is essential.

Protecting Child Audiences

If the available evidence suggests that children represent a vulnerable audience, what can be done to help them contend with marketing messages? There have traditionally been three methods employed to protect young audiences: teaching children about advertising, encouraging parents to intervene, and enacting policy to limit marketing to children.

The first of these approaches has been to teach children about advertising in the hopes that this will increase their advertising literacy (Eagle, 2007; Gunter, Oates, & Blades, 2005). Typically, these interventions focus on teaching children about advertiser tactics with the ultimate goal of increasing children's advertising skepticism and persuasion knowledge which is then believed to help children become more critical consumers (Rozendaal *et al.*, 2011). Unfortunately, however, the available evidence indicates that these interventions are frequently not successful in changing children's responses to marketing. Specifically, while these interventions do increase children's advertising literacy (Hobbs & Frost, 2003; Roberts, Christenson, Gibson, Mooser, & Goldberg, 1980), there is little evidence that these interventions subsequently affect children's consumer behavior (e.g., Brucks, Armstrong, & Goldberg, 1988; Chernin, 2007; Christenson, 1982).

The second approach used to protect children is to encourage parents/guardians to intervene and help children process commercial messages (i.e., parental mediation). Parental mediation works by encouraging parents/guardians to voice concerns about advertiser messages with their children in order to help teach the child to be more careful when considering marketing appeals (Buijzen & Mens, 2007). More importantly, research shows that parental mediation can influence children's consumer behavior (Buijzen, 2007). However, this method to limit the impact of advertising to children is not without issue. First, with the growing popularity of mobile and new media it is becoming harder to monitor children's media use which makes it more difficult for parents to intervene (Spiteri Cornish, 2014). Second, research on parent responses to marketing appeals reveals that they are not immune to marketing tactics (Harris, Thompson, Schwartz, & Brownell, 2011; Vaala & Lapierre, 2014) which might influence how they help their own children.

The last method is through public policy whereby governments restrict how marketers reach children, this can include limiting certain types of appeals (e.g., licensed characters), the types of products marketed to children, restricting when advertisers can target children, and/ or limiting the amount of time that is dedicated to advertising to children (Kunkel & Wilcox, 2012). Across the globe, there is a great deal of variation in how the law is used to regulate advertising to children. For example, in Norway, marketers are entirely forbidden from targeting children with their appeals. In the Netherlands, the government does not allow advertisers to use product placement in any program targeted to children under 12. Finally, in Greece, toy advertisements cannot be shown before 10 P.M.

With regard to the United States, there are very few legal statutes in place as it relates to children and advertising although there are some limitations in place regarding how much time per hour can be dedicated to commercials during children's programming (Kunkel & Gantz, 1992). However, for the most part, advertising to children in the United States is overseen by an organization called the Children's Advertising Review Unit (CARU; Kunkel & Wilcox, 2012). CARU is an industry group made up of advertisers that is affiliated with the Better Business Bureau and is responsible for reviewing advertiser practices and if marketers are following their own voluntary guidelines. These guidelines instituted by CARU spell out what kinds of claims may be used, what sort of sales pressure advertisers can employ, and what disclosures ought to be put in place; yet, evidence is mixed regarding the stringency of this agency's oversight (Fried, 2006; Grubbs Hoy, Childers Carpenter, & Morrison, 2012; Kunkel & Gantz, 1993). (See Chapter 2 for a thorough discussion of the regulation of children's media.)

Advertising and New Media

One of the greatest future challenges related to children and advertising is understanding how new media will shape children's advertising environment and what sorts of effects there will be. This is particularly important, as for the first time in history; we have a generation of young people that have not known life without the Internet. In fact, research looking at children's screen use over time shows that, as both Internet access and speed has increased, time spent online has similarly increased. A report by Common Sense Media found that children eight-years-old and under spend an average of 1 hour and 55 minutes per day consuming screen media (Rideout, 2013). Of that, 26 minutes is devoted to computers and mobile devices (as of 2013), a 5-minute per day increase from 2011. Conversely, from 2011 to 2013 television, DVDs, and video games all decreased in use. (For a detailed discussion of young people's online activities, see Chapter 16.)

More importantly, as mobile devices have increased in popularity, children are often using them without adult supervision. For example, by the time children reach preschool, 3 out of 4 children have their own mobile devices (Kabali *et al.*, 2015). Moreover, this same study found that parents use such devices to occupy their children when they are otherwise indisposed as 75% of parents indicated that they have given their child a device to keep them busy. Other research has found that of all the time children spend on new media devices, parents only co-play with their children 25–29% of the time (Rideout, 2014b).

As new media devices become more commonplace and children's exposure becomes more isolated, advertisers are developing new techniques and capitalizing on old techniques. Children are exposed to advertisements in a number ways; such as advergames, pop-up/banner ads, sponsored posts/videos, paid ads, and company profiles on social media. With these new advances, advertisers have an entirely new way to reach children with almost no checks and balances.

As it stands now, the only federal law in regards to children and online advertising is the Children's Online Privacy Protection Rule (COPPA; Federal Trade Commission, 2013). The rule requires that any operator of a child-directed site that collects information about children (under thirteen-years-old) is required to notify and receive permission from a parent. Yet, keeping online marketers accountable is a daunting task, and while there are examples of marketers having been caught violating this rule (Federal Trade Commission, 2016), there is evidence that marketers often flout it (Dahl, Eagle, & Baez, 2009).

Beyond this one law, advertisers largely have free reign on what they can produce for children. For example, many products offer advergames on their website for children to play. Advergames are free games that young people can play; yet, the entire game functions as an extended advertisement. A report by the Kaiser Family Foundation found that most child-targeted websites had more than one advergame, while the average was 4.5 games per site, some sites offered as many as 22 games (Moore, 2006). The games sampled in the study also featured a great deal of branded content as logos, brand characters, and/or packages were found in every advergame, with some going so far as to make the children watch a full-length TV commercial during game play. Moreover, many of the games tried to appeal to children by offering special deals or even requiring the child to create a membership to continue playing (Moore, 2006).

Video streaming is another element of the Internet that has added uncertainty to the world of advertisements. For example, in February of 2015 Google released YouTube Kids (YTK), a streaming service and app for mobile devices. This app is advertised as a kid friendly and catered to the young child's streaming experience. However, this app is ad-supported so children watching are subjected to watching advertisements (Ads in YouTube Kids, 2016). The Campaign for Commercial Free Childhood (CCFA) filed a complaint against Google's YTK in 2015 because they found the app was not as kid friendly as it was purported to be.

For example, companies like Coca-Cola had pledged to not show any advertisements to children under 12, yet while watching YTK 47 Coca-Cola commercials, 11 promotional videos, and 2 product placements were found (Kang, 2015). On the podcast Marketplace Tech, Professor Dale Kunkel addressed the fact that Google is using algorithms to select content appropriate for children and is failing because a simple search on the app can bring up topics on violence and abuse (Johnson, 2015). Previously, child content was limited to media produced and intended for children that were specifically chosen by humans and not computers. With companies eliminating the use of a person selecting content for children, even filtered content for children is not limited to actual appropriate material. The problem is that when parents see claims such as kid friendly or family friendly, they are often lead to believe the content is appropriate for their children and that is not always the case.

Lastly, advertising in these new media formats presents a number of additional challenges to children beyond what children encounter in traditional older media formats. First, there is evidence showing that children have more difficulty detecting whether they are being sold to in these newer settings (Owen, Lewis, Auty, & Buijzen, 2013) and children seem to be less critical in their evaluations of these advertisements when they recognize them (Rozendaal, Slot, van Reijmersdal, & Buijzen, 2013). Second, when looking at the marketing of food products, the nutritional quality of products marketed in new media environments are often less healthy compared to products marketed on television (Harris, Speers, Schwartz, & Brownell, 2012).

Conclusion

Children are one of the most sought after demographics by marketers both for their value as consumers and for what they contribute to household spending. However, targeting children with marketing messages is viewed by many as controversial as there are significant links to negative outcomes regarding children's health and well-being and it is not altogether clear that children are fully capable of understanding marketing messages. Moreover, while there are things that can be done to protect children, due to changes in children's media environment and current laissez-faire attitudes regarding policy many families and children are "on their own".

Discussion Questions

1. In a world where children are constantly being sold to, how do you think this affects their experiences as they grow up? For example, one of the common tropes in children's advertising is to associate owning the advertised product with popularity, how might these types of appeals impact young audiences?

2. Thinking about your own experience growing up with advertising, when do you think you had a firm grasp of what advertisements were really trying to do? Do you think that changed how you reacted to commercial messages?

3. How did you react to advertising as a child? Do you recall ever wanting the products that you had seen advertised? How did your parents respond to your requests for products?

Exercises

1. Conduct a content analysis on one hour of children's television with a focus on the advertisements. Take note of the products that are advertised, the appeals that are used, and/or how children and adults are portrayed in these advertisements.

2. Spend an hour surfing websites for child-targeted products (e.g., cereals, toys). Examine how advertisers try to engage children in these online environments. In addition, explore how advertisers disclose information related to protecting children's privacy.

3. Take a close look at the cereal aisle in your local supermarket. How do companies try to appeal to child consumers with their product packaging? How do they appeal to parents? How do "sugary" cereals differ from "non-sugary" cereals?

Note

1. The authors would like to thank Hailey Hunter and Madison Meeks for their feedback on this chapter.

References

Ads in YouTube Kids. (2016). *YouTube Kids parental guide*. Retrieved from https://support.google.com/youtubekids/answer/6130541?hl=en&ref_topic=6130504

Anderson, P., de Bruijn, A., Angus, K., Gordon, R., & Hastings, G. (2009). Impact of alcohol advertising and media exposure on adolescent alcohol use: A systematic review of longitudinal studies. *Alcohol and Alcoholism, 44*(3), 229–243. doi:10.1093/alcalc/agn115

Banet-Weiser, S. (2007). *Kids rule!: Nickelodeon and consumer citizenship*. Durham, NC: Duke University Press.

Best, J. R., & Miller, P. H. (2010). A developmental perspective on executive function. *Child Development, 81*(6), 1641–1660. doi:10.1111/j.1467-8624.2010.01499.x

Borzekowski, D. L. G., & Robinson, T. N. (2001). The 30-second effect: An experiment revealing the impact of television commercials on food preferences of preschoolers. *Journal of the American Dietetic Association, 101*(1), 42–46. doi:10.1016/S0002-8223(01)00012-8

Brucks, M., Armstrong, G. M., & Goldberg, M. E. (1988). Children's use of cognitive defenses against television advertising: A cognitive response approach. *Journal of Consumer Research, 14*, 471–482. doi:10.1086/209129

Buijzen, M. (2007). Reducing children's susceptibility to commercials: Mechanisms of factual and evaluative advertising interventions. *Media Psychology, 9*(2), 411–430. doi:10.1080/15213260701291361

Buijzen, M., & Mens, C. (2007). Adult mediation of television advertising effects. *Journal of Children and Media, 1*(2), 177–191. doi:10.1080/17482790701339233

Buijzen, M., Schuurman, J., & Bomhof, E. (2008). Associations between children's television advertising exposure and their food consumption patterns: A household diary-survey study. *Appetite, 50*(2–3), 231–239. doi:10.1016/j.appet.2007.07.006

Buijzen, M., & Valkenburg, P. M. (2003). The effects of television advertising on materialism, parent–child conflict, and unhappiness: A review of research. *Journal of Applied Developmental Psychology, 24*(4), 437–456. doi:10.1016/S0193-3973(03)00072-8

Calvert, S. L. (2008). Children as consumers: Advertising and marketing. *Future of Children, 18*(1), 205–234. doi:10.1353/foc.0.0001

Chamberlain, L. J., Wang, Y., & Robinson, T. N. (2006). Does children's screen time predict requests for advertised products? Cross-sectional and prospective analyses. *Archives of Pediatrics & Adolescent Medicine, 160*(4), 363–368. doi:10.1001/archpedi.160.4.363

Chernin, A. (2007). *The relationship between children's knowledge of persuasive intent and persuasion: The case of televised food marketing* (pp. 1–187) (Ph. D. dissertation, University of Pennsylvania, Philadelphia). Retrieved from http://repository.upenn.edu/dissertations/AAI3292015/

Christenson, P. G. (1982). Children's perceptions of TV commercials and products: The effects of PSAs. *Communication Research, 9*(4), 491–524. doi:10.1177/009365082009004001

Cross, G. (2002). *An all-consuming century: Why commercialism won in modern America*. New York, NY: Columbia University Press.

Cross, G. (2004). *The cute and the cool: Wondrous innocence and modern American children's culture*. New York, NY: Oxford University Press.

Dahl, S., Eagle, L., & Baez, C. (2009). Analyzing advergames: Active diversions or actually deception. An exploratory study of online advergames content. *Young Consumers, 10*(1), 46–59. doi:10.1108/17473610910940783

Donohue, T. R., Henke, L. L., & Donohue, W. A. (1980). Do kids know what TV commercials intend. *Journal of Advertising Research, 20*(5), 51–57.

Duke, J. C., Lee, Y. O., Kim, A. E., Watson, K. A., Arnold, K. Y., Nonnemaker, J. M., & Porter, L. (2014). Exposure to electronic cigarette television advertisements among youth and young adults. *Pediatrics, 134*(1), e29–e36. doi:10.1542/peds.2014–0269

Eagle, L. (2007). Commercial media literacy: What does it do, to whom—And does it matter? *Journal of Advertising, 36*(2), 101–110. doi:10.2753/JOA0091-3367360207

Federal Trade Commission. (2013). Children's online privacy protection rule: Final rule amendments. *Federal Register, 78*(12), 3972–4014.

Federal Trade Commission. (2016). *Federal Court Finds Amazon liable for billing parents for children's unauthorized in-app charges* [Press Release]. Retrieved from https://www.ftc.gov/news-events/press-releases/2016/04/federal-court-finds-amazon-liable-billing-parents-childrens

Fried, E. J. (2006). Assessing effectiveness of self-regulation: A case study of the Children's Advertising Review Unit. *Loyola of Los Angeles Law Review, 39*(1), 93–138.

Gantz, W., Schwartz, N., Angelini, J. R., & Rideout, V. (2007). *Food for thought: Television food advertising to children in the United States.* Menlo Park, CA: Kaiser Family Foundation. Retrieved from https://kaiserfamilyfoundation.files.wordpress.com/2013/01/7618.pdf

Grabe, S., Ward, L. M., & Hyde, J. S. (2008). The role of the media in body image concerns among women: A meta-analysis of experimental and correlational studies. *Psychological Bulletin, 134*(3), 460–476. doi:10.1037/0033-2909.134.3.460

Grubbs Hoy, M., Childers Carpenter, C., & Morrison, M. (2012). The evolution of self-regulation in food advertising. *International Journal of Advertising, 31*(2), 257–290. doi:10.2501/IJA-31-2-257-290

Gunter, B., Oates, C., & Blades, M. (2005). *Advertising to children on TV: Content, impact, and regulation.* Mahwah, NJ: Lawrence Erlbaum Associates.

Harris, J. L., Speers, S. E., Schwartz, M. B., & Brownell, K. D. (2012). US Food Company Branded Advergames on the Internet: Children's exposure and effects on snack consumption. *Journal of Children and Media, 6*(1), 51–68. doi:10.1080/17482798.2011.633405

Harris, J. L., Thompson, J. M., Schwartz, M. B., & Brownell, K. D. (2011). Nutrition-related claims on children's cereals: What do they mean to parents and do they influence willingness to buy? *Public Health Nutrition, 14*(12), 2207–2212. doi:10.1017/S1368980011001741

Henry, H. K. M., & Borzekowski, D. L. G. (2011). The nag factor: A mixed-methodology study in the US of young children's requests for advertised products. *Journal of Children and Media, 5*(3), 298–317. doi:10.1080/17482798.2011.584380

Hobbs, R., & Frost, R. (2003). Measuring the acquisition of media-literacy skills. *Reading Research Quarterly, 38*, 330–355. doi:10.1598/RRQ.38.3.2

Institute of Medicine. (2006). *Food marketing to children and youth: Threat or opportunity.* Washington, DC: National Academies Press.

John, D. R. (1999). Consumer socialization of children: A retrospective look at twenty-five years of research. *Journal of Consumer Research, 26*(3), 183–213. doi:10.1086/209559

Johnson, B. B. (2015, May 19). Marketplace Tech for Tuesday, May 19, 2015 [Audio podcast]. *Marketplace.* Retrieved from http://www.marketplace.org/shows/marketplace-tech/marketplace-tech-tuesday-may-19-2015

Kabali, H. K., Irigoyen, M. M., Nunez-Davis, R., Budacki, J. G., Mohanty, S. H., Leister, K. P., & Bonner, R. L. (2015). Exposure and use of mobile media devices by young children. *Pediatrics, 136*(6), 1044–1050. doi:10.1542/peds.2015–2151

Kang, C. (2015, November 24). YouTube Kids app faces new complaints over ads for junk food. *New York Times*, p. B1. Retrieved from http://www.nytimes.com/2015/11/25/technology/youtube-kids-app-faces-new-complaints.html?_r=0

Kline, S. (1993). *Out of the garden: Toys, TV and children's culture in the age of marketing.* Toronto, ON: Garamond Press.

Knorr, C. (2014). *Sneaky ways advertisers target kids.* Retrieved from https://www.commonsensemedia.org/blog/sneaky-ways-advertisers-target-kids

Kunkel, D. (2010). Mismeasurement of children's understanding of the persuasive intent of advertising. *Journal of Children and Media, 4*(1), 109–117. doi:10.1080/17482790903407358

Kunkel, D., Castonguay, J. S., & Filer, C. R. (2015). Evaluating industry self-regulation of food marketing to children. *American Journal of Preventive Medicine, 49*(2), 181–187. doi:10.1016/j.amepre.2015.01.027

Kunkel, D., & Gantz, W. (1992). Children's television advertising in the multi-channel environment. *Journal of Communication, 42*(3), 134–152. doi:10.1111/j.1460–2466.1992.tb00803.x

Kunkel, D., & Gantz, W. (1993). Assessing compliance with industry self-regulation of television advertising to children. *Journal of Applied Communication Research, 21*(2), 148–162. doi:10.1080/00909889309365363

Kunkel, D., & Wilcox, B. (2012). Children and media policy: Historical perspectives and current practices. In D. G. Singer & J. L. Singer (Eds.), *Handbook of children and the media* (pp. 569–594). Thousand Oaks, CA: Sage Publications.

Kunkel, D., Wilcox, B. L., Cantor, J., Palmer, E., Linn, S., & Dowrick, P. (2004). *Report of the APA task force on advertising and children.* Washington, DC: American Psychological Association.

Lapierre, M. A. (2015). Development and persuasion understanding: Predicting knowledge of persuasion/selling intent from children's theory of mind. *Journal of Communication, 65*(3), 423–442. doi:10.1111/jcom.12155

Lapierre, M. A. (2016a). Emotion regulation and young children's consumer behavior. *Young Consumers, 17*(2), 168–182. doi:10.1108/YC-11-2015-00566

Lapierre, M. A. (2016b). *Persuasion knowledge and executive function: Links to children's consumer behavior.* National Communication Association Conference, Philadelphia, PA.

McNeal, J. U. (2007). *On becoming a consumer: The development of consumer behavior patterns in childhood* (1st ed.). New York, NY: Butterworth-Heinemann.

Mittell, J. (2003). The great Saturday morning exile: Scheduling cartoons on television's periphery in the 1960s. In C. A. Stabile & M. Harrison (Eds.), *Prime time animation: Television animation and American culture* (pp. 33–54). New York, NY: Routledge.

Moore, E. S. (2006). *It's child's play: Advergaming and the online marketing of food to children.* Menlo Park, CA: Kaiser Family Foundation.

Moore, E. S., & Rideout, V. (2007). The online marketing of food to chldren: Is it just fun and games? *Journal of Public Policy & Marketing, 26*(2), 202–220. doi:10.1509/jppm.26.2.202

Moses, L. J., & Baldwin, D. A. (2005). What can the study of cognitive development reveal about children's ability to appreciate and cope with advertising? *Journal of Public Policy & Marketing, 24*(2), 186–201. doi:10.1509/jppm.2005.24.2.186

Oates, C., Blades, M., & Gunter, B. (2002). Children and television advertising: When do they understand persuasive intent? *Journal of Consumer Behaviour, 1*(3), 238–245. doi:10.1002/cb.69

Ogden, C. L., Carroll, M. D., Kit, B. K., & Flegal, K. M. (2014). Prevalence of childhood and adult obesity in the United States, 2011–2012. *JAMA, 311*(8), 806–814. doi:10.1001/jama.2014.732

Opree, S. J., Buijzen, M., & Valkenburg, P. M. (2012). Lower life satisfaction related to materialism in children frequently exposed to advertising. *Pediatrics, 130*(3), 486–491. doi:10.1542/peds.2011-3148

Owen, L., Lewis, C., Auty, S., & Buijzen, M. (2013). Is children's understanding of non–traditional advertising comparable to their understanding of television advertising? *Journal of Public Policy & Marketing, 32*(2), 195–206. doi:10.1509/jppm.09.003

Rideout, V. (2013). *Zero to eight: Children's media use in America 2013.* San Francisco, CA: Common Sense Media. Retrieved from https://www.commonsensemedia.org/research/zero-to-eight-childrens-media-use-in-america-2013

Rideout, V. (2014a). *Advertising to children and teens: Current practices.* San Francisco, CA: Common Sense Media.

Rideout, V. (2014b). *Learning at home: Families' educational media use in America.* New York, NY: Joan Ganz Cooney Center at Sesame Workshop.

Roberts, D. F., Christenson, P., Gibson, W. A., Mooser, L., & Goldberg, M. E. (1980). Developing discriminating consumers. *Journal of Communication, 30*(3), 94–105. doi:10.1111/j.1460-2466.1980.tb01996.x

Rozendaal, E., Lapierre, M. A., van Reijmersdal, E. a., & Buijzen, M. (2011). Reconsidering advertising literacy as a defense against advertising effects. *Media Psychology, 14*(4), 333–354. doi:10.1080/15213269.2011.620540

Rozendaal, E., Slot, N., van Reijmersdal, E. A., & Buijzen, M. (2013). Children's responses to advertising in social games. *Journal of Advertising, 42*(2–3), 142–154. doi:10.1080/00913367.2013.774588

Serazio, M. (2013). *Your Ad Here: The Cool Sell of Guerrilla Marketing.* New York, NY: New York University Press.

Spiteri Cornish, L. (2014). "Mum, can I play on the internet?": Parents' understanding, perception and responses to online advertising designed for children. *International Journal of Advertising, 33*(3), 437–473. doi:10.2501/IJA-33-3-437-473

Vaala, S. E., & Lapierre, M. A. (2014). Marketing genius: The impact of educational claims and cues on parents' reactions to infant/toddler DVDs. *Journal of Consumer Affairs, 48*(2), 323–350. doi:10.1111/joca.12023

Ward, S., Wackman, D. B., & Wartella, E. (1977). *How children learn to buy: The development of consumer information processing skills.* Beverly Hills, CA: Sage Publications.

White, M. C. (2013, April). American families increasingly let kids make buying decisions. *Time.* Retrieved from http://business.time.com/2013/04/11/american-families-increasingly-let-kids-make-buying-decisions./

PART 3

The Kids:
Youth, Culture & Media

CHAPTER 15

Just How Commercialized Is Children's Culture?

Matthew P. McAllister and Azeta Hatef

It feels like Christmas morning as a young boy, dressed in an Iron Man costume, unwraps an egg-shaped gift to reveal a Captain America figurine. The young boy, who goes by the username CKN Toys, moves on to the next gift; looking at the camera with a big smile, he says, "I wonder what's inside." So does the audience. He continues to unwrap each present, showcasing four other Marvel Avengers figurines. But, this is not Christmas morning and the young boy is no amateur.

The phenomenon is called "unboxing," and it has become one of the most popular video genres on YouTube. CKN's unboxing of the new Spider-Man battery-powered car amassed over 140 million views through 2016 (CKN Toys, 2016). The popular videos are a cross between home-family videos and the Home Shopping Network, where viewers vicariously experience the joys of receiving gifts, as young children display the newest gadgets and toys. CKN Toys and other young online talent like EvanTubeHD know their products and have the presence of professional salespeople.

For young online stars like EvanTubeHD, these videos have become a lucrative opportunity. The video's star has signed with Maker Studio, which falls under The Walt Disney Company umbrella (Maker Studios, 2016), and currently has 11 channels among YouTube's Top 100 (Cohen, 2016). (Toys "R" Us has its own channel, too.) Hosts of the unboxing channels unveil new products to accompany the latest film releases, including toys for *Cars*, *Star Wars*, and *Frozen*. Before viewers watch the unboxing of these toys, though, they see commercials for brands such as the Disney film *Moana*.

These videos, then, encompass commercialism and promotion at virtually every level and in interconnected ways: wearing branded clothing, displaying new brands, sponsored channels, explicit commercials, and connections to corporate ownership. And the main incentives for watching?: the mystery of the gift-reveal and then the subsequent emotional display from the kids—the "wondrous innocence" (Cross, 2004)—over receiving their new commodities. The message of the videos, then, complement perfectly the surrounding commercialization.

Sponsored gift-unwrapping videos may seem extreme, but they actually are fairly indicative of the current state of children's media and culture, in which the logic of licensing, selling, and commodification is fundamental to the creation—and often the messages—of high-profile cultural texts for kids, cultural texts that are also surrounded by explicit product commercials and media promotions. So let's now answer the title question of this chapter: kids' culture in the United States is pretty darned commercialized. By "commercialized" we mean the involvement of advertising or product promotion in the creation or funding (direct or indirect) of media and cultural phenomena (see the discussion in Mosco, 2009). Of course, much of our culture—kids' and adults'—is commercialized: we see ads everywhere, and much of our media is funded and influenced by advertising. But to say that children's culture is commercialized doesn't quite get at the extreme level of commercial involvement. Again like a lot of adult culture, kids' culture is really *hyper*commercialized (to use a term from McChesney, 1999). Advertising, marketing, and selling pervade nearly all elements of modern kids' culture. The claim that modern children's culture is commercialized (even when using the *hyper* prefix) is not in much dispute: just about everyone agrees on this. In dispute are the differences this may make, and the ways commercialism may harm or help (or both) kids and society generally.

This chapter will try to do several things. First, it will offer a brief history of commercialism in children's culture. Then, it will discuss some of the recent factors that seem to increase, or at least encourage in new ways, commercialism in modern kids' media. Finally, some of the relevant issues and debates of commercialization in modern kids' culture will be touched upon. Just to make things manageable, the discussion here will focus on the U.S. experience, arguably the most commercialized of all countries in terms of its media.

Historical Precedents

Historical reviews of children's culture argue that commercialization and licensing have been a part of this culture since virtually the beginnings of the modern industrialized age (see, for example, Cross, 2004; Kline, 1993). The Yellow Kid, one of the first regularly appearing characters in a U.S. newspaper comic strip, in the late 1800s, for example, spun off a large number of authorized and bootleg merchandise. This precedent led the way for even heavier commercial integration of later popular characters such as Buster Brown, originally a comic-strip character that later became so commercialized that its enduring legacy was as a children's shoe mascot (Cross, 2004; Gordon, 1998). Popular characters were licensed to different media. Superman appeared in comic books, newspaper comic strips, film serials, radio (and later television) programs, and even a novel. In the same vein, icons that were originally created for advertising could also be licensed as toys or other products, such as the Campbell Soup kids (Cross, 2004).

One trend that has developed is the gradual use of children's culture to sell products directly to children. Early industrialized toys and games tended to target parents as the market more than children themselves. There were exceptions to this, even in the early 1900s, however. Children's magazines were economically designed to sell to children early on; beginning in the 1930s and '40s, comic books and radio also produced content for kids that was advertising supported (Cross, 2004). Sometimes the advertising would bleed over into the content, such as a

Superman comic-book story that featured a real tie-in licensed toy—the Krypto-Ray Gun—as a plot device (Gordon, 1998). Radio, as a sponsored medium in which advertisers often acted as program producers, would even more fundamentally blur the commercial into the program as a way to sell to kids (Asquith, 2014). This is why Ralphie, in the 1983 movie *A Christmas Story*, experiences such a crushing loss of innocence when decoding a secret message from the radio program *Little Orphan Annie*, prompting him to exclaim, "'Be sure to drink your Ovaltine.' Ovaltine? A crummy commercial? Son of a bitch!"

These dynamics increased dramatically with the rise of broadcast television. When looking at the history of kids' TV programming, the level of commercialism has ebbed and flowed with both the regulatory environment of the time as well as industrial and technological trends. In the late 1940s and early 1950s, many early kids' television programs were "sustaining," meaning that they had no advertising or sponsor. However, even this noncommercial strategy had a commercial purpose: early television companies saw children's programming as a way to entice parents to buy television sets (Pecora, 1998). Such very early nonadvertised programming may also have been designed as a tactic to convince (or, perhaps, con) the FCC and other regulators into thinking that this new medium—a federally licensed medium—would be "responsible" to the public interest.

This promotional coyness did not last long, and as the sponsorship model grabbed hold of children's programming, viewers saw a level of commercial-program integration that was crude both in its explicitness and in its lack of coherent marketing strategy. Techniques such as "host selling"—where human or puppet hosts of programs would tout their sponsor's product—and "integrated commercials"—skits or other program segments featuring sponsors' products—were commonplace (Alexander, Benjamin, Hoerrner, & Roe, 1998; Samuel, 2001). Kids would soon get used to selling as part of the show, such as *Howdy Doody*'s Buffalo Bob Smith touting Wonder Bread (Samuel, 2001).

With the 1955 debut of *The Mickey Mouse Club* on ABC and the various toy merchandise that followed, the links between toys and children's programming strengthened. Companies such as Mattel used kids' shows to sell directly and year-round to children, and increased the number of licensed products based upon children's programming as well as visually oriented toys that looked good on television (Cross, 2004; Kline, 1993). Although the 1960s saw the single-sponsorship model gradually erode, the migration of children's network programming to Saturday morning was primarily in response to kids' marketers' need to efficiently reach specialized niche audiences (Mittell, 2004). A potentially more activist stance by the Federal Communications Commission and Federal Trade Commission in the late 1960s and '70s helped somewhat to keep growing commercialism in check, but a movement toward free-market ideologies in the late 1970s—reinforced by the election of Ronald Reagan as president—ended any significant federal challenges (Cross, 2004; Niesen, 2015). Beginning in the early 1980s, even modest industry self-regulation of children's TV programming was virtually eliminated (Johnson & Young, 2003; Kunkel, 2001). (See Chapter 2 for a history of the regulation of children's media and Chapter 14 for a discussion of the role and effects of advertising in children's media.)

The 1980s, then, saw a greater integration of toys and culture that influenced later legislation but also established models of strategic synergy that still exist today to perhaps an even greater extent (Pecora, 1998). Licensing activity in the film industry beginning in the late 1970s played a key role. The nature and success of Star Wars toys, according to historian Gary Cross, "helped to change the meaning of play" by offering not just Luke Skywalker and Darth Vader action figures, but practically everyone in that whole galaxy far, far away. The prolific Star Wars toy line promised near-complete duplication of characters and sets from the films such that "the child was invited to stage scenes from the movies, to play a god orchestrating a miniature world of high-tech adventure" (Cross, 2004, p. 158).

Other toy companies could not help notice the success of the Jedi. Some companies altered the formula by turning (1) from film to TV and (2) from a stance that was reactive to cultural trends to one that was profoundly proactive. Implementing what Thomas Engelhardt (1986) called "The Shortcake Strategy," toy companies would develop toy lines that were created to be turned into television programs. The toys, then, come first, the TV shows second. Such product lines—like Care Bears, Masters of the Universe, G.I. Joe (the post-Vietnam, Cobra-hating version) and of course Strawberry Shortcake—were comprised of multiple characters and emphasized the importance of teamwork, both illustrated by the plots of programs. The purpose of the TV show, then, was to promote the toys: they were "program-length commercials," the small-fry version of infomercials. Product commercials for the toys also aired during the programs, just in case kids didn't get the message. This era helped to legitimize the large amount of licensed-based programs we still see today, such as Lego-based programming like *Ninjago: Masters of Spinjitzu*.

Another consequence was a regulatory backlash that, as explained in Chapter 2, resulted in the Children's Television Act of 1990. This legislation implemented or reasserted rules, and applied to both cable and broadcast television for children. The act placed several restrictions on commercialism, including a limit on the amount of time devoted to product commercials; the mandated use of "bumpers" or program separators, designed to separate programs from commercials; and the elimination of "program-length commercials." However, as a result of industry lobbying, the definition of this last concept is not nearly as restricted as it could be. Instead of being defined as TV shows based on toys (which would bump off shows like *Ninjago: Masters of Spinjitzu*), the term is instead defined as "a program associated with a product in which commercials for that product are aired" (quoted in Kunkel, 2001). A show based on Ninjago is okay, but no commercials for Ninjago-based Legos during Ninjago the program on The Cartoon Network. Later in that decade and addressing the Internet, the Children's Online Privacy Protection Act of 1998 (COPPA) restricted websites both in terms of collecting information about users under thirteen and therefore sharing such information to third-party marketers without explicit, verifiable parental consent.

So things have to be better than they were in the 1950s, right? The Children's Television Act, after all, is a sweeping piece of regulation that applies to both ABC and Nickelodeon. We no longer see "host selling" on children's television as a consequence. Online data collection about kids is also regulated. But if things should be better, then why do critics say that the single biggest change in consumer culture since the 1990s—at any level—has been marketers' "imperative to target kids" (Schor, 2004, p. 12), or that even since 2005 "advertising and marketing to children has become intensified" (Carlson & Clarke, 2014)? It's because, despite legislation like the Children's Television Act or COPPA, the commercialization of children's culture has increased, even dramatically, since the 1980s. The next section explains a few of the reasons why this is so.

The Modern Context of Kids' Commercialism

This section will focus on three elements that increase the pressure to blur differences between culture and commercial with children's media: (1) recent incentives to create "aggressive" advertising, (2) the growth of synergistic, mega-media corporations, and (3) the proliferation of new media (creating new marketing and media-selling venues).

First, part of the reason we're seeing increased commercialization in children's culture is that, as noted at the beginning of this chapter, we are seeing this accelerated movement in all of culture, not just kids' (West & McAllister, 2013). New advertising philosophies like integrated marketing seek to coordinate promotional techniques such as traditional advertising, public relations and event sponsorship. Digital media have also siphoned advertising revenue from traditional media like network television. These traditional media, then, might be willing to strike permissive deals with advertisers given their desperation to avoid becoming mediated dinosaurs, leading to strongly commercialized programming such as the *Victoria's Secret Fashion Show*. Such factors also make reaching desirable audiences who are willing to spend—like kids!—even more valuable.

A second trend that is strongly linked to this commercial push but also has its own promotional trajectory is the continued domination of coordinated media licensing, what in the 1990s was called "synergy" (McAllister & Proffitt, in press). Synergy encourages media corporations to grow by acquiring different media outlets in which licensed brands can be produced, distributed, and exhibited. From an entertainment point of view, then, a synergistically pure media conglomerate would own different subsidiaries dealing with books, comic books, film, recorded music, television, video games, and websites. Such corporations, then, are promotionally oriented, with one subsidiary, through shared licensing, promoting the other subsidiaries (and often the corporate brand as a whole). While *Star Wars* may have shown the economic value of prolific toy and licensing output, it was 1989's *Batman* that spotlighted how one corporation (at that time Warner Communications) can move a character license effectively through different internally owned media outlets, creating one massive, multimedia "commodity inter-text" (Meehan, 1991).

We routinely see media companies exploiting their outlets to coordinate their licenses. Disney, owner of *Star Wars*, will use their owned networks ABC and ESPN to promote the latest release in the franchise. *The Big Bang Theory*, produced by Warner Television, features t-shirts and action figures from DC superheroes in virtually every episode: both Warner Television and DC are owned by Time Warner.

A third factor in the enhanced commercial/promotional ethos of kids' culture is the use of digital media technologies. Obviously, the media landscape has changed dramatically since the 1980s with the creation and diffusion of digital media such as social media, video-game systems, on-demand media, and mobile media like smartphones with downloadable media options. Although through 2016 advertisers for children's brands still emphasize traditional media spending such as television and magazines (Kim, Williams, & Wilcox, 2016), digital options have all significantly influenced how brands and media corporations operate. Digital media serve multiple functions. They can be integrated into the larger corporate synergy, promoting other properties. They can be sold or upgrades can be sold, generating direct-sales revenue. They can display product commercials, generating advertising revenue. They have led to their own versions of aggressive marketing, as digital media like social media blur the distinctions between advertising and web environments, creating "guerrilla marketing," "native advertising," and "content marketing" that often are difficult to distinguish *as* advertising (Einstein, 2016; Serazio, 2013). And all of them are key players in the commercialization of children's culture.

Given these factors, what are some of the ways that we see children's culture being commercialized in the modern age?

Categories of Kids' Commercialization

The Commercial Logic of Media Systems

Let's just start out with the basic one: unsurprisingly, sales are at the heart of children's culture. This is obvious to see when we're talking about "direct" sales—like kids buying, or influencing their parents to buy, video games, apps, and on-demand movies. But most children's media, in some way, is also supported by advertising sales. The history of broadcasting shows that commercial interests fundamentally shaped the development of radio and television (McChesney, 1993). When kids (or any audience members) watch TV, they are being sold to advertisers (Smythe, 1977). Child viewers are "hailed" as consumers by the system, not as children to be educated or publics to be engaged. Commercial interests, then, will do and say whatever is in their legal rights (and sometimes beyond such rights) to persuade kids to purchase or influence a purchase. Media companies are economically rewarded to support that commercial imperative; economically, programs are subordinate to the ads. So although the television industry generally is concerned about declining television viewing and declining ratings, children's television networks such as Nickelodeon and Cartoon Network saw an increase in advertising revenues in the mid-2010s (Lafayette, 2014, 2015). So-called "flanker networks"—affiliated outlets like Nick Jr., Nick Toons, Disney Junior, and Disney XD—have created more opportunities to advertise to children with television (Katz, 2014). Networks that at one time were commercial-free or with limited commercials—such as Boomerang and Disney Channel—have added or increased advertising (Katz, 2014). In addition, watching children's programming on these networks' apps via tablets and other mobile devices allows advertisers connected to these programs to reach children outside of the home (Poggi, 2016).

Given the economic incentives of making children's entertainment friendly to advertising, it is no surprise that commercials and programs look and sound alike, and often share similar kid-appealing themes of fun adventure, kid empowerment, and "kids rule," anti-adult values. This leads to a flow of commercial and promotional images that often seem to merge (McAllister & Giglio, 2005). During a November 26, 2016 airing of *SpongeBob SquarePants* on Nickelodeon, for example, viewers saw the end of a cartoon that immediately went into a 4:15-minute stretch of animated images not unlike (and in fact sometimes exactly like) SpongeBob. In order, these were: a promotion for the animated *The Loud House* holiday special; the results of a Nick.com-based contest involving viewers choosing between SpongeBob and Lincoln Loud (thus tying the program with the promotion that followed); paid commercials for Shopkins miniature-kitchen-food toys for girls, Pokémon video games, Super Wings toy airplanes, Kellogg's Frosted Flakes (with Tony the Tiger), the Barbie Pop-Up Camper (in pink, naturally), the Nerf Terrascout, Animal Jam toy pets ("The more you adopt the more you unlock exclusive content!" on a tie-in website, the ad promises), the upcoming premiere of the Disney film *Moana*, the Monster High Deluxe High School toy set; then more promos for Nick video games featuring characters like SpongeBob, an upcoming episode of *Henry Danger*, and the Nickelodeon Halo Awards, before immediately going back to an episode of SpongeBob. Two of the toy commercials are further connected with each other as viewers are told by an announcer that the products are "available at ToysRUs!"

Finally, toy companies themselves may be program producers. Hasbro, for example, produces several programs on the cable network Discovery Family that essentially serve as content marketing for these toy brands, including *Transformers: Rescue Bots, My Little Pony: Friendship is Magic,* and *Littlest Pet Shop.*

The Power of the Media Brand

Children's media companies do not just carry other companies' advertising, they also have their own products to advertise and promote. In this case, media companies use children's culture to "brand" themselves. They sell their own products with messages and appeals that, like commercials, exploit kids' desires and need for autonomy (White & Preston, 2005; Sandler, 2003). This has several implications. First, many commercials/promotions for synergistic products (like for *Moana*) will air on subsidiary networks (ABC and Disney Channel). But it will also mean that the shows themselves can be multi-level promotions. The Disney Channel program *K.C. Undercover* promotes by its existence any merchandise connected to it. It also promotes Disney (since the official title of the program is *Disney K.C. Undercover*) and the singing career of its star, Zendaya, who sings the program's theme song, whose songs are played on Radio Disney and the Radio Disney app, and who hosted the 2015 Radio Disney Music Awards (Olson, 2015).

Similarly, the Cartoon Network program *Batman: The Brave and the Bold* promoted not just Batman, but the fundamental premise of the show was team-ups featuring Batman's adventures with second-tier superheroes such as Red Tornado and Blue Beetle; toys, video games, and comic books tied to the show featured characters that matched the specific animation style—and sometimes plot developments of specific episodes—on the program (Roman & McAllister, 2012).

New Integration, Old Policy

Although such legislation as the Children's Television Act and COPPA (see Chapter 2 for details on these policies) place some limits on some media, there are plenty of loopholes in the system, loopholes that are enacted by new technologies and new corporate trends. The branding of promos and separators are such loopholes. Similarly, while the FCC bans the narrowly defined "program-length commercials" on cable and broadcast TV, no such restriction exists on media like the Internet and apps. This works both for licenses that were originally media-oriented, and licenses that were also originally toys or even advertising mascots.

Websites often combine media characters, product advertisers, and shopping opportunities in ways that virtually eradicate these differences. These included branded online environments like Disney's Club Penguin or BarbieWorld that embedded multiple layers of commercialism and promotion as kids explore these digital worlds. Grimes (2015) argues that such games pioneered commercial techniques such as "micro-transactions" where players buy upgrades or attractive items, and that companies use such branded game environments for market research, brand promotion, and new product testing. Advanced kid players often serve as "brand ambassadors" for long-term immersion in the game and for the perks of spending money on upgrades. Other scholars have noted that traditional commercial techniques that are banned on television, like host-selling, are not uncommon on kids' websites and digital games (Bucy, Kim, & Park, 2011).

Dangers and Dilemmas

Often, when we lecture about these issues to students, a question that may be asked is, "So what? Does it really hurt that kids are sold to, and that there's a blurring of the commercial with the culture?" It is true, as we'll see, that there is not complete agreement about this issue among scholars of society and culture. But many believe that these commercial characteristics are harmful, a position to which we are sympathetic.

The mix of the commercial and the cultural, adding in modern marketing research techniques, may make the construction of promotional messages especially manipulative and strategic, involving consistent messages that celebrate consumption in a variety of media. With new commercial forms such as advergames, researchers have found that children have a difficult time recognizing them as forms of advertising (An, Jin, & Park, 2014). Some critics argue that heavy immersion in commercial/consumer culture can lead to the cultivation of commodity-influenced self-concepts that are fraught with potential social and economic division and insecurity, vulnerable to the commercial message, and therefore potentially harmful to well-being (Schor, 2004). The consistent "pro-kid, anti-adult" message found in children's media and commercials, coupled with the "nag factor" commercialism encourages, may add stress to the household (Schor, 2004). The drive for ever more efficient niche marketing may entice media creators and marketers to target ever-younger potential consumers, even those less than a year old (Linn, 2004). Products that are sold on television may be physically harmful, such as foods high in sugar and fat (Carlson & Clarke, 2014). Even non-advertising on-demand systems like Netflix still carry children's programming that are licensing and promotionally based, such as the TV programs *Angry Birds* (from the popular game app) and *Max Steele* (based on a Mattel action figure) and movies *Monster High: Boo York, Boo York* (2015) and *Lego: The Adventures of Clutch Powers* (2010), both based on toys. Another argument has to do with the potential effect of environmental waste on the planet that commodity culture encourages (Jhally, 2000), especially when such values are inculcated at a young age and could lead to long-term materialist values (Opree, Buijzen, van Reijmersdal, & Valkenburg, 2014).

Some scholars dispute that a commodity-based children's culture is all bad, however. While recognizing the ideological dilemmas of commodity culture, Ellen Seiter (1993) argues that niche marketing can open up spaces for some groups such as young girls, who otherwise may be undervalued or to a large degree ignored in a predominantly patriarchal culture. Both Seiter and David Buckingham (2000) note the critical stance kids may bring to commercialism, and even the creative power of play with licensed-driven toys and the shared community that kids can construct with them. Maya Götz, Dafna Lemish, Amy Aidman, and Hyesung Moon (2005) conclude from their international, ethnographic study of children's play that commercially supported television viewing does not seem to significantly restrict children's imagination; such results, however, may have been more clear outside of the United States. Although media and toy brands like Bratz are highly commercialized (McAllister, 2007), Hains (2012) observes unexpected creativity among kids playing with these "problematic" dolls. Buckingham (2000) further argues that critics of toy-based media content do not understand historical trends that have always blurred the toy-media connection in the industrial age or the complexities of the market.

What to do about the dangers of commercialism in kids' culture is also complex and multidimensional. Critics such as Juliet Schor (2004) and Susan Linn (2004) suggest multifaceted approaches, including activist- and community-group alliances, media literacy programs, the support of alternative and children-created media, parental awareness and mediation, and increased lobbying for more assertive legislation for children's consumer rights and against excessive commercialism. Although it's likely that he would be in favor of many of these ideas, Buckingham (2000) warns against the "wag of the finger" approach to children and their culture, especially with media literacy programs. He argues that when adults bad-mouth to kids the commercial culture that kids take pleasure in, it reinforces the distance between kids and adults and becomes a self-defeating teaching tactic. In a "back-at-ya" response, though, Shirley Steinberg and Joe Kincheloe (2004, p. 10) argue that stances like Buckingham's are too dismissive of media literacy efforts that reveal manipulative techniques and that such stances even encourage a "pedagogy of nihilism" that justifies educational apathy about commercialism and underplays the gross power discrepancy between corporate marketers and children.

Going back to our opening example of unboxing, viewers may enjoy the unvarnished review of products, but the videos, which appear as entertainment programming, are essentially extended commercials, and are embedded in multi-layered promotions, commercials, and sponsorships. This example illustrates that the resources of the children's cultural industries—fed by and integrated with the children's commercial industries—are formidable and, we believe, quite destructive on the whole. Scholars have argued that anti-commercial critics often seem engaged in unreasonable and emotional "moral panics" that blind complexities (Götz and colleagues [2005] make such charges against anti-TV critics, for instance). When we see the incredible level of commercialism that drives all of culture—not just for kids—we will admit that, yes, we're a little bit worried, even sometimes panicked, about the percolation of advertising into various aspects of children's culture.

Discussion Questions

1. In what ways do entertainment media for children integrate advertising and brands in the viewing experience?

2. How do large corporations that specialize in children's media try to brand themselves to children? What themes and symbols do they use in this branding?

3. What are recent digital examples of hyper-commercialism or hyper-promotion? What messages do these promotions send to kids about the connection of advertising and media content?

4. What are some of the most important negative consequences of the commercialization of children's culture? What are some positive consequences?

Exercises

1. Find a schedule of Saturday-morning television programs targeted at children. How many of the programs are based upon licensed properties? Be sure to list programs based upon established media characters as well as programs based upon toys or other children's products.

2. Watch an hour of children's television, noting especially what websites, games and apps are advertised or promoted during this time. Does television encourage kids to immerse themselves in digital commercial environments?

3. Examine a branded app aimed at kids, like apps for Marvel superheroes. In what ways are the brand promoted within the app?

References

An, S., Jin, H. S., & Park, E. H. (2014). Children's advertising literacy for advergames: Perceptions of the game as advertising. *Journal of Advertising, 43*(1), 63–72. doi:10.1080/00913367.2013.795123

Asquith, K. (2014). Join the club: Food advertising, 1930s children's popular culture, and brand socialization. *Popular Communication, 12*, 17–31. doi:10.1080/15405702.2013.869334

Alexander, A., Benjamin, L. M., Hoerrner, K., & Roe, D. (1998). "We'll be back in a moment": A content analysis of advertisements in children's television in the 1950s. *Journal of Advertising, 27*(3), 1–9. doi:10.1080/00913 367.1998.10673558

Buckingham, D. (2000). *After the death of childhood: Growing up in the age of electronic media.* Cambridge: Polity.

Bucy, E. P., Kim, S. C., & Park, M. C. (2011). Host selling in cyberspace: Product personalities and character advertising on popular children's websites. *New Media & Society, 13*(8), 1245–1264. doi:10.1177/1461444811402485

Carlson, L., & Clarke, B. (2014). Reassessing the current state of advertising to children. *International Journal of Advertising, 33*(3), 429–436. doi:10.2501/IJA-33-3-429-436

CKN Toys. (2016, March 28). *Unboxing new Spiderman battery-powered ride on Super Car 6V Test Drive Park Playtime Fun Ckn Toys.* Retrieved from https://www.youtube.com/watch?v=he8nz5tAZrw&t=94s

Cohen, J. (2016, November 16). *Top 100 most subscribed YouTube channels worldwide – October 2016.* Retrieved from http://www.tubefilter.com/2016/11/16/top-100-most-subscribed-youtube-channels-worldwide-october-2016/

Cross, G. (2004). *The cute and the cool: Wondrous innocence and modern American children's culture.* New York, NY: Oxford University Press.

Einstein, M. (2016). *Black ops advertising: Native ads, content marketing, and the covert world of the digital sell.* New York, NY: O/R Books.

Engelhardt, T. (1986). The shortcake strategy. In T. Gitlin (Ed.), *Watching television* (pp. 68–110). New York, NY: Pantheon.

Gordon, I. (1998). *Comic strips and consumer culture, 1890–1945.* Washington, DC: Smithsonian Institution Press.

Götz, M., Lemish, D., Aidman, A., & Moon, H. (2005). *Media and the make-believe worlds of children: When Harry Potter meets Pokémon in Disneyland.* Mahwah, NJ: Lawrence Erlbaum.

Grimes, S. M. (2015). Playing by the market rules: Promotional priorities and commercialization in children's virtual worlds. *Journal of Consumer Culture, 15*(1), 110–134. doi:10.1177/1469540513493209

Hains, R. C. (2012). An afternoon of productive play with problematic dolls: The importance of foregrounding children's voices in research. *Girlhood Studies, 5*(1), 121–140. doi:10.3167/ghs.2012.050108

Jhally, S. (2000). Advertising at the edge of the apocalypse. In R. Andersen & L. Strate (Eds.), *Critical studies in media commercialism* (pp. 27–39). Oxford: Oxford University Press.

Johnson, M. D., & Young, B. M. (2003). Advertising history of televisual media. In E. L. Palmer & B. M. Young (Eds.), *The faces of televisual media: Teaching, violence, selling to children* (2nd ed., pp. 265–285). Mahwah, NJ: Lawrence Erlbaum.

Katz, A. J. (2014, December 15). As Disney and Nick falter, flanker nets and rivals give chase. *Broadcasting & Cable,* p. 19.

Kim, K. K., Williams, J. D., & Wilcox, G. B. (2016). "Kid tested, mother approved": The relationship between advertising expenditures and "most-loved" brands. *International Journal of Advertising, 35*(1), 42–60. doi:10.1080/02650487.2015.1079947

Kline, S. (1993). *Out of the garden: Toys and children's culture in the age of TV marketing.* London: Verso.

Kunkel, D. (2001). Children and television advertising. In D. G. Singer & J. L. Singer (Eds.), *Handbook of children and the media* (pp. 375–393). Thousand Oaks, CA: Sage.

Lafayette, J. (2014, March 10). In the Nick of time, kids market gets rolling. *Broadcasting & Cable,* pp. 12–13.

Lafayette, J. (2015, November 16). How Cartoon grows its grip on a new generation. *Broadcasting & Cable,* p. 20.

Linn, S. (2004). *Consuming kids: Protecting our children from the onslaught of marketing and advertising.* New York, NY: Anchor.

Maker Studios. (2016). *About.* Retrieved from http://www.makerstudios.com/#about

McAllister, M. P. (2007). "Girls with a passion for fashion": The Bratz brand as integrated spectacular consumption. *Journal of Children and Media, 1*(3), 244–258. doi:10.1080/17482790701531870

McAllister, M. P., & Giglio, J. M. (2005). The commodity flow of U.S. children's television. *Critical Studies in Media Communication, 22*(1), 26–44. doi:10.1080/0739318042000331835

McAllister, M. P., & Proffitt, J. (in press). Media ownership in a corporate age. In L. Wilkins & C. G. Christians (Eds.), *The Routledge handbook of mass media ethics* (2nd ed.). Mahwah, NJ: Lawrence Erlbaum.

McChesney, R. W. (1993). *Telecommunications, mass media, and democracy: The battle for the control of U.S. broadcasting, 1928–1935.* New York, NY: Oxford University Press.

McChesney, R. W. (1999). *Rich media, poor democracy: Communication politics in dubious times.* Urbana, IL: University of Illinois Press.

Meehan, E. (1991). "Holy commodity fetish, Batman!" The political economy of a commercial intertext. In R. E. Pearson & W. Uricchio (Eds.), *The many lives of the Batman: Critical approaches to a superhero and his media* (pp. 47–65). New York, NY: Routledge.

Mittell, J. (2004). *Genre and television: From cop shows to cartoons in American culture.* New York, NY: Routledge.

Mosco, V. (2009). *The political economy of communication* (2nd ed.). Thousand Oaks, CA: Sage.

Niesen, M. (2015). From gray panther to national nanny: The kidvid crusade and the eclipse of the US Federal Trade Commission, 1977–1980. *Communication, Culture & Critique, 8,* 576–593. doi:10.1111/cccr.12100

Olson, C. A. (2015, April 22). Zendaya keeps her cool preparing to host Radio Disney Music Awards. *Billboard.* Retrieved from http://www.billboard.com/articles/columns/pop-shop/6538998/zendaya-host-radio-disney-music-awards-2015

Opree, S. J., Buijzen, M., van Reijmersdal, E. A., & Valkenburg, P. M. (2014). Children's advertising exposure, advertised product desire, and materialism: A longitudinal study. *Communication Research, 41*(5), 717–735. doi:10.1177/0093650213479129

Pecora, N. (1998). *The business of children's entertainment.* New York, NY: Guilford.

Poggi, J. (2016, March 7). Kids networks pitch immersive experiences. *Advertising Age,* p. 6.

Roman, Z., & McAllister, M. P. (2012). The brand and the bold: Synergy and sidekicks in licensed-based children's television. *Global Media Journal, 12*(20), 1–15. Retrieved from http://lass.calumet.purdue.edu/cca/gmj/index.htm

Samuel, L. R. (2001). *Brought to you by: Postwar television advertising and the American dream.* Austin, TX: University of Texas Press.

Sandler, K. S. (2003). Synergy nirvana: Brand equity, television animation, and Cartoon Network. In C. A. Stabile & M. Harrison (Eds.), *Prime time animation: Television animation and American culture* (pp. 89–109). New York, NY: Routledge.

Schor, J. B. (2004). *Born to buy.* New York, NY: Scribner.

Seiter, E. (1993). *Sold separately: Children and parents in consumer culture.* New Brunswick, NJ: Rutgers University Press.

Serazio, M. (2013). *Your ad here: The cool sell of guerilla marketing.* New York, NY: New York University Press.

Smythe, D. W. (1977). Communications: Blindspot of Western Marxism. *Canadian Journal of Political and Social Theory, 1*(3), 1–27.

Steinberg, S. R., & Kincheloe, J. L. (2004). Introduction: Kinderculture, information saturation, and the socio-educational positioning of children. In S. R. Steinberg & J. L. Kincheloe (Eds.), *Kinderculture: The corporate construction of childhood* (2nd ed., pp. 1–47). Boulder, CO: Westview.

West, E., & McAllister, M. P. (2013). Introduction. In M. P. McAllister & E. West (Eds.), *The Routledge companion to advertising and promotional culture* (pp. 1–8). New York, NY: Routledge.

White, C. L., & Preston, E. H. (2005). The spaces of children's programming. *Critical Studies in Media Communication, 22*(3), 239–255. doi:10.1080/07393180500201678

CHAPTER 16

How Are Internet Practices Embedded in Teens' Everyday Lives?

Susannah R. Stern and Olivia A. Gonzalez

Jade wakes up on a Monday morning to the sound of her favorite music streaming on her smartphone. As she lies in bed, she scrolls through Instagram, "liking" her friends' pictures from their weekend camping trip. She scrunches up her face, takes an ugly selfie with her phone camera, and sends it to her best friend on Snapchat. Then she climbs out of bed, takes a shower, and exchanges a few text messages with her friends while getting ready for school. Before heading to breakfast, she glances quickly at a weather app to see if she needs a raincoat. When she sits down at the breakfast table, her dad asks her how yesterday's Algebra test went; Jade quickly navigates to her math teacher's course website to check her score. The rest of breakfast time is spent scanning her favorite news sites to prepare for her current events quiz. Before she knows it, a text from her friend tells her it's time to meet to walk to school. It's 7:30 A.M.

Jade's morning routine reflects just a few of the many ways that digital practices are embedded in the everyday lives of American teenagers. In fact, digital media have become essential for full participation in social, educational, and civic life. The Internet links teenagers to one another, to their schools and communities, and to the public culture more broadly. Because many teenagers today have grown up with smartphones and wired computers, they move seamlessly between websites, apps and platforms as they navigate the expectations and adventures of adolescence. This chapter will discuss what teenagers are up to online, as well as describe what we are learning about the affordances and costs associated with their digital practices.

Internet Access and Ownership

With the help of laptops, tablets, and especially mobile phones, most teenagers lead Internet-saturated lives. Ninety-two percent of American teens between the ages of 12–17 report going online every day, typically using a mobile device (Lenhart, 2015). Smartphones, in particular, allow Internet access anywhere and anytime, helping to explain how a fourth of teens say they go online "almost constantly" (Lenhart, 2015). Teenagers are more likely than ever to own the devices that enable them to go online; over two-thirds of all teenagers own their own smartphone, and more than four-fifths own a desktop, laptop or tablet computer. Not surprisingly, teens from higher income families and whose parents have more education are most likely to own Internet-connected devices (Lenhart, 2015).

Although nearly all teenagers across the country can use the Internet at home, school, or a public library, inequities in Internet usage remain. These days, the inequities are less about access, and more about how easy that access is. For example, about 5 million households in America with children between the ages of 6–17 do not have high-speed Internet service at home. A disproportionate share of those households are low-income and rural, and predominantly Black and Hispanic (Horrigan, 2015). Teens who don't have broadband service at home have less chance to play around, research, and socialize online, with important implications for their education, social lives, and future employment options. Some school districts have outfitted school buses with Wi-Fi routers, parking them in rural and low-income neighborhoods so that local teens can complete their homework (Clapman, 2016), but such programs are rare. Inequities also exist in how teens are compelled and encouraged to use Internet-connected devices. For instance, teens from wealthier families tend to use the Internet more to search for information or read news, compared to teens in poorer families, who spend more time chatting or playing video games (OECD, 2016). Calling attention to these access and usage disparities, Martin and Ito (2015) point out that "young people who lack digital fluency and full access will always be a step behind their more connected peers."

Although the rest of this chapter will primarily focus on what we know about teens with consistent and convenient Internet access, we feel it is important to forefront these inequities from the outset. It can be easy to assume that all teenagers access the Internet whenever they want and with comparable levels of familiarity and expertise. Omitting discussion of American teens who cannot easily and consistently access the Internet renders existing inequities invisible, and thus less likely to be addressed.

What Are Teens Doing Online?

These days, discussions about teen Internet use frequently focus on how much time teenagers spend on smartphones, tablets and computers. But it is much more interesting to consider the wide range of activities and uses for which they employ the Internet. Although it is impossible to offer a complete inventory, we organize teens' digital practices into three frequently overlapping categories: (1) socializing & self-presenting; (2) consuming entertainment; and (3) information seeking.

Socializing and Self-Presenting

Similar to other new technologies over the years, the Internet was initially heralded as a tool that young people would avail themselves of to gain valuable, employable skills. The Internet, it was predicted, would help to restructure adolescence into a period of disciplined information seeking, increased world awareness, and greater productivity. Despite debates over whether such premonitions have come to fruition, the current reality is that teenagers primarily use the Internet for social reasons. Although adults often rue this "unproductive" use of their teens' screen time, it's important to remember that managing social relationships and playing around with self-expression styles is as developmentally functional as it is fun.

These days, much of the socializing teens do online takes place on social media. Social media has become an umbrella term to refer to social network and video sharing sites, blogging platforms, and similar tools that enable participants to create and share their own content (boyd, 2014). Four-fifths of American teens use social media (Lenhart, Smith, Anderson, Duggan, & Perrin, 2015), whether on computers, tablets, or increasingly, on mobile phones. Currently, the most popular social media used by teens are Facebook, Instagram, Snapchat, Twitter and Google+ (Lenhart *et al.*, 2015). Although all social media are designed to connect people, each social media platform is slightly different. On Facebook, for example, teenagers can post information about themselves and their current sentiments, as well as read their friends' posts. Snapchat, alternatively, allows teens to send one another messages, typically images that disappear after viewing. Teens' choices about which social media they use at any given time depend not only on their Internet access and device ownership (e.g., whether or not they have a smartphone), but also where the people with whom they want to socialize congregate (boyd, 2014).

Why are social media so popular with teens? Our research and review of relevant literature indicates that teenagers use social media for the same reasons they employ more traditional means of communication. They want to maintain and develop relationships, present themselves, and participate in public life.

In many ways, social media offer real advantages in accomplishing these tasks. Social media allow teenagers to be in touch with family and friends frequently, without limitations of geography, transportation, or mutual availability. The variety of ways to communicate—including text, videos, photos, and cut-and-pasted pop culture artifacts—allows teens to be both strategic and playful about how they socialize with one another. Conveniently available for many teens on smartphones as well as computers, social media can be perused while doing any number of different activities, such as homework or watching television; indeed, for most teenagers today, multi-tasking is the new normal.

On social media, teens can also interact with a much larger number of people than they would otherwise. For many teens, this sense of connection to a greater community leads them to feel more included and supported (Davis, 2012; Reich, Subrahmanyam, & Espinoza, 2012). More opportunities to communicate with one's friends seems to make teens feel closer with one another (Gardner & Davis, 2013; Lenhart *et al.*, 2015). For teenagers who find it difficult to disclose their personal feelings in face-to-face situations, communicating on social media enables them to control their interactions and posts and avoid the anxiety of not knowing how others will react (Davis, 2012; Valkenburg & Peter, 2012). Finally, the Internet provides opportunities for young people with similar interests or lifestyles to interact with one another, regardless of geography. Indeed, more than half of teens ages 13–17 have made a new friend online (Lenhart *et al.*, 2015). Opportunities to meet new friends online can be especially valuable for teenagers who do not experience a welcoming community or satisfying relationships offline (Gardner & Davis, 2013). Online communities can also offer sources of support that are missing in teens' offline lives (e.g., Sherman & Greenfield, 2013).

Social media not only afford teenagers convenient and appealing ways to socialize, but they also offer teenagers substantial control over how they present themselves while socializing online. Goffman (1959) advanced the idea that all social interactions are inherently performative, as people aim to shape others' impressions of them. Self-presentation is particularly important during adolescence, a time when young people deliberate who they are and who they wish to be. Social media enable teens to be strategic about what they share, omit or exaggerate, as well what mode of presentation they use to represent themselves (e.g., a photo, a quote, or poem). Seventeen-year-old Dylan, for instance, hoping to project himself on Instagram as artsy and hip, offers a carefully curated selection of black and white images of himself at alternative music concerts. In keeping with his theme, he intentionally avoids posting any content about the mundane activities that consume much of his everyday life, like working at the grocery store or babysitting his little sister. As they make such self-presentation choices, teenagers engage in valuable self-reflection and identity work (Stern, 2008).

Online, teens alter their self-presentations depending on who they want or expect to encounter them. One way they do this is by using different social media platforms for different audiences. Only very best friends might see the ugly selfie fourteen-year-old Jade posts on Snapchat, while parents and her larger school community might see pictures of her accepting her soccer trophy posted on Facebook. In spaces where anonymous or pseudonymous expression are possible (e.g., Tumblr), teens are more free to offer presentations of themselves that are less conventional or accepted (e.g., as transgender or pro-ana). Studies show that as they make their decisions, teens consider who they want to connect with, how long they want their posts to last, the level of curating they want to undertake, and how much publicity they desire (e.g., Agosto, Abbas, & Naughton, 2012; Marwick & boyd, 2014; Mesch & Baker, 2010).

Consuming Entertainment

Watching television and movies, listening to music, reading books and magazines, and playing video games have been popular pastimes for teens for decades. What's different today is that all of these media can now be accessed through Internet-enabled devices, such as computers, tablets and smartphones. The fact that so many devices deliver content may help explain how the average American teenager spends 9 hours each day consuming entertainment (Common Sense Media, 2015). Despite their many options, teenagers say they most enjoy and most frequently engage in listening to music and watching television (Common Sense Media, 2015). However, teens may be watching favorite TV shows on Netflix, rather than on cable or satellite television, or streaming their favorite music on Spotify, rather than listening to music recordings they own. Teens also take advantage of entertainment content that is uniquely available on the Internet, such as user-generated "fail" videos (short videos depicting unsuccessful events, like skateboard wipeouts) and professional music videos posted to YouTube (Defy Media, 2016).

Teens don't just watch and listen to entertainment media, but they also spend considerable time keeping up with news about popular culture, celebrities, professional athletes and fashionable trends. Staying informed allows teenagers to gain and maintain social status among friends and peers while nurturing their own interests. Many teens follow their favorite celebrities, teams, and shows on social media; by reading tweets and posts that seem to come straight from their idols' mouths, they feel as though they share a personal relationship that heightens teens' sense of belonging and importance. Moreover, engagement in interest-driven entertainment consumption helps some teenagers develop a meaningful sense of identity. Borca, Bina, Keller, Gilbert, and Begotti (2015), for example, describe how adolescent boys they studied were able to develop meaningful identities as sports experts by using the Internet to read sports commentary, view videos of athletic events and interviews, and analyze statistics about teams and athletes.

Not all of teens' entertainment consumption online is passive. In fact, most teens also enjoy interactive entertainment online, including playing video games, participating in fantasy sports leagues, and completing quizzes and surveys. Online gaming has received the most attention from adults and scholars, likely because the vast majority of teens play games. Online video games, in particular, allow players to connect with others within the context of a game, despite being separated by geographic boundaries. Sitting alone in his bedroom, thirteen-year-old Jason can play World of Warcraft with his next door neighbor Wyatt, but also with countless other players across the globe. In fact, online games are specifically designed to encourage and facilitate interaction among co-players. For this reason, scholars and players argue, online games constitute a distinctive environment characterized by social, rather than solitary, play (Kowert, Domahidi, Festl, & Quandt, 2014).

Indeed, although older generations tend to think of teen video gamers as reclusive and isolated, researchers have found that the appeal of online games for many teens is simply hanging out with offline and online friends in a social setting (Kowert & Oldmeadow, 2013). Many online games have a voice connection capability allowing players to talk to each other while they play, and some teens report using separate online platforms, such as Skype, to connect with others while they play (Lenhart *et al.*, 2015). Because online games encourage teamwork, conversation, strategizing, and banter, they play a meaningful role in friendship formation and maintenance for many teens, especially boys. Not only do boys play online games more frequently, but they are also more likely to have made new friends through online games and to report that gaming makes them to feel closer to their existing friends (Lenhart *et al.*, 2015). Socializing within online gaming spaces also makes some teens feel safer, more confident, and more comfortable than when they interact in face to face contexts (Kowert & Oldmeadow, 2013).

Information Seeking

Rapid search capabilities, twenty-four-hour availability, and private browsing combine to make the Internet the first place that young people turn for a broad array of information. Directed Internet searches help teens with everything from health maintenance to homework to shopping. Online information-seeking is even embedded into everyday conversations, as friends and family interrupt their dialogues with Google searches about relevant topics (e.g., "What time does the movie start tonight?" or "How big is the Grand Canyon?") Such queries are made incredibly quick and convenient with the help of smartphones, which three-quarters of American teens own or can access (Lenhart, 2015). For teens today, looking things up online feels natural, and many teenagers are reassured that answers and diverse perspectives are only a few keystrokes away.

Questions about bodies and health are a normal part of adolescence, and many of them are answered or at least addressed on the Internet. Eighty-four percent of teens report accessing health information online, with search engines like Google as the typical starting place for inquiries. Primarily, teens seek information on preventative self-care, such as exercise and nutrition (Wartella, Rideout, Zupancic, Beaudoin-Ryan, & Lauricella, 2015). Take Mark, for example, who has decided that he wants to try out for his high school's varsity basketball team. He knows he needs to develop his leg strength to earn a spot on the team, so he Googles "speed and strength training for basketball." His search unearths dozens of articles and videos that teach him how to set up his own training program and nutrition plan to help him achieve his goals. The Internet helps Mark acquire his informational needs independently and efficiently. More than a third of teens report changing their behavior in response to health information they find online (Wartella *et al.*, 2015).

About a third of teens also use online resources to assess their symptoms, diagnose ailments, and to determine if medical conditions warrant treatment from a doctor (Wartella *et al.*, 2015). Because the Internet can be navigated privately, it may be particularly useful to teens who view discussions with doctors, parents, and peers with apprehension. Teens who are concerned about mental health issues like depression consult the Internet for facts and guidance, and about a fifth of teenagers report using the Internet to research other hard-to-discuss topics, like sexually transmitted diseases and puberty (Lenhart, 2010; Wartella *et al.*, 2015).

Not all of teens' online health information queries are directed toward information sites, nor are they explicitly geared toward finding out facts about bodies or health care. Rather, it has also become common for young people to use the Internet to learn more about and engage in conversations about sexual norms, attitudes and experiences. Online communities, websites and even YouTube videos provide spaces for young people to discuss homosexuality and transgenderism, teenage pregnancy, and living with sexually transmitted infections, among other identities (e.g., Hiller, Mitchell, & Ybarra, 2012). Teens who encounter the stories other teens and adults share about their experiences often report feeling less alone, less aberrant, and more supported (e.g., Wuest, 2014).

Homework assignments and school research also figure prominently into teens' online information-seeking practices. Consider the case of Alejandro, who has been assigned a group project on tobacco use for Health class that is due tomorrow. Because he and his classmates are busy afterschool with sports and jobs, they collaborate online that night. Communicating on Facebook and by text, they agree to develop a shared Google Document, which each group member adds to and edits as the night progresses. For his part, Alejandro toggles back and forth between the course website describing the project, various medical websites he has located on tobacco-related diseases, and the Google document itself, where he synthesizes what he is learning. By accessing online resources and collaborating virtually, Alejandro and his peers are able to complete the project by the time they go to bed.

This example illustrates how teens today use the Internet to collaborate and locate information that historically required visits to the library and in-person meetings. Teens today, however, are three times more likely to use online resources than library resources when conducting research (Kaiser Foundation, 2011). Virtual collaborations using social media and other digital platforms not only expedite group work outside of class, but they also seem to facilitate learning within the classroom (Khan, Wohn, & Ellison, 2014). Schools and teachers increasingly integrate online resources and platforms to disseminate information and resources to their students. Many students keep track of their grades online, submit homework online, and communicate with their teachers and peers through online message platforms. And for teenagers who are interested in higher education or exploring vocational paths, the Internet is central to learning more about course offerings, expenses, and job qualifications.

Two-thirds of teenagers use the Internet to seek out information about news, politics, and current events (Lenhart, Purcell, Smith, & Zickuhr, 2010). Increasingly, rather than browse news sites, teenagers rely on social media (e.g., Twitter, Snapchat, and Instagram) to preselect news stories that might interest them. For example, Snapchat provides "featured stories" for teen users to view specific news articles posted by companies such as *Buzzfeed*, *Cosmopolitan*, *The Economist*, *National Geographic*, and *CNN* (Godlewski, 2016). Friends and family also post stories on their social media that become visible on teens' own feeds, working as somewhat of an endorsement for news that is relevant and important. Teens play a similar role in their own social media when they "like" a story or post a link. These types of news consumption patterns influence what and how contemporary teenagers think about news and current events.

Finally, teens use the Internet as a resource for shopping. In fact, half of teens go online to make purchases (Lenhart *et al.*, 2010). Online, teens have greater access to products than they typically do in their nearby geographic communities, and searching for specialty items (e.g., a prom dress) can take too much time and scheduling coordination. Teens rely heavily on their social networks to inform their purchasing decisions. Social media sites such as Instagram and Twitter offer information about new products, details about fashion trends, celebrity endorsements, and tailored advertisements. Mobile devices compel teens to use messaging and social media platforms to quickly and easily solicit the opinions of their friends and social networks regarding online sales or new brands and trends. More than half of teenagers believe that social media influences their online spending (Kaplan, 2013).

Why Do People Worry about Teen Internet Use, and Is There Any Evidence That These Concerns Are Warranted?

Online, teens have considerable autonomy to do, say, and go where they wish. This type of freedom is precisely what concerns many adults. Indeed, despite the fact that most adults agree that the Internet is vital to young people's social and academic lives, they harbor significant fears about what digital media are doing to young people and what young people are doing with digital media. In fact, a majority of American parents of teens indicate they are concerned about their teens' online activities and their potential impacts in the short and long term (Madden *et al.*, 2013). The research community has begun to address an array of the most common concerns. We offer a brief summary of some of these concerns here.

Access to Inappropriate or Problematic Content

One of the most enduring concerns raised in connection with teen Internet use is the easy access it provides to inappropriate or problematic content. Sites and services that promote eating disorders, bomb making, hate groups, gambling, alcohol, smoking, and pornography are among the most heavily criticized. Teens who intentionally seek information of these sorts can easily find an abundance of visual and textual content that can be unhealthy or even dangerous. Unintentional experiences with such content is also troubling, because young people can be caught off guard at ages and times when they may be ill-equipped to understand or handle what they have seen.

Most of the research focusing on inappropriate content has centered on pornography. Pornography is pervasive online, and motivated teenagers have little trouble finding an array of sexually explicit content ranging from nudity to violent and gruesome depictions of misogynist sexual interactions. While it is clear that many adolescents use pornography, prevalence rates vary greatly across existing studies. Cumulatively, the existing research paints a portrait of *frequent* teen porn users as male, sensation seekers, at more advanced pubertal stages, and who have weak or troubled family relations (Peter & Valkenburg, 2016). Adolescent pornography use is associated with more permissive sexual attitudes and tends to be linked with stronger gender-stereotypical sexual beliefs. Using pornography also appears to be related to the occurrence of sexual intercourse, greater experience with casual sex behavior, and more sexual aggression (Peter & Valkenburg, 2016). Pornography can offer teen viewers scripts for suitable body type and sexual performance that offer unrealistic expectations for both male and females (Lofgren-Martenson & Mansson, 2010). Teenagers themselves express concern about the emotional effects of experiencing pornography as a dominant model of relationship (Gardner & Davis, 2013).

Online Safety & Privacy

Another frequently voiced concern regarding teen Internet use is the possibility that unsuspecting teens will be lured into dangerous relationships or sexual interactions with online predators. Online, nonverbal cues are absent, potential consequences seem distant, and correspondence can take place pseudonymously. These features can facilitate interesting new relationships and conversations among young people, but many worry that they may also lead to potentially risky situations. The popular press is notorious for highlighting sensational but rare instances in which online teens are stalked by predators. boyd (2014) and others argue that risks posed by online strangers have been overblown, creating unnecessary and widespread panic while detracting attention from a minority of teens who are particularly vulnerable. Teens most at risk are those who have previously been abused, who have had problems in school or at home, and who engage in risky offline behavior (Wolak, Evans, Nguyen, & Hines, 2013).

Part of the concern that adults harbor about online predators stems from their worry that teenagers today share too much and have no sense of privacy. Teenagers are, in fact, sharing more information about themselves on social media than they did in the past. For example, more than half of teens include photos of themselves, their school names, the cities they live in and their email addresses on social media (Madden *et al.*, 2013). However, recent explorations of teens' privacy perceptions and behaviors indicate that they are actually quite judicious and thoughtful about their online disclosures and content sharing. For example, most teenagers conscientiously restrict the amount and types of information they put online, and the majority take advantage of available privacy settings (Madden *et al.*, 2013). They make deliberate choices about which digital communication tools to use when they desire more privacy (e.g., texting vs. Facebook). And the majority have sought advice about how to manage their online privacy (Lenhart *et al.*, 2013).

Nonetheless, teens acknowledge the tension they feel between the desire to protect their personal privacy and the social pressure to share (Agosto & Abbas, 2017). For example, the desire to receive more positive feedback (e.g., more "likes" on Instagram) can compel teens to accept as friends people they might not otherwise accept, and thus reveal more of their own personal content to a larger audience. Actions like these compromise their privacy to some extent, but the tradeoff is considered to be worthwhile (boyd, 2014). Balancing the often conflicting demands of public participation and privacy regulation is an on-going and often onerous task for contemporary teenagers.

Social Interaction and Well-Being

Does socializing online, at "arm's length," diminish the quality of teens' relationships and impede their social skills? The idea that teenagers who are constantly connected and always in touch might actually be *less* connected is quite controversial, especially because it runs counter to the promise of the Internet. Turkle (2011) argues that although digital media enable teens to multi-task and communicate with many people, their communication exchange does not support the kinds of deep connection that truly sustain and nourish relationships. Moreover, there is concern that teenagers who avoid the messiness of face-to-face or voice encounters also miss out on the kinds of multifaceted engagement that are needed for true closeness and intimacy. For example, teenagers increasingly begin and end relationships on social media, and they frequently send text messages because they perceive voice conversations to be too intrusive (Gardner & Davis, 2013). Some teenagers immerse themselves in online games, thus preempting opportunities for engagement, however awkward, in real life contexts (Kowert *et al.*, 2014). Even when teenagers are face-to-face with their friends, the constant barrage of notifications from their social media and mobile phones distract them from their in-person conversations (Gardner & Davis, 2013).

It's not just the superficiality of digital communication that concerns some scholars, but also the idea that teenagers' self-presentations in digital spaces encourage them to focus on superficial identity displays, rather than deeper identity exploration. Some adults worry that when teenagers focus so much on how they appear to others, they have less time and inclination to focus on their inner lives, to quietly self-reflect, and to engage with their own personal struggles and aspirations. The emotional labor involved with determining how to negotiate audiences, and to attract the right kinds of attention while avoiding the wrong kinds, can be substantial (boyd, 2014). What other explorations and adventures are displaced by teens' "packaging of the self" online (Gardner & Davis, 2013)? And does the culture of curated self-presentations increase teens' feelings of loneliness, anxiety and incompetence? Initial evidence suggests that teenagers who compare themselves to others online often feel worse after spending time on social media, perhaps because no one else seems ever to be depressed, confused, or even just bored (e.g., Lee, 2014).

As researchers address these questions, what becomes increasingly clear is that the answers lie not in the digital technologies, but rather in how and why they are used. Gardner and Davis (2013) articulate how digital devices can be used in ways that are both enabling or limiting for young people. When teenagers use them as "springboards to new experience and areas of knowledge, meaningful relationships and creative expression," digital media can positively enhance teenagers' lives. Yet when teenagers "look to their apps and devices first before looking inside themselves or reaching out to a friend," digital devices can thwart healthy development and nurturing relationships (p. xiii).

Conclusion

This chapter merely scratches the surface in its effort to illuminate the many ways in which Internet practices are embedded in teenagers' everyday lives. The Internet clearly plays an essential role in many of the most basic tasks of contemporary adolescence, from socializing to keeping entertained to seeking information. We still have a great deal to learn about the extent to which teenagers' digital practices facilitate and impede normal and healthy development. Teenagers approach their Internet practices with a diversity of personal contexts and histories, psychological and personal traits, intentions for engagement, and technological and expressive abilities. Listening to the diverse experiences of individual teens promises one fruitful avenue toward further understanding of the role of the Internet in their lives.

Discussion Questions

1. To what extent are digital media embedded in the lives of contemporary teenagers? What advantages do those with easy and constant access to the Internet have over other teens?

2. Why are social media and video games so popular with American teens? Are there any reasons you can think of that the authors neglected to mention? If so, what are they?

3. To what extent do you find the various issues presented in this chapter to be concerning? Which issue(s) do you see as most concerning, and why? How might these concerns be addressed within peer groups, families, at school, or elsewhere?

4. Based on your personal experiences as an online teenager, what would you add to this chapter about how the Internet is embedded into young people's everyday lives? Is your online experience well represented in this chapter? What did the chapter get right, and what did it get wrong or miss altogether?

Exercises

1. Leave your phone, computer, and other digital devices at home for a day. Pay attention to how other people interact (or don't) as a consequence of their digital participation. Take notes throughout the day after considering the following prompts:

    a. What do you notice that is not usually visible to you?
    b. How do you feel about how your friends, peers, parents and others act with their technology?
    c. How do you feel about your interactions with others; are they more or less rewarding?
    d. What do you miss without your digital media, and what are you glad to leave behind?
    e. Consider your experience. Will you do anything differently in your own life, now that you have spent a day without digital media? How easy will it be to make changes?

2. Make a list of all the things you love/appreciate about the role of digital media in your everyday life. Now make a list of all the things that you *don't* like or that trouble/concern you. Which list is longer? Do you notice any patterns? Now compare it with a friend's list. How much overlap is there between likes and dislikes? Is there anything you could do together to address the things you mention in the "dislike" list? (e.g., put phones away during lunch).

References

Agosto, D., & Abbas, J. (2017). 'Don't be dumb – that's the rule I try to live by': A closer look at older teens' online privacy and safety attitudes. *New Media & Society, 19*(3), 347–365. doi:10.1177/1461444815606121

Agosto, D., Abbas, J., & Naughton, R. (2012). Relationships and social rules: Teens' social network and ICT selection practices. *Journal of the American Society for Information Science and Technology, 63*(6), 1108–1124. doi:10.1002/asi.22612

Borca, G., Bina, M., Keller, P., Gilbert, L., & Begotti, T. (2015). Internet use and developmental tasks: Adolescents point of view. *Computers in Human Behavior, 52,* 49–58. doi:10.1016/j.chb.2015.05.029

boyd, d. (2014). *It's complicated: The social lives of networked teens.* New Haven, CT: Yale University Press.

Clapman, L. (2016). Wi-Fi enabled school buses leave no child offline. *PBS Newshour.* Retrieved from http://www. pbs.org/newshour/bb/wi-fi-enabled-school-buses-leave-no-child-offline/

Common Sense Media. (2015). *The Common Sense Media census: Media use by tweens and teens.* Retrieved from https://www.commonsensemedia.org/research/the-common-sense-media-use-by-tweens-and-teens

Davis, K. (2012). Friendship 2.0: Adolescents' experiences of belonging and self-disclosure online. *Journal of Adolescence, 35,* 1527–1536. doi:10.1016/j.adolescence.2012.02.013

Defy Media. (2016). *Acumen report: Youth video diet.* Retrieved from http://www.defymedia.com/acumen/acumen-report-youth-video-diet/

Gardner, H., & Davis, K. (2013). *The App generation.* New Haven, CT: Yale University Press.

Godlewski, N. (2016, June 21). Teens are getting almost all of their news from Snapchat and Twitter these days. *Business Insider.* Retrieved from http://www.businessinsider.com/how-do-teens-get-news-2016-6

Goffman, E. (1959). *The presentation of self in everyday life.* New York, NY: Anchor Books.

Hiller, L., Mitchell, K., & Ybarra, M. (2012). The Internet as a safety net: Findings from a series of online focus groups with LGB and non-LGB young people in the United States. *Journal of LGBT Youth, 9*(3), 225–246. doi:10.1080/19361653.2012.684642

Horrigan, J. (2015). *The numbers behind the broadband 'homework gap'.* Washington, DC: Pew Research Center. Retrieved from http://www.pewresearch.org/fact-tank/2015/04/20/the-numbers-behind-the-broadband-homework-gap/

Kaiser Foundation. (2011, February 18). *Teens online.* Retrieved from http://www.education.com/reference/article/Ref_Teens_Online/

Kaplan, M. (2013). *Teenage online shopping trends.* Retrieved from http://www.practicalecommerce.com/articles/4073-Teenage-Online-Shopping-Trends

Khan, M. L., Wohn, D. Y., & Ellison, N. B. (2014). Actual friends matter: An Internet skills perspective on teens' informal academic collaboration on Facebook. *Computers & Education, 79,* 138–147. doi:10.1016/j.compedu.2014.08.001

Kowert, R., Domahidi, E., Festl, R., & Quandt, T. (2014). Social gaming, lonely life? The impact of digital game play on adolescents' social circles. *Computers in Human Behavior, 36,* 385–390. doi:10.1016/j.chb.2014.04.003

Kowert, R., & Oldmeadow, J. (2013). (A) Social reputation: Exploring the relationship between online video game involvement and social competence. *Computers in Human Behavior, 29*(4), 1872–1878. doi:10.1016/j.chb.2013.03.003

Lee, S. (2014). How do people compare themselves with others on social network sites? The case of Facebook. *Computers in Human Behavior, 32,* 253–260. doi:10.1016/j.chb.2013.12.009

Lenhart, A. (2010). *Social media and mobile Internet use among teens and young adults.* Washington, DC: Pew Research Center. Retrieved from www.pew.org

Lenhart, A. (2015). *Teens, social media, and technology overview 2015.* Washington, DC: Pew Research Center. Retrieved from http://www.pewinternet.org/2015/04/09/teens-social-media-technology-2015/

Lenhart, A., Madden, M., Cortesi, S., Gasser, U., Duggan, M., Smith, A., & Beaton, M. (2013). *Teens, social media, and privacy.* Washington, DC: Pew Research Center. Retrieved from http://www.pewinternet.org/2013/05/21/teens-social-media-and-privacy/

Lenhart, A., Purcell, K., Smith, A., & Zickuhr, K. (2010). *The Internet as an information and economic appliance in the lives of teens and young adults.* Washington, DC: Pew Research Center. Retrieved from http://www.pewinternet.org/2010/02/03/part-4-the-internet-as-an-information-and-economic-appliance-in-the-lives-of-teens-and-young-adults/

Lenhart, A., Smith, A., Anderson, M., Duggan, M., & Perrin, A. (2015). *Teens, technology and friendships.* Washington, DC: Pew Research Center. Retrieved from http://www.pewinternet.org/2015/08/06/teens-technology-and-friendships/

Lofgren-Martenson, L., & Mansson, S. (2010). Lust, love, and life: A qualitative study of Swedish adolescents' perceptions and experiences with pornography. *Journal of Sex Research, 47,* 568–579. doi:10.1080/00224490903151374

Madden, M., Lenhart, A., Cortesi, S., Gasser, U., Duggan, M., Smith, A., & Beaton, M. (2013, May 21). *Teens, social media, and privacy.* Washington, DC: Pew Research Center. Retrieved from http://www.pewinternet.org/2013/05/21/teens-social-media-and-privacy/

Martin, C., & Ito, M. (2015, May 5). *Teens without smartphones encounter a new digital divide.* Retrieved from http://theconversation.com/teens-without-smartphones-encounter-a-new-digital-divide-40947

Marwick, A., & boyd, d. (2014). Networked privacy: How teenagers negotiate context in social media. *New Media & Society, 16*(7), 1051–1067. doi:10.1177/1461444814543995

Mesch, G. S., & Baker, G. (2010). Are norms of disclosure of online and offline personal information associated with the disclosure of personal information online? *Human Communication Research, 36,* 570–592. doi:10.1111/j.1468–2958.2010.01389.x

OECD. (2016). Are there differences in how advantaged and disadvantaged students use the Internet? *PISA in Focus, 64*, 1–4. doi:10.1787/5jlv8zq6hw43-en

Peter, J., & Valkenburg, P. (2016). Adolescents and pornography: A review of 20 years of research. *The Journal of Sex Research, 53*(4–5), 509–531.

Reich, S. M., Subrahmanyam, K., & Espinoza, G. (2012). Friending, IMing, and hanging out face-to-face: Overlap in adolescents' online and offline social networks. *Developmental Psychology, 48*, 356–368. doi:10.1037/a0026980

Sherman, L., & Greenfield, P. (2013). Forging friendship, soliciting support: A mixed-method examination of message boards for pregnant teens and teen mothers. *Computers in Human Behavior, 29*, 75–85. doi:10.1016/j.chb.2012.07.018

Stern, S. (2008). Producing sites, exploring identities: Youth online authorship. In D. Buckingham (Ed.), *Youth, identity, and digital media* (pp. 95–118). Cambridge, MA: The MIT Press.

Turkle, S. (2011). *Alone together: Why we expect more from technology and less from each other.* Cambridge: MIT Press.

Valkenburg, P., & Peter, J. (2012). Online communication among adolescents: An integrated model of its attraction, opportunities, and risks. *Journal of Adolescent Health, 48*(2), 121–127. doi:10.1016/j.jadohealth.2010.08.020

Wartella, E., Rideout, V., Zupancic, H., Beaudoin-Ryan, L., & Lauricella, A. (2015). *Teens, health, and technology.* Retrieved from http://cmhd.northwestern.edu/wp-content/uploads/2015/05/1886_1_SOC_ConfReport_TeensHealthTech_051115.pdf

Wolak, J., Evans, L., Nguyen, S., & Hines, D. A. (2013). Online predators: Myth versus reality. *New England Journal of Public Policy, 25*(1), article 6. Retrieved from http://scholarworks.umb.edu/nejpp/

Wuest, B. (2014). Stories like mine: Coming out videos and queer identities on YouTube. In C. Pullen (Ed.), *Queer youth and media cultures* (pp. 19–33). London: Palgrave Macmillan.

CHAPTER 17

How Are Young People Connecting with Their Families through Mobile Communication?

Sun Sun Lim and Yang Wang

In the past decade, mobile communication devices such as smartphones and tablet computers have encroached so intensively into people's daily routines that they have become a veritable extension of the human body (Ling & Donner, 2013). In particular, these personally-used, internet-enabled portable devices facilitate constant communication with close intimates and distant acquaintances, thus enabling a lifestyle of "perpetual connectivity" wherein the boundaries between absence and presence, near and far, and private and public are blurred (Licoppe, 2004).

This blurring of boundaries takes on special significance within the household as families come to grips with the new connectivities within and beyond the home, meshing as they do with family lifestyles, routines, practices and value. While mobile communication technology heralds new possibilities for real-time family connection and micro-coordination of daily activities, this same technology can also introduce unforeseen risks and burdensome expectations of constant availability, thus fomenting anxieties, tensions and conflicts between family members, especially parents and children (Clark, 2012; Mascheroni, 2014). The ease of accessibility and personally-owned nature of mobile technology devices is another issue, as young people tap the enhanced affordances of mobile technology to carve out expanded social networks, manage personal and peer identities, and strive for independence from parental controls (Green, 2003; Ling, 2000; Thulin & Vilhelmson, 2009). Parents in turn seek to oversee their children's mediated experiences, even to the extent of imposing rigorous time restrictions, closely monitoring their daily mobile technology use, and even surreptitiously reviewing the contents of their children's devices (Clark, 2012; Lim & Soon, 2010; Livingstone & Helsper, 2008). In such a context, tensions and misunderstandings are likely to emerge as parents and children may disagree over the degree of autonomy youths can enjoy in their mobile communication, as well as over the nature and extent of parental supervision.

This chapter will explain how young people, primarily adolescents, connect with their families through mobile communication, and it will also delve into the complexity of parent–child negotiations that may emerge as a result. Specifically, it will focus firstly on the use of mobile technology by youths to communicate with their families, peers, and individuals beyond their immediate milieus, as well as the multifarious roles these technologies play in their everyday life. It will then look into parental concerns about their children's vulnerability to negative impacts from these mobile devises, and in turn, their proactive strategies of supervising children's technology use within the domestic sphere. Moreover, this chapter will also discuss how youths and their parents negotiate tensions and conflicts that emerge in the presence of mobile information and communication technologies (ICTs), so as to maximize benefits of technologies on youth and nurture intimate family relationships.

Youths' Communication Needs and Wants

Young people today are among the most avid and proficient users of mobile communication, possessing their own mobile devices from an early age. Although still under the care of their parents, young people are also eager to establish themselves as independent individuals with their own peer networks. Personally-owned mobile technologies thus assume particular significance for youths in that they allow them to stay in continuous contact with their parents for daily coordination, while enabling them to carve out an autonomous space to engage in independent socialization (Clark, 2009, 2012; Devitt & Roker, 2009; Ling & Yttri, 2002).

Bonding with Family

Young people's interactions with their parents, whether borne out of compulsion or intrinsic motivation, have been significantly influenced by the emergence of mobile communication. With their facility for constant connectivity, parents were quick to recognize the value of mobile phones in helping them monitor their children's whereabouts in the interest of safety (Devitt & Roker, 2009; Williams & Williams, 2005). Mobile communication technologies thus serve as "metaphorical umbilical cords" (Ling & Yttri, 2006, p. 226) between young people and their parents, cherished for the security they offer, but villainized for inculcating dependency (Clark, 2012; Ling & Yttri, 2002, 2006).

Indeed, young people's communication with parents over mobile devices focuses largely on practical issues such as routinized reporting of whereabouts and coordination of daily activities. In particular, adolescents tend to keep their parents informed about where they are, when they will return home as well as who they are staying with, in order to ensure their safety and relieve their parents of anxieties (Devitt & Roker, 2009; Ling & Yttri, 2006). Mobile communication also enables real-time and spontaneous adjustments of plans and activities between youths and their parents, such as rearrangement of transportation, emergency notifications and seeking permission to stay out late (Ling & Yttri, 2002). For example, if a teenager bumps into a friend after school, she can contact her parents immediately with her smartphone, whether via phone call, text message or instant message (IM) applications, to seek permission to "hang out" with her friend and return home later than usual.

While acknowledging the convenience of family coordination via mobile technology, young people tend to regard such communication as tedious obligations. This is self-evident in the fact that most of the time parents, as opposed to their children, are the ones who initiate mediated conversations and speak more (Green, 2003; Ling & Yttri, 2006). Indeed, frequent contacts from parents, especially when youths are socializing with peers, are viewed as overbearing and intrusive, and will likely arouse annoyance and anger among adolescent children in particular (Clark, 2012; Ling & Yttri, 2006).

Connecting with Peers

Besides connecting with families, mobile communication technology is more often and more intensively used by youths to forge and sustain friendships with peers. In the transition from adolescence to emerging adulthood, young people invariably gravitate towards their peers and away from their parents and family (Lim, 2016). Mobile communication, which guarantees exclusive access and private conversations, is thus a boon for youths who want to be accessible to peers but insulated from parental oversight (Clark, 2009, 2012; Ling & Yttri, 2002, 2006).

As with their communication with family via mobile devices, a significant proportion of mediated exchanges between youths and their peers center around the coordination of daily activities and the discussion of practical issues. Specifically, young people usually stay in contact with each other on a daily or even hourly basis to discuss mundane topics such as where they are, what they are doing, when and where to meet, and provide real-time help when their peers get into trouble (Ling, 2000; Ling & Yttri, 2002). Another trait of mediated communication within adolescent peer groups is the prevalence of "small talk" that may take the form of gossip, jokes and anecdotes (Ling & Yttri, 2002). In these conversations, what is being said is less important than the reciprocity of communication itself. The mere fact that they are chatting with large networks of friends affirms their sense of acceptance and popularity within peer groups, widely perceived as a status symbol among youths of varying ages (Green, 2003; Johnsen, 2003).

However, the gratifications from peer relationships come with burdens, too. Young people today have to remain available and responsive to contacts from their friends, anytime and anywhere, in expectation of reciprocal acknowledgment and strengthening emotional bonds, with a view towards reproducing their status within the virtual community. Sometimes a mere delay in replying to a message can be regarded as indifference and strain relational bonds, or tensions can easily escalate when a request for conversation is accidentally overlooked (Johnsen, 2003).

Interacting with Strangers

Mobile communication technologies are also frequently used by youths to explore diverse social contexts and interact with people beyond their immediate milieus. Connected to the rest of the world via a panoply of ICT devices and online social networks, young people today can meet and befriend strangers from all over the world without even stepping out of their homes. This flexibility in social communication as well as the sense of empowerment it brings is unprecedented.

In general, youths are inclined to interact with two types of strangers via mobile devices. The first type consists of the "like-minded" people who share common interests or face similar pressures (Clark, 2012). For example, a teenager who is enthusiastic about game design but fails to find like-minded acquaintances within her immediate social circle may actively reach out to larger networks of people online who share his passion. The second type comprises people whom youths serendipitously encounter in the mediated space. For example, a young boy may trade views with strangers about parent–child relationships on a public online discussion forum. Although young people are reported to spend increasing amounts of time socializing with strangers online, prior research shows that they rarely seek to develop these interactions into face-to-face friendships, but instead maintain stable and continuous online communications with them (Livingstone & Bovill, 2001).

Parents cite contact with strangers as among the riskiest online behaviors, besides other potential dangers such as cyberbullying, phone frauds, stalking and harassment (Devitt & Roker, 2009; Huisman, Edwards, & Catapano, 2012; Mascheroni, 2014). Hence, parents with such concerns are motivated to closely supervise their children's daily interactions with people outside of their immediate social circles. In this regard, it is extremely challenging for parents to supervise their children's use of internet-enabled mobile communication devices given that they are personally-owned and highly portable. Yet young people use these very devices to extend their social networks beyond the realms that their parents would permit (Clark, 2012; Mascheroni, 2014).

Value of Mobile Communication Technology for Young People

In light of the crucial roles mobile communication plays in the lives of young people, we can discern three types of value this technology offers them: pragmatic, emancipatory, and symbolic.

Pragmatic value. As the preceding discussion amply demonstrates, mobile communication technologies serve as pragmatic tools for youths to seek help during emergencies, and make real-time and nuanced coordination of daily activities with families and peers (Ling & Yttri, 2002). In particular, remaining available to parents and assuring them of their safety is seen as a basic responsibility of a decent child (Williams & Williams, 2005), whilst staying in constant connection with peers allow youths to become mature, sociable and well-accepted by peers as they transition from childhood to adulthood (Clark, 2012; Green, 2003).

Emancipatory value. In providing constant connectivity and perpetual contact, mobile communication paradoxically shackles young people to their parents, while enabling them to acquire independence as well (Green, 2003). Through personalized use of communication technologies, young people can override their parents as gatekeepers, and experience the world and establish broader social networks in their own capacity as individuals (Green, 2003; Ling & Yttri, 2006). In this sense, mobile communication technologies embody and grant young people leeway from omnipresent parental control into the more autonomous sphere wherein they can make their own decisions.

Symbolic value. Mobile communication technologies are also rich with symbolic meaning and become potent signifiers of personal identity and social status, especially towards one's peers (Ling & Yttri, 2002, 2006). Through choosing mobile devices of certain brands and appearances, contacting certain groups of people, and using certain language styles in mediated communication, young people can intentionally reshape their images to cater to peer groups that they are in or hope to join, so as to gain acceptance and enhance their standing within these groups (Clark, 2012; Green, 2003; Ling & Yttri, 2002, 2006). For young people, mobile ICTs are therefore more than merely functional communication technologies and are instead material and symbolic totems of autonomy, independence, personal identity and growth.

Parental Interventions

When new technologies emerge, their impact on time-honored lifestyles, practices and values are always viewed with trepidation, often triggering moral panics that are fueled by adverse media coverage and alarmist social commentary. (Refer to Chapter 3 for more information on moral panics about youth media.) The growing proliferation and use of mobile communication technologies have similarly sparked parental concerns about their potentially detrimental impacts on young people, especially in light of the highly personalized and always-on communication these portable devices enable (Lim, 2016; Mascheroni, 2014).

Motivated by these concerns, parents have been known to actively mediate their children's mobile communication technology use, often by imposing rules on usage and content consumption. Some parents leverage these very technologies to monitor their children's whereabouts, activities and peer interactions.

Concerns and Anxieties

Parental concerns and anxieties usually focus on two general aspects, namely social isolation caused by ICT addiction and the risks that young people may be exposed to via ICTs.

As young people are spending increasing amounts of time on their mobile devices, parents are likely to worry about their children's preference for mediated interaction over family interactions and other social activities. Parents have been known to blame mobile technologies for taking their children's time away from family life, and consequently, reducing the quality of family relationships over time (Clark, 2012; Clark, Demont-Heinrich, & Webber, 2005). Mobile devices are also reported to encroach on the time that young people could better spend on more productive activities, such as schoolwork, household chores, outdoor sports, social communication and so forth (Clark, 2012; Clark et al., 2005; Shepherd, Arnold, & Gibbs, 2006). In this sense, while mobile communication technologies can help youths to socialize with broader social circles and properly maintain various relationships, they may finally end up physically isolating themselves in their bedrooms as their time is monopolized by mediated interactions instead of face-to-face family communication.

Besides the negative outcomes of addiction, parents also tend to keep watchful eyes on potential risks that their children may be exposed to, either intentionally or inadvertently, via mobile ICTs. In particular, parents have expressed strong concerns over the negative influence of inappropriate content, especially those containing violent and pornographic elements (Clark et al., 2005; Haddon, 2012; Mesch, 2006). Of even greater parental concern is children's mediated communication with strangers online, which is often mentioned in relation to unforeseen threats to children's safety, such as cyber-bullying, phone frauds, disclosure of personal data to online predators and so on (Devitt & Roker, 2009; Haddon, 2012; Lim, 2016; Mesch, 2006). These anxieties are further exacerbated by the prevalence of internet-enabled and personally-used portable mobile communication devices that do not lend themselves easily to parental oversight.

Parental Mediation

In view of the potential risks and negative implications of mobile ICTs, parents seek to assume active roles in mediating their children's ICT use practices, so as to maximize beneficial effects while mitigating undesirable impacts.

Parents are reported to employ a range of approaches to supervise and regulate their children's use of ICTs. Some parents rely heavily on restrictive rules to ensure that their children use technological devices in appropriate manners and punishing them when these rules are violated. In particular, parents tend to formulate a series of rules regarding appropriate ICT use such as the time and duration for accessing ICTs, permitted locations for use, as well as online activities that are encouraged or forbidden (Haddon, 2012; Lim & Soon, 2010; Mascheroni, 2014). Similarly, some parents also set regulations about the types of information or websites that their children are not allowed to access beforehand and enforce these regulations by tracking their online traces and checking messages on their phones without their children's knowledge (Clark *et al.*, 2005; Devitt & Roker, 2009; Haddon, 2012).

Other parents prefer to exercise oversight and supervision when their children are using communication technology. In this way, parents can have a better understanding of their children's preferences and lived experiences in the mediated world, identify potentially problematic behaviors and develop improvised strategies of regulation. There are also parents who undertake active mediation by engaging in interpretive and expressive communications with their children during their screen time. Specifically, they usually encourage their children to share their online experiences, while offering advice on the selection of content, and discuss appropriate attitudes towards communication technology with a view towards cultivating their children's critical thinking about technologies and steering them away from potentially risky people and communications (Haddon, 2012; Lim, 2016; Livingstone & Helsper, 2008).

Parental mediation of children's technology use is an ongoing and dynamic process that involves intensive negotiation and emotional labor for both parents and children. Different parents are likely to adopt different intervention approaches depending on their parenting styles and the characteristics of their children, whilst the same parent may also employ different strategies as the immediate context of children's ICT consumption changes.

Parental Surveillance

While mobile communication technologies empower youths to cultivate a social life beyond direct parental oversight, they also stretch the time-space boundary of parental control in an unprecedented fashion, to the point that it can be regarded as surveillance. Constantly connected to their children via mobile phones, these parents not only require their children to provide regular updates on their safety and schedules, they also call or send messages to them from time to time and interrogate in detail about their activities, whereabouts and companions, regardless of their children's availability (Devitt & Roker, 2009; Williams & Williams, 2005).

Some parents also look up their children's phone logs, visiting online histories and profiles on social network sites (SNS), usually without their children's consent, to gain insights into their social circles, activities beyond the home, as well as emotions and feelings (Devitt & Roker, 2009; Lim & Soon, 2010; Mascheroni, 2014). For these parents, online trails serve as a window to their children's personal spaces that are otherwise private. Parents sometimes also resort to surveillance software to track their children's whereabouts and monitor their mediated communications via ICTs (Clark, 2012; Haddon, 2012; Lim, 2016). As a result, mobile communication technologies can be veritable surveillance tools for parents to invade and gain control over their children's personal life, breaching their privacy and eroding the trust between them and their children (Mascheroni, 2014; Williams & Williams, 2005).

Challenges of Parental Mediation

The rapid evolution of mobile communication technologies and young people's avid embrace of the same have posed new challenges for parents to exercise effective mediation. First, the growing portability of ICTs and personally-owned nature of mobile communication devices allow young people to immerse themselves in online experiences in relative isolation, thus undermining parents' ability to implement direct mediation. Second, parents often lack sufficient technological expertise to properly understand the mediated environment which their children inhabit, let alone provide guidance for their children. They must constantly keep pace with technological developments, acquire new knowledge and broaden the purview of parental oversight. This often results in the erosion of parental authority over their children and the compromise of parental influence on children's socialization process (Clark, 2009, 2012; Mesch, 2006). Third, parents also face the dilemma of being uninvolved or overinvolved in their daily supervision of children's time with ICTs. On the one hand, in view of youths' vulnerability to potential risks related to ICT use, parents cannot grant their children full freedom in experiencing the technology-mediated space without appropriate parental oversight. On the other hand, however, parents also seek to avoid becoming the overbearing parents who interfere too much in their children's personal life via ICTs and consequently create conflicts between them (Clark, 2012). In this context, parents usually seek to strike a proper balance between these two extremes, although not always successfully.

Parent–Child Tensions Surrounding Mobile Communication Technology Tensions and Negotiations

In many families, tensions between young people and their parents emerge due to sharp differences in their respective perceptions and experiences of mobile communication technologies, as well as divergences in the range and efficacy of parental mediation over children's consumption of these devices. While youths tend to fully applaud the rich affordances of various technological devices, parents usually maintain an ambivalent attitude wherein they appreciate the convenience brought by these technologies on the one hand, yet also remain vigilant about their potentially negative effects on children's well-being and quality of family life on the other hand (Clark, 2009, 2012). Intergenerational divergences in relation to mobile ICTs also reflect on distinct purposes and routines of using these devices by youths and their parents. Specifically, for most parents, mobile devices are merely meaningful as pragmatic tools for daily communication and coordination, while for young people, they are indispensable parts of everyday life which not only serve practical purposes but also of symbolic and expressive values (Clark, 2012; Ling & Yttri, 2002, 2006). Sometimes these divergences can become blasting fuses of parent–child conflicts, especially when mobile ICTs are intensively used by young people for "unproductive" activities such as gaming and chatting, instead of or "beneficial" purposes such as learning and relationship management (Clark, 2012; Mascheroni, 2014).

In this context, parents and children have to engage in constant negotiations about these tensions, usually with a host of strategies and emotional exchanges, so as to better incorporate various mobile ICTs into family life and explore appropriate ways of connecting with each other in the presence of new technologies. Indeed, tensions often emerge between parents and children over the extent of autonomy the latter can enjoy in using mobile devices, and the appropriate rules and boundaries of parental control. In particular, the mediation practices implemented by parents as an effort to protect their children from potential risks are often interpreted as an invasion of privacy and an attempt to curtail freedom by young people, and consequently give rise to discomfort, hostility and rebellion over time (Clark, 2012; Mesch, 2006). In the face of strict parental control, a large proportion of youths develop various tactics, either overtly or secretly, to elude and resist unwanted surveillance. Popular evasive tactics include using mobile devices surreptitiously, outside the realm of parental oversight, switching off or muting phones to deliberately "miss" phone calls from parents, blocking phone numbers of parents, deleting messages and online web histories (Clark, 2009, 2012; Devitt & Roker, 2009; Ling & Yttri, 2002, 2006; Mascheroni, 2014). In this ongoing game of control and evasion, mobile technologies actually serve as the invisible yet fraught battleground for residual parental authority and the growing adolescent autonomy.

Strategies for Parent–Child Connections

Intergenerational tensions derived from the adoption of mobile communication technologies can erode parent–child relationships, and therefore require constant negotiation in the domestic sphere.

For parents, the first step towards improved parent–child interactions is trying to understand and navigate the mediated environment that their children inhabit, while remaining open-minded to the children's needs for mobile mediated communication and other forms of online access (Clark, 2012; Lim, 2016). To this end, parents need to build a relationship of trust with their children and purposefully create an expressive atmosphere at home concerning the consumption of mobile communication technology. One parental strategy is to initiate conversations about technology and engage in shared online activities, such as watching videos and playing games on mobile devices (Clark, 2012; Lim & Soon, 2010; Shepherd *et al.*, 2006). Through casual chats and shared activities, parents and children can exchange their experiences in the mediated world and discuss appropriate values and behavior, thereby helping to defuse parental concerns over negative impacts of mobile communication technology on their children, while enhancing young people's trust of and closeness with their parents. Some parents also ask their children to teach them about new functionalities of mobile technologies that they are less knowledgeable about (Clark, 2009, 2012; Correa, 2014; Kiesler, Zdaniuk, Lundmark, & Kraut, 2000). Instead of eroding parental authority, this "bottom-up transmission" (Correa, 2014) can actually become an opportunity for parents and children to enjoy cozy family time together and achieve mutual understanding in the process.

Children can also play their part. Above all, young people must put themselves in the shoes of their parents, seek to understand parental concerns about the ever-changing mediated environment, and at least to some degree, show respect for their seemingly overbearing monitoring practices. In particular, they need to be mindful of the potential risks they may be exposed to via mobile devices, and exercise self-regulation so as to evade malicious people and inappropriate contents in their day-to-day use of these devices (Clark, 2012). They should also seek to remain in regular contact with their parents to ensure them their safety and facilitate basic coordination of family life with mobile communication technology, which is increasingly regarded as a basic obligation of children in many contemporary families.

Conclusion

Mobile communication technology has firmly entrenched itself within many households today, providing families with a variety of opportunities to remain connected with each other for daily coordination and expressive interaction. In particular, the constant connectivity bestowed by these technologies allows instrumental and emotional communication between family members despite their physical separation, thus serving to boost family cohesion and nurture intimacy. But for all of the blessings mobile communication technology can bring to family life, they can also trigger tensions and conflicts between parents and children. The negotiation between young people and their parents surrounding mobile ICTs is never a one-off effort, but a dynamic and emotionally-laden process that involves dialogue, persuasion, compromise, built on a relationship of honesty and trust.

Discussion Questions

1. What roles do peers play in young people's lives and how does mobile communication support these roles?

2. Compared to older technologies such as the television or desktop computer, how do mobile communication devices such as smartphones and laptops make parental mediation more challenging?

3. How can parents seek to better inform themselves about young people's media consumption practices and needs?

4. Drawing on your own experience, do you feel if parental concerns about their children's mobile communication use reasonable or misplaced?

5. How can parent–child tensions of mobile communication use be alleviated?

Exercises

1. Draft a parent–child contract on the child's use of mobile devices that you feel is reasonable to both parties, and that takes into account the child's needs and the parent's concerns.

2. Surf the internet for articles that offer parents advice on how to manage their children's use of mobile communication technologies. Critique the advice. Is it realistic and useful? How would you improve on it?

References

Clark, L. S. (2009). Digital media and the generation gap: Qualitative research on US teens and their parents. *Information, Communication & Society, 12*(3), 388–407. doi:10.1080/13691180902823845

Clark, L. S. (2012). *The parent App: Understanding families in the digital age.* Oxford: Oxford University Press.

Clark, L. S., Demont-Heinrich, C., & Webber, S. (2005). Parents, ICTs, and children's prospects for success: Interviews along the digital "access rainbow". *Critical Studies in Media Communication, 22*(5), 409–426. doi:10.1080/07393180500342985

Correa, T. (2014). Bottom-up technology transmission within families: Exploring how youths influence their parents' digital media use with dyadic data. *Journal of Communication, 64*(1), 103–124. doi:10.1111/jcom.12067

Devitt, K., & Roker, D. (2009). The role of mobile phones in family communication. *Children & Society, 23*(3), 189–202.

Green, N. (2003). Outwardly mobile: Young people and mobile technologies. In J. E. Katz (Ed.), *Machines that become us: The social context of personal communication technology* (pp. 201–217). London: Transaction Publishers.

Haddon, L. (2012). Parental mediation of internet use: Evaluating family relationships. In E. Loos, L. Haddon, & E. Mante-Meijer (Eds.), *Generational use of new media* (pp. 13–30). Farnham: Ashgate.

Huisman, S., Edwards, A., & Catapano, S. (2012). The impact of technology on families. *International Journal of Education and Psychology in the Community, 2*(1), 44–62. doi:10.1001/archsurg.140.11.1058

Johnsen, T. E. (2003). The social context of the mobile phone use of Norwegian teens. In J. E. Katz (Ed.), *Machines that become us: The social context of personal communication technology* (pp. 161–169). London: Transaction Publishers.

Kiesler, S., Zdaniuk, B., Lundmark, V., & Kraut, R. (2000). Troubles with the Internet: The dynamics of help at home. *Human-Computer Interaction, 15*(4), 323–351.

Licoppe, C. (2004). "Connected" presence: The emergence of a new repertoire for managing social relationships in a changing communication technoscape. *Environment and Planning D: Society and Space, 22*(1), 135–156. doi:10.1068/d323t

Lim, S. S. (2016). Through the tablet glass: Mobile media, cloud computing and transcendent parenting. *Journal of Children & Media, 10*(1), 21–29. doi:10.1080/17482798.2015.1121896

Lim, S. S., & Soon, C. (2010). The influence of social and cultural factors on mothers' domestication of household ICTs – Experiences of Chinese and Korean women. *Telematics and Informatics, 27*(3), 205–216. doi:10.1016/j.tele.2009.07.001

Ling, R. (2000). "We will be reached": The use of mobile telephony among Norwegian youth. *Information Technology & People, 13*(2), 102–120. doi:10.1108/09593840010339844

Ling, R., & Donner, J. (2013). *Mobile phones and mobile communication.* Cambridge: John Wiley & Sons.

Ling, R., & Yttri, B. (2002). Hyper-coordination via mobile phones in Norway. In J. Katz & M. Aakhus (Eds.), *Perpetual contact: Mobile communication, private talk, public performance* (pp. 139–169). Cambridge: Cambridge University Press.

Ling, R., & Yttri, B. (2006). Control, emancipation, and status: The mobile telephone in teens' parental and peer relationships. In R. Kraut, M. Brynin, & S. Kiesler (Eds.), *Computers, phones, and the internet: Domesticating information technology* (pp. 219–234). Oxford: Oxford University Press.

Livingstone, S., & Bovill, M. (2001). *Families and the internet: An observational study of children and young people's internet use.* Retrieved from http://eprints.lse.ac.uk/21164/1/Families_and_the_internet_-_an_observational_study_of_children_and_young_people's_internet_use.pdf

Livingstone, S., & Helsper, E. J. (2008). Parental mediation of children's internet use. *Journal of Broadcasting & Electronic Media, 52*(4), 581–599. doi:10.1080/08838150802437396

Mascheroni, G. (2014). Parenting the mobile internet in Italian households: Parents' and children's discourses. *Journal of Children and Media, 8*(4), 440–456. doi:10.1080/17482798.2013.830978

Mesch, G. S. (2006). Family characteristics and intergenerational conflicts over the Internet. *Information, Communication & Society, 9*(4), 473–495. doi:10.1080/13691180600858705

Shepherd, C., Arnold, M., & Gibbs, M. (2006). Parenting in the connected home. *Journal of Family Studies, 12*(2), 203–222. doi:10.5172/jfs.327.12.2.203

Thulin, E., & Vilhelmson, B. (2009). Mobile phones: Transforming the everyday social communication practice of urban youth. In R. Ling & S. Campbell (Eds.), *The reconstruction of space and time: Mobile communication practices* (pp. 137–158). New Brunswick, NJ: Transaction.

Williams, S., & Williams, L. (2005). Space invaders: The negotiation of teenage boundaries through the mobile phone. *Sociological Review, 53*(2), 314–331. doi:10.1111/j.1467–954X.2005.00516.x

CHAPTER 18

Snoops, Bullies and Hucksters
What Rights Do Young People
Have in a Networked Environment?

Valerie Steeves

In 2009, the students attending high schools in Lower Merion School District in Pennsylvania were supplied with school-bought laptops to help them with their schoolwork. A few months later, sophomore Blake Robbins was called into the Assistant Principal's office and disciplined for "improper behavior in his home." The school provided a photograph as evidence, showing Blake sitting in his bedroom eating brightly colored candies that the Assistant Principal had mistakenly identified as illegal drugs. The photo had been taken when—unbeknownst to Blake or his parents—the school had activated the laptop's webcam after school hours. Moreover, the photo was just one of over 66,000 photos of students that the school board had surreptitiously collected by remotely turning on laptop webcams, sometimes snapping pictures of individual students as frequently as once a minute. In Blake's case, the school also had photos of him chatting with friends on instant messaging, sleeping, and standing in his bedroom shirtless after he got out of the shower (*Robbins v. Lower Merion School District*, 2010).

Blake felt strongly that his rights had been violated so the Robbins family sued the school board on behalf of all the students who had been monitored, and eventually the school board agreed to pay $610,000 in damages. But one of the key reasons why the school board settled the case was the fact that they had failed to notify Blake and his parents that they would be watching him. What if Blake or his parents had signed a user agreement that told them the school board could activate the webcam randomly? What would Blake be able to do then to protect his privacy, his ability to access information, and his desire to pursue his education? What rights does Blake have as a young person hanging around with his friends, enjoying a quiet moment in his bedroom, doing his homework, watching a video and playing an online game when all of those activities take place on devices that can let others monitor his every move?

This chapter addresses these questions, by providing an overview of the kind of rights young people have in networked environments. The networked part is important because, as Blake's case demonstrates, networked technologies blur the lines between young people's school lives, social lives, work lives and home lives, and make it easy for others—teachers, parents, peers, marketers—to cross those lines in ways that shape the kinds of online opportunities young people have.

The chapter starts by outlining the rights children enjoy under the United Nations *Convention on the Rights of the Child*. It then looks at a number of examples, starting with Blake's case, to examine the kinds of laws and policies that various countries have passed to protect those rights. These laws and policies fall into two categories: 1) constitutional protections for privacy and 2) information rights. I argue that attempts to promote young people's rights in a networked environment in these two categories have been shaped by two sets of tensions. The first is the tension between the desire to protect children from offensive online content, on the one hand, and the commitment to respect young people's ability to make their own decisions about the media they access, on the other hand. The second is the tension between the commitment to dignity and cultural autonomy, and the competing desire to create rules that ensure technology companies can continue to generate profits from the vast pools of data that networked technologies generate. Although policymakers will continue to be pulled between these competing poles, I conclude by suggesting that expressly grounding laws in a rights-based approach will better enable us to create a legislative framework that will enable young people to fully enjoy the benefits of networked technologies.

The *Convention on the Rights of the Child*

There is an old adage that, if you ask a lawyer a question, the answer is always, "It depends". In our case, the answer to the question "what rights do young people have in a networked environment?" depends on the location of the child. This is because specific countries have different legal frameworks and seek to protect the interests of young people in different ways. At the same time, there is remarkable international agreement about children's rights, most notably expressed in the United Nations *Convention on the Rights of the Child* (CRC). As the child's rights non-governmental organization Humanium notes, "No other international treaty has provoked such a consensus on the part of governments" (Humanium, n.d.). As such, the CRC is a good starting point for any discussion of children's rights.

The CRC was adopted in 1989 and has been ratified by every member-state of the United Nations, except the United States.[1] The Convention builds on previous human rights declarations and covenants that set out legal, political, social and economic rights for all persons, including children. However, the CRC recognizes that, because they are not yet physically and mentally mature, children[2] have unique needs that entitle them to "special care and assistance" (Preamble). States are accordingly required to "ensure the child such protection and care as is necessary for his or her well-being" (Art. 3(2)). The CRC also requires that all institutions, whether public or private, that seek to provide this care and assistance should consider first and foremost the "best interests of the child" (Art. 3(1)).

Interestingly, media, and by extension, networked technologies, play a prominent role in the CRC. Before 1989, media had only been included in human rights instruments in the context of freedom of expression (Steeves, 2007). For example, when the *Universal Declaration of Human*

Rights was adopted by the United Nations in 1949, it stated that persons have the right to seek out and share information and ideas *through any media* (Art. 19, emphasis added). The drafters of the CRC included a similar provision in 1989: under Article 13, the child's right to free expression includes the "freedom to seek, receive and impart information and ideas of all kinds, regardless of frontiers, either orally, in writing or in print, in the form of art, or *through any other media of the child's choice*" (emphasis added). However, Article 17 of the CRC goes further, and expressly recognizes "the important function performed by the mass media" in children's lives; states are accordingly required to proactively make sure children can access information from a range of national and international sources, especially information "aimed at the promotion of [the child's] social, spiritual and moral well-being and physical and mental health."

Information, and the media a child uses to access information, are therefore implicitly linked to a variety of other rights enshrined in the CRC, including: freedom of thought, conscience and belief (Art. 14); freedom of association (Art. 15); the right to education (Art. 28) in general and to education to support the development of the child's personality, cultural identity and values in particular (Art. 29); the right to engage in play (Art. 31); and the right to participate in cultural and artistic life (Art. 31). Under Article 16, a child also has the right to be protected from "arbitrary or unlawful interference with his or her privacy, family, home or correspondence." This right to privacy is often seen as a proto-right, because a loss of privacy chills the child's ability to exercise those other rights, like freedom of speech, and discourages social, cultural and political participation (Regan, 1995). Accordingly, the CRC recognizes that both access to information and privacy are "central to the child's ability to develop a sense of self and participate in community life, and the media are seen as a valuable tool to promote both access and the child's personal development" (Steeves, 2007, p. 126).

When the CRC was adopted in 1989, the Internet was still nascent and had yet to enter the public consciousness. However, as early as 1996, the United Nations Committee on the Rights of the Child began to talk about children's media rights in the context of networks, noting that "new technologies" both extend and threaten children's rights. On the one hand, the Committee concluded that the Internet is the ideal medium for children because it provides them with access to cultural information, supports their education, and gives them a platform to exercise their free speech. On the other hand, the Committee worried that access to networked technologies would also put children in danger, from both offensive content and ill-intentioned strangers (Williams, 1997).

This bifurcation between promise and peril is a common theme when it comes to children's use of any technology; just think of the prolonged (and continuing) debates over the potential negative effects of television and video games on young people's development. But for our purposes, it is important to note that it is also a constant *within* children's rights. As discussed above, the CRC requires that states both protect the welfare of children and empower them as active agents capable of making their own decisions (Franklin, 1995; Smith, 2007). This tension is particularly acute with respect to media, as the CRC both encourages the dissemination of information for the child's social, cultural and educational benefit, and points to the need for guidelines to protect children from information that could harm their well-being (Hammarberg, 1997). Even the notion of protection in a media-saturated environment is complicated by the express need to balance protective measures with the child's freedom of expression and the important role of parents in a child's upbringing (Art. 17).

As the next section demonstrates, this bifurcation between promise and peril also plays out in domestic laws designed to regulate children's online spaces.

From Rights to Remedies—Translating CRC Rights into Domestic Laws

The CRC is a legally binding international treaty. That means that the states that sign and ratify the treaty are committed to ensuring that their domestic laws are compatible with its provisions. In a sense, this means that CRC rights can trump other laws by providing a benchmark to judge whether or not a particular law or policy is consistent with the commitment to treat all persons with dignity. If a law or policy fails to meet that benchmark, then "…it is wrong for officials to act in violation of that right, even if they (correctly) believe that the community as a whole would be better off if they did" (Dworkin, 2009, p. 335). In other words, the individual's right trumps the government's policy, even if the policy advances some communal good.

However, playing that trump card can be difficult. Although rights are "entitlements", they are also open to interpretation, and can be "promoted or resisted differently, depending on the meaning they hold for particular people—most particularly for children and young people, and the persons who have the most contact with them and power over them" (Smith, 2007, p. 147). To demonstrate how these entitlements can provide young people with remedies, I now examine the two types of domestic laws that have been used most frequently to protect children's online rights: 1) constitutional protections for privacy; and 2) information rights in data protection regimes.

Constitutional Protections for Privacy

Constitutional protections for privacy provide excellent remedies to push back against state laws and policies that violate children's rights, especially in a networked environment where government agents can both monitor children and capture the data trail they leave as they chat, play, or do homework online. However, privacy is a double-edged sword: it is also often drawn into the debate around the promise and peril of networked technologies, because it arguably creates an environment where children can exercise their autonomy as independent actors, on the one hand, and be put at risk of harm by exposure to content and persons outside the protected arena of the home, school and community, on the other hand.

In Europe, constitutional provisions regarding privacy typically mirror the same language as Article 16 of the CRC, guaranteeing freedom from interference with privacy, home and family life. Some European states also have additional protections. The German Supreme Court, for example, has interpreted the general personal rights set out in the German constitution to include the right to informational self-determination; this means that constitutional law in Germany guarantees German citizens the right to decide if and how their personal information may be collected, used or disclosed by organizations that process data electronically. Other non-European Western states, such as the United States and Canada, do not have constitutional protections for privacy *per se*. However, their courts have interpreted constitutional provisions disallowing unreasonable search and seizure in a way that protects an individual's reasonable expectation of privacy. Laws and policies that violate these rights are unconstitutional and, as such, have no force or effect.

To see how this plays out for children in networked spaces, let's look back to our opening example. Lower Merion School District's commitment to providing all students with access to networked laptops was intended to advance students' rights to access to information and education, in keeping with Articles 13 and 28 of the CRC. As the Superintendent of Schools noted at the time, a personal laptop "[enables] an authentic 21st Century learning environment… enhances opportunities for ongoing collaboration, and ensures that all students have 24/7 access to school based resources and the ability to seamlessly work on projects and research at school and at home. The result: more engaged, active learning and enhanced school achievement" (cited in *Robbins v. Lower Merion School District* Class Action Complaint, 2010, p. 6).

Given the convergence enabled by networked technologies, the same laptops also arguably created opportunities for Lower Merion students to freely associate with others, exercise free speech, play, and participate in cultural and artistic life. Again, this is in keeping with the call of the United Nations Committee on the Rights of the Child to use "new technologies" to advance CRC rights, such as access to information, culture and play.

However, the same technology that had such promise to enhance children's rights also created an opportunity for the school to put Blake under surveillance, in effect violating Blake's right to privacy under Article 16. The school argued that this was necessary to protect its property from theft, and to ensure that Blake was not violating school rules. However, from Blake's perspective, the protective aspects were overshadowed by the humiliation and embarrassment he experienced because of his loss of privacy (*Robbins v. Lower Merion School District* Class Action Complaint, 2010), so he sued the School District. But in order to obtain a remedy from the School District, Blake needed to be able to point to a violation of American law to support his suit. Since the School District was a government agency, and the collection of data electronically constitutes a "search," Blake argued that its actions violated his right to be free of unreasonable search and seizure under the Fourth Amendment.[3]

The Fourth Amendment is not an absolute guarantee that a citizen's privacy will never be infringed, and American courts have allowed schools to conduct searches when school officials reasonably suspect that the student has committed some violation (*Morse v. Frederick*, 2007). Indeed, most countries expect schools to keep an eye on students in order to protect them from harm, in keeping with Article 3 of the CRC.

However, two factors make this a very weak argument in Blake's case. The first is that the School District was not monitoring Blake on school property, but in his home. And as the ACLU argued in its brief in the case, "The right to privacy inside one's own home 'is sacrosanct.' The 'right of a man to retreat into his own home and there be free from unreasonable government intrusion [stands at] the very core of the Fourth Amendment'" (*Robbins v. Lower Merion School District* Brief of Amicus Curiae, p. 2). The second is that the School District did not notify Blake or his parents in advance, or obtain their consent to the monitoring. In the circumstances, it is no surprise that the School Board decided to settle the lawsuit and stop its practice of remotely activating laptop cameras: the language of rights and rights violations was deeply embedded in the jurisprudence dealing with the Fourth Amendment, so Blake's right to privacy trumped other concerns, including the school's ability to protect its property from theft and enforce its rules.

What is perhaps surprising is that, in spite of the *Robbins* case, electronic surveillance on the part of schools has grown exponentially, most notably under the aegis of cyberbullying laws. These laws, now found in 46 states and the District of Columbia, "implicitly provide schools with the authority to…[develop] a system for comprehensively monitoring students' online and electronic activity…to reach into students' lives while they are at home, work, the mall or other non-school places and gather electronic data on the students in the name of learning about cyberbullying activity" (Suski, 2014, pp. 67–68). Whereas in Blake's case, privacy was sacrosanct, in the case of cyberbullying, fears about the potential harm young people could experience appear to have trumped children's rights to free expression and association.

Again, this mirrors the tension between the need to protect children from harm and the need to position children as rights-bearers, entitled to free speech, free association and participation in cultural and political life. However, in this case, fear of harm has overshadowed other rights concerns, arguably leading to overly protective regimes that constrain young people's abilities to enjoy the benefits of networked communication. For example, two girls in Canada were disciplined for racist bullying when they compared tans after Spring break. Even though they were best friends who were simply talking about their vacations, their school's zero tolerance approach to bullying trumped their free speech (Steeves, 2012).

Because of outcomes like this, Fisk concludes that many school cyberbullying initiatives have "reconfigure[d]…the everyday social practices of youth" as suspicious in and of themselves (Fisk, 2014, p. 567). Ironically, the need to protect children from this suspicious behavior has shut down opportunities for young people to access educational sites that have been incorrectly identified by school filters as problematic, curtailing students' ability to access information of educational value (Fisk, 2014; Johnson, Riel, & Froese-Germain, 2016; Suski, 2014).

Certainly young people report a real frustration with the level of surveillance and adult paranoia they encounter in networked spaces (Fisk, 2014; Steeves, 2012). However, it is arguably a breach of their CRC rights as well. As noted above, privacy is a particularly important CRC right because it enables young people to exercise other rights. Certainly in the educational context, "cyberbullying laws, though well meaning, vastly expand school authority…to such a degree that, in many cases, schools' authority to conduct surveillance of students is nearly without bounds," seriously curtailing students' rights to speech and association (Suski, 2014, pp. 64, 68). Protective monitoring may also interfere with the significant percentage of children (78%) who use networks to learn about news, health issues or relationships (Steeves, 2014a), violating their right to access information. Accordingly, tipping the balance so heavily in favor of online protection misses half the equation, inadvertently working against young people's full enjoyment of their CRC rights.

Information Rights

In addition to constitutional protections for privacy, young people can use data protection laws to help advance their rights in networked spaces. Data protection regimes give individuals some control over the information that is collected about them electronically. Although each country has its own version, data protection laws typically include some or all of the following 10 principles:

- **Identifying Purposes**: The organization should inform the individual why it is collecting the individual's personal information (i.e. the purpose for collection).
- **Consent**: The organization should obtain the individual's consent to the collection.
- **Limiting Collection**: The organization should only collect that information which is necessary to fulfill the purpose stated at the time of collection.

- **Accuracy**: The organization should ensure the information is accurate, complete and as up-to-date as required by the purpose for collection.
- **Limiting Use, Disclosure and Retention**: The organization should only use or disclose the information for the purpose for which it was collected, unless it first obtains the individual's consent. Once the purpose is fulfilled, the organization should delete the information.
- **Access**: An individual should be able to access his or her own information, and to have any inaccurate information corrected.
- **Safeguards**: The organization should use safeguards to protect the information and keep it secure.
- **Openness**: The organization should make its practices and policies regarding information management readily accessible.
- **Accountability**: An organization should be accountable for how it manages other people's personal information. That means that there should be a particular person in the organization who is responsible for ensuring that the organization complies with its own policies and that the principles are followed.
- **Challenging Compliance**: An individual should be able to contact that person with a complaint should the organization fail to comply with any of these principles.

As with the CRC, there is a remarkable international consensus behind this kind of legislation. Over 100 countries around the world have enacted comprehensive data protection regimes (Privacy International, n.d.) and others, like the United States[4] and the European Union, have created specific laws to protect children's information, most notably by requiring parental consent for the collection of information from children under the age of 13 (Jasmontaite & De Hert, 2015). Depending on the country, these regimes regulate the collection, use and disclosure of personal information on the part of both governments and the private sector.

Private sector collection is particularly important in the context of children's rights because young people are often early adopters of new technologies, and unwittingly drop terabytes of data as they do their schoolwork, chat with friends and share photos on networked platforms. For its part, the private sector collects this data because it is extremely valuable; the Boston Consulting Group estimates the market in personal data will generate an economic benefit to companies of 330 billion Euros (approximately U.S. $350 billion) *per year* by 2020 (BCG, 2012).

Research suggests that a growing number of children are aware that corporations collect the information they generate online. However, they typically assume this information is primarily used to determine what advertisements are served to them. Although young people may think this collection is "creepy," they often assume the ads have no effect on them. Many also see this as the cost of using social media, as they know that if they do not allow it, they will not be able to use the sites they rely on to communicate and explore (Steeves, 2012).

However, advertising is only the tip of the iceberg, as young people's online data is increasingly being batched and analyzed by algorithms for a variety of purposes. For example, there are a number of companies that offer services designed to help schools identify students who are "at risk" of participating in cyberbullying and harassment. Although these are private sector players (and therefore protections like the Fourth Amendment do not apply), they typically use the language of policing to describe their services. Safer Schools Together (SST), for example, talks about "threat assessment training," and links "digital threat assessment" to other issues, like "guns and gangs." It also promotes the sharing of information between the public and private sectors. For example, one testimonial from a police officer stated: "[SST training] has made me more confident in identifying early warning signs and opened me up to realizing I must share info with other agencies" (Safer Schools Together, 2016). This in effect takes data out of the public arena (where it is protected by constitutional constraints on state surveillance) into the marketplace (where it can be used to generate profits).

These companies typically "scrape" the Internet, collecting anything students may have posted on social media sites (Shade & Singh, 2016). The data the companies collect are then run through algorithms that use mathematical formulae to identify what SST calls "worrisome online behavior" (Safer Schools Together, 2016). If the algorithm determines that the young person is engaged in bullying or violence, or appears to be depressed, a report is sent to the principal so the student can be disciplined. Most problematic from a rights perspective is the way this algorithm can inadvertently code for bias, first assuming that personal characteristics like race and socio-economic status correlate with criminality, for example, and then identifying racialized children living in poverty as at risk of being criminals (Gandy, 2009).

Data protection is designed to enable consumers to challenge the corporate use of their information. Students caught up in this monitoring could ask to see what information is being collected about them, and demand that any inaccurate information be corrected. They could also argue that they, or their parents, never consented to the collection, or to this particular use. However, these rights have been weakened by corporate reliance on terms of use policies that often include large, catch-all terms designed to give the corporation maximum freedom to use the information as they see fit. Accordingly, even though surveys repeatedly indicate that very few young people or their parents read the terms of service for the platforms they use (see, for e.g., Pew Research Center, 2014), and, even when they do, the majority of policies use technical and legal language that is difficult to understand (Steeves, 2016), the terms are accepted when the child or his or her parent clicks on "accept."

It is noteworthy that in a Canadian survey of over 5,000 children between the ages of ten and seventeen years of age, 95% of respondents felt that marketers should not be allowed to access the information they post on social media. The percentage rose to 99 with respect to locational information (Steeves, 2014b). This suggests that the current business model that equates disclosure on the site with consent to its monetization may be out of keeping with young people's preferences.

An additional hurdle to obtaining a remedy in this case is the argument that these services are protective; children are posting information publicly so harvesting that information to ensure that they do not fall prey to bullies, criminality or depression is an acceptable invasion of their online privacy. Once again, discourses around online risks and the need to protect young people—from themselves as much as from ill-intentioned others—are called upon to justify an extreme level of surveillance and control (Bailey & Steeves, 2013), and the monetization of children's information is legitimized.

However, there is a growing recognition of the impact of this kind of collection on children's rights. As Jasmontaite and De Hert (2015) note, early data protection laws were primarily focused on economic goals; however, over the past decade, judicial decisions in the Court of Justice of the European Union have given children's rights a fundamental place in European law, and this has made a significant difference to European data protection regimes. From this perspective, data protection laws are first and foremost an expression of privacy as a human right, and as such they have become a key tool to protect children not only from bullies, but also from "economic exploitation" (Jasmontaite & De Hert, 2015, p. 23). The importance of a human rights perspective is also seen in the European Commission's Agenda for the Rights of the Child, which underscores the importance of pursuing both protection *and* empowerment, and warns that the failure to protect children's information may destroy the trust and confidence that are needed if children are to "make the most of online technologies" (European Commission, 2016).

Whether or not data protection is up to the task is yet to be determined. O'Brien (2014) argues that too much of data protection regulation has been driven by the needs of corporations, and that excessive attention on safety has obfuscated the competing importance of children's online participation (see also Steeves, 2016). Moreover, relying on simple age limits (such as requiring parental consent for children under 13), i.e. "[r]epresenting children as *always and only* victims" (O'Brien, 2014, p. 756), also fails to take into account the importance of children's evolving capacity, a key feature of the CRC itself (see also Jasmontaite and De Hert, 2015). The corrective is "to consider children as rights-bearers in this context, and to respect children's right to participation…[this] would be to provide safe and supporting opportunities for children to develop their own skills in negotiating the (*sometimes* risky) online world" (O'Brien, 2014, p. 756).

Conclusion

In sum, children's rights have been particularly difficult to fulfill because of "the ease with which rights, framed as rhetorical flourish, are dispensed with in the name of…safety" (O'Brien, 2014, p. 749), and reshaped by the needs of government agencies and the private sector for their own purposes. A rights-based approach is accordingly important, even in the case of the United States which has not yet ratified the CRC, because it recognizes "the respect [rights] bearers are entitled to. To accord rights is to respect dignity" (Freeman, 2007, p. 8).

The commitment to dignity, which is at the heart of the CRC, provides an alternative discourse that helps frame digital policy as a "'site of struggle' characterised by competing 'interests'…[to denaturalize] the prevailing power dynamic" that privileges the needs of government agencies and the private sector over the needs of children (O'Brien, 2014, p. 750). If children's rights in a networked environment are to be made meaningful, a rights-based approach is a first step to ensuring that young people have a voice in the design of the networked tools that shape their lives.

Discussion Questions and Exercises

1. In 1999, as part of the CRC's ten-year anniversary celebrations, UNICEF issued the Oslo Challenge calling on 1) governments, 2) children's organizations, 3) media professionals, 4) children and young people, 5) the private sector, and 6) parents, teachers and researchers to take steps to ensure that young people's online rights are respected.
    Read the Oslo Challenge at https://www.unicef.org/magic/briefing/oslo.html and answer the following questions:

(a) How have children's online rights changed since 1999?

(b) How well have the six groups listed above lived up to their obligations under the Oslo Challenge?

(c) What new approaches, if any, are needed to ensure that children can enjoy their online rights in the future?

2. Digital literacy initiatives typically seek to develop three related competencies in children: the ability to 1) use, 2) understand, and 3) create with networked technologies. Visit MediaSmarts' Digital Literacies Fundamentals page at http://mediasmarts.ca/digital-media-literacy-fundamentals/digital-literacy-fundamentals and answer the following questions:

(a) How do these competencies promote children's rights?

(b) Which is the most important and why?

3. Young people can and do use networked technologies to advance their rights and the rights of others. Visit the Pushback Timeline at http://www.equalityproject.ca/get-involved/pushback/ and select three examples. Did networked technologies create the problem these young people were trying to solve? Did networked technologies make it easier for these young people to organize and protect their rights and the rights of others? Why or why not?

Notes

1. The United States signed the treaty in 1995 but Congress has yet to ratify it.
2. A child is defined in s. 1 of the CRC as "every human being below the age of 18 years unless under the law applicable to the child, majority is attained earlier."
3. The Class Action Complaint also refers to breaches of specific legislation protecting the privacy of electronic communications that are consistent with the Fourth Amendment.
4. See the Children's Online Privacy Protection Act 1998, 15 U.S.C. §§ 6501–6506.

References

Bailey, J., & Steeves, V. (2013). Will the real digital girl please stand up? In H. Koskela & J. M. Wise (Eds.), *New visualities, new technologies: The new ecstasy of communication* (pp. 41–66). Surrey: Ashgate Publishing.

BCG. (2012). *The value of our digital identity.* Retrieved from www.libertyglobal.com/PDF/public-policy/The-Value-of-Our-Digital-Identity.pdf

Children's Online Privacy Protection Act 1998, 15 U.S.C. §§ 6501–6506.

Dworkin, R. (2009). Rights as trumps. In A. Kavanagh & J. Oberdiek (Eds.), *Arguing about law* (pp. 335–344). New York, NY: Routledge.

European Commission. (2016). *An EU agenda for the rights of the child.* Retrieved from http://ec.europa.eu/justice/fundamental-rights/rights-child/eu-agenda/index_en.htm

Fisk, N. (2014). "…when no one is hearing them swear": Youth safety and the pedagogy of surveillance. *Surveillance & Society, 14*(4), 566–580.

Franklin, B. (1995). The case for children's rights: A progress report. In B. Franklin (Ed.), *The handbook of children's rights: Comparative policy and practice* (pp. 3–22.). London: Routledge.

Freeman, M. (2007). Why it remains important to take children's rights seriously. *International Journal of Children's Rights, 15*(5), 5–23. Retrieved from https://doi.org/10.1163/092755607x181711

Gandy, O. (2009). *Coming to terms with chance: Engaging rational discrimination and cumulative disadvantage.* New York, NY: Routledge. Retrieved from https://doi.org/10.4324/9781315572758

Hammarberg, T. (1997). Children, the UN Convention and the media. *International Journal of Children's Rights, 22*(1), 748–775. Retrieved from https://doi.org/10.1163/15718189720493636

Humanium. (n.d.). *The convention on the rights of the child: Signatory states and parties to the convention.* Retrieved from http://www.humanium.org/en/convention/signatory-states/

Jasmontaite, L., & De Hert, P. (2015). The EU, children under 13 years, and parental consent: A human rights analysis of a new, age-based bright-line for the protection of children on the Internet. *International Data Protection Law, 5*(1), 20–33. Retrieved from https://doi.org/10.1093/idpl/ipu029

Johnson, M., Riel, R., & Froese-Germain, B. (2016). *Connected to learn: Teachers' experiences with networked technologies in the classroom.* Ottawa: MediaSmarts/Canadian Teachers' Federation.

Morse v. Frederick, 551 U.S. 393 (2007). doi:10.4135/9781604265774.n892

O'Brien, W. (2014). Australia's digital policy agenda: Adopting a children's rights approach. *International Journal of Children's Rights, 15*(5), 5–23. Retrieved from https://doi.org/10.1163/15718182-02204004

Pew Research Center. (2014). *What Internet users know about technology and the web: The Pew Research Center's web IQ test.* Retrieved from http://PI_Web-IQ_112514_PDF.pdf

Privacy International. (n.d.). *Data protection.* Retrieved from https://www.privacyinternational.org/node/44

Regan, P. M. (1995). *Legislating privacy: Technology, social values and public policy.* Chapel Hill, NC: University of North Carolina Press.

Robbins v. Lower Merion School District. Class Action Complaint. (U.S. Dist. E.D. Pa. Feb. 11, 2010). Retrieved from https://archive.org/stream/RobbinsV.LowerMerionSchoolDistrictpdf/robbins17_djvu.txt

Robbins v. Lower Merion School District. Brief of *Amicus Curia* American Civil Liberties Union of Pennsylvania supporting issuance of injunction (U.S. Dist. E.D. Pa. Feb. 11, 2010). Retrieved from https://www.aclupa.org/download_file/view_inline/600/210/

Safer Schools Together. (2016). *Home page.* Retrieved from http://saferschoolstogether.com/

Shade, L. R., & Singh, R. (2016). "Honestly, we're not spying on kids": School surveillance of young people's social media. *Social Media + Society, 2*(4), 1–12. Retrieved from https://doi.org/10.1177/2056305116680005

Smith, A. B. (2007). Children and young people's participation rights in education. *International Journal of Children's Rights, 15*, 147–164. Retrieved from https://doi.org/10.1163/092755607x181739

Steeves, V. (2007). The watched child: Surveillance in three online playgrounds. In V. Pinero (Ed.), *Proceedings of the international conference on the rights of the child* (pp. 119–140) Montreal: Wilson Lafleur. El niño observado: vigilancia en tres sitios de juegos de niños en Internet. In V. Pinero (Ed.), *Actas de la Conferencia Internacional sobre los Derechos del Niño.* Buenos Aires: Universidad de Buenos Aires.

Steeves, V. (2012). *Young Canadians in a wired world, phase III: Talking to youth and parents about life online.* Ottawa: Media Smarts.

Steeves, V. (2014a). *Young Canadians in a wired world, phase III: Life online.* Ottawa: Media Smarts.

Steeves, V. (2014b). *Young Canadians in a wired world, phase III: Online privacy, online publicity.* Ottawa: Media Smarts.

Steeves, V. (2016). Now you see me: Privacy, technology and autonomy in the digital age. In G. DiGiacomo (Ed.), *Current issues and controversies in human rights.* Toronto: University of Toronto Press.

Steeves, V. (2016). *Terra Cognita*: The surveillance of young peoples' favourite websites. In T. Rooney & E. Taylor (Eds.), *Surveillance and childhood.* Surrey: Ashgate Publishing.

Suski, E. F. (2014). Beyond the schoolhouse gates: The unprecedented expansion of school surveillance authority under cyberbullying laws. *Case Western Reserve Law Review, 65*(1), 63–119.

UN General Assembly, *Convention on the Rights of the Child*, 20 November 1989, United Nations, Treaty Series, 1577, 3. Retrieved from http://www.refworld.org/docid/3ae6b38f0.html

Williams, N. (1997). The theme day of the Committee on the Rights of the Child on "Children and Media". *International Journal of Children's Rights, 5*(2), 263–266. Retrieved from https://doi.org/10.1163/15718189720493645

CHAPTER 19

How Do Social Differences Influence Young People's Media Experiences?

Vikki S. Katz

Immigration and intermarriage are two of the most powerful drivers of increased social diversity in the United States. One-quarter of U.S. children is Hispanic; another 14% are Black, and 5% are Asian (Child Trends, 2014; Kids Count, 2014). In addition, the proportion of children who are either the U.S.-born children of immigrants or are immigrants themselves increased from 18% to 25% between 1994 and 2014 (Child Trends, 2014). Added to this diversity is the promise of more to come; by 2013, one in eight new marriages in the United States was between different-race spouses (Wang, 2015).

The racial, ethnic, and cultural diversity in the United States has increased concurrently with profound growth in income inequality. By 2014, close to half (44%) of U.S. children were living in low-income families. But not all children are equally likely to be among them; 65% of Black children and 62% of American Indian and Hispanic children are low-income, compared with 31% of White and 30% of Asian children. And more than half (54%) of children with immigrant parents are growing up in low-income homes, compared with 40% of those with U.S.-born parents (Jiang, Ekono, & Skinner, 2016).

It seems obvious that these forms of social diversity can, in turn, affect how young people interact with media. For example, children who speak multiple languages can select from both mainstream and ethnic media offerings (Matsaganis, Katz, & Ball-Rokeach, 2011). In an increasingly fragmented media landscape, young people of all racial and ethnic backgrounds are drawn to channels and platforms that resonate with their personal experiences (Louie, 2003; Oh, 2013; Tynes, Reynolds, & Greenfield, 2004). Family income also affects many aspects of media experience, ranging from the kind of technology young people can afford to own, to whether they can access the skill-building opportunities that enable them to use these devices meaningfully (Helsper & Eynon, 2010; Katz & Gonzalez, 2016).

Nevertheless, since the popularization of movies and radio in the early part of the twentieth century, the majority of research on children, adolescents, and media has focused on the concerns and behaviors of White, middle (and upper-middle) class, young people (Alper, Katz, & Clark, 2016; Wartella & Reeves, 1985). Over the last two decades, researchers have worked to correct that imbalance by documenting how social differences, including race/ethnicity, immigrant generation, and social class affect children's experiences with media and technology. Since these are three of the most prominent dimensions of social difference covered in the existing literature, I focus on them in this chapter. Of course, there are many others; gender is a prominent example, and is covered in detail in Chapter 11.

Researching Social Diversity, Children, and Media

Prior studies have consistently reported that Black and Hispanic youth consume more media than their White counterparts. Most recently, Common Sense Media (2016) found that, on average, Black tweens and teens spend 11 hours and 10 minutes *daily* with media outside of school. This is more than two extra hours a day than their Hispanic (8:51) and White (8:27) counterparts. The largest proportion of that time is spent with TV and videos; Black teens and tweens average four and one-half hours (4:33) per day, Hispanics about one hour less (3:22), and Whites just under three hours (2:56).

Why do these differences between racial and ethnic groups exist in the first place, and why have they persisted over time? A partial answer lies in different access to various forms of media and to TV in particular. An earlier study of children (ages eight to eighteen) found that 84% of Black and 77% of Hispanic youth have a television set in their bedroom, compared with 64% of White and Asian youth (Center on Media and Human Development, 2011). Among those with a bedroom TV, Black and Hispanic youth are also significantly more likely to have premium channels (42% and 28%, respectively) than White (17%) and Asian (14%) youth. Black and Hispanic households also report more background television exposure; 78% of Black and 67% of Hispanic youth reported that the TV is "usually" on during dinner, compared with 58% of Whites and 55% of Asians (Center on Media and Human Development, 2011). Of course, these numbers don't explain *why* Black and Hispanic youth grow up in in more screen-centric families; they indicate only that these differences exist.

The relationship between race/ethnicity and social class is another partial explanation for these group differences. I noted above that nearly two-thirds of Black and Hispanic children are low-income, which is another form of social difference that is consistently associated with higher media use. Specifically, Common Sense Media (2016) found that lower-income teens (i.e., those in households reporting incomes less than $35,000 per year) spend two hours and 45 minutes more with media on an average day than higher-income teens (i.e., those in households earning more than $100,000 annually; 10:35 versus 7:50). For time spent with TV specifically, the difference between these two income groups is approximately 90 minutes on an average day (4:14, compared with 2:41).

How much of the time that Black and Hispanic youth spend with media can be attributed to racial/ethnic differences, and how much is explained by family income? The picture is complicated still further by other forms of social difference that relate closely to family income, including family structure and parents' level of education. Children growing up with a single parent or whose parent(s) have limited formal education also spend more time with media per day than children in two-parent households or those with college-educated parents (Center on Media and Human Development, 2011).

An additional, important dimension of social difference for children's media experiences is whether they have U.S.-born or immigrant parents; one in four U.S. children is now in the latter category. A representative survey of U.S. adolescents with parents from Central America,[1] Mexico, the Dominican Republic, and China found that only 20% of teens watch television "mainly alone," and that they were most likely to watch alongside parents and siblings (Louie, 2003). By contrast, a general study of U.S. teens during the same time period found that more than one-third watched TV "mainly alone," and that they frequently watched with peers (Rideout, Foehr, Roberts, & Brodie, 1999). As I will discuss in more detail later, there are important differences between shared and individual media experiences for how young people assign meaning to media content and rituals.

In addition, because children of immigrants generally watch television with their parents, it is hardly surprising that much of that content is in their parents' primary language. However, there are interesting differences based on the family's country of origin. The majority of Dominican-, Central American-, and Mexican-origin youth report that they watch Spanish-language TV channels more than one-half of the time. Children of Chinese origin report that less than one-quarter of their TV time is in Chinese, and teens of Haitian origin watch English-language media almost exclusively (Louie, 2003). The author offers two explanations for these patterns. The first is that youth of Chinese origin report more private computer ownership and spend more of their media time with computers than TV, thus making their viewing habits qualitatively different from Spanish-speaking groups.

The second explanation relates to availability of ethnic media for different language groups. *Telemundo* and *Univision* are two of the largest media conglomerates in the United States, and Spanish-language media are by far the largest, U.S. ethnic media market (Louie, 2003). While Chinese-language media are prominent in the United States, they are more heavily print-based than visual. There is a much smaller media marketplace for speakers of Haitian Creole (Matsaganis *et al.*, 2011). The broader range of ethnic media offerings available for Spanish-speaking families may make it easier to agree on content that all members find enjoyable.

Getting Beyond the Numbers

Statistics alert us to differences between young people's media experiences but may not offer clear explanations for *why* those differences exist and endure over time. Qualitative research relies on interviews, in-person observations, and other open-ended and participatory methods to better understand these kinds of dynamics.

Qualitative studies have suggested that elements of social class, including family income, parental education and occupation, and family structure work together to influence how children, siblings, and parents orient themselves to media use. Researchers who use qualitative methods do not separate media use from who families are, what challenges they face, and the strengths that they apply to addressing those challenges. As such, these scholars argue that patterns of media use reflect and are dynamically related to families' social characteristics.

Amy Jordan's (1992) classic study of social class and media use offers an explanation for why parents' occupations influence media use patterns. She argues that although most quantitative studies, such as those detailed earlier in this chapter, focus on how much time children or parents spend with media, they do not assess parents' orientations to time itself. Jordan found that parents who do shift work have schedules and routines that are externally (rather than internally) imposed. By definition, shift workers also do not bring work home to complete outside of office hours. Parents in professional occupations often do so, and, in the process, they are "carrying the notion that 'time is money' into the home" (Jordan, 1992, p. 377). As a result, these parents are more likely to consider time as a commodity that should be carefully spent. Therefore, they are more likely to treat extensive media use without a productive purpose (such as completing a homework assignment) as wasting time. Another factor, which supports the link Jordan makes between parents' occupation and media use, is that shift work often involves unpredictable scheduling practices (Henly & Lambert, 2014). This makes it more likely that children will spend time with media with little parental supervision (Austin, Knaus, & Meneguielli, 1997; Warren, Gerke, & Kelly, 2002).

Thus, parents' occupation can have an influence, and occupations are closely related to parents' educational attainment and to their income. Lynn Schofield Clark (2012) considers all of these factors to explain that social differences between working class parents and professional families result in different parenting "ethics" related to media practices. She describes the media strategies of professional parents as an *ethic of expressive empowerment*. This involves limiting children's technology time to "productive" purposes that emphasize skills development (e.g., learning to code) or support other individualized pursuits of excellence, such as mastering the violin. These limitations on technology use are a logical extension of broader parenting practices that aim to provide their children with extensive opportunities to develop skills and interests, for example, through after-school soccer, dance, or music classes. Annette Lareau (2003) calls these forms of parental investment (which are usually financially impossible for lower-income families) *concerted cultivation*, because these parents consciously try to cultivate their children's capabilities to convert existing familial social advantages into life successes as they grow up.

Clark (2012) contrasts this approach with the *ethic of respectful connection*, which she documents as guiding the media experiences of lower-income, native-born, and immigrant families. Again, aligning her findings with Lareau's earlier work (2003), Clark notes that, although lower-income parents also work hard to ensure their children's successes in school and life, they prioritize raising children who are loyal and caring toward their families and communities. In accordance with those values, Clark documents that lower-income families are more likely to consider "media time" as "family time," which leads them to privilege television and other shareable screens over more privatized forms of media use.

The result is that members of lower-income and immigrant families are more likely to act as *interpretive communities* (Mayer, 2003), in that members help each other to understand and integrate media content, which they consume together. Of course, interpretive communities do not have to be family members; they can also be other trusted individuals, including peers. However, for youth in immigrant families, in particular, (and in low-income families more broadly), the evidence shows that close relatives frequently act as interpretive communities.

These intensive family exchanges around media are reinforced by other forms of sharing that are part of everyday life in a lower-income household. Lower-income youth are more likely to share media devices with other family members than are higher-income young people, particularly expensive new devices, like tablets and laptops (Clark, 2012; Rideout & Katz, 2016). They are also more likely to share space. Scholars have documented how higher-income tweens and teens (especially girls) develop *bedroom cultures*, using technology to help establish their bedrooms as separate, private worlds within their homes (Livingstone, 2007). Most lower-income youth have neither the personal physical space nor private ownership of devices to enact such boundaries, even if they would like to. As a result, sharing is more likely to be a fundamental element of media experiences in lower-income families than in higher-income ones.

Sharing space, devices, and media experiences can facilitate deep trust among family members. Clark (2011) suggests that parents and children in lower-income families frequently collaborate to learn with technology together. In my own work, I've examined these dynamics by documenting how tween and teen children of immigrants *broker* their parents' media connections. Adults who are low-income, have limited formal education, and/or are not proficient in English have less experience with technology than other groups (Rideout & Katz, 2016), so their children can enable them to more easily connect with devices and content than they would be able to do alone. When children of immigrants broker their parents' connections *to* an unfamiliar digital device, they often also broker content available *through* that device by translating it into their parents' language and explaining its cultural significance, to the best of their abilities (Katz, 2010, 2014).

Although it may appear that children are acting alone when they play these brokering roles for their parents, they are not. To illustrate this point: a child may teach a parent how to send text messages, but that same child might rely on a parent to help him/her decide how to respond to a hurtful text message received from a classmate. In multiple studies, I have found that parents and children collectively contribute to the success of children's brokering activities by bringing their distinctive skills and capabilities to the table. Child brokers bring their relatively greater facility with English, U.S. popular culture and cultural norms, and digital devices; parents bring their life experience and understanding of their children's and family's needs (Katz, 2014; Katz, Moran, & Gonzalez, 2017). Together, they trade expert and learner roles to support each other in learning about and developing skills that enhance their ability to use technology.

These learning exchanges are not limited to digital technologies. Vicki Mayer (2003) documented how Mexican-American youth and their immigrant mothers and grandmothers watched soap operas (*telenovelas*) on TV and formed an interpretive community, which facilitated intergenerational language learning and cultural exchange. In a similar way, Meenakshi Durham (2004) showed how daughters of Indian immigrants treated viewing TV content from India with their parents as an essential element of their cultural education. Their parents considered mainstream depictions of U.S. high school life an alarming education about things against which they needed to protect their daughters' virtue. Durham's findings are a good reminder that not all family interactions around media and technology are cooperative. For example, children of North African immigrants in France admitted to secretly repositioning the family satellite dish to receive more French TV stations, as opposed to the diasporic channels their parents preferred that they watch (Hargreaves & Mahdjoub, 1997).

Interpreting Social Differences

Taken together, this evidence clearly shows that social differences influence young people's media experiences. Researchers not only need to document how young people's experiences vary across dimensions of social difference; they must also interpret what those differences mean. The *what*—that differences exist—is only the first step; the *why* is equally important. Differences themselves are neutral; assessments about what those differences mean might not be. In the following sections, I discuss some common ways that researchers have worked to explain their findings.

Defining "Normal" Media Use

A fundamental question in interpreting research results is whose behaviors get treated as the norm against which other groups are compared. Earlier in this chapter, I pointed out that the majority of research on children and media has focused on White, higher-income youth. As a result, the media behaviors of those children and families have often been treated as the standard against which other groups are compared.

This framing raises at least two fundamental concerns. The first, as discussed above, is that differences in media behaviors between diverse families are complicated. There are real and legitimate reasons why working class, racial and ethnic minority, and/or immigrant children and parents might have different orientations to media. A problem with treating one set of people or practices as "normal" is that everything outside of that definition, by natural consequence, is treated as abnormal. Research that documents differences in how much time White and non-White families spend with media and how closely parents supervise children's media use have frequently been released to the public without additional context to explain those differences. Journalists who report de-contextualized research findings have often adopted a *deficit* perspective of these children and families. They question the capability of parents to guide their children's media use or conclude that lower-income children "waste time" with technology, whereas their higher-income counterparts supposedly use technology more constructively (e.g., Richtel, 2012).

Sometimes the assessment that one set of practices is better for children's development than others draws from strong evidence. For example, young children in low-income households (who, as discussed previously, are disproportionately children of color) are exposed to more background television than wealthier and White children (Thompson & Tschann, 2016). Background television is hard for young children to ignore and impedes learning processes by interrupting their play (Linebarger, Barr, Lapierre, & Piotrowski, 2014). Background television exposure at age two is also associated with significantly increased aggression and attention problems at age five (Martin, Razza, & Brooks-Gunn, 2012). These are compelling reasons for trying to reduce background television exposure for all young children. Echoing a similar concern, the American Academy of Pediatrics recently argued that more screen time among older children displaces time from other crucial developmental activities, such as exercise, play, and in-person social interactions (AAP Council on Communications & Media, 2016).

However, drawing firm conclusions about both of these subjects requires consideration of the broader contexts of children's lives. More than two-thirds (69%) of children with a single parent are low-income (Jiang *et al.*, 2016). Among low-income single mothers, those with depressive symptoms are most likely to report high levels of child television exposure (Ansari & Crosnoe, 2015). Deborah Linebarger and her colleagues (2014) also found that parenting style influences how background television affects children. If background television provides over-extended mothers with the short breaks they need to subsequently be more engaged with their children, the picture becomes more complicated; is a young child more adversely affected by background television or by having an anxious, stressed parent?

In a similar way, more screen time can be a protective strategy for parents of older children. Lower-income children of color are disproportionately likely to live in urban neighborhoods, which generally have less safe, high-quality, outdoor spaces (Baksh, 2011; Telles, Sawyer, & Rivera-Salgado, 2011). Researchers have found that low-income parents in dangerous neighborhoods sometimes respond to those threats by prioritizing purchases of expensive technology to entice their children to stay within the safe confines of their homes (Livingstone, 2007; Katz, 2014). A low-income, Mexican-American mother, whom I interviewed years ago, told me, "Kids get shot on my block. At least when my kids watch TV, I know they are safe." Her experience is obviously not the reality of every low-income parent, but a consideration of her decision-making process makes it easier to understand why her family's media practices look different from someone who lives in a wealthier, safer community. Contextualizing parents' decision-making in this way also makes it harder to claim with confidence what qualifies as the "right" set of parenting practices for children's media use.

An additional problem with normalizing the practices of one demographic group is that it can obscure social realities. What image comes to mind when I ask you to picture a "normal" or "typical" American family? Responses to this question by my undergraduate students over many years are almost totally uniform: they picture a family with two married parents, two children, and a dog. If I ask them to specify the family's race and where the family lives, the answer is almost always that the family is White and lives in a house with a white picket fence. This "normal" depiction is a specific family formation (married adults with children), race (White), and social class (the white picket fence being stereotypically middle class).

Now guess what percentage of U.S. children grow up in a nuclear household. You may be surprised that it is only 41% of children—less than half. The same proportion grows up with a single mother, father, or with extended family members. The remaining 18% grow up in adoptive families, stepfamilies, or in "other" family configurations (U.S. Census Bureau, 2013). Combined with the statistics I presented earlier about U.S. children's racial/ethnic and income diversity, it is clear that the stereotype of a "normal" American family is anything but typical. Assumptions about "normal" media practices, therefore, are not typical either.

Understanding Overlapping Forms of Social Difference

Another aspect of interpreting findings is deciding how to account for multiple forms of social difference that people experience simultaneously. In quantitative studies, researchers routinely "control" for the effects of certain demographic differences in order to analyze others. For example, a researcher interested in how teens' time with media varies by their family's income level will control for other demographic variables, such as race/ethnicity and family type, to be able to focus specifically on income. Controlling for a variable is the statistical equivalent of holding it constant, so that the researcher can assess (all else being equal) how much variance in teens' time spent with media is explained by variations in their household income. There are also more sophisticated statistical methods for measuring how forms of social difference interact with and influence each other to affect media experiences among diverse young people.

Intersectionality is a prominent, qualitative analytical approach for understanding multiple forms of social difference simultaneously (Crenshaw, 1989). The underlying concept is that a person's identity is not simply the sum of its component identifications. That is, understanding the experience of a lower-income, Chinese-American, teenage, female is more than the independent effects of her social class, ethnicity, age, and gender on her life experiences. An intersectional approach would require considering how all of these facets of her identity are dynamically linked to each other.

Intersectionality's second key component is a concern with social inequality; it assumes that forms of social exclusion (such as racism, classism, xenophobia, and sexism) intersect and potentially compound each other. Kimberlé Crenshaw initially coined the term to understand how racism and sexism intersected in the lives of Black women. Her contention was that a consideration of the impacts of racism and sexism separately would not accurately capture their experiences. This concern becomes particularly interesting for considering how certain dimensions of an individual's social identity confer privilege relative to his/her peers, whereas others confer relative disadvantage. In an article I co-authored with Meryl Alper and Lynn Schofield Clark, we offered this illustration:

> Consider, for example, that a financially well-off, native-born family with a child who has disabilities experiences both privilege and oppression. On the one hand, this family's social positioning and disposable income makes it possible to access and purchase new media technologies designed to assist their child. On the other, this family faces systemic challenges that other privileged families do not, but still likely encounters less barriers than a low-income family whose child has the same condition. (Alper *et al.*, 2016, p. 100)

This example shows how an intersectional approach creates possibilities for analyzing the meanings of social differences among young people and their media experiences. A researcher whose sole interest is in how family income affects technology use might fail to consider how a wealthy family with a child who has disabilities is less privileged, relatively speaking, than another wealthy family whose children do not face such challenges. On the other hand, a researcher focused on disability and technology use who neglects to analyze how wealthier families are relatively privileged, compared with poorer ones whose children have the same conditions, would offer incomplete (and likely quite inaccurate) conclusions.

Intersectionality, therefore, offers some important tools for considering children and families on their own terms by attempting to account for how people actually *live* their varied forms of social difference. Although some aspects of our identities may be more salient to us in certain circumstances than others (Tajfel & Turner, 2004), we live the different aspects of our identities in the intertwined ways that intersectionality suggests. The qualitative studies profiled earlier in this chapter offer these kinds of assessments. For example, Mayer (2003) focuses on how gender, age, social class, and immigrant generation are woven together in the media experiences that lower-income Mexican-American teenage girls share with their mothers and grandmothers, and how those experiences affect their linguistic and cultural identity development.

For every strength of a methodological or analytical approach in research, however, there are also weaknesses. Intersectionality can ably document forms of social difference, but social commonalities are harder to trace. Consider, for example, the individuals in Figure 19.1.

Lauren   Jesse   Camila

Figure 19.1: Explaining Intersectionality. Source: Cassie Peng

Lauren is White and from a lower-income family, Jesse is Hispanic and also from a lower-income family, and Camila is from a higher-income, Hispanic family. These three teens differ from each other along dimensions that, as we now know, are predictive of their media experiences. But, can we assess whose experiences are more similar using an intersectional approach? Are Lauren and Jesse more alike because they are both lower-income, or are Jesse and Camila more alike because they are both Hispanic? Although we have not discussed in this chapter how gender affects media experiences (see Chapter 11) Lauren and Camila may share similarities in this regard as well. An intersectional approach is able to describe what makes these three young people different from each other, but is limited when it comes to explaining or measuring their potential commonalities.

Explaining Social Difference and Addressing Social Inequality

In this chapter, I have focused explicitly on social differences in youths' media experiences and hinted that research links some kinds of social difference to social inequality related to, for example, income and parental education. This distinction is critical, because whereas differences are not inherently concerning, inequalities are. Which research approaches permit the most accurate documentation of social differences, in order to reduce social inequalities among young people?

Researchers who examine social differences related to social inequalities bear responsibility for how their conclusions may be interpreted or used by others. Ideally, well-designed, executed, and analyzed studies will inform efforts to reduce unequal access to social opportunities for young people from diverse backgrounds. For example, as technology is increasingly integrated into new learning models, both in and out of school, ensuring that all children have equitable access to those benefits becomes increasingly crucial (Rideout & Katz, 2016). However, researchers do not always carefully consider how findings that highlight social differences can reinforce stereotypes and further disadvantage groups that already face a range of social challenges. Researchers run this risk when the media behaviors of less privileged children are compared with those who are wealthier and White without adequate contextualization.

How, then, can research on diversity, youth, and media endeavor to contribute to the first group of outcomes rather than the second? Because all of the research methods and modes of analysis profiled in this chapter have strengths and weaknesses, one way would be to combine various methods thoughtfully within a single study. As Chapter 7 discusses in more detail, the strengths of one research approach can compensate for the weaknesses of another. Mixed-method designs allow researchers to *triangulate* their results and explain findings that would otherwise feel incomplete (Denzin, 1978; Johnson, Onwuegbuzie, & Turner, 2007). When data collected via different methods produce complementary results, the researcher can be more confident that her study findings accurately reflect young people's experiences. That accuracy (also referred to as *validity*) is key to developing programs and policies that effectively address young people's needs.

Researchers' confidence in the accuracy of their findings is also important because young people's relationships with media are often subject to *moral panics* (see Chapter 3). Claims about the diversity of young people's media experiences, what they mean, and what should be done about them, therefore, need to be well-supported by evidence. They need to be carefully explained to a variety of concerned audiences, including parents, educators, policymakers, and, of course, young people themselves.

Discussion Questions

1. The introduction to this chapter notes that the majority of research on children, adolescents, and media has focused on White, middle, or upper-middle class, young people. Select another chapter in this book on a topic you found particularly interesting and re-read it with this issue in mind. If that chapter discusses research that accounts for social differences among young people, consider how that broader focus affects your understanding of the topic. If that chapter does not include such studies, provide a well-reasoned argument for what researchers could be missing about their chosen topic by studying a relatively homogenous group of young people.

2. Review the section of this chapter about definitions of "normal" media use. With two classmates, discuss whether the notion that implicit value judgements of normal/non-normal media behaviours have real consequences resonates with you (or does not), and explain your reasoning either way.

3. Although this chapter focuses primarily on social differences, it also hints at the importance of identifying similarities among young people's media experiences. Re-read the discussion of intersectionality and consider this tension; why is it important for researchers to not only identify what makes young people different, but also to consider how they are alike?

Exercises

1. Identify a dimension of social difference that is *not* covered in this chapter and explain why you think it relates to differential experiences with media. Begin with some basic online research to assess how common that dimension of diversity is among young people today. Then, consult journals in communication and across the social sciences available through your university library that publish research on children and media. (The *Journal of Children and Media* is a good place to start!). How much scholarly attention has your chosen dimension of diversity received? What methods have primarily been used to study it; what have researchers found so far? Do their findings relate your chosen topic to the dimensions of social difference that *are* covered in this chapter, and if so, in what ways?

2. The research reviewed in this chapter is U.S.-centric, but issues related to social diversity and young people's media experiences are, obviously, international. Select a dimension of social difference that *is* covered in this chapter that you find particularly interesting. Review research available through your university library on how that dimension has been treated by researchers in one or more non-U.S. contexts. Consider differences in how studies have been conducted and how findings have been analyzed; what do those distinctions between research traditions reflect about how social differences are defined and experienced in those countries, as compared with in the United States?

3. Re-read Chapter 7 which discusses research methods, and the last section of this chapter, which discusses methodological consequences for addressing social inequalities among diverse young people. How do the contents of Chapter 7 relate to the discussion of what

responsibilities researchers bear for how their data and analyses are interpreted by others?

Note

1   The designation "Central American" refers to adolescents whose families had migrated from Nicaragua, El Salvador, Honduras, or Guatemala (Suárez-Orozco, Suárez-Orozco, & Todorova, 2008).

References

Alper, M., Katz, V. S., & Clark, L. S. (2016). Researching children, intersectionality, and diversity in the digital age. *Journal of Children and Media, 10*(1), 107–114. doi:10.1080/17482798.2015.1121886

American Academy of Pediatrics Council on Communications and Media. (2016). Media use in school-aged children and adolescents. *Pediatrics, 38*(5), e20162592. doi:10.1542/peds.2016–2592

Ansari, A., & Crosnoe, R. (2015). Children's elicitation of changes in parenting during the early childhood years. *Early Childhood Research Quarterly, 32*(3), 139–149. doi:10.1016/j.ecresq.2015.03.005

Austin, E. W., Knaus, C., & Meneguelli, A. (1997). Who talks to their kids about TV: A clarification of demographic correlates of parental mediation patterns. *Communication Research Reports, 14*(4), 418–430. doi:10.1080/08824099709388685

Baksh, S. (2011, June 15). Media overload? A look at exactly how much youth of color consume. *Colorlines.* Retrieved from https://www.colorlines.com/content/media-overload-look-exactly-how-much-youth-color-consume

Center on Media and Human Development. (2011, July). *Children, media, and race: Media use among White, Black, Hispanic and Asian American children.* Northwestern University. Retrieved from http://static1.1.sqspcdn.com/static/f/1083077/14689973/1318952548830/Children+Media+and+Race.FINAL.pdf?token=N5og98s7yg0emHLR8JmGNo3AwNE%3D

Child Trends. (2014, July). *Racial and ethnic composition of the child population: Indicators on children and youth.* Retrieved from http://www.childtrends.org/?indicators=racial-and-ethnic-composition-of-the-child-population

Clark, L. S. (2011). Parental mediation theory for the digital age. *Communication Theory, 21*(4), 323–343. doi:10.1111/j.1468–2885.2011.01391.x

Clark, L. S. (2012). *The parent app: Understanding families in the digital age.* Oxford: Oxford University Press.

Common Sense Media. (2016). *The Common Sense census: Media use by tweens and teens.* Retrieved from https://www.commonsensemedia.org/sites/default/files/uploads/research/census_researchreport.pdf

Crenshaw, K. (1989). Demarginalizing the intersection of race and sex: A black feminist critique of antidiscrimination doctrine, feminist theory and antiracist politics. *University of Chicago Legal Forum, 140,* 139–167.

Denzin, N. K. (1978). *The research act* (2nd ed.). New York, NY: McGraw-Hill.

Durham, M. (2004). Constructing the "new ethnicities": Media, sexuality and diaspora identity in the lives of South Asian immigrant girls. *Critical Studies in Media Communication, 21,* 140–161. doi:10.1080/0739318 0410001688047

Hargreaves, A., & Mahdjoub, D. (1997). Satellite television viewing among ethnic minorities in France. *European Journal of Communication, 12,* 459–477. doi:10.1177/0267323197012004002

Helsper, E. J., & Eynon, R. (2010). Digital natives: Where is the evidence? *British Educational Research Journal, 36*(3), 503–520. doi:10.1080/01411920902989227

Henly, J. R., & Lambert, S. (2014). Unpredictable work timing in retail jobs: Implications for employee work-life outcomes. *Industrial and Labor Relations Review, 67*(3), 986–1016. doi:10.1177/0019793914537458

Jiang, Y., Ekono, M., Skinner, C. (2016, February). *Basic facts about low income children.* National Center for Children Living in Poverty. Retrieved from http://www.nccp.org/publications/pub_1145.html

Johnson, R. B., & Onwuegbuzie, A. J., & Turner, L. A. (2007). Toward a definition of mixed methods research. *Journal of Mixed Methods Research, 1*(2), 112–133. doi:10.1177/1558689806298224

Jordan, A. B. (1992). Social class, temporal orientation, and mass media use within the family system. *Critical Studies in Media Communication, 9*(4), 374–386. doi:10.1080/15295039209366840

Katz, V. S. (2010). How children use media to connect their families to the community: The case of Latinos in Los Angeles. *Journal of Children and Media, 4*(3), 298–315. doi:10.1080/17482798.2010.486136

Katz, V. S. (2014). *Kids in the middle: How children of immigrants negotiate community interactions for their families.* New Brunswick, NJ: Rutgers University Press.

Katz, V. S., & Gonzalez, C. (2016). Toward meaningful connectivity: Using multilevel communication research to reframe digital inequality. *Journal of Communication, 66*(2), 236–249. doi:10.1111/jcom.12214

Katz, V. S., Moran, M., & Gonzalez, C. (2017). Family learning with technology in lower-income US families. *New Media & Society.* Advance online publication. DOI: 10.1177/1461444817726319

Kids Count. (2014). *Annie E Casey Foundation.* Retrieved from http://datacenter.kidscount.org/

Lareau, A. (2003). *Unequal childhoods: Class, race and family life.* Berkeley, CA: University of California Press.

Linebarger, D. L., Barr, R., Lapierre, M. A., & Piotrowski, J. T. (2014). Associations between parenting, media use, cumulative risk, and children's executive functioning. *Journal of Developmental & Behavioral Pediatrics, 35*(6), 367–377. doi:10.1097/DBP.0000000000000069

Livingstone, S. (2007). From family television to bedroom culture: Young people's media at home. In E. Devereux (Ed.), *Media studies: Key issues and debates* (pp. 302–321). Thousand Oaks, CA: Sage Publications.

Louie, J. (2003). Media in the lives of immigrant youth. *New Directions for Youth Development, 100,* 111–130.

Martin, A., Razza, R. A., & Brooks-Gunn, J. (2012). Specifying the links between household chaos and preschool children's development. *Early Child Development and Care, 182*(10), 1247–1263. doi:10.1080/03004430.2011.605522

Matsaganis, M. D., Katz, V. S., & Ball-Rokeach, S. J. (2011). *Understanding ethnic media: Producers, consumers and societies.* Thousand Oaks, CA: Sage Publications.

Mayer, V. (2003). Living telenovelas/Telenovelizing life: Mexican-American girls' identities and transnational telenovelas. *Journal of Communication, 53*(4), 479–495. doi:10.1111/j.1460–2466.2003.tb02603.x

Oh, D. C. (2013). Mediating diasporas and fandom: Second-generation Korean American adolescent diasporas, identification, and transnational popular culture. *The Communication Review, 16*(4), 230–250. doi:10.1080/10714421.2013.839588

Richtel, M. (2012, May 12). Wasting time is new divide in digital era. *New York Times.* Retrieved from http://www.nytimes.com/2012/05/30/us/new-digital-divide-seen-in-wasting-time-online.html

Rideout, V., Foehr, U., Roberts, D., & Brodie, M. (1999). *Kids and media @ the new millennium.* Menlo Park, CA: Henry J. Kaiser Foundation.

Rideout, V. J., & Katz, V. S. (2016). *Opportunity for all? Technology and learning in lower-income families.* New York, NY: Joan Ganz Cooney Center at Sesame Workshop.

Suárez-Orozco, C., Suárez-Orozco, M. M., & Todorova, I. (2008). *Learning in a new land: Immigrant students in American society.* Cambridge, MA: Harvard University Press.

Tajfel, H., & Turner, J. C. (2004). The social identity theory of intergroup behavior. In J. T. Jost & J. Sidanius (Eds.), *Political psychology: Key readings* (pp. 276–293). New York, NY: Psychology Press.

Telles, E., Sawyer, M. Q., & Rivera-Salgado, G. (Eds.). (2011). *Just neighbors? Research on African American and Latino relations in the United States.* New York, NY: Russell Sage Foundation.

Thompson, D. A., & Tschann, J. M. (2016). Factors contributing to background television exposure in low-income Mexican–American preschoolers. *Maternal and Child Health Journal, 20*(9), 1835–1841. doi:10.1007/s10995-016-1986-0

Tynes, B., Reynolds, L., & Greenfield, P. M. (2004). Adolescence, race, and ethnicity on the Internet: A comparison of discourse in monitored vs. unmonitored chat rooms. *Journal of Applied Developmental Psychology, 25*(6), 667–684. doi:10.1016/j.appdev.2004.09.003

U.S. Census Bureau. (2013). *Families and households.* Retrieved from https://www.census.gov/topics/families/families-and-households.html

Wang, W. (2015, June 12). *Interracial marriage: Who is 'marrying out'?* Pew Research Center. Retrieved from http://www.pewresearch.org/fact-tank/2015/06/12/interracial-marriage-who-is-marrying-out/

Warren, R., Gerke, P., & Kelly, M. A. (2002). Is there enough time on the clock? Parental involvement and mediation of children's television viewing. *Journal of Broadcasting & Electronic Media, 46*(1), 87–111. doi:10.1207/s15506878jobem4601_6

Wartella, E., & Reeves, B. (1985). Historical trends in research on children and the media: 1900–1960. *Journal of Communication, 35*(2), 118–133.

CHAPTER 20

How Do We Move Toward a Global Youth Media Studies?

Divya McMillin

Media targeted to young consumers portray protagonists as autonomous decision-makers, superheroes even, as they swiftly unravel the mysteries behind products and dilemmas and produce quick and magical solutions. Fascinating, then, is dominant theory on youth and media that is shrouded in a "moral panic" where youth are seen as vulnerable and at-risk, incapable of informed decision-making, with every need filled by a predatory marketplace. Such a protection-ist approach, argue critical media scholars, leaves us ill-equipped to understand the complexity of the media worlds of young consumers across the globe. A global approach to youth media studies is one that pays close attention to the *interdependencies* of systems and cultural contexts, to unique differences in media content, and to the ways in which media products are actually appropriated and accommodated locally. It is critical of the *neoliberal market approach* that constructs the market as free and open, with consumers having equal and informed access to a range of products and possessing autonomous purchasing power (see Herman & McChesney, 2003, for a critique of this approach) and cautious of the *determinist approach* that assumes consumer actions are determined by the type of media product they use.

Clearly the active or passive construction in the respective neoliberal and determinist ap-proaches is limiting to our understanding of youth consumers. The rich possibilities in between are exciting areas for development. As you develop your own research questions on youth and media, this chapter encourages you to think about the theory or theories that are best suited for your analysis, while paying close attention to the gaps to be filled especially in our current globalizing environment of interconnected, social, and interactive technologies.

This chapter takes us on journey through theory in youth media studies. It is an interdis-ciplinary adventure where we move through fields of education, psychology, anthropology and communication. We will encounter various foundational texts that often populate graduate studies in media; these are suggested here for further reading. The purpose is to identify the similarities in strains of thinking, and more importantly, weave together a productive and contemporary global framework for the media scholar to embark on her or his own empirical work in the field. We begin with foundational works on youth.

Ages and Stages vs. Contextual Approaches

The study of childhood and adolescence have long been the prerogative of the fields of psychology and education. Moreover, historian Paula Fass (2008) points out that childhood and youth are studied through a Western lens because it is in the Western hemisphere that theory in the field has emerged. So, for example, dominant thinking on the possibilities of the human being is influenced by such thinkers as John Locke (1632–1704) and John Dewey (1859–1952). Locke's *An Essay Concerning Human Understanding* positioned the human mind as a blank slate at birth; experience defined cognitive development. Observation of such cognitive development provided a way to understand processes of knowledge acquisition. Dewey's collection of essays titled *Thought and Its Subject-Matter* provided insights on how children learn. His 1899 work, *The School and Society*, is still considered an authority on how democracy can be achieved, and, Fass (2008) argues, shaped social development in the Western world. In psychology, Jean Piaget (1896–1980) proposed the cyclical and dialectical stages of individual cognitive development (sensorimotor, preoperational, concrete operational, and formal operational) stages. (Refer to Chapter 6 for more information on this approach.) Erik Erikson (1902–1994) identified eight phases of psychosocial development, as a departure from Sigmund Freud's (1856–1939) psychosexual stages of oral (birth–two years), anal (two–four years), genital (three–six years), latency (six years–puberty), and mature genital (puberty to adulthood and beyond). Erikson's phases follow with variation: basic trust versus mistrust (infancy); autonomy versus shame and doubt (toddlerhood); initiative versus guilt (kindergarten phase); industry versus inferiority (six years–puberty); identity versus role confusion (teenage years); intimacy versus isolation (young adulthood); generativity versus stagnation (midlife adulthood); and finally, ego-integrity versus despair (old age). Taken together, these theories regard the child as an autonomous individual who develops cognitively through a logical sequence of "ages and stages" toward the achievement of adult maturity and rationality. Childhood then is a process of becoming. Adulthood is the finished state where development is regarded as having ceased. Childhood is measured against adulthood standards of rationality, morality, and restraint. (Refer to Chapter 7 for more information on this as well as a discussion on how this impacts the methodological choices made by children's media researchers.) You can appreciate here the connection to the neoliberal market approach that views the individual as being able to exercise independent choice in the marketplace.

The direct relation between developmental stage and individual action is termed the *biological determinist approach*, and it was Philippe Ariès (1914–1984) who created a shift in this mode of thinking. In his *L'Enfant et la Vie Familiale sous l'Ancient Régime* (1960) translated as *Centuries of Childhood* (1962), Ariès argued that childhood was a historical construction, quite absent as a concept in medieval times and at best, a notable phase among the upper classes. Among the lower classes, young children were very much part of the labor force, socialized to adult roles and responsibilities out of economic necessity. The industrial environment of mid-1800s Europe is a stark example of the exploitation of children for factory labor. In the early twentieth century, *Coming of Age in Samoa* (1928) by anthropologist Margaret Mead (1901–1978) placed culture, not the individual, at the heart of how development should be understood. She noted that the socialization of children is crucial to sustain a culture from generation to generation. Although both Ariès and Mead have been widely criticized for the validity of their data and interpretations, they contributed to a fundamental shift in how individual development was studied. Their emphasis on context and culture as opposed to biological determinism marked an invaluable turn in the study of childhood and adolescence.

Adding substantively to the effort to move away from stage-focused development in psychology is Carol Gilligan, whose colleague at Harvard, Lawrence Kohlberg is noted for the construction of three stages of moral development, deriving from Piaget: preconventional (birth–nine years), conventional (nine–twenty), and postconventional (twenty years and beyond). Gilligan's *In A Different Voice* (1982) argued that not only did Freud, Piaget, Erikson, and even Kohlberg limit into narrow stages how development actually occurs, they also based their observations primarily on males. Girls were quite excluded from these theories of development causing many of their differences from the norm to be characterized as aberrations or instabilities.

Approaches to the study of childhood and youth are now increasingly international and interdisciplinary. Anthropology, developmental psychology, law, history, education, and sociology are some of the fields that scholars draw from to study the various aspects in an individual's journey from childhood to adulthood. Despite the interdisciplinarity, Balagopalan (2008) states that two trends dominate the field. First, childhood is still measured universally against a Western bourgeois ideal. Bourgeois refers generally to middle class aspirations, that is, the desire for advancement or upward mobility through materialism. Seen in this light, the normalization of the Western bourgeois childhood is a self-evident truth where the child is not seen as an economic contributor to the family but an object of nurture and care. The child has to be indulged with products that symbolize rites of passage, that is, that mark development from one stage to the other. Those environments that deviate from this ideal are regarded as impoverished and even abusive. Balagopalan argues for the second, more realistic approach that takes into consideration "multiple childhoods." The emphasis here is on differences in cultural contexts. This is a far more useful approach where history and culture are considered to have significant impact on how the child is socialized through various stages.

The early biological determinist approach is echoed in the work of early mass communication scholars who proposed a direct-effects *media determinist approach*. Also aptly termed the magic-bullet theory, proponents of this approach collectively known as the Frankfurt School, connected World War I and II propaganda content and effects to post-war television and advertising where audiences were regarded as vulnerable to all-powerful media messages. The critical turn in media studies most notably emerged in Great Britain in the mid-1950s with the establishment of the New Left, a group of scholars who argued that the Frankfurt School scholars, in their critique of a mass produced culture that was "dumbing down" consumers, were creating an artificial distinction between "high" and "low" cultures. Three pivotal texts, Richard Hoggart's *The Uses of Literacy* (1957), Raymond Williams' *Culture and Society* (1958), and E. P. Thompson's *The Making of the English Working Class* (1963), emerged at this time and demonstrated that popular or so-called "low culture" were actually expressions of youth identity and institutional resistance. In brief, the popular was political. These texts set the foundations for British cultural studies through the Center for Contemporary Cultural Studies (CCCS) at the University of Birmingham in the late 1970s. Between 1968 and 1979 under the leadership of

Stuart Hall, several anthologies were produced that focused on youth as subcultures employing unique forms of expression and style to establish identity through resistance (Hall & Jefferson, 1976; Hall, Hobson, Lowe, & Willis, 1980).

Further works took a closer look at the institutional effects on youth identities and the ways in which youth used media to resist institutional demands. For example, Willis' *Learning to Labour* (1977) is an influential treatment of the role of schools in preparing children for the labor force in ways that reinforce and perpetuate class divisions. Hebdige's (1979) *Subculture: The Meaning of Style* is an examination of how youth resist social order symbolically; signs of resistance come together to produce the subculture. The texts, however, were critiqued for their masculinist, monolithic constructions of class issues with little attention to ethnic differences. McRobbie's *Feminism and Youth Culture* (1991) is path-breaking in this context and argued that work on youth subcultures excluded the experiences of women. Although disbanded in July 2002 amid much controversy, the CCCS provides important frameworks by which we understand the ideological contexts of the production and consumption of media texts.

Using the broad tenets of British cultural studies and its attention to contexts and the role of ideology in creating those contexts, Buckingham (2000) argued for a shift in how children and youth were studied. He summarized that childhood—and by extension, adolescence—should be considered a social, not biological, category that is historically, socially, and culturally variable. It should also be seen as a class-based phenomenon (where this stage was a prerogative of middle and upper classes), or as a symbol of a mythical Golden Age, a Garden of Eden where children could play freely. The general themes surrounding childhood crept into youth studies: its definition as a development category generating sociological concerns of deviance, legitimizing various "moral panics," and sanctioning multiple strategies of control. (Refer to Chapter 3 for a detailed discussion of this phenomenon.).

In the late 1990s and 2000s, attention shifted to how girls receive these messages (see Durham, 1999) and how girls produce media (Kearny, 2006). The media environment has expanded to include interactive communication technologies. Studies have shown that girls use these avenues with greater frequency and for more varied purposes than boys (Clark, 2002). As Mazzarella and Pecora (2007) have noted, the field of Girls' Studies, while gaining currency in the United States, does bear a bias toward "middle-class white girls in Western countries" (p. 117). A few scholars are changing this trend (Durham, 2002; McMillin, 2005; Valdivia, 2008), but concepts of childhood and adolescence continue to be drawn from Western theory.

How, then, are we equipped to study youth in various parts of the world? Obviously, we need a more critical and inclusive focus on youth in globalization. Young people, particularly in developing countries, face vast opportunities for employment in newly liberalized economies; yet these opportunities are for the most part, casual and temporary connections to the labor market. What is required is an understanding of youth mobility and the "ways in which they are agents of change and produce the new conditions for their lives" (Dolby & Rizvi, 2008, p. 5). The dominant strains of youth studies that examine them as consumers or audiences of popular technologies and media leave little room for the examination of youth as bodies of labor. Developed within media centric environments in developed economies, such studies largely neglect the economic and political conditions that shape youth identity worldwide.

Connecting Youth Studies, Media Studies, and Globalization

Globalization is an umbrella term for interlinked processes of financial deregulation and the mobilization of capital across a networked world. The definition offered by Roland Robertson (1995) is still widely used in a variety of scholarship on the subject. Robertson defines globalization as "a concept (that) refers both to the compression of the world and the intensification of our consciousness of the world as a whole" (p. 8). The projection of globalization as an empowering space that awards myriad choices in previously constricted environments is now routinely criticized. Developing economies are becoming quite vocal in renewing anti-colonialist stances, decrying the aggressive expansion of multinational corporations (MNCs) in labor-rich, safety-poor environments. Media scholars note that consumerism advances at a hectic pace even in impoverished environments because so-called new and diverse commodities merely repackage time-tested sexist and racist stereotypes. Youth are considered to be the primary consumers of "universalized" or Westernized modes of dress, speech, and music, imbibing these in the same temporal frame all across the world (Real, 1996; Walker, 1996).

The question of youth agency assumes prime importance in this context. The United Nations presents in its May 2015 report on *Youth Population Trends* that one out of every six individuals is between fifteen to twenty-four years of age, putting the youth population at 1.2 billion worldwide. This population is projected to decline in Europe, North America and parts of Asia, and increase in Africa, overall continuing the trend noted in 2008 that placed a majority of the world youth population in the global south (Jeffrey, 2008). Education and employment are high priorities naturally, and combined with decreasing youth populations in the global north, increased south-north migration will be very much part of the immediate future. Investment in youth is recognized as a high priority for national governments, particularly in developing economies, yet such investment follows the preferences of entrenched systems of patriarchy where, for the most part, it results in the elevation of a narrow group of mainly young men who have achieved a globally competitive education and who can move across elite institutions for highly paid salaried positions. This class of youth is desired by Euro-American businesses and innovative headhunting strategies are launched in the urban areas where such youth live in the global south. Of these young people, a small percentage is represented by women, who face complex politics of consumption, where the body continues to be the primary site through which desire and vulnerabilities are conveyed (Lukose, 2005). A second stratum of youth, generally between fifteen and nineteen years, is denied secondary school education; these are more likely to be poorly paid manual laborers in the industry, urban homes, or agricultural fields. Emerging economies around the world are witnessing a rapid increase in the numbers of youth who fall in between: they are educated, yet unemployed.

Scholars of global media describe youth environments as fragmented and shifting, with young consumers simultaneously inhabiting multiple worlds and feeling isolated (Nuttall, 2008). Spaces for the expression of dynamic youth identities are a complex blend of gender, class, religious, ethnic, national, and orientation positions, facilitated by the wide variety of local, national, and global television programming available to the average viewer. In the research on youth media practices around the world, we can once again detect strains of the active or passive construction of the subject, placed in a context of "connectivity" or "fragmentation," respectively. Under the connectivity position, individuals are assumed to occupy a borderless world, able to respond as active subjects to the tantalizing call of multinational products and job opportunities. Under the fragmentation position, the individuals are regarded as uncritically following market imperatives. Endless accumulation of capital is the priority, leading to the degeneration of individuality and heritage (Applbaum, 2000). The current overcrowding in cities and redundant education in postcolonial economies converge into a "moment of danger" (Venn, 2006, p. 1) for youth, where strategies of colonialism are very much alive; their forms are more pervasive, subversive, and totalizing. Despite these strains, global media studies expands how we approach youth and media in three significant ways as flagged at the beginning of this chapter: attention to viewing context, to differences in format and content, and to variations in how media are used.

First, the *conditions* of viewing play a significant role in how messages are interpreted, note several scholars of global media studies, injecting caution in the assumption that viewing experiences of audiences in the global north may be generalized to those in the global south. For example, Algan (2003) reminds us from her studies in southeast Turkey that roadside television, internet cafes, video parlors and radios in the marketplace allow for communal and public media consumption in ways that are quite different from the domestic, usually isolated consumption in Western environments. To cite another example, the cinematic experience in India can be quite intense, with audience members singing along to catchy song and dance sequences which are often released even before the movie hits the theaters, making for a collective, emotionally charged event (Srinivas, 2002). Describing fieldwork in Brazil, Tufte (2000) writes that television viewing often takes place in front of the house because most homes regard the corresponding street space as part of the domestic space of the living room itself. My own extensive fieldwork in urban and semi-urban India has revealed a dynamic matrix of consumer behaviors. Living room space of lower income homes is generally considered community space; residents open their doors to neighbors for shared prime time watching, and closed doors are often seen as a sign of hostility (McMillin, 2005). Further, a *TV Characters* study that included extensive fieldwork among teens in the four global cities of Bangalore, New York, Johannesburg, and Munich, demonstrated that various *mediating systems* were at play, not just as conventional media technologies, but, as structures of family, peers, school, and religion as well. This prompts the global media scholar to stay away from arguing for "authentic" cultural positions but to develop methodologies that allow us to examine the dynamic flows between how teens live their daily lives, interacting with media technologies as part of their everyday rituals (McMillin, 2009).

Also, in terms of content, non-Western case studies reveal a high level of religious and political themes on television across genres, not typical in Western viewing contexts. Religious programming, religion-themed apps, and movies with religious overtones are not uncommon, with mythological stories serving to further political causes where those in the religious majority occupy positions of power. For example, Lila Abu-Lughod (2005) has written extensively about the use of religion to foster national and citizen identity through television in Egypt. Abrahamian (1999), Kraidy (2003), Rodriguez (2003) and Tomaselli and Teer-Tomaselli (2003) have written similarly bringing forward case studies from Iran, Lebanon, Southern Chile, and South Africa, respectively. Viewers have to have cultural literacy to understand the symbolism of the programming, as in the case of the wildly popular Hindu epic, the *Ramayana,* in Nepal (Burch, 2002). The use of Hindu epics to impart lessons to youth on ideal individual-to-family relationships and, by extension, citizen-to-nation relationships, has been richly described by such scholars as Mankekar (2002) and Rajagopal (2001), urging us to appreciate the powerful role of the media around the world as they connect to local contexts and desires and as they offer extensions of viewer's individual habits and social rituals. Once again, the *TV Characters* study provided powerful evidence that teens across the world have intensely personal relationships with their favorite television shows and video games; these facilitate explorations of self, allow for safe self-expression, and spark ambitions for upward mobility as well as actions toward social and political justice (McMillin, 2009).

Finally, global media studies draw our attention to the remarkable ways in which media are used by youth for activism. This moves our understanding of media beyond a site for pleasure and entertainment, to one of purpose as well, where the active user exerts agency for far-reaching social change. Examples here are abundant, as in the case of young Chinese women protesting state monitoring of the internet (Yang, 2003; see also Lagerkvist, 2011) and of Indian youth launching a Facebook campaign where supporters across the globe could join the page, *Consortium of Pub-Going, Loose and Forward Women* and virtually deliver a pair of pink panties to symbolically shame the fundamentalist Shri Ram Sena group behind the 2009 attacks on young, unmarried women in local city pubs. Kang (2016) provides powerful examples of candlelight youth vigils mobilized through the internet in South Korea to push for democracy.

The significance of the global approach to youth media studies is that it goes beyond examples in international locales; it is attentive to the *interdependencies* of political, economic, and cultural systems that produce local experiences. Audiences, media industries, and media products and content are not just anchored in nationalized contexts as would be the prerogative of a comparative *international* lens, but in the dynamic nodes of interconnection. Political and economic relationships between countries produced through shared histories of colonialism, for example, would provide a crucial backdrop to examine the residual effects or new patterns of colonialism (termed *neocolonial)* experienced in contemporary environments. The postcolonial approach is a practical and useful one that places at the center of analysis a recognition of the interdependencies engendered through colonialism that result in much of the landscape we inhabit today. It is described briefly below to urge more studies on youth and media in the global south, with specific focus on *displacement,* that is, how consumer experiences differ or are displaced by dominant narratives of consumption that arise from Western user contexts.

The Postcolonial Approach

To make youth studies relevant in globalization, we need a framework that is global in its vision, scrutinizes history, and flags contemporary practices on a temporal, spatial, and ideological map. The critical approach that examines questions of power and social hierarchies that we have encountered earlier in this chapter lends itself most usefully for the study of youth across the world. While the origins of this approach are credited to the Frankfurt Scholars who were keenly concerned with class differences, and demarcations of "high" and "low" culture produced through media, it grows more robust and relevant in how it is developed by feminist media scholars (as cited in previous sections) and postcolonial scholars, whose work will be described in this section.

Postcolonial scholars have developed a framework that radically shifts the Western-oriented perspective critiqued at the beginning of this chapter and argue that the developmental stages led to "universal" categories of childhood, adolescence, and adulthood, relegating as backward, or underdeveloped, those who did not conform to these constructions. Postcolonial theory fundamentally exposes the "West" and "East" as ideological rather than geographical categories. Edward Said, whose book *Orientalism* (1979) was a thorough treatment of the ways by which colonized peoples and their lands were manipulated, tagged, and organized for colonizer psychic and material gain, is credited with laying the groundwork for this theory. Postcolonial studies was developed to address the imprints of colonialism on the culture of postcolonial societies. "Postcolonial" refers to the actual material conditions of formerly colonized societies. It pertains to a global condition after colonialism that produced various blocs of allegiance as, for example, the "third world," and to the discourse about these conditions that offers a way to view the global condition (Dirlik, 1996; Mongia, 1996).

The postcolonial framework allows us to see similarities between conceptualizations of communities in developing parts of the world and of "universal" childhood and adolescence. Natives in the colonies were likened to children, requiring discipline and direction by, for example, the Spanish theologians toward the Indians in the Americas in the sixteenth century or by the Europeans toward Africans in the eighteenth and nineteenth centuries. The evolutionary model likened non-Western "primitives" with European children, and many of these "Age-based relationships continue today to be centrally connected with the racial/ethnic hierarchies developed under colonialism and imperialism, linking race, gender, and age with far-flung global relationships within the intimate economy of the home" (Cole & Durham, 2007, pp. 7–8). Postcolonial theory, used appropriately, pushes for analysis beyond the limitations of polarities and impels scrutiny of the interrelated mechanisms that perpetuate the power differentials of colonialism. This critique is important because it is the keen attention to class and its texturing by ethnicity, gender, nationality, and so on that expand youth studies to global contexts.

Use of this framework in youth media studies is still emerging, pointing to the need for more empirically grounded analyses that take into account colonial histories and residual trends in the globalizing present. Black, Khoo, and Iwabuchi's (2016) anthology *Contemporary Culture and Media in Asia* is a rich collection of essays, that, for example, examine representations of minorities in youth films in Hong Kong and role of the multitalented Taiwanese girl group S.H.E (with music albums, television drama appearances, and commercials to their credit), in the emergence of Girl Power in the Chinese market.

Conclusion

This chapter has taken us through various trends in theory on youth and media and has argued for contextually rich analyses that pay close attention to social differentiations and identity positions. This is a particularly urgent need since scholarship on new interactive media experiences such as gaming, for example, harkens back to the "moral panic" of the 1960s and 70s. Youth media environments are not dominated by any one medium as it was by television, just about a decade ago. With hand held technologies, computers, and gaming connectivities, youth have access to a wider variety of media products and mediated contexts than ever before. We need to understand youth as agents of change, with the ability to produce new conditions for their lives. While studies on the impact of new media on youth development are important and warranted, this chapter ends on a note of hope and enthusiasm that they will highlight both the positive and negative, be culturally sensitive, recognize youth as mobile and dynamic, *as well as market-led*. Such holistic studies will open up new methodologies to understand the rich media worlds inhabited by young consumers around the world.

Discussion Questions

1. What do we mean by "determinist" models of development or media consumption? How do these limit our understanding of youth as consumers?

2. What were the contributions of feminist scholars such as Carol Gilligan and Angela McRobbie to the study of youth and media?

3. How does the global approach advance the ways we may study youth consumerism and media practices around the world?

4. How would you develop a method to study youth consumers in a country in the global south? What would be some key considerations?

Exercises

1. Divide your group into two sub groups, with one taking a "passive consumer" approach and the other taking an "active consumer" approach. Develop at least four points each by which you would argue for or against warning labels on explicit (i.e. high sexual and violence content) video games.

2. Write a short narrative (one paragraph) on your media habits. Share and discuss with members of your group. What contextual details emerged, that is, what did you learn about your group member's media environment, home life, and interests? What questions remained? Without posing these questions, think through how you would find those answers from a broader group. Write that down, you are beginning to create method from context!

3. Find a current news story from your go-to news source about youth media in the global south. What assumptions about the audience do you think the author is making? What stereotypes and ideologies emerge, if any? What theoretical approach is the author's angle most reminiscent of?

References

Abrahamian, E. (1999). *Tortured confessions: Prisons and public recantations in modern Iran.* Berkeley, CA: University of California Press.

Abu-Lughod, L. (2005). *Dramas of nationhood: The politics of television in Egypt.* Chicago, IL: University of Chicago Press.

Algan, E. (2003). The problem of textuality in ethnographic media research: Lessons learned in southeast Turkey. In P. D. Murphy & M. W. Kraidy (Eds.), *Global media studies: Ethnographic perspectives* (pp. 23–39). New York, NY and London: Routledge.

Applbaum, K. (2000). Crossing borders: Globalization as myth and charter in American transnational consumer marketing. *American Ethnologist, 27*(2), 257–282. doi:10.1525/ae.2000.27.2.257

Balagopalan, S. (2008). Memories of tomorrow: Children, labor, and the panacea of formal schooling. *Journal of the History of Childhood and Youth, 1*(2), 267–285. doi:10.1353/hcy.0.0005

Black, D., Khoo, O., & Iwabuchi, K. (2016). *Contemporary culture and media in Asia.* New York, NY: Rowman and Littlefield.

Buckingham, D. (2000). *After the death of childhood: Growing up in the age of electronic media.* Cambridge: Polity.

Burch, E. (2002). Media literacy, cultural proximity and TV aesthetics: Why Indian soap operas work in Nepal and the Hindu diaspora. *Media, Culture, and Society, 24*(4), 571–579. doi:10.1177/016344370202400408

Clark, L. S. (2002). U.S. adolescent religious identity, the media, and the "funky" side of religion. *Journal of Communication, 52*(4), 794–811. doi:10.1111/j.1460–2466.2002.tb02574.x

Cole, J., & Durham, D. (2007). Introduction: Age, regeneration, and the intimate politics of globalization. In J. Cole & D. Durham (Eds.), *Youth, age and family in the new world economy* (pp. 1–28). Bloomington, IN: Indiana University Press.

Dirlik, A. (1996). The postcolonial aura: Third World criticism in the age of global capitalism. In P. Mongia (Ed.), *Contemporary postcolonial theory: A reader* (pp. 294–321). New Delhi: Oxford University Press.

Dolby, N., & Rizvi, F. (2008). *Youth moves: Identities and education in global perspective.* London: Taylor and Francis.

Durham, M. G. (1999). Articulating adolescent girls' resistance to the mediated feminine ideal. *Psychology & Marketing, 19*(2), 211–233. doi:10.1080/07491409.1999.10162421

Durham, M. G. (2002). Out of the Indian diaspora: Mass media, myths of femininity, and the negotiation of adolescence between two cultures. In S. R. Mazzarella & N. O. Pecora (Eds.), *Growing up girls: Popular culture and the construction of identity* (pp. 193–208). New York, NY: Peter Lang.

Fass, P. (2008). The world is at our door: Why historians of children and childhood should open up. *Journal of the History of Childhood and Youth, 1*(1), 11–31. doi:10.1353/hcy.2008.0016

Gilligan, C. (1982). *In a different voice: Psychological theory and women's development.* Cambridge, MA: Harvard University Press.

Hall, S., Hobson, D., Lowe, A., & Willis, P. (Eds.). (1980). *Culture, media, language.* London: Hutchinson.

Hall, S., & Jefferson, T. (Eds.). (1976). *Resistance through rituals: Youth subcultures in post-war Britain.* London: Hutchinson.

Hebdige, D. (1979). *Subculture: The meaning of style.* New York, NY: Routledge.

Herman E. S., & McChesney, R. (2003). The rise of the global media. In L. Parks & S. Kumar (Eds.), *Planet TV: A global television reader* (pp. 21–39). New York, NY and London: New York University Press.

Hoggart, R. (1957). *The uses of literacy.* Harmondsworth: Penguin.

Jeffrey, C. (2008). "Generation nowhere": Rethinking youth through the lens of unemployed young men. *Progress in Human Geography, 32*(6), 739–758. doi:10.1177/0309132507088119

Kang, J. (2016). *Igniting the Internet: Youth and activism in postauthoritarian South Korea.* Honolulu, HI: University of Hawaii Press.

Kearny, M. C. (2006). *Girls make media.* New York, NY: Routledge.

Kraidy, M. M. (2003). Globalization avant la lettre? Cultural hybridity and media power in Lebanon. In P. D. Murphy & M. W. Kraidy (Eds.), *Global media studies: Ethnographic perspectives* (pp. 276–296). New York, NY and London: Routledge.

Lagerkvist, J. (2011). *After the Internet, before democracy competing norms in Chinese Media and society.* Bern: Peter Lang.

Lukose, R. (2005). Consuming globalization: Youth and gender in Kerala, India. *Journal of Social History, 38*(4), 915–935. doi:10.1353/jsh.2005.0068

Mankekar, P. (2002). Epic contests: Television and religious identity in India. In F. D. Ginsburg, L. Abu-Lughod, & B. Larkin (Eds.), *Media worlds: Anthropology on New Terrain* (pp. 134–151), Berkeley, CA: University of California Press.

Mazzarella, S., & Pecora, N. (2007). Girls in crisis: Newspaper coverage of adolescent girls. *Journal of Communication Inquiry, 31*(1), 6–27. doi:10.1177/0196859906294712

McMillin, D. C. (2005). Teen crossings: Emerging cyberpublics in India. In S. Mazzarella (Ed.), *Girl wide web: Girls, the Internet, and the negotiation of identity* (pp. 161–178). New York, NY: Peter Lang.

McMillin, D. C. (2009). *Mediated identities: Television, youth, and globalization.* New York, NY: Peter Lang Publishing.

McRobbie, A. (1991). *Feminism and youth culture.* Boston, MA: Unwin Hyman.

Mongia, P. (1996). Introduction. In P. Mongia (Ed.), *Contemporary postcolonial theory: A reader* (pp. 1–18). Oxford: Oxford University Press.

Nuttall, S. (2008). Youth cultures of consumption in Johannesburg. In N. Dolby & F. Rizvi (Eds.), *Youth moves: Identities and education in global perspective* (pp. 151–179). New York, NY: Taylor and Francis.

Rajagopal, A. (2001). *Politics after television: Hindu nationalism and the reshaping of the public in India.* Cambridge: Cambridge University Press.

Real, M. R. (1996). *Exploring media culture: A guide.* Thousand Oaks, CA: Sage.

Robertson, R. (1995). Mapping the global condition: Globalization as the central concept. In M. Featherstone (Ed.), *Global culture: Nationalism, globalization and modernity* (pp. 15–30). London: Sage.

Rodriguez, C. (2003). The bishop and his star: Citizen's communication in Southern Chile. In N. Couldry & J. Curran (Eds.), *Contesting media power: Alternative media in a networked world* (pp. 177–194). Lanham, MD: Rowman and Littlefield Publishers.

Said, E. (1979). *Orientalism*. New York, NY: Vintage.

Srinivas, L. (2002). The active audience: Spectatorship, social relations and the experience of cinema in India. *Media, Culture and Society, 24*(2), 155–173.

Thompson, E. P. (1963). *The making of the English working class*. New York, NY: Vintage.

Tomaselli, G. T., & Teer-Tomaselli, R. (2003). New nation: Anachronistic Catholicism and liberation theology. In N. Couldry & J. Curran (Eds.), *Contesting media power: Alternative media in a networked world* (pp. 195–208). Lanham, MD: Rowman and Littlefield Publishers.

Tufte, T. (2000). The popular forms of hope: About the force of fiction among TV audiences in Brazil. In I. Hagen & J. Wasko (Eds.), *Consuming audiences? Production and reception in media research* (pp. 275–300). Cresskill, NJ: Hampton Press.

Valdivia, A. N. (2008). Popular culture and recognition: Narratives of youth and Latinidad. In N. Dolby & F. Rizvi (Eds.), *Youth moves: Identities and education in global perspective* (pp. 179–193). New York, NY: Taylor and Francis.

Venn, C. (2006). *The postcolonial challenge: Towards alternative worlds*. London and New Delhi: Sage.

Walker, C. (1996). Can TV save the planet? *American Demographics, 18*(5), 42–48.

Williams, R. (1958). *Culture and society, 1780–1950*. New York, NY: Columbia University Press.

Willis, P. (1977). *Learning to labor: How working class kids get working class jobs*. Farnborough: Saxon House.

Yang, G. (2003). The Internet and the rise of a transnational Chinese cultural sphere. *Media, Culture and Society, 25*(4), 469–490. doi:10.1177/01634437030254003

Contributors

Chelsie Akers is a Ph.D. candidate in the Department of Communication at the University of Arizona. Her research interest are new technology, mass media, and media effects specifically among children and adolescents. Her research on social support through computer mediated communication and text message interventions among teens has appeared in *American Journal of Health Promotion, Human Communication Research, and Journalism and Mass Communication.*

Alison Alexander (Ph.D., Ohio State University) is Professor and Senior Associate Dean for Academic Affairs in the Grady College of Journalism and Mass Communication at the University of Georgia. She is a past editor of the *Journal of Broadcasting & Electronic Media.* She conducts research in the areas of media and family, audience research, and media economics.

J. Alison Bryant (Ph.D., University of Southern California) leads the Research Center for AARP. Prior to AARP, she was the founder and co-CEO of PlayScience, a research and design firm that led innovation around branding, content creation and development in the kids and family space; and Senior Director of Digital Research & Strategy for the Nickelodeon/MTV Networks Kids & Family Group. She has also been an assistant professor of communication at Indiana University. She has three edited books and over 30 research articles and chapters.

Moniek Buijzen (Ph.D., University of Amsterdam) is Professor and Chair of Communication Science, Radboud University. Her research focuses on young (media) consumers within the paradigm of positive communication science. In 2013 she received a prestigious ERC Consolidator Grant for a 5-year research project investigating the implementation of health campaigns via youths' social networks. Her work has been recognized by several awards from international communication associations. In addition, Buijzen is co-initiator of Bitescience.com, an online portal for worldwide academic research on young consumers.

Sahara Byrne (Ph.D., University of California), is Associate Professor in the Department of Communication at Cornell University where she is Director of Undergraduate Studies. Her research addresses the unintended effects of persuasive messaging, youth, and health communication, and has been published in a range of academic journals including *Health Communication, Journal of Children and Media, Journal of Computer-Mediated Communication* and more. Her recent focus is on why youth resist campaigns intended to prevent them from engaging in risky behaviors.

Sherri Hope Culver (MLA, University of Pennsylvania) serves as Director, Center for Media and Information Literacy (CMIL) at Temple University and Associate Professor, School of Media and Communication. Sherri serves on the Board of the National Association for Media Literacy Education. She is author of the book, *The Media Career Guide* and served as co-editor of the *Media and Information Literacy and Intercultural Dialogue Yearbook* published by UNESCO/UNAOC from 2013–2015.

Rebecca N. H. de Leeuw (Ph.D., Radboud University) is Assistant Professor of Communication Science at the Behavioural Science Institute, Radboud University. She devotes her research to the role of parenting and media in relation to kindness and well-being in children and adolescents. Her research belongs to the field of positive media psychology.

Olivia A. Gonzalez is an undergraduate research scholar at the University of San Diego, where she is earning her Bachelor of Arts in Communication Studies. Olivia is writing her senior thesis on the motivations and implications of teenagers' creation, consumption, and dissemination of Internet memes.

Rebecca C. Hains (Ph.D., Temple University) is Professor of Advertising and Media Studies at Salem State University. Her research on gender and children's media culture has been published in journals such as *Popular Music and Society*, *Girlhood Studies*, and the *Journal of Communication Inquiry*. She is the co-editor of the anthology *Princess Cultures: Mediating Girls' Imaginations and Identities* and the author of the books *The Princess Problem* and *Growing Up with Girl Power: Girlhood on Screen and in Everyday Life*.

Azeta Hatef is a doctoral candidate in the College of Communications at Penn State. Her research centers international human rights, global media systems, as well as gender and diversity in the media. Her most recent work focuses on the democratizing effects of social media among marginalized communities.

Renee Hobbs (Ed.D., Harvard University) is Professor of Communication Studies at the University of Rhode Island, where she directs the Media Education Lab, whose mission is to improve the practice of media literacy education through scholarship and community service. Hobbs co-directs the Graduate Certificate Program in Digital Literacy and is the co-editor of the *Journal of Media Literacy Education,* the official publication of the National Association for Media Literacy Education.

Keisha L. Hoerrner (Ph.D., University of Georgia) is Professor and Associate Dean in the College of Undergraduate Studies at the University of Central Florida. She previously served as Dean of University College at Kennesaw State University (GA). Her early research interests focused on children and media as well as media law. After moving into administration, her research interests transitioned to student success initiatives in higher education.

Kyra Hunting (Ph.D., University of Wisconsin) is an assistant professor at the University of Kentucky, where she teaches media arts and studies. Her research on genre, children's media, and audiences has been published in scholarly journals including *Spectator, Quarterly Review of Film and Video, Communication Review, Transformative Works and Culture,* and the *Journal of Popular Culture,* as well as multiple anthologies.

Nancy A. Jennings (Ph.D., University of Texas at Austin) is Associate Professor and Undergraduate Director in the Department of Communication at the University of Cincinnati. She is also the Director of the Children's Education and Entertainment Research Lab (CHEER). She has published a book, *Tween Girls and Their Mediated Friends,* focusing on girls and their relationships with media characters. She has published on other topics including virtual environments, children's advertising, families and media, and media violence.

Vikki S. Katz (Ph.D., University of Southern California) is an Associate Professor in Communication, and Affiliate Graduate Faculty in Sociology, at Rutgers University. Her research focuses on media and technology use among low-income and immigrant children and their families, and has been funded by the Bill & Melinda Gates Foundation and the Russell Sage Foundation. You can learn more about her work and find copies of her publications at vikkikatz.com and digitalequityforlearning.org.

Matthew A. Lapierre (Ph.D., University of Pennsylvania) is Assistant Professor in the Communication Department at the University of Arizona. His primary research focuses on how development affects children's understanding of advertising messages and their susceptibility to such messages. He also conducts research on parent–child communication related to consumer purchasing. His research has appeared in the *Journal of Communication, JAMA Pediatrics, Public Health Nutrition, Pediatrics,* and *Media Psychology.*

Dafna Lemish (Ph.D., Ohio State University) is Associate Dean of Programs and Professor at the School of Communication and Information at Rutgers University, founding editor of the *Journal of Children and Media;* and a Fellow of the International Communication Association (ICA). She is author or editor of numerous books and articles on the role of media in children's lives and on gender representations and identity, including most recently: *Children and Media: A Global Perspective* (Wiley, 2015).

Sun Sun Lim (Ph.D., LSE) is Professor of Media and Communication and Head of Humanities, Arts and Social Sciences at the Singapore University of Technology and Design. She studies social implications of technology domestication by young people and families, charting the ethnographies of their Internet and mobile phone use. Her recent research focuses on understudied and marginalised populations including youths-at-risk, migrant workers and international migrant students. She has authored more than 60 book chapters and articles. Her latest books are *Mobile Communication and the Family: Asian Experiences in Technology Domestication* (Springer, 2016) and *Asian Perspectives on Digital Culture: Emerging Phenomena, Enduring Concepts* (Routledge, 2016).

Sharon R. Mazzarella (Ph.D., University of Illinois at Urbana-Champaign) is Professor of Communication Studies at James Madison University. She is editor/co-editor of seven academic anthologies, including the recently published *The Mediated Youth Reader* (Peter Lang, 2016). In addition, she is editor of the book series Mediated Youth (Peter Lang)—a series dedicated to publishing trailblazing academic books on cultural studies of youth. Her research has been published in a range of academic journals, and she currently is completing a book examining the news media's role in contributing to a moral panic about girls growing up too fast.

Matthew P. McAllister (Ph.D., University of Illinois at Urbana-Champaign) is Professor of Communications in the Department of Film-Video and Media Studies at Penn State. His research focuses on political economy of media and critiques of commercial culture. He is the co-editor of *The Routledge Companion to Advertising and Promotional Culture* (with Emily West, 2013) and *The Advertising and Consumer Culture Reader* (with Joseph Turow, Routledge, 2009).

Divya McMillin (Ph.D., Indiana University Bloomington) is Professor of Global Media Studies and Executive Director of the Institute for Global Engagement and Global Honors Program at the University of Washington Tacoma. She is author of *International Media Studies* (Blackwell, 2007), *Mediated Identities: Youth, Agency, and Globalization* (Peter Lang, 2009), and co-editor of *Place, Power, Media* (forthcoming). Her research on media globalization and audiences has resulted in numerous top-tiered journal articles, book chapters, and conference and keynote presentations.

Jessica Taylor Piotrowski (Ph.D., University of Pennsylvania) is an Associate Professor in the Amsterdam School of Communication Research at the University of Amsterdam where she serves as the Director of the Center for Research on Children, Adolescents, and the Media. Her research investigates how children are affected by media, focusing upon the cognitive and socio-emotional benefits of media. She is the co-author *Plugged In: How Media Attract and Affect Youth* (Yale University Press, 2017).

Erica Scharrer (Ph.D., Syracuse University) is Professor in the Department of Communication at the University of Massachusetts Amherst, where she studies media content, opinions of media, media effects, and media literacy, especially regarding the topics of gender and violence. She's the editor of the Media Effects/Media Psychology volume of the *International Encyclopedia of Media Studies* (Wiley Blackwell, 2013) and a past chair of the Children, Adolescents, and Media division of the International Communication Association.

Cyndy Scheibe (Ph.D., Cornell University) is Professor of Psychology at Ithaca College, and serves as the Director of the Center for Research on the Effects of Television Lab and Archive. She is also Executive Director and Founder of Project Look Sharp, a media literacy initiative of Ithaca College, and co-author of the book *The Teacher's Guide to Media Literacy: Critical Thinking in a Multimedia World* (2012, Sage/Corwin).

Valerie Steeves (Ph.D., Carleton University) is Full Professor in the Department of Criminology at the University of Ottawa in Canada. She is the co-leader of The eQuality Project, a 7-year partnership funded by the Social Sciences and Humanities Research Council of Canada exploring young people's experiences of privacy and equality in networked spaces. She is also the lead researcher of the multi-year study Young Canadians in a Wired World, which has been collecting data on young people's online experiences since 1999.

Susannah R. Stern (Ph.D., University of North Carolina) is currently a professor in the Department of Communication Studies at the University of San Diego. Her research examines the intersections of adolescent development, media use and popular culture. She is particularly interested in how young people explore identity and express themselves in digital spaces. She has published her work in top communication journals and shares her work at academic conferences, youth organization, and with parents, teachers, and the press.

Yang Wang is a Ph.D. candidate in the Department of Communications and New Media, National University of Singapore. Her research interests focus on ICTs domestication of transnational households, digital media use and gender identity, as well as everyday politics of Chinese netizens.

Ellen Wartella (Ph.D., University of Minnesota) is the Sheikh Hamad bin Khalifa Al-thani Professor of Communication and Professor of Psychology, Human Development and Social Policy, and Medical Social Sciences at Northwestern University. She is Director of the Center on Media and Human Development and Chair of the Department of Communication Studies. She is a leading scholar of the role of media in children's development and serves on a variety of national and international boards and committees on children's issues.